NERDS 2.0.1

NERDS 2.0.1

A BRIEF HISTORY OF THE INTERNET

Stephen Segaller

TV Books

NEW YORK

Nerds 2.0.1: A Brief History of the Internet is the companion book to the television series "Nerds 2.0.1—A Brief History of the Internet" on PBS. The series was produced by Oregon Public Broadcasting.
Host—Robert X. Cringely
Series Producer—Stephen Segaller
Executive Producer—John Gau

Publisher's Cataloging-in-Publication Data
Segaller, Stephen.
 Nerds 2.0.1 : a brief history of the Internet / Stephen Segaller. — 1st ed.
  p. cm.
 Includes index.
 ISBN: 1-57500-106-3

 1. Internet (Computer network)—History. I. Title.
TK5105.875.I5S44 1998   004.678
           QBI98-66871

TV Books, L.L.C.
Publishers serving the television industry.
1619 Broadway, Ninth Floor
New York, NY 10019
www.tvbooks.com

For my mother, Joyce Segaller,
who first planted a love of words,
starting with *Mesembryanthemum*

Contents

Acknowledgments

The *Triumph of the Nerds* VENTURE began, like many television projects, over a large gin and tonic. In the bar of the George Hotel in Edinburgh, Scotland, during the 1993 Edinburgh International Television Festival, I got together with my friend and colleague John Gau, doyen of British independent television producers, to talk coproduction. John had just returned from his summer vacation on Cape Cod where he had passed the time reading *Accidental Empires,* by Robert X. Cringely. Using his signature accolade for a viable TV project, John declared the book "a cracking good yarn."

Bob Cringely had helpfully included his telephone number in the book, so it was not a major research assignment to locate him. Our first question was whether the witty irreverence of his writing could be adapted into television. Could Cringely do on camera what he can do on paper—tell a good story and entertain the audience at the same time? In April 1994, we shot some sample videotape that demonstrated that Bob could. He was quite the most accomplished television novice we had ever encountered. So, armed with a sample tape, we took a mere fifteen months to round up the funds to produce the series, for a variety of broadcasters starting with PBS in the United States, Channel 4 in Britain, and the ABC in Australia.

Our first Nerds TV series, *Triumph of the Nerds*, was based substantially on Bob's excellent book, and any reader wishing to delve more deeply into the history and evolution of the personal computer would do well to read *Accidental Empires: How the Boys of Silicon Valley Make Their Millions, Battle Foreign Competition, and Still Can't Get a Date.* The series was expertly directed by Paul Sen, photographed by John Booth, and edited by Mike Duxbury. John Gau and I were executive producer and series producer, respectively. It was broadcast in Britain in April 1996 and in the United States in June 1996, with the happy result that PBS immediately commissioned a sequel. *Nerds 2.0.1: A Brief History of the Internet* is the result.

This book includes a small amount of material from the first series, but mostly tells a different, parallel narrative to that originally presented in *Accidental Empires*. Nevertheless, this book and its author owe a great debt to the original storytelling vigor and wit of Bob Cringely. Without John Gau—whose choice of beach reading is as excellent as his judgment in all other matters of editorial quality—none of these ventures would have occurred.

Other acknowledgments should begin, of course, with the more than seventy interviewees who generously gave their time, memories, and knowledge to our effort to portray the history of computer networking in *Nerds 2.0.1*. Added to the sixty-plus interviews we conducted for *Triumph of the Nerds*, we have now assembled a significant oral history archive of the digital age, and we are immensely grateful to all those who willingly took part.

It takes an army to create a television series, and everyone who contributed to the making of *Nerds 2.0.1* has equally contributed to the production of this book. I will attempt to acknowledge *everyone* at the peril of omitting *someone*. Bruce Barrow edited the series with great skill and intelligence, and still greater calm; Greg Bond shot the great majority of the videotape with patience, vision, and energy. Gene Koon deserves a special mention for having recorded all but a tiny fraction of the audio for both series, always reliably and with good humor. Brett Wood and Wendy Revak shot some of the pictures, with great confidence and style. John Booth directed some important sequences for the series and did so beautifully. Michael Bard, our composer, added immensely to the final flavor of the series by composing music which echoed the times, tastes, and tones of the pictures in a masterful fashion.

My production team deserve special praise for enduring the long, long grind from original, incoherent series concept to final delivery. Gino Del Guercio, a fine producer in his own right, undertook to serve as line producer for this series, and made a great contribution editorially and creatively. Mark Dorgan, who has the dubious distinction of having worked with me for almost five years, brought his calm competence to bear whenever called upon. Catherine Wilson joined us to help resolve last-minute logjams and delivery deadlines, and learned fast. Above all, Cyndee Readdean fulfilled the role of associate producer of the series with unfailing good humor, thoughtfulness, and sheer hard work. She chased details and paperwork, invoices and schedules, relentlessly, not only throughout production of the series, but also during the writing of this book. Her talent for cajoling strangers to loan her vintage computers, flawless antique sports cars, and grungy VW buses—even a golden retriever for a TV camco—is just astounding.

At Oregon Public Broadcasting (OPB), I would like to acknowledge the support and encouragement of my senior management colleagues Maynard Orme, Debbi Hinton, and John Lindsay, both for our joint efforts to create excellent television productions, and for agreeing to let me take a short break from production and development activity to write this book.

Many more people at OPB contributed to *Nerds 2.0.1*, in a variety of ways: Carrie Christopher (who created the graphic design for the series) and Neil Blume (who executed some of it); Rosalie Edmonds (who typed every word of more than seventy interview transcripts); online editor Howard Beckerman; producer/stand-in narrator Jim Leinfelder; business manager Susan Smith (who tracked the budget around the globe); and engineers John Scoon, John Frazee, and Dave Fulton (who can fix Apple Powerbooks like no one else). Chris Zier helped in various ways to get computers to work right in front of the camera—no small task.

As I have noted in the Introduction, there is a growing array of books discussing the impact, meaning, and dangers of the Net and the digital age. There are relatively few that recount its development and history. Of the latter, one was particularly useful to us in researching *Nerds 2.0.1*. This was *Where Wizards Stay Up Late*, by Katie Hafner and Matthew Lyon. For readers who wish to know much more, in both narrative and technical detail, about the creation of the ARPAnet, it is to be highly recommended. I have, however, endeavored to tell a much wider story in these pages, with reference only to our own interviews and original documentary sources.

Television programming of quality is expensive, and *Nerds 2.0.1* was fortunate to enjoy the financial support of two admirable institutions: PBS, the Public Broadcasting Service, of which Oregon Public Broadcasting is a member; and the Alfred P. Sloan Foundation, which provides grants to enhance the public understanding of science and technology. At PBS, I wish to thank for their support of the Nerds ventures Ervin Duggan, Kathy

Quattrone, John Hollar, John Wilson, Sandy Heberer, Mary Jane McKinven, and Glenn Marcus. At the Sloan Foundation, program officer Doron Weber made it painless and pleasant to seek and acquire funding for our project. The Sloan Foundation also supported the writing and production of this book, for which I offer additional thanks.

I am grateful to Peter Kaufman, the publisher of TV Books, and Keith Hollaman, editorial director, for seeing the potential value in this companion book and bending editing and publishing schedules beyond breaking point to print it to coincide with our broadcast date on PBS. I also owe a significant debt to Len Kleinrock, professor of computer science at UCLA, who kindly undertook to read the manuscript and offered invaluable suggestions and technical corrections to the low-tech author.

These pages would not be complete without my acknowledging the advice, friendship, and mentoring of three men: John Callaway, formerly director of the Benton Fellowship at the University of Chicago, and a model exponent of public television journalism (or any other kind) at WTTW in Chicago; Professor Marvin Zonis of the Graduate School of Business at the University of Chicago, whose eclecticism, intellectual firepower, and hospitality it has been my privilege to enjoy; and Dr. Harry Wilmer, founder and president of the Institute for the Humanities at Salado, Texas—a wise and beloved man.

Finally, but no less important, I want to record my heartfelt thanks to my family for their support, love, and patience. For many months, they saw far less of me than I wanted; less, I think, than they would have wanted. To my wife, Merrill; my son, Adam; and my daughter, Coco, I can offer only a simple thank you—for accepting with such good grace that to make a TV series and write a companion book (just like in Silicon Valley), "you can work any eighty hours a week you like." I owe you all, and I owe you everything.

While the content of the book has been largely based upon interviews we recorded for our series, other material kindly loaned by our interviewees, and a variety of published sources, the selection, interpretation, and opinions expressed here are my own. If there are factual errors, they are mine.

Introduction
Very, Very Long Legs

JEFF BEZOS, FOUNDER OF AMAZON.COM, the online bookstore, says this about the contrast between his solid products and the intangible medium in which the transactions are processed: "I think there's a sort of a fundamental irony that we're using bits to sell atoms. And, yeah, it's a little wacky. But it works and it's extremely efficient and people recognize the value."

It is a statement that neatly captures both the tone and the attitude of the most dynamic and rapidly growing industry in history. The language is a mixture of the technical, the juvenile, and the profit-motivated. But it is this geeky pragmatism that has transformed a technology once reserved for computer scientists in research laboratories into a global medium of instantaneous communications—and commerce. If the invention and propagation of the personal computer in all its forms was the Triumph of the Nerds, then the evolution of the wired world is truly the Glory of the Geeks. How it got to be that way is the subject of this book.

Of course, there's also "sort of a fundamental irony" in writing a book at all on this subject. But as long as computers take many seconds to boot up and minutes to print more than a couple of pages, the book has a user-friendliness that's unbeatable.

Just ask Jeff Bezos: he sold $87 million worth of these cumbersome old devices last year, without the trouble or overhead of either a bookstore or a printed catalog. Amazon's 1997 results—a net loss of just over $9 million, $6 million *worse* than the previous year—was greeted on Wall Street as a triumph, and the stock shot up. The company is valued at about $1.6 billion at the time of writing. Not for its earnings, but for its rate of growth and potential reach. In 1996, Amazon had sales of less than $16 million. The following year, sales rose by almost ten times, to $148 million. In the final quarter of its fiscal year, Amazon's customer accounts grew 50 percent, to $2.26 million. But in the Internet economy, 15 percent growth a month is barely worthy of comment.

According to the U.S. Commerce Department report of April 1998, *The Emerging Digital Economy*, "The Internet's pace of adoption eclipses all other technologies that preceded it. Radio was in existence thirty-eight years before fifty million people tuned in; TV took thirteen years to reach that benchmark. Sixteen years after the first PC kit came out, fifty million people were using one. Once it was opened to the general public, the Internet crossed that line in four years."

The speed with which the Internet industry is evolving, and the Internet marketplace is growing, guarantees that this book, like any reference text, will become dated. However, it is the only work so far to attempt a general history of the wired and networked world, and the Internet's thirty years of development represent a solid and intriguing preamble to its current, ever-accelerating growth. As John Doerr, leading Silicon Valley venture capitalist, observes, "Think of this as just a few milliseconds after the Big Bang. We only barely discern the fundamental laws of physics, the business models that are going to work. And it's got very, very long legs because, unlike the PC, it leverages the top line. It helps us entertain and inform and educate and inspire and sell and make community, even make meaning out of life and out of death. And that's a far more powerful dynamic than cranking out memos and doing financial analyses with a spreadsheet."

The Department of Commerce, not prone to hyperbole, lines up the statistics of Internet growth thus:
- Fewer than 40 million people worldwide were connected to the Internet in 1996. A year later, the figure had more than doubled, to 100 million people.
- In the same year, domain names registered rose from 627,000 to 1.5 million.
- Cisco Systems (the leading manufacturer of routers, a key element of the Internet's own infrastructure) made $100 million worth of sales on the Internet in 1996. In 1997, its Internet sales totalled $3.2 billion.
- In 1998, it takes only 100 days for the Internet's volume of traffic to double.

As a consequence, this book, like the television series it accompanies, makes no effort to predict the likely outcome of events unfolding today. All it can attempt is a reasonable stab at recounting the events of the recent past and an explanation of why they unfolded as they did.

In fact, another "sort of a fundamental irony" can be found in the fact that this volume may be in danger of adding to a growing, but not very appealing category of books that extol in linear, analog, page-by-page fashion the elusive appeal and importance of the non-linear, digital, interactive communication phenomenon. A welter of these volumes—slim books, making broad claims—have been appearing since the rise of the World Wide Web in 1994; collectively they represent a compelling argument for the utility of history over futurology.

Those who cover this industry on an hourly, daily, or weekly basis long ago exhausted the supply of metaphors and superlatives with which to describe a working environment of twenty-hour days, intense rivalries, and immense rewards. The rate of growth is breathtaking in the short term, unsustainable in the long term. In the 1950s, it was calculated that if long-distance phone traffic continued to increase at the same rate for twenty years, every American citizen would have to be employed as a telephone operator. (What happened to them, by the way?) But between the short term and the long term, there is a lot of market capitalization to be generated. And an immense churning of talent and stress. Rohit Khare, a twenty-two-year-old wunderkind of the World Wide Web Consortium, claims that in the Web universe, "a person with two years' experience has gotten more experience in Web years than someone who's got twenty years of the previous generation of programming. That's a bit of an overstatement, but Web years are a wonderful curiosity to the general public and an actual health threat to those who work in the industry."

Other than for children in science class, or those wanting to get jobs in software development, learning *how* the Internet works may not be of any real value. For users of the Internet, its *use* is the point, not its mechanics. There will be a minority of people who really do care about the encoding of words into digits; the capsulizing of batches of digits into packets; the labeling of packets; their distribution by electrical impulse along copper wires, coaxial cables, fiber-optic cables, or radio waves; the redirection of packets to their final destination; their reassembly into ordered streams of digits by IMPS (the original network switches) and nodes, and later by hubs and servers; and the retranslation of digits into words appearing as pixels on a screen. Some people will care about that, and they may come away from reading this book feeling undernourished. Others, like the author, may prefer just to accept (uneasily) that it simply does work—like the internal combustion engine, or photosynthesis, or a flea circus.

I am not a technologist or scientist, but a journalist. I once produced (with the aid of my psychologist wife) a television series on the life and work of C. G. Jung. After seeing these films, a prominent Jungian analyst concluded that filmmaking was like anthropology. The task, he said, was to enter a more or less closed community, in which people spoke their own language, observed their own customs and rituals, enjoyed and perpetuated arcane feuds, shared a set of far-from-universal beliefs and secrets, and claimed to have a special understanding of the human condition. Having gained their confidence, the filmmaker settled down to trying to capture their worldview; and then returned to the outside world to offer a report to the wider community. This kind of television documentary is indeed a little like anthropology; and the self-enclosed world of the nerds and geeks is no less baffling to the outsider, perhaps more so, than that of analytical psychology.

My job here, as in our television series *Triumph of the Nerds* and *Nerds 2.0.1*, is to tell a coherent and enlightening story of a cultural phenomenon that is truly changing many aspects of many people's lives. The technology is inseparably a part of the story, but the emphasis here is on the people who did it, the ideas they were pursuing, the ambitions they shared, and its meaning to them at the time and in retrospect. In the modern, Western, industrialized nations at least, the advent of the universal syntax of www. and dotcom appears to be startlingly rapid and deeply entrenched.

The story we now try to tell is how it got to be that way. In producing our television series *Nerds 2.0.1*, we have had the good fortune to be granted access to almost all of the pioneers, inventors, and prime movers who made the Internet and the wired world happen, from unsung researchers who are most comfortable in white laboratory coats, to tycoons and corporate executives whose faces routinely appear on covers of the world's newsmagazines. Much of this story, therefore, will be told in the words of the people who did the work... and changed the world. Like Frank Heart, the manager of the original development team that first connected computers together into a network: "It feels wonderful. I think it's incredibly exciting. It's the kind of thing where now you go down the street to your neighbors, who never knew what a computer was in the days you were doing this, and they're all of a sudden experts at using the Web, and I think that's a lot of fun. So, it's quite nice."

Drawing on the interviews given by more than seventy people for our television series, this book will recount the history and evolution of networking from the time before it existed until approximately yesterday. The story lasts roughly forty years, and the book is divided into four parts, by decade.

It is inevitable, in presenting a historical review of events, that one identifies a starting point, milestones, and continuing trends as a way of organizing and rationalizing the material that is mostly accurate, partly arbitrary. This case is no exception.

The earliest beginnings remind us of a historical truth and a modern one: American technology has been driven by the urge to explore and open the frontier, and the perennial desire for personal communication that works ever more easily, across longer distances. Thus the first antecedent of modern networking can be identified as Samuel Morse, whose eponymous code consists of timed pulses of electricity. He chose to transmit over electrical wires, which can only transmit a pulse, or no pulse: on or off. That binary choice is the fundamental basis of all "digital computing." The digits are 1 and 0, on and off. The difference is that today they travel billions of times faster.

On May 24, 1844, Morse sent his famous message "What hath God wrought?" to a receiver thirty-seven miles away in Baltimore. He assigned his patents to the Magnetic Telegraph Company, which signed up licensees. By 1851, there were fifty competing telegraph companies, and Western Union was formed by a merger of a dozen of these. By 1866, Western Union had over four thousand offices—opening a new office about every other day—and became the first communications giant in U.S. history. That pace of growth comes close to rivaling the uptake of the Net.

Looking back, on the eve of the new century and millennium,

it seems apparent that the revolution in computing derives most
directly from the mid-century war, when technology was most
fully engaged in the service of military efforts. World War II gave
birth to radar, cryptographic machines, battlefield communications methods, and a pace of operations that combined to create
a legacy in computer science. Problem-solving, communications,
automation, and remote command-and-control processes all resulted from the impetus of wartime necessity. Among the first pioneers of the world of networking, Dr. Vannevar Bush left a
legacy that can be clearly traced. Bush was the wartime director
of the Office of Scientific Research and Development in the Roosevelt and Truman administrations, was closely involved in the
Manhattan Project, and was appointed the first director of the National Science Foundation in 1950. His July 1945 article in the
Atlantic Magazine, "As We May Think," describing a "memex"
device that today would be called a laptop or palmtop computer,
inspired the first postwar generation of computer scientists (before they had that name) to experiment with ways of using computing power to augment human efficiency.

These trends might have remained truly a backwater of academic thought and laboratory experimentation had it not been for
the Cold War, which provided the next great historical impetus.
The Sputnik launch, on October 4, 1957, brought the importance
of science to defense to everyone's attention. While the space race
was to become the most visible, even glamorous representation of
the Cold War struggle, and technology in itself a weapon of Cold
War rivalry, the seeds of computer networking—sown at the same
time—can be argued to have had more lasting, profound, and
widespread consequences. Both space exploration and networking programs got started around the turn of the decade, and both
proceeded towards their ultimate success in 1969. Networking
was a bold experiment in the 1960s.

The hyperbolic growth of the Internet suggests that a brief history is timely. With Net usage doubling every hundred days, the
vast majority of users come to the Net in its Web-faced, graphical, media-savvy form. Many of them perhaps will be surprised
to learn that the Net has been thirty years in the making, and that
for the first fifteen years it was as obscure as any other Pentagon-
funded backwater of research. The earliest pioneers are still

mostly at work in the field, or just old enough to retire by choice. In a way, the Net is both older and younger than it seems; its beginnings came before most present-day users were born, but its heyday, so far, has come in the nineties. One entity links both origins and apogee: the United States government, in both executive and legislative branches.

Reading source materials, and interviewing early participants, one senses a surreal contrast between the image of the Department of Defense (DoD) as a funding source for the earliest adventures in networking, and the ideology of many of the people (though not all) who thought networking important. Who would expect to see the DoD described in *Rolling Stone*, on December 7, 1972—of all times, a month after Richard Nixon's reelection—as "enlightened"? The ethos of the sixties and seventies, usually thought of as "hippie" but almost interchangeable with "hacker," had a significant effect on the evolution of computer networking and its uses. Computer science was a cool new area to be working in, with so little history that one central figure claimed that most of computer science could be mastered in one year of close attention. Networking was funky in the 1970s.

The historical trends and milestones are categorized quite neatly by decade. Sputnik in the fifties spawned the beginnings of networking experiments; and the ARPAnet, the first fledgling academic and governmental computer network, was developed in the sixties. The ethos of the sixties helped promote and distribute more widely the gospel of networking. As Steve Jobs points out, "The sixties really happened in the seventies." The late seventies and early eighties marked the next major milestone of network expansion, caused by the invention of the personal computer.

In some respects, the story of the Internet owes nothing to the personal computer, for network experiments predate any form of personal computer by at least a decade. Yet without the PC (a term whose coining is claimed by the networker par excellence Stewart Brand), networking might have remained stuck in the limited enclaves of computer-science departments, federally funded research projects, and a few large corporate ventures. But it was not so much the PC as a *personal* device that in the eighties multiplied the value and reach of networking; rather, it was the PC as a *business* machine, whose utility was multiplied when the prospect of networking and connecting data became real. The IBM PC, launched in 1981; the Sun Microsystems workstation in 1982; the Apple Macintosh in 1984; and IBM clones led by Compaq in 1983 coincided with the deregulation of financial services in the United States and Europe. Increasingly powerful desktop computers, especially when networked to share and exchange information, were a key tool of the financial industry in the decade that later earned the smear slogan "Greed Is Good." Networking became professional in the 1980s.

The personal computer generation had begun in about 1978, with the introduction of the first computer that was truly personal, affordable, and usable by almost anyone—the Apple II. So anyone born after 1970, into a family with the funds and imagination to equip the home with an Apple (or a Tandy, Commodore, Osborn, etc.) can be considered a member of the PC generation. In the late eighties and early nineties, these kids were in college, having lived with computers all their lives. And it was among this community, of people entirely at home with computers as tools and toys, that a cool new medium, accessible *only* by computer, began to take hold.

By the 1990s, computer science was no longer a field that could be learned in one year of close attention. It was established, and produced people who suddenly became immensely rich. Despite the best efforts of many self-confessed "nerds" to speak a language other people cannot understand, the results of computer science began to be widely understood. Two milestones of the nineties portray the half-accidental, half-predictable evolution of the Net. The first was the World Wide Web, created by the individual brilliance of one information technology consultant, an Englishman named Tim Berners-Lee, in a nuclear research laboratory in Europe. The second was the Mosaic browser, or Web browser, developed by university students from the PC generation in an out-of-the-way campus that just happened to house one of the vertebrae on the National Science Foundation's powerful supercomputer network backbone. In both cases, these efforts betray the classic nerd trait of deep impatience at things that don't work as well as they should, or (they imply) as their finely tuned brains would accommodate more easily.

In 1992, the Net was freed by the U.S. government of its noncommercial restrictions and became a medium not just for information, but for commerce. (Although the Net is not strictly an American entity, so much of its technology has evolved in the United States that it has been de facto American from the start. All internationally based Web site addresses end with a two-digit country designation like *uk* or *fr*, while American-based sites have no such suffix.) Suddenly people with money (advertisers) and merchandise (everyone from Amazon to Z. Z. Top) wanted to promote a medium that was previously reserved for connoisseurs of a sort. The predictable result was a vast increase in awareness of the Net, together with an inevitable tidal wave of digital dross. But the commercial impulse, and its effective underwriting of the medium in all its expressions, has probably done more good than harm. General use is subsidized by the commerce, but no one is forced to participate in the commerce. One may still use the Net for its social, informational, and artistic content. In the 1990s, the Net became a mass, ubiquitous phenomenon.

So this is a story in which the government is the good guy. Networking began as a U.S. government experiment, and twenty-four years later networking was empowered (or prostituted) as a mass medium for commerce by an act of the United States Congress. At no time in the story have the supposedly restrictive instincts of government been allowed to limit networking, and its exponential growth has been facilitated by the hands-off attitude of the government officials who took charge or took an interest.

Despite the military/diplomatic origins of the Sputnik-provoked ARPAnet, the experimental mainframe network that provided the fundamental roots of all subsequent computer networking, its protocols were always in the public domain, its activities were unclassified, and its architects either by chance or design belonged to that school of thought that said computers can be used to assist people and improve their lives. Thirty years later, a variety of outcomes can be claimed for the Net, from the suggestion that the booming information-technology sector is responsible for a negative 1 percent trend in U.S. inflation, as the Department of Commerce states, to the less measurable, but widely believed argument that the Net was responsible for facilitating social and political liberation in places as diverse as Myanmar, Russia, and China. The narrative comes almost full circle: a

Pentagon program prompted by Cold War rivalry has evolved into a communications medium that helps overthrow, or at least publicize the activities of, tyrants. Today's tyrants are attempting to restrict or dominate computer networks, almost certainly in vain.

One of the most striking themes in the history of networking is the fact that each new breakthrough is, on closer examination, a repetition, a new way of solving much the same problem over and over again. The core problem of getting computers to communicate with each other is, by definition, one of compatibility. As the network grows bigger, incompatibilities must be overcome. As separate networks present the prospect of interconnection, compatibility hurdles arise. And as the pressure grows to connect all data resources together and make them universally accessible, the key technological obstacle is incompatibility. While the value and user-friendliness of networked computers is also driven by speed, memory, bandwidth (known to lay people as capacity or power), and interface design (how the screen looks to the user), none of these matters without a compatible platform of hardware and software.

Thus a number of episodes in this book tell a somewhat similar story: how the ARPAnet overcame the challenge of connecting computers made to different specifications by different manufacturers; how both the Stanford University Network and Cisco Systems linked disparate hardware in different departments or locations; and how the first Mosaic browser and the World Wide Web both provided software solutions to "translate" material from anywhere into a common language of words, images, and addresses.

Cumulatively, the wealth-generation of the Net thunders on. Our interviews with those who have started companies, raised venture funding, taken their ventures public, and ridden the information-technology wave on a rising tide of investor funding, driving the Dow Jones and NASDAQ exchanges upwards, all demonstrate the astonishing vigor and profitability of Internet-driven businesses. Carnegies, Mellons, and Rockefellers were surely never as accessible, frank, and direct about profits as the founders of Amazon, Excite, Sun, Cisco Systems, or 3Com. But the revolution of their products and technology is the wealth-creating engine of the world, at least into the beginning of the next century. What is so different about this revolution, however, is the low price of entry.

To industrialize a nation, a century ago, required a massive physical infrastructure, the import or extraction of huge amounts of raw materials, large amounts of capital to create and build industry, and decades of amortizing those costs before productivity and profitability repaid them. In the information economy, the cost of the infrastructure keeps dropping. Geographical, physical barriers that used to obstruct or raise the cost of imports are largely irrelevant. Citizens and governments alike can get online for very modest investments, and there's no catching-up required. Today's neophyte user starts with much the same access to the Net as someone who has been online since the ARPAnet first ticked into existence in 1969. The accumulated knowledge of how the Net used to work when it was *difficult* is of no further use now that it is *easy*. This has a curious effect on employment patterns and career paths in high technology. It may be no advantage, or could even be a disadvantage, to have twenty years of experience because that experience probably relates to an obsolete technology.

In the 1970s, when hippies weren't protesting about the Vietnam War they were worrying about multinational corporations and "cultural imperialism." The concern was that white Anglo-American culture and the English language were going to overrun the world to the detriment of ethnicity and minority identity elsewhere. The Internet has definitively delivered on that prognosis.

English *is* the language of the Internet, and predominantly of the computer and software industries. The accelerating spread of the Net is only going to deepen and strengthen this reality. It has interesting consequences, in that well-educated Anglophone engineers—most notably in India but also in Hong Kong, Singapore, Malaysia, and elsewhere—find themselves in great demand for employment in Silicon Valley, Boston, Austin, and Seattle. However, only Silicon Valley has a really thriving cricket league, populated by batting and bowling programmers from South Asia. This trend might continue and grow, pending a greater liberalization of professional immigration rules by Congress. Another trend may accelerate: the use of the Internet to enable the import of programmers' work, not programmers. The industry generally calls this "outsourcing." Many American companies have established contracting relationships or full-scale subsidiary ventures in India—typically in Bangalore, where English is spoken, engineering education is of high quality, and Internet connections have perfected telecommuting and the twenty-four-hour workday.

On May 18, 1998, the U.S. Department of Justice, in the person of Attorney General Janet Reno, gave the Internet the ultimate accolade of legitimacy and maturity, by bringing suit for anti-competitive practices in the browser market against Microsoft. It was not Microsoft's de facto monopoly in the personal computer operating system market, but its giveaway Web browser that attracted the attention of the federal regulators. Had anyone at the Justice Department heard of "browsers" five years earlier? Still, all the details of the case were there for anyone to survey, at http://www.usdoj.gov.

There's no ready conclusion to this story, neither the Bill Gates/Uncle Sam confrontation nor the onrushing Internet narrative. The day this manuscript is completed, it becomes outdated. Growth will race on, though it must level off at some point. Before that happens, some information technology boosters argue there will be a twenty- to thirty-year "long boom" in the stock markets. But this brief history—in identifying trends and milestones of the past, with insights and perspectives of the pioneers—can only aim to help show how things have been, and hint at what might come next.

Appendices provide the reader with a cast of characters, a timeline of events, and a glossary of technical terms that need to be defined. There is also a selection of photographs, provided mostly by the pioneers whose story is told in these pages.

A note on vocabulary: in everyday speech in 1998, the terms "Internet," "Net," and "Web" have become almost completely interchangeable. All three convey in general all the data one can reach by computer modem, wherever it may be. In referring to this general resource, I too have used the terms interchangeably, especially in later chapters. Separately, the terms "ARPAnet," "Internet," and "World Wide Web" refer to specific technological entities, created at particular times in the chronology, and I have used them accordingly. I hope that the difference between specific language in the narrative and generic use in quotation and interpretation is clear.

This book is an oral history—anecdotal, selective, and impressionistic—that attempts to present a coherent, broadly chronological account of a history spanning four decades. Because this book relies primarily on interviews, and secondarily on published sources, it is clear that for any one piece of the story the interested reader has a choice of more detailed and more technical books—on the ARPAnet alone, the impact of the Cold War on American science, the ups and downs of Xerox Palo Alto Research Center, and so on. Since 1994, we have been interviewing the pioneers of both the personal computer industry and the networking industry. From more than 120 interviews, we have tried to assemble two coherent television series and one useful book to provide what one Internet professional refers to as "strong consensus and working code." The material here is a synthesis of memories, interpretation, and anecdote, but a strong consensus of narrative does emerge. Whether the author has produced "working code," the reader may decide.

Part One

The 1960s:
Inventing
the Wheel

Chapter One
A Testing Time

Looking back, with four decades' perspective, we see the creation of the Internet as one of the twentieth century's most productive accidents. For a modern medium of communications and commerce to have been planned, executed, expanded, and ultimately liberated by an agency of the government seems most unlikely. Yet this is indeed the story of the almost seamless evolution of a government-funded efficiency experiment named ARPAnet into the ubiquitous, commercial, hip media space known as the Web. Bob Taylor, the man who can most truly claim to have activated the era of computer networking, occupied a desk in the Pentagon where it all began. As he explains, "Computers were first born as arithmetic engines, but my own view, and the view of some other people as well, is that they're much more interesting and powerful as communication devices because they mediate human-to-human communication."

So it has been proved. The seeds of the Internet were planted by the U.S. government in the wake of nationwide concern over the Soviet launch of *Sputnik*. But the soil had already been tilled, fertilized, and watered by a prior succession of federal government and military research programs that were based at the engineering powerhouse of MIT, the Massachusetts Institute of Technology, and its rural outpost, Lincoln Laboratory. Lincoln Laboratory was the academic, experimental location for both research and researchers who had what it took to build a computer network. In later phases of the ongoing development of computer networking, the focus and developmental momentum would shift to commercial entities such as Bolt Beranek & Newman (BBN) in Cambridge, Massachusetts, or the Palo Alto Research Center of Xerox Inc. in California; and back to academic centers at the Stanford Research Institute, the University of California at Los Angeles, the University of Hawaii, and the National Center for

Supercomputing Applications at the University of Illinois, Champaign-Urbana. Along the way, companies such as Microsoft, Novell, Sun Microsystems, 3Com, Cisco Systems, and Netscape would all play important roles. But the nursery in which the seeds germinated was Lincoln Lab, a few miles out in the countryside beyond Cambridge.

The Cold War was the context for Lincoln's research funding. By the late 1940s, the Soviet Union had both long-range bombers and the atomic bomb—which meant that they could, in theory, deliver a nuclear weapon to the mainland United States. President Harry Truman's administration asked the U.S. Air Force to develop a defense system to detect and counteract airborne attack. The Department of Defense called upon MIT to assist in this effort, and in 1951, MIT founded Lincoln as a "Laboratory for Air Defense." Its mission: to develop an air defense system that could detect, identify, intercept, and direct resources against hostile aircraft. This capability became known as DEW (for "Defense Early Warning"). In 1951, Lincoln Lab hired behavioral psychologist J.C.R. Licklider to work in a non-defense area. Forty-six years old, "Lick," as he urged everyone to call him, started the lab's human-engineering group.

Most projects at Lincoln focused on DEW work. Lincoln took over from MIT's Project Whirlwind, one of the earliest computers. While the navy had supported computer research at Harvard, the army had funded the development of ENIAC (the computer that later evolved into Remington Rand's UNIVAC) at the University of Pennsylvania. At MIT, both the navy and the air force had supported Project Whirlwind. One of the graduate students who worked on Whirlwind at Lincoln Lab was Frank Heart, who would later become the project manager for the ARPAnet (the first network of mainframes):

It was a part of MIT that did some of the very best computer R&D in that period of time, and a lot of the people who were later involved in the ARPAnet and the Internet worked at Lincoln at one time or another. Larry Roberts worked at Lincoln, I worked at Lincoln. Dave Walden and others that followed me to BBN worked at Lincoln. One thing about Lincoln was it was a source of people. But also that was a place that was doing some of the very best work of connecting computers to phone lines, and trying to use computers to handle real-time data coming from antennas or seismic arrays or submarines or ocean sensing devices or anything else. And so the people got a lot of experience connecting computers to real systems and real phone lines. That was the source of the expertise which got my group in a position to work on the ARPAnet contract.

Whirlwind was succeeded at Lincoln Lab by the SemiAutomatic Ground Environment (SAGE), another defense venture with momentous consequences for the networking of computers. This new air defense system required many of the same features, and thus expertise, that an experimental computer network would in due course demand, particularly digital communications, real-time software applications, networking, and a completely reliable computer. SAGE, as the experiment was officially designated in July 1954, could locate and mobilize a variety of defenses against incoming enemy bombers, but not against missiles. It lacked any interception capacity; as long as the enemy didn't possess intercontinental ballistic missiles, it was theoretically adequate to defend the United States. SAGE operated from 1960s to mid 1980s, initially with vacuum-tube computers and room-sized memory banks. It resulted in a network of inter-operating computers across the United States—arguably the first computer network.

The official history of Lincoln Lab, a glossy, illustrated hardcover volume entitled "MIT Lincoln Laboratory—Technology in the National Interest" makes the huge claim that SAGE spun off both the computer and digital communications industries. Certainly IBM was the prime contractor for SAGE computers and used that expertise in part to shift from being a business machines specialist to become the world's biggest commercial computer manufacturer. The SAGE division of Lincoln Lab, 485 employees in all, was spun off by MIT to become the MITRE Corporation in 1959. Similarly, the System Development Division of the Rand Corporation, in Santa Monica, California, which SAGE contracts had enlarged until it was bigger than all the rest of the company, had already mutated into the System Development Corporation, with a thousand employees, in 1956.

More spin-offs were to follow. At Lincoln Lab, another of the ultimate pioneers of ARPAnet, Larry Roberts, and someone who would make a key theoretical contribution, Wesley Clark, worked on building the first transistorized computers, prototypes of the TX0 and TX2. Among the many SAGE alumni who went on to founding roles in computer technology and business were Kenneth Olsen and Harlan Anderson, who exploited their SAGE experience to start the Digital Equipment Corporation, which pioneered computers that were smaller and cheaper than IBM-type mainframes, and were thus generically known as "mini-computers," though nothing about these machines could yet be described as "personal." The TX-0 computer evolved into the Digital PDP-1, and the TX-2 was the prototype of the PDP-6 and PDP-10. More significantly, the TX-2 was commercialized as the cornerstone of Digital and later used in the very first computer networking experiment, predictably carried out at Lincoln Lab, by Larry Roberts.

Roberts' friend Len Kleinrock—who would in due course assume another key role in the development and proliferation of computer networking at UCLA—also worked on TX-2 at Lincoln Lab, having attended MIT on full scholarship. Kleinrock had gone to the legendary Bronx High School of Science, after an unusual introduction to the world of engineering—a comic book. At the age of six, Leonard Kleinrock was reading a Superman comic at his family's apartment in Manhattan, when, in the centerfold, he found plans for building a crystal radio. To do so, he needed his father's used razor blade, a piece of pencil lead, an empty toilet paper roll, and some wire. None of these were difficult to find. In addition, he needed an earphone, which he promptly appropriated from a public telephone booth.

The one remaining part required was something called a "variable capacitor." For this, young Leonard convinced his mother to take him on the subway down to Canal Street, the center for radio electronics. In one of the stores, he asked the clerk for a variable capacitor. After some debate about the size, which forced the six-year-old to confess his inexperience, the clerk sold him just what he needed. Kleinrock built the crystal radio. When "free" music came through the earphones—without batteries, without power—an engineer was born.

After Bronx Science, Kleinrock found he could not afford to attend even the tuition-free City College of New York, so he enrolled in their evening session program while working full time as an electronics technician and engineer. Five-and-a-half years later, he graduated and won a full graduate fellowship to attend MIT in the Electrical Engineering Department.

In 1959, Kleinrock proposed doing his Ph.D. thesis on communications networks. In 1961, while at MIT, he wrote a report that analyzed data flow in networks. A short quotation from that report: "The nets considered consist of nodes that receive, sort, store, and transmit messages entering and leaving by way of the links."

According to Roberts, Kleinrock's theoretical contribution on the method of digitizing and transmitting information, which was to become known as "packet switching," was another key plank in the ARPAnet platform: "Kleinrock published the first papers in '59 or '61 on packet switching in terms of the packet technology.... Kleinrock is very much not understood for what his contribution was back then. But he did [the] initial research in his Ph.D. thesis."

As Kleinrock himself recalls: "Well, it all began when I started as a graduate student at MIT. I reached a point where I wanted to do a Ph.D. I was made aware of a problem that the military was having in what we now call data networking—sending messages around in a reliable way, in a hostile environment, efficiently. So I started doing some research in data networks and my Ph.D. dissertation basically uncovered the underlying principles of packet switching, of message switching, of burst communications, of data networking."

Kleinrock completed this Ph.D. research at the end of 1962, and in doing so he laid the foundation for packet switching, the key invention for the technology of today's Internet.

Kleinrock may have missed a golden opportunity while at MIT. In 1957, his first summer at MIT, Kleinrock worked for Ken Olsen, who offered him a job in his start-up venture: "Ken Olsen was head of our group. That summer he formed Digital Equipment Corporation and he asked me to join him and, of course, I didn't because I wanted to get my graduate degrees, which I still consider a smart move; after all, I would not have invented the Internet technology if I had left graduate school at that point."

The seriousness with which these pioneers set about exploring the limits of technology contrasts with the sheer fun they found in fooling with great big expensive machines. A common theme is the fact that mere graduate students always had to work on the machines at times when more exalted members of the department didn't want access to the computers. So Len Kleinrock, once again, found himself propping his eyes open in front of the TX-2.

> Lincoln Laboratory sent me to MIT on a scholarship program in order to run my simulation, and I needed the machine quite heavily. There was one major transistorized computer there called the TX-2. I would get it from midnight to 7:00 A.M. four days a week. But they were not contiguous days so it totally destroyed my sleeping habits.
>
> One night, late, I was really beat and I was running the machine and all alone in this room. You'd get to know every sound and every sight. And I heard a sound that I didn't recognize. It was a 'Psssssss!' I began to get very worried. There I was, responsible for a million-dollar machine and it was in my charge right now making strange sounds. So I looked around.... The TX-2 was an experimental machine so parts of the machine were missing every so often. As I looked around, there was an empty slot where a piece of the machine had been removed to be repaired, and my eyes raised up and I looked at that slot and looking back were two eyes! And son of a gun, it was Larry Roberts! He had snuck in behind the machine... scared the hell out of me.

The responsiveness of the SAGE system was made necessary by the uncertainty of Cold War brinkmanship. In the mid-1950s, only *aircraft* early warning systems were required. SAGE represented a technological development that would prove significant in both the theory and practice of the computer networks that were to appear a decade later—namely, speed. The difference can be found between two types of computer processors. First, there are those that do things only when instructed, and that feed results back to the programmer when they're done, generally known as batch processing; and second, there are those that process information in "real time," so the operator and the computer are in constant consultation, and both input and output vary according to rapid change and interaction between machine and operator. The latter, using a computer "as an extension of the human mind," was the beginning of what J.C.R. Licklider called "Man-Computer Symbiosis."

In August 1957, the U.S.S.R. test-fired an Intercontinental Ballistic Missile (ICBM). Two months later, the announcement of the launch of Sputnik—demonstrating that the Soviet Union also had the capacity to launch rockets into earth orbit—shook the U.S. defense establishment (and its technology researchers). Sputnik I was launched on October 4, 1957, and shortly afterwards President Eisenhower convened a meeting of his Presidential Science Advisory Committee. At a presidential press conference, Eisenhower played down both Sputnik (he had been advised as far back as 1955 that it was possible) and the ICBM launch (he denied that the Unites States' own Strategic Air Command was obsolete).

A month later, Sputnik II was launched, but by then the American political response was in full swing. On November 7, James R. Killian Jr. (then president of MIT) was appointed as presidential science advisor and quickly became known as America's "missile czar."

Sputnik had caused a worldwide sensation and sent shock waves through the U.S. administration. Newsreels of the time show Moscow's citizens lining up to use powerful telescopes to observe their nation's technological prowess, and fashionable Muscovite ladies having battery-operated orbiting satellites inserted into their beehive hairstyles.

Within two weeks of Sputnik II, Killian testified before Congress about the progress of U.S. ballistic missile programs. By the end of the year, President Eisenhower decided to set up a "single manager" for all defense research, partly to eliminate inter-service rivalry, partly for efficiency. On January 7, 1958, President Eisenhower requested funds from Congress to set up the Advanced Research Projects Agency (ARPA).

While the Sputnik shock was a challenge and an opportunity for Eisenhower to take forceful action, it represented a political lever for the vice president, Richard M. Nixon, to use in his advance campaign for the Republican presidential nomination and in his ultimate campaign against Democratic nominee John F. Kennedy.

Nixon responded to Sputnik in terms of national anxiety and patriotism: "The Soviet Union is exploiting this day after day with their propaganda.... This is a testing time for the United States of America, a testing time not only to see if we have the faith in our system of government but also to see whether or not the people of the U.S.—in addition to wanting protection for their rights and their privileges—are willing to assume their responsibilities, which are essential if we are to continue to have economic progress, and progress in all the other fields which spell national greatness. I have no doubt as to the outcome of this struggle because I know that you have an infinite faith in the rightness of our system."

The Soviet capacity to launch missiles into orbit, with its threatening offensive implications, became a part of Nixon's rhetorical weaponry. By the time of the presidential campaign in 1960, the "missile gap"—exaggerating the difference between Soviet and American weapons arsenals—became an issue Kennedy had to deal with by outbidding Nixon on his own Cold War turf. The legacy would be mixed: as president, Kennedy inherited the disastrous Bay of Pigs invasion plans as a legacy of Eisenhower, yet was unable to disown the venture for fear of seeming "soft on Communism"; and Kennedy committed the country to an acceleration of the space race.

With an appropriation of $520 million, and a planned budget four times as large, approved as a line item in an air force appropriations bill, ARPA opened for business as the government's unitary research agency for all space and strategic missile research. Thus obscure academics suddenly found themselves on the Cold War's front line.

A geologist with an Abe Lincoln beard, Severo Ornstein was one of them. He landed his first job in computing as early as 1952 after accosting a fellow rock climber in a parking lot: "I looked in the back window of a car and there was a climbing rope. I looked up the owner of the car, who turned out to be a guy at MIT who had been working at Whirlwind (the early computer project)."

Ornstein had been thinking that interpreting seismographic information was work that a computer ought to be able to do: "Whirlwind was just going great guns at that point. MIT was just opening Lincoln Lab. The next thing we knew, we were bored with our work and we went on a ski trip up to New England, and he said as he left, 'You know enough about computers by now from our conversations, perhaps you can get a job too.' So I wrote and the next thing I knew I was working at Lincoln."

Ornstein went to work at Lincoln Lab on the initial research phase of the SAGE air defense system, thus becoming a member of a rare new breed: computer programmer: "Well, there were none then. If you said you were a programmer you had to explain what that might be to anyone that you met. It's really quite remarkable now. It's become so embedded. But there were only a handful of computers in the country at that time."

Sputnik forced people like Ornstein into the limelight: suddenly science became acknowledged as having public, indeed national importance: "It created a considerable stir. And we, of course, felt quite good about that because it was clear that the area that we had chosen to work in was going to get more attention. Science for a long time before that had not had a particularly good name. It had not been a big deal. And I think there was a sudden realization that it maybe was important after all. And that made people feel good."

As Bob Taylor, who would later initiate ARPA's great network experiment, recalls, "ARPA was created in response to Sputnik. Sputnik surprised the nation and the world. Eisenhower told the secretary of defense, 'I don't want to be surprised like this again, the nation shouldn't be surprised like this again.' So they wanted an agency created to fund especially promising high technology—risky funding, in some sense, so that they not be caught by surprise again. NASA was not in existence yet, but the early NASA programs were created in ARPA."

ARPA's half-billion-dollar budget didn't last. Although ARPA was placed under the management of the Defense Department (and later acquired a D for Defense and became DARPA), later in 1958 a separate, civilian agency was created to undertake all the space and missile research, which amounted to the lion's share of the funds. Consequently, the National Aeronautics and Space Administration (NASA) received its own appropriation of funds and stepped away from Pentagon supervision. The ARPA budget was left at around $150 million, and the research functions that remained were primarily those in computer science, high-technology research, and information processing.

Space got most of the money, and all the attention, as goals were set and achieved. Project Mercury was launched at the same time as NASA was set up, in 1958. The first of two manned suborbital flights, Freedom 7 (carrying Alan Shepard), took place on May 5, 1961.

In the same month, President Kennedy announced Project Apollo, which was the second major technological response to the Soviet threat and to continuing demonstrations of apparent Soviet superiority in space research. Before Congress on May 25, Kennedy requested additional funding for space programs, for this experiment in science and deliberate boost to national pride: "I believe that this nation should commit itself to achieving the goal before this decade is out, of landing a man on the moon and returning him safely to earth. No single space project of this period will be more impressive to mankind."

NASA's first orbital flight (with a chimpanzee on board) took place on November 29, 1961; the first manned orbital flight with John Glenn making his mark as America's first astronaut, just three months later, on February 20, 1962.

Kennedy was the cheerleader for a venture that would dominate American media attention for the rest of the decade, more so than any event other than his own assassination. At Rice University in Texas on September 12, 1960, the day after a spectacular Saturn rocket launch, the president cast the Space Race in blunt terms of Cold War rivalry: "We have vowed that we shall not see space governed by a hostile flag of conquest but by a banner of freedom and peace. We have vowed that we shall not see space filled with weapons of mass destruction but with implements of education.... We have vowed...to become the world's leading spacefaring nation. We choose to go to the Moon in this decade and do the other things not because they are easy but because they are hard, because that goal will serve to organize and measure the best of our energies and skills, because that challenge is one we are willing to accept, one we are unwilling to postpone, and one we intend to win."

While Kennedy was seizing the spotlight with a glamorous and daring assignment, the technologists and researchers of ARPA were exploring a variety of new technological avenues for a category broadly described as "information processing." Under a succession of visionary leaders, mostly still unknown and unrecognized, the Information Processing Techniques Office (IPTO) would prove to be the division of ARPA that would in fact build the foundations of the networked information economy which surrounds us today.

The first director of IPTO was J.C.R. Licklider, the prophet of the "intergalactic computer network," who was hired by the first director of ARPA, Jack Ruina. Five years earlier, "Lick" had moved from Lincoln Lab to join Bolt, Beranek & Newman in Cambridge. In 1960, Lick had published a memorable and influential paper, "Man-Computer Symbiosis," in which he had set out some of the prophetic ideas he had for such implementation of computers.

He summarized the main aims thus: "1) to let computers facilitate formulative thinking as they now facilitate the solution of formulated problems, and 2) to enable men and computers to co-operate in making decisions and controlling complex situations without inflexible dependence on predetermined programs.

Computing machines will do the routinizable work that must be done to prepare the way for insights and decisions in technical and scientific thinking."

Later in the paper, Lick continues, "The other main aim is closely related. It is to bring computing machines effectively into processes of thinking that must go on in 'real time,' time that moves too fast to permit using computers in conventional ways. Imagine trying, for example, to direct a battle with the aid of a computer.... Obviously the battle would be over before the second step in its planning was begun."

Bob Taylor was to succeed Licklider at ARPA. Licklider was proposing, perhaps for the first time, the type of "interactive computing" that every user of a personal computer now takes for granted. But when it was proposed, it was largely impossible: an act of the imagination. As Taylor says, "When you're punching holes in cards, you are not doing interactive computing. Because in those days to work with a computer you had to go punch a bunch of holes in either paper tape or cards. Then you had to take these cards to the computer room and turn them over to someone usually with a white coat on. That's called batch processing. It's not interactive computing. It's like writing letters to people long distance rather than talking to someone. [Interactive computing was] where you would type something onto your terminal and the computer would type something back to you."

Clearly, the "Symbiosis" would be assisted by the experience of those at Lincoln who, like Licklider, had been exposed to real-time computing—the nearest thing to interactive computing then available. Yet, while Lick could define how symbiosis *should* work, the task of designing how it *would* work lay in the realm of speculation. He wrote: "It seems reasonable to envision, for a time ten or fifteen years hence, a 'thinking center' that will incorporate the functions of present-day libraries together with anticipated advances in information storage and retrieval and the symbiotic functions suggested earlier in this paper. The picture readily enlarges itself into a network of such centers, connected to one another by leased-wire services. In such a system, the speed of the computers would be balanced, and the cost of the gigantic memories and the sophisticated programs would be divided by the number of users."

Thus was the sketch of a computer network proposed, in 1960, nine years before it became an experimental reality. Larry Roberts would become another of Lick's successors at ARPA, but it was at Lincoln Lab that he was first inspired by Licklider's contagious vision:

> Lick had this concept of the intergalactic network which he believed was everybody could use computers anywhere and get at data anywhere in the world. He didn't envision the number of computers we have today by any means, but he had the same concept—of all of the stuff linked together throughout the world, that you can use a remote computer, get data from a remote computer, or use lots of computers in your job. The vision was really Lick's originally. None of us can really claim to have seen that before him nor [can] anybody in the world. Lick saw this vision in the early sixties. He didn't have a clue as how to build it. He didn't have any idea how to make this happen. But he knew it was important, so he sat down with me and really convinced me that it was important and convinced me to move into making it happen.

But Lick was not satisfied with dreaming up mere computer networks; we should note also that by this time Len Kleinrock had designed, analyzed, and simulated a full computer network. Another aspect of the symbiosis Lick planned was a pen-based computer, like the Apple Newton or Palm Pilot. His paper described it thus:

Desk-Surface Display and Control

The man should be able to present a function to the computer, in a rough but rapid fashion, by drawing a graph. The computer should read the man's writing, perhaps on the condition that it be in clear block capitals, and it should immediately post, at the location of each hand-drawn symbol, the corresponding character as interpreted and put into precise type-face. With such an input-output device, the operator would quickly learn to write or print in a manner legible to the machine. The "other engineer" [the computer] would be a precise draftsman, a lightning calculator, a mnemonic wizard, and many other valuable partners all in one.

Furthermore, Licklider planned to cut directly to a symbiotic function—"Automatic Speech Production and Recognition"—which even today the largest software and hardware companies are struggling to master. What Bill Gates calls "the natural interface"—computers that listen, speak, and learn—was an early goal for Licklider, but for a reason that today seems more quaint than technological: "In large part the interest stems from realization that one can hardly take a military commander or corporation president away from his work to teach him to type."

Licklider had moved from Lincoln Laboratory to the small Cambridge consulting firm Bolt, Beranek and Newman. (Like the identity crisis of ARPA/DARPA over its "D" for Defense, BBN alumni interchangeably use or drop the ampersand. Ergo, BB&N = BBN.) BBN had been founded by MIT engineers in 1948 as an architectural acoustics firm, but as time went by it became a computer research organization as well. Some of its research and development work was commissioned by ARPA, and BBN earned a footnote in history (the headlines were to come later) by buying the first PDP-1 computer manufactured by Digital Equipment, serial number #1. It cost the monstrous sum of $150,000.

Licklider was recruited to BBN by founder Leo Beranek. The two had worked together at both Harvard and MIT. Lick started work at ARPA on October 1, 1962, and was charged with devising uses for computers other than as tools for computation. In early 1963, he wrote a memorandum proposing that ARPA's IPTO division contrive to have computer "centers netted together" with an "agreed language, or agreed conventions for asking 'what language do you speak?'" In the same year, Lick invited Robert Taylor, then a manager at NASA, to join a committee he headed of government program managers who were all funding computer research. Thus Licklider "networked" with academic and corporate computer scientists, a loose assembly that earned the nickname "Intergalactic Computer Network."

Despite the name, ARPA's plans remained earthbound, unlike NASA's spectacular ventures. As NASA launched America's first men into space in 1961 and 1962, the scientists at the Pentagon, deprived of the space portfolio, concentrated on computers. Compared with the glamour of the moon mission, computer research was something of a Cinderella. For the rest of the decade the space race would get all the media's attention—but even Cinderellas go to the ball in the end.

Computers circa 1963 were far from glamorous—they were the size of small apartments, and had neither screens nor keyboards. Their use was strictly rationed and only a few people got anywhere near them. But Licklider saw their growing and accelerating potential. As he stated in a television interview in the 1970s, "The computer technology has been moving in a way that nothing else that people have ever known has moved. Here is a field that gets a thousand times as good in twenty years."

Lick was thinking big about the future of networking at a time when there was only a handful of computers anywhere in the world, and decades before the personal computer would arrive. He recognized that as computer efficiency continued to accelerate, the breakthrough would come by creating access for more people at once: distributed computing. "Specialized hardware facilities tend to be expensive, but very efficient. On the other hand, if they can be distributed, then specialized hardware facilities can be very effective and can allow us to do things that we couldn't otherwise do."

Bob Taylor, like Licklider, was trained as an experimental psychologist, and his earliest career was devoted to brain research and the auditory nervous system. As he tells it, "I got interested in computing before there was computer science. And I wound up, through a bizarre set of circumstances, in a management rather than a technical role, having to do with computer research."

Bob Taylor joined NASA in 1961 as a manager of technology research. Born in Texas, the son of a minister, Taylor has an outstanding reputation as a manager who could identify and motivate the most talented researchers in the service of a common goal. His is the ultimate blue-chip resumé for the computer age: NASA, ARPA, Xerox PARC, Digital's Systems Research Center. Taylor came to Washington with a background in computer technology at the defense contractor Martin Marietta, and, after submitting a research proposal to NASA, was invited to join NASA as a program manager in their Office of Advanced Technology and Research. As he recalls: "Kennedy had gotten elected very recently, and he made a lot of people in my generation think for the first time seriously about working for the government, whereas previously a lot of people I know, myself included, would never have thought of working for the government. He changed people's values with regard to how you could make a difference."

Until 1965, Lick's division of ARPA had a more military name: Command & Control Research. In that year, it became the Information Processing Techniques Office, and Licklider was succeeded by Ivan Sutherland, a pioneer in the field of computer graphics, inventor of the "Sketchpad" device, yet again from MIT. Ivan Sutherland hired Bob Taylor to become associate director of IPTO, and in early 1966, Taylor succeeded Sutherland, to control probably the world's largest computer research budget.

Despite the rapid turnover of directors, one constant remained at ARPA: an unprecedented and unrivaled freedom in the defense and research community to select and fund experimental projects with almost no red tape. As Taylor remembers, "It was amazing for a government enterprise to be so unbureaucratic. With most government funding, there are committees who decide who gets what and who does what. In ARPA, that was not the way it worked. The person who was responsible for the office that was concerned with that particular technology, in my case, computer technology, was the person who made the decision about what to fund and what to do and what not to do."

While Taylor was not handicapped by red tape, he did need to find the right people to put into practice the vision of distributed, interactive computing that Licklider had planted in his mind. The core of talent at Lincoln Lab was clearly an asset, and some of those people had moved elsewhere. But the itinerary seemed mostly confined to the orbit of MIT—the campus itself, Lincoln Lab, and Bolt, Beranek & Newman in Cambridge.

Severo Ornstein, after half a dozen years at Lincoln Lab, was in his words, "beginning to grow a little weary of working always on air defense and air defense–related projects; and wanted to do something that was more directly of benefit to mankind. In particular, we were interested in medical work."

Lincoln Lab had been approached by the National Institutes of Health, which was interested in using computers in a variety of research tasks, in a number of disciplines within medical science. But Lincoln was not interested in medicine. So Ornstein—somewhat disillusioned with the military—and several colleagues left Lincoln Lab, first for MIT itself, then for the Midwest: "We didn't want to be under the thumb of the academics. So we left MIT, and I went with a shrinking group of people to Washington University in St. Louis. We worked there for a number of years building a bridge between the engineering school and the medical community."

But Ornstein "hated St. Louis with a passion." So he called a friend from Lincoln Lab: "I had worked with Frank Heart at Lincoln, at one time earlier on, and he was by then at BBN and so fairly naturally I tended to gravitate to where he was. I had also contacted Ivan Sutherland, who was at Harvard at the time, and I was offered a position there, and also at BBN. I taught at Harvard just on the side while I was working at BBN."

It had taken BBN founder Dick Bolt some effort to recruit Frank Heart to the company. A computer systems engineer at MIT, Heart had taken MIT's first-ever computer programming course in 1951, his senior year. Frank Heart had left Lincoln Lab as an expert in real-time systems "built for when the physical world demands a response within fractions of seconds," like radar tracking data sent to SAGE, or seismic information in an earthquake. Heart moved from Lincoln Lab to BBN in 1966 to work on the same specialty Ornstein pursued in St Louis—computers in medicine. As Heart recalls, "When I came [to BBN], I was extracted from Lincoln at some difficulty to work on a thing called the hospital computer project, which was an attempt to apply computers to hospital data processing. BBN had a contract with NIH and was working with Massachusetts General [Hospital] and that project was having difficulties. I was supposed to help rescue it. I arrived sort of in time to help officiate at its funeral about a year later."

Within less than a year, the BBN staff would have a new challenge, which would define its members' career paths, and those of thousands, possibly millions of others. But one key appointment had to be put in place before networking's formative age could be set in motion. Bob Taylor, as director of the IPTO at ARPA, had begun to take concrete steps to make Licklider's network idea take shape. It may not have been intergalactic, but interstate, or even intercity, would be a vast step. So in 1966, Taylor tried to hire Larry Roberts, then just twenty-eight, from Lincoln Lab.

Roberts had seen Ornstein and Heart leave, had become firm friends with Len Kleinrock, understood Kleinrock's pioneering theoretical work, and, most importantly, had just completed the first-ever networking experiment connecting two distant computers. Inevitably, the experiment was funded by ARPA, indeed by Taylor himself, and involved the experimental TX-2 at Lincoln and a computer in Santa Monica that had already earned a thoroughbred pedigree from an early networking experiment. This was the air force's Q-32 mainframe at System Development Corporation (SDC), the Rand Corporation spin-off in Santa Monica, California. The Q-32 had been purchased to back up the DEW (Defense Early Warning) system pioneered at Lincoln, and was operated under a contract that Licklider had been hired by ARPA to manage. As Roberts notes, "The TX-2 was where I did the first network experiment. I was excited about trying to find out how to link computers together because Licklider had told me his vision and I was looking for a way to do that and so I set up an experiment between Lincoln and SDC to try the first network experiment."

Roberts and his colleague Tom Marill published a paper describing the experiment, one of the earliest scriptures of the networking religion. So Roberts was Taylor's perfect candidate, except for the fact that he loved his job, and didn't want to go to Washington. Taylor offered him the program director's job for the yet-to-be-built experimental network, and the probable future succession to Taylor's own position, as director of IPTO. Roberts declined, and according to various accounts, he did so at least six times, while consulting his friend Len Kleinrock for advice. (Kleinrock, Sutherland, and Roberts had all been classmates at MIT/Lincoln Lab as they pursued their Ph.D.s in related, frontier research areas.) But Bob Taylor wasn't taking no for an answer. He enlisted the forceful support of his boss, ARPA's second director Charlie Herzfeld. The versions of the story mostly coincide, and they testify to the determination, imagination, and cunning of Taylor.

Roberts recalls that he was happy doing his ARPA-funded research at Lincoln, and was not about to move. So, as Bob Taylor admits, "I blackmailed Larry Roberts into coming to ARPA to be a program manager. And he was the primary architect of the ARPAnet. I say blackmail because I got the money to start the project in February of 1966 from my boss, Charlie Herzfeld, and then I asked Larry to come down and be the program manager, and no, he wanted to stay at Lincoln Lab and be a researcher."

Len Kleinrock found himself advising Roberts on his career path: "I remember Larry talking to me one day in Lexington near Lincoln Laboratory in his little Volkswagen. It was a snowy day. We're sitting in this car and he says, 'Len, should I take that job? Will it do me good?' I said, 'Take it. You can't miss.'"

Taylor was persistent: "So I kept trying and trying and failing and failing and then one day in the fall of that year [1966], after failing since February, I had an idea. I went in to see Charlie Herzfeld and I said, 'Charlie, doesn't ARPA fund 51 percent of Lincoln Laboratory at MIT?' He said, 'Yeah.' And I said, 'Well, you know this networking project that I want to do, I'm having a hard time getting the program manager that I want and he works at Lincoln Lab.' I said, 'Would you call Gerry Dinneen'—the director of Lincoln Lab—'and ask him to get Larry Roberts in his office and tell Larry Roberts that it would be in Larry Roberts' best interest and Lincoln Lab's best interest if Larry would just come down and take this job?' And Charlie said 'Sure.' And while I was in his office, he picked up the phone and talked to Gerry Dinneen. I could hear Charlie's end of it and it was a short conversation."

Roberts heard the other end of the conversation, in the director's office at Lincoln Lab: "Bob got Herzfeld to call up the head of Lincoln and say, 'Well, we have 51 percent of your money. Why don't you send Roberts down here as fast as you can?' And the head of Lincoln called me in and said, 'It'd probably be a nice thing for all of us if you'd consider this.'"

Bob Taylor stood back to watch his plans unfold: "And Charlie hung up the phone at the end of the conversation and smiled and said, 'Well, we'll see what happens.' Two weeks later Larry accepted the job."

Roberts found his fate sealed thus: "And [Dinneen] actually counseled me it might be helpful for my career, and so on, and it was. So, I took his advice and I went down to ARPA and it was actually quite beneficial because I got to make it happen."

Kleinrock was the next domino to fall: "So they dragged Larry to Washington to basically make this happen. It turns out there was a lot of pressure behind the scenes. He took the job and he was charged with making this happen. So the first thing he did was bring me in because he was well aware of the work I did at MIT, being classmates. In fact, we shared an office together."

Thus Roberts arrived at the Pentagon, age twenty-nine, ready to implement a plan that would have technological repercussions for a generation or more. Bob Taylor, Larry Roberts, Len Kleinrock, Frank Heart, Severo Ornstein, and others were ready, in their undemonstrative engineers' fashion, to change the world.

Chapter Two
Something Seductive

W<small>HEN</small> B<small>OB</small> T<small>AYLOR</small> "BLACKMAILED" Larry Roberts into leaving Lincoln Lab and coming to work for ARPA in Washington, he was just warming up. Before long he would be blackmailing whole university computer research departments to join in his proposed fledgling computer network, the ARPAnet. Taylor was a manager, not an engineer or systems designer, and he believed that Roberts—with the triple-crown credentials of Bachelor's, Master's, and Ph.D. degrees, all from MIT—had the technical expertise to define and execute the project. As Bob Taylor observes: "One of the reasons that this program manager business was so important is because most of the way we had been working up until that time in my office at ARPA was to just take in proposals that were, by and large, unsolicited and let other people propose and we would then dispose."

Now Taylor and Roberts would be launching an initiative that ARPA would both propose and dispose, and their university department "clients" would have to be persuaded to accept. At Christmastime 1966, when Roberts arrived in Washington, Taylor already had a plan for an experimental network, linking big, expensive university mainframe computers. The technological state of play in the early 1960s saw computers confined to the unwieldy punch-card–driven monsters that only select technicians could touch.

Many of these unwieldy monsters had been purchased with ARPA funds, and were commissioned to carry out research on a variety of government programs, military and otherwise—especially so since Sputnik—in science and technology. As computers became identified as useful tools for research, so universities wanted their own, and they applied to the Information Processing Techniques Office at ARPA for the funds to buy mainframes of their own. Bob Taylor saw a budget problem in the making, as each institution wanted as good a computer as the last, plus all the upgrades and improvements made since. As Len Kleinrock describes the problem, "In the mid-sixties [ARPA managers] were supporting a large number of PIs (Principal Investigators) doing research. They'd come to a researcher and they'd say, 'We want you to do research for us.' And so we'd say, 'Fine, you want me to do computer research? Buy me a computer.' So they were buying computers like mad. Each time they bought somebody a computer, the good scientist would alter it and put special applications and packages and hardware on it, so when they came to yet a new guy he would say not only 'Buy me a computer,' but 'I want all the capability that all of these other guys have.' And pretty soon ARPA said, 'We can't afford this.' And they conceived of the idea of putting these machines into a network. The justification being I could then use your machine and use your applications at your location."

Taylor's remedy was a radical one: in order to create the proposed network, ARPA would have to commission the creation of a new technology, which thus far consisted only of theoretical work, to enable distance-access to shared computer resources—instead of installing the desired equipment at every site.

Len Kleinrock, who had already made a notable personal contribution by encouraging Larry Roberts to take the job in Washington, had done the theoretical work that defined the technology of the proposed network in 1960–61 while working alongside Roberts at MIT. Both were graduate students. Kleinrock was a theoretician of queuing theory, and had simulated the behavior of a computer network without having a real network to study. In December 1962, Kleinrock had completed his research project at MIT. Although he was offered a number of research positions, including one at Lincoln Lab, he received an invitation to UCLA and was immediately offered a faculty position. At the time, he thought, "If I don't like it, I can come right back to Lincoln Lab. I tried it. I liked it. The rest is history. I never went back. I've been here for thirty-six years now."

Computer networking began thirty years ago because a Pentagon bureaucrat wanted to save money. If there was a Eureka! moment that propelled the network from theory into concrete planning, it occurred in Bob Taylor's office at the Pentagon: Room 3D-200 (3rd floor, D ring, room 200). As befits the director of information processing techniques, Taylor had a terminal linking him to each of three mainframes, funded by ARPA, at three distant locations.

Each of these terminals in Taylor's office was connected to time sharing systems. ARPA had funded mainframe computers for research at many big universities and research establishments such as Harvard, MIT, UCLA, and Stanford. They were too big, too expensive, and too jealously guarded by men in white coats for personal use in real time. One of the ways in which computers were made more accessible, and cost was amortized, was by the invention of "time sharing." This science-fiction notion allowed multiple computer users to be served by one computer, which could process data fast enough to create the illusion of serving everyone at once. The users could even submit and process data from terminals, using local or long-distance telephone lines. Bob Taylor explains: "Many users were connected to the same computer, and every individual user had the illusion that the computer was just serving that user. The computer was fast enough so it could serve you and move to the next person and the next person and the next person and come back to you and you were never aware of the fact that it left you."

Despite the fact that by late 1990s standards these machines were monolithic, slow, and absurdly limited in processing power, time sharing provided a great improvement at the time, in speed and accessibility.

Time sharing, was, in Len Kleinrock's words, "the rage of the 1960s." Somewhat inevitably, J.C.R. Licklider had built one of the first time sharing systems, on the first $150,000 Digital PDP-1, which BBN had purchased. It was on this time sharing experience that he based his observations of "Man-Computer Symbiosis." One result of time sharing was that vastly more people, legitimately or otherwise, were beginning to get access to what nerds at least might call "the romance of computers"—people such as Vinton G. Cerf, another ultimately important figure in the saga of networking, who with Bob Kahn would later define the protocols that enabled separate networks to merge into the Internet.

In 1960, Vint Cerf was seventeen years old, as was his best friend from Van Nuys High School, Steve Crocker, who managed to get an introduction to Michel Melkanoff, then chairman of the

Electrical Engineering Department at UCLA. Somehow Crocker got permission to use the UCLA Bendix G15 (a computer, not a washing machine) during the summer. As Vint Cerf recalls, he and his pal Steve went to work: "This machine is about the size of a couple of refrigerators. And it doesn't have the kinds of terminals we're accustomed to today. It has this thing called a Flexowriter, which takes paper tape in and you punch holes in it and then it prints the stuff out. So you program it by punching a tape and you feed the tape into a little slot and it gets sucked into the machine and interpreted, and then it does its calculations and it punches the answers out on some more tape, and you take that back and put it in the Flexowriter and print out the answers."

On Crocker and Cerf's first foray to UCLA, the computer department's doors were locked. Undaunted, and confident that permission to use the computer also covered breaking-and-entering, they climbed up the outside of the building through an open third-floor window.

> We programmed the machine to do a particularly interesting exponential calculation, and then we went off for a pizza, because we calculated it would take a certain amount of time. We taped the doors open. When we got back we expected a lot more paper tape to be out of the machine. There was only about two or three feet. We went, "Oh, heck, the program must have bombed." But we discovered that all the paper tape was actually inside the machine because it had fouled on the little tray that carries it in. We had a quarter of a mile of paper tape inside the machine. So we rolled it all up finally and we printed out the answer and plotted it very carefully, got the answers we were interested in. Well, that turned me on to computers. I was just fascinated by the idea that you could actually make this thing do anything you wanted as long as you could figure out how to program it.

In 1961, Vint Cerf entered Stanford as an undergraduate, majoring in math while taking every computer science course available. At the time, Stanford had no undergraduate major in computer science. The notion of time sharing, and a PDP-1 computer, had both arrived from Massachusetts: the PDP-1 was the

first time-shared machine on the campus. By the time Vint Cerf
graduated, he had concluded that he did not want to be a mathe-
matician, but that he wanted to do something serious with computers. So he went to work for IBM and spent two years with IBM
from 1965 to 1967 in Los Angeles. Next, Cerf became one of Len
Kleinrock's graduate students at UCLA, with a special fascination
for computers, and especially the beguiling magic of long-range
computing: "There's something seductive about being able to do
something in one place, in Los Angeles, and have an effect someplace else—in Boston or at Stanford or somewhere else. The idea
of being able to create an environment that bursts the bounds of
the computer and reaches across the network and has some interaction with some other piece of software elsewhere—for me,
anyway—it's just totally fascinating."

Time sharing was a useful, if partial, solution to the access
problem that dominated computing until the advent of the truly
personal computer in 1978. With the connection of multiple terminals as input-output devices, the exclusive scheduling of computer time by the hour was made obsolete. Terminals could be
close to the mainframe, or distant, using telephone lines to communicate. So some inroads were made on both space and time
limitations to 1960s computing. But any single terminal was connected only to its own mainframe system. To resist the budget
pressure of requests for new, separate mainframes, Bob Taylor
began to think laterally: "I was sitting in my office in the Pentagon and to communicate with people at Santa Monica I had to sit
down at this terminal here, and if I wanted to talk with the people, or the computer in Berkeley, I had to get up from this terminal and go over and sit at another terminal, go through a different
protocol, a different command language. The same for MIT. So,
the obvious question is, wait a minute.Why don't we have one
terminal and have all of these places interconnected?"

In these uninspiring surroundings, Bob Taylor's brainwave was
the first step towards today's wired and webbed world, though at
the time Taylor at least was unaware of Kleinrock's research that
had analyzed how to make it all work. While he acknowledges
that the ARPAnet was his idea, he makes no more of a claim than
to say "I was in a job that called for it."

We'll pause now to consider the social habits of 1960s geeks like

Larry Roberts, the man Bob Taylor brought to the Pentagon to devise the specifications of the ARPAnet, and his friend and queueing expert Len Kleinrock. These are applied mathematicians—and for fun and profit, they applied their mathematics not only to their Pentagon-funded and university research, but also to gambling. These are people who live and breathe numbers—not just in computer science, but on playing cards and roulette wheels as well.

To Larry Roberts, gambling is an intellectual challenge: "The appeal is basically to break the system, to be smart, to learn how to do it. If I can't break the system, I'm not interested in gambling. I don't see much benefit in it for its own sake because I know too much about statistics; but for the sake of learning how to count and find a true advantage at the cards, that's interesting."

"How to count" in this context is a specialized activity. In blackjack, players can attempt to count how many cards of each number have been played, thereby improving their likelihood of predicting the next card. The goal is to get a hand with a total of 21. But casino blackjack is played with at least four decks: 208 cards to try to track. Len Kleinrock explains with a story of a prodigious card-counter: "I got a call one summer from a young man who had just gotten his degree in economics. This guy was a terrific player. His mental capacity was such that he could memorize every card that went out. And he could particularly remember how many 3s and 4s were left. We went to Las Vegas together. We're playing there. He has 17 showing. There were very few cards left in the deck. And he indicates to the dealer to hit him, which nobody does. You never hit 17. The dealer told him 'You don't hit 17.' He said, 'Hit me.' Dealer said, 'You don't hit 17.' 'Hit me.' 'You don't hit 17.' So he says, 'Goddamn it, give me the 4!' And he gave him the 4, he got his win."

Len Kleinrock describes his motivation for playing blackjack as "the enormous thrill of pitting my brain against the entire might of the Mafia." Larry Roberts also knows how to count. He designed a counting system for blackjack "before anybody else did high-low counting. In the '70s, I was busy going to Las Vegas and when I was there, earning money. And I did very well over time, until they changed the number of decks. I could work up to four decks but six decks makes it almost impossible."

Len Kleinrock says that he and Roberts "always liked puzzles and challenges and, of course, Las Vegas presented a wonderful challenge. We wanted to expand our horizons beyond blackjack. We were going after roulette. Roulette is a wonderful game, where you average a nickel loss on every dollar you bet, by and large, if it's fair. But if the wheel is a little off or if you can detect where the ball is relative to the wheel, Newtonian mechanics tells you where the ball is going to fall. So we developed a system to just measure the ball and the wheel. You just have to predict which half of the wheel the ball will fall on and you've got 2-to-1 odds in your favor. But we needed some data. So Larry and I went to Las Vegas, and we needed to measure the speed of the ball."

Larry Roberts was using scientific research notions: "I wanted to record the sound of the wheel and use the sound of the wheel and the Doppler shift that was on the wheel to find out when the ball would fall."

Len Kleinrock was the accomplice: "So Larry put a microphone in his hand, wired to a recorder inside his jacket, and wrapped his arm as if he had a broken arm. And he put his arm next to the wheel. I was the decoy. I was there gambling and drawing attention to me. And so Larry's measuring and the ball's going, he's trying to measure it. Trouble is, I started winning. And now the croupier started noticing me and he saw Larry and me walk in together. So I'm winning, I'm a buddy with Larry, and Larry's hand is right next to the wheel wrapped up like a mummy."

Roberts now became the object of some unwelcome attention: "The pit boss came by as he started seeing him winning and me and my bandaged hand near the wheel, and he said 'Now, what's wrong with your hand?' And I said, 'Well, I burned it.' And he said, 'Well, would you like it broken off?'"

Len Kleinrock remembers that "At that point we decided we'd better leave. And we knew we couldn't explain this so we got up and we hightailed it out of there as fast as we could."

According to former student Vint Cerf, Kleinrock's capacity for instant mathematics goes far beyond blackjack and roulette, into the classroom:

> Len is one of those unbelievably energetic, enthusiastic, and smart people that you have to see . . . lecture to believe. I took queueing theory classes from Len. That was a real

honor. He would write on the board faster than most people can write and, moreover, this was mathematical equations. You might imagine that he'd simply memorized all this stuff, he'd done it so many times. No: he was actually doing the calculus in his head as he would go along and the reason we'd know that is that he'd make mistakes every once in a while. Not very often, but every once in a while you'd catch him and he'd fix it and go on. Len was able to look at a mathematical equation, a result from one of these complicated queueing analyses, and then walk through each term of the thing and explain intuitively what it was that was going on.

Roberts himself wasn't new to networking, at least conceptually. In 1962, he had attended a military-sponsored conference organized by Licklider at The Homestead resort in Virginia. As he recalled at a celebratory, reminiscence-filled conference arranged by Len Kleinrock at UCLA in August 1989 (oddly named "Act One"), to celebrate the twentieth anniversary of the birth of the ARPAnet: "We sat around in the evening, and we talked about where the future was and what the future was. Well, time sharing was old by 1962. We had done them. So I figured the future was with this global networking Lick was talking about. So I decided I ought to get into that and start working on that."

In 1967, as Bob Taylor and Larry Roberts embarked on planning the ARPAnet, there was probably as much relevant talent at the small consulting firm of Bolt, Beranek & Newman as at any of the major universities. Approaching its twentieth anniversary, BBN had added computer communications research to its main portfolio of acoustic engineering applications, both civilian—like designing the architectural acoustics for the new United Nations headquarters building in New York, and for concert halls at Lincoln Center—and military, such as detecting the sound of submarines.

J.C.R. Licklider had moved from BBN to ARPA, and the connection between the two places remained strong. BBN had started trying to hire Frank Heart away from Lincoln Lab in 1965 to take charge of their new hospital computer project. Heart had completed his master's degree while working on the Whirlwind project's real-time systems at MIT, and had transferred with it to

Lincoln Lab, where he built antennae and radar systems. Heart was attracted to working somewhere which pursued nonmilitary, social applications for computers.

Robert Kahn, who would play important roles in the planning of both ARPAnet and (with Vint Cerf) the evolution of the Internet, was an MIT professor of electrical engineering. He was temporarily attached to work at BBN's "information sciences" division—a commercial counterpart to the Pentagon's IPTO. "I had joined them in October of 1966, and began working on computer networking shortly after I had gotten there. BBN at the time was largely in the architectural acoustics business. And they were building a small state-of-the-art practice in computing. I think I was one of the first, if not the first, to really be from the communications arena."

Meanwhile Severo Ornstein had completed his circuit from Lincoln Lab, to MIT, to St Louis, and ultimately back to Cambridge, by getting himself hired by Frank Heart to work at BBN. As a hardware expert, it would be his role to design the special interface computer that would prove to be the structural key to the ARPAnet. And a young California-born programmer, Dave Walden, who was hired by Frank Heart from Lincoln Lab, would become the point man for software.

Throughout the 1960s, all of these computer experts, both civilian and government, were working in near-total obscurity. Computer science was a nascent field, and the idea of networking was widely discounted as being either technically or financially impossible. Information processing had noodled along in the quiet style of most government-funded activities, almost a decade since ARPA had been established. Other priorities at the Pentagon were getting vastly more attention. The Vietnam War was immersing the nation in controversy and pain, on the one hand; the regular milestones of the NASA space program were amazing and uniting the land, on the other. As a Pentagon official with the temporary and honorary rank of one-star general, Bob Taylor found himself processing information on several tours of duty in South Vietnam.

President Johnson's White House had been embarrassed by newspaper stories that publicized conflicting reports from different branches of the services. It was a war in which statistics, in particular the "body count," were a matter of great controversy, and the Pentagon's own statistics were in conflict. LBJ asked Secretary of

Defense Robert McNamara to fix the problem. The secretary called on the director of ARPA, knowing that ARPA had some computer research going on, and the director of ARPA, still Charlie Herzfeld, called Bob Taylor: "I went out there, and I took with me officers from the army, the navy, and [the] air force—one each—who knew something about their inventory control and reporting systems. We found that all the services used different definitions of what they were reporting, and different forms. There was no standardization, so it was no wonder they didn't agree when all these reports got back to the White House. So I created a project to build a new inventory-reporting control system, and [ARPA] created something called the Data Management Agency in Vietnam. After that, Johnson got a singular report rather than multiple reports. Whether or not he got more truth, I have no idea. I hope so."

While Vietnam caused national and generational divisions, NASA's Gemini and Apollo programs mined an enthusiastic, even jingoistic streak in America. The astronauts hit the headlines and dominated primetime television consistently. Unmanned rockets were followed by the manned Gemini projects, and John Glenn's stardom as the first American in space. Gallingly again, the Russians did it first. But soon enough, Glenn's triumph was succeeded by a roll call of firsts: the first space-docking, the first space walk, the first orbit of the Moon. By 1968, the Gemini program had been succeeded by the Apollo missions, which would fulfill JFK's promise to put a man on the Moon by the end of the decade.

Like his predecessors Licklider and Sutherland, Bob Taylor had recognized the incompatibility problem of his three office terminals. Meanwhile, IPTO contractors were requesting ever higher capital expenditures for mainframe computer installations, from half a million dollars and up per location. Determined to attempt his radical solution—actually to do what Licklider had dreamed—Taylor approached ARPA director Charlie Herzfeld. He proposed a test network of four nodes, building up to a dozen. "Charlie Herzfeld, when I went in to see him in that short conversation to get approval for the project, took a million dollars out of somebody else's budget right there. And he said, 'Okay, you got a million dollars. Go.' He was wonderful."

It was only once Taylor had the funds approved that he was

able to press Larry Roberts to join the project. It may have been theoretical, and it had never been done before, but it had a budget. Among the experts, experimenters, and theoreticians who began to discuss executing the plan, there was a variety of opinions: both about the purpose of the network, and about its desirability.

Some believed the most useful benefit of a network would be *load sharing*: effectively an extension of time sharing that would allow processing to be shifted from a busy computer to an idle one, or to be scheduled and executed simultaneously on more than one computer. The range of time zones across the United States facilitates this option. Others thought that *data sharing* would be most important. The network would allow people scattered around the country, but all interested in the same kind of research, to share and exchange data. A third function, communication between the people at the different sites, was not much discussed, though Bob Taylor regarded it as the starting point for building the ARPAnet: "I thought the principal use of the network would be to allow people who were separated geographically to discover and then exploit common interests. That's what I thought it was for. And that's what I still think it's for. There are many people on the Internet who just are there because they want to explore, they want to see if they can find someone who, like themselves, is a specialist in the duckbill platypus."

As Taylor observes, both load-sharing and data-sharing advocates "were quite surprised at the amount of use of the ARPAnet for message passing, me sending a message to you, you sending a message to me. I was surprised that they were surprised, but many of these people in print have said that ARPA was caught unawares that communication would be such a strong part of the ARPAnet—when, in fact, the reason for building the ARPAnet was for communication."

In 1967, with funding and a hand-picked manager in place, the ARPAnet program began to take shape. Larry Roberts, the engineer, was given day-to-day responsibility for the design, resources, and recruitment activities by Bob Taylor, the manager. One of the first tasks was winning the hearts and minds of the proposed ARPAnet's constituency, the PIs (Principal Investigators) at research departments that had been funded by ARPA, and that therefore controlled their computing resources locally, and those at departments who still hoped to have their shiny new mainframe paid for by ARPA. To the former group, the prospect of a network brought with it the risk of "outsiders" meddling in their private computer center. To the latter, it brought the unwelcome implication that ARPA would build the network instead of buying the mainframes they wanted. Larry Roberts describes his uphill struggle to win support for the plan: "They thought that this was something that they didn't need. They had their computer, they had their resources. They wanted to work on their own thing at their own location and they didn't see any need to talk to anybody anywhere else. They thought that this was going to be the worst thing that ever happened. Because their computer that they were carefully guarding, that they had all worked so hard to buy, or to get me to buy, was now going to be potentially used by somebody else and all their computer time was going to be used up."

Vint Cerf recalls there was "tremendous resistance" from ARPA-sponsored research groups on the grounds that it was a waste of money: "The trouble was that ARPA was asked repeatedly to buy the best computing equipment for each one of the universities on the grounds that you couldn't do good quality computer science without the best computers. And they couldn't afford to keep doing that every year for every place. And so the question was, how do I hook them together to do resource sharing, which was the original motivation for the ARPAnet."

Larry Roberts recruited Len Kleinrock to be a cheerleader for the network experiment. He in turn contacted all nineteen of the potential ARPAnet sites, and he too found a profound reluctance from most of these locations: "They couldn't imagine allowing the hoi polloi from less upscale groves of academe soiling their mainframe with mere workaday research data. Though they could imagine wanting to get their hands on other people's computer resources, as they never had enough. Larry was doing a similar thing from his side. The typical response was, 'Why?' I said, 'Well, look, you'll be part of a network and you can use other people's computers and they can use yours.' They said, 'No, nobody can use mine. It's overloaded already. A hundred percent right now. Don't touch me.' And I said, 'But you can have access to other people.' They were not interested."

But Kleinrock pushed harder: "I asked them how much they

might use other nodes, for example the modeling and simulation capability at UCLA. They typically replied, 'I have no idea,' and I would ask if they would like two or three teletypes to my machine. They would reply, 'Yeah, two or three.' After I received all this 'data,' I published a paper about the design of computer networks and published the traffic matrix numbers I had extracted from these researchers as a 'sample' traffic matrix."

Frank Heart confirms the widespread reluctance: "The primary goal was resource sharing. And initially, some of the universities that had these host sites weren't incredibly enthusiastic. They would say, 'Why do I want to let anybody else use my computer? I'm busy enough right here. I don't want to share anything at that other guy's site anyway. We've got our own fish to fry.'"

Larry Roberts observed a regional bias: "We actually had more conservatism on the East Coast. When I looked for sites that were willing to start, the four West Coast sites were interested and excited to be involved. And the East Coast sites, like MIT, said, 'Well, I don't want you to touch my computer.' So we went with the ones that were cooperative, and those happened to be out here."

Bob Taylor had demonstrated in his novel approach to hiring Larry Roberts that he would resort to helpful pressure in order to achieve his goals. The solution to the widespread reluctance was some old-fashioned arm-twisting by IPTO and ARPA. Since the proposed network centers were all ARPA-supported, ARPA had some leverage over their future funding—and used it.

Len Kleinrock witnessed the blackmail: "People were totally unwilling to do it. However, each of these sites was being supported with hundreds of thousands, millions of dollars a year, by ARPA. And ARPA said, 'You're going to join this network.' And sure enough, they did."

As Frank Heart recalls, "They got more enthusiastic fairly rapidly, partly because ARPA was supporting them and ARPA *wanted* them to be enthusiastic. Well, that's a strong way to get someone to be enthusiastic. But, in addition, they got interested so, you know, in a while that problem, kind of concern over it went away and they were very supportive and interested."

Taylor delegated the network planning to Larry Roberts, who began exploring the technology options for building a four-node network with a half-second response time. The number, and speed, and all other aspects of how the network would be built were a creative mixture of arbitrary decisions, heated debate, and technical efficiency. According to Len Kleinrock, the half-second response time was defined by a general desire that the response must be as fast as if the remote user and the computer were in the same room—and by "a Berkeley researcher named Herb Baskin, a time sharing hack. He pounded his fist on the table and said, 'If this network can't support a half-second response time, by God it won't be a suitable network.' So we specified a half-second response time."

One of Roberts' first tasks was to conduct a study of the cost-per-message of a variety of existing communications systems, and to compare that with the projected cost of ARPAnet messages. As Roberts describes it, "Telegrams were very expensive. We went down to telex, which was the low-speed data of the time, and then WATS telephone was something like $1.50 a megabit, and there was a service called Data-50, a switch fifty-kilobit service. Then we designed the ARPAnet and that came down to about thirty cents a megabit. You could mail a computer tape a lot cheaper, but we figured that was a little bit slow in response time."

A meeting was convened in Ann Arbor, Michigan, early in 1967, which served primarily to reveal the widespread lack of interest in the proposed network from principal investigators funded by ARPA. Among the exceptions to this apathy was Douglas Engelbart. Another crucial computer pioneer, and one of the earliest advocates and experimenters in networking, Engelbart was then at Stanford Research Institute, working on ARPA-funded projects. He welcomed the plan as a long-overdue element of his own Lickliderish vision of computers as instruments of human intellect augmentation.

Doug Engelbart was a naval radar technician in 1945, stationed in the Philippines, when he read an *Atlantic Monthly* article entitled "As We May Think," discussing future information-management technologies. The author, Vannevar Bush, was first chairman of the National Advisory Committee on Aeronautics, then of the National Defense Research Committee, and lastly of the Office of Scientific Research and Development—all under President Roosevelt. Bush's article was an informed speculation about futuristic technologies, including the "memex," a mechanized device that would operate as an enlarged, intimate supplement to human memory.

Engelbart devoted himself to making this happen. He got a job at Stanford Research Institute (SRI), and attracted funding from Bob Taylor (while at NASA), then from Licklider and Taylor at ARPA. Engelbart called his laboratory the "Augmented Human Intellect Research Center," or "Augmentation Research Center" (ARC). Among the fruits of Engelbart's research was the invention of the computer "mouse" under a grant from NASA on Bob Taylor's watch, and a landmark demonstration in 1968 of networked computers and videoconferencing. Engelbart specializes in being about twenty years ahead of his time and getting recognition long after he has despaired of anyone's understanding his innovative thinking.

Larry Roberts began to write a plan for the network, for the first time naming it "the ARPAnet," and the report was published as a paper at the ACM (Association for Computing Machinery) conference in Gatlinburg, Tennessee, in late 1967. The paper was received with some polite interest. At the same meeting, another paper was presented by the British researcher Roger Scantlebury of National Physical Laboratory (NPL), proposing the design of a "packet-switched" network.

Two years earlier, in 1965, Donald Davies of NPL had started notes on "packet switching" and gave a lecture about using this technology to build a new, public, nonmilitary communications network in Britain—an Internet. As a result, the U.S. Department of Defense contacted him, and put him in touch with Paul Baran at Rand. Davies was a graduate of Imperial College, London, who had joined Professor Alan Turing's team at the National Physical Laboratory in 1947. He had spent part of 1954 at MIT, and in 1965 he had visited MIT's Project MAC time sharing experiment. Larry Roberts had also met Davies in London in 1965.

Davies and his colleague Roger Scantlebury had been working on a parallel track to Len Kleinrock and others. At the meeting, Larry Roberts learned from Scantlebury of the work of Paul Baran, an American computer scientist, funded by the Pentagon, who had been working on data communications networks eight years earlier.

Paul Baran was preaching the value of what he called "distributed communications" at the Pentagon as early as 1960. In 1959,

Baran had joined the Rand Corporation, where he started to research "the major problem facing the country in defense." At the height of the Cold War, two years after Sputnik, the two superpowers had both offensive nuclear weapons and highly vulnerable defenses. As Baran observed at the UCLA Act One conference in 1989, "with two paranoid countries staring each other down, there is the realization that if one country fired off its weapons first, it would have a very, very much greater chance of surviving, which made for a very unstable situation."

The essence of the problem was this: if the country attacked had a military command-and-control communications system that could survive a nuclear attack, retaliation could be ensured. The deterrent effect of certain retaliation became known in the Nixon years as "MAD"—or mutually assured destruction. But in 1960, as Baran explained, "all the communications networks at the time were centralized. So the challenge was to come up with a network that had no central node and had perfect switching, so signals were able to find their way through the network."

Baran rejected both "centralized" and "decentralized" network models in favor of a "distributed" structure—though at the time he didn't know how to build one. (A centralized structure has one command center and many small outposts; a decentralized structure has several major centers and many outposts; a distributed structure has nothing but outposts, with "central" functions distributed among all of them.) Baran identified the same technical problems that the ARPAnet would have to overcome almost a decade later: how to guarantee that messages reached their destination, how to confirm they had done so, how to avoid traffic overloads, and—in case of war—how to ensure the functioning of the network survived the destruction of significant parts.

Baran proposed digital information traffic at a time when communications was all analog. He referred to the information being sent as "message blocks," and designed a store-and-forward network of "hot-potato routing." He was unaware of Kleinrock's work, which had successfully simulated the design of store-and-forward networks. The name "hot potato"described a process resembling how one juggles a hot potato from hand to hand; Baran created a method in which messages were passed from node to node, while no one node was responsible for end-to-end traffic.

In 1965, RAND recommended to the U.S. Air Force that they build a distributed switching network, as a research-and-development venture first, and later make it operational.

As a true pioneer, Baran encountered a series of roadblocks that would be raised again for the ARPAnet: a lack of interest from the experts in the existing technology, and scorn or fear from those with something to lose. Baran recalled in 1989, at Act One: "The hardest people to convince were really competent analog transmission engineers. They knew their business, and they knew it couldn't possibly work. Someone from another department said 'What in hell is somebody in computer science [doing] screwing around with communications? That's *our* business.' So at that time, computers and communication were far, far apart. AT&T was the monopoly at the time, and they were the people that had to be convinced. And they took two attitudes. One was 'It can't possibly work.' Then, 'If it did work, damned if we're going to put a competitor in the business with ourselves.'"

In response to RAND's formal proposal in 1965 to build the network, the air force established a committee to review and recommend its implementation. In 1966, the project was passed, much like a hot potato, to the Defense Communications Agency. As Baran remembers, "This was a difficult one, because the agency had just formed, and it had zero technical capacity at the time . . . [which] almost guaranteed that it [the project] would not work."

Baran's experience could not have been more different from the near-miraculous capacity to make decisions and allocate budgets that Bob Taylor and ARPA, operating out of the same building, would later enjoy. But in 1966, Baran was out of luck. "So I recommended to my friends in the Department of Defense, and we decided, that the best thing to do was not proceed with that program. We'd put it in ice and wait for some more competent organization to show up."

On returning to Washington, Larry Roberts found documentation on Baran's hot-potato network gathering dust at ARPA, that more competent organization. While the starting point for Baran, network survivability in nuclear war, was of no interest to Roberts, the data communications theories were of interest. As Roberts recalls, "I found the pile of classified reports in the safe back at the office. I had a meeting with Paul the following year and found the concept of hot-potato routing interesting. Later, when I wrote the ARPAnet RFP, I included a suggestion about this type of routing." Ultimately however, neither Baran nor the hot potato played a significant role in the building of ARPAnet.

Larry Roberts began to plan the technical specifications for the network, while consulting colleagues and trying to build support for both the creation and the use of the network. One key technical contribution was made, ironically, by a computer scientist who didn't want to participate.

One decision was to settle on the first four willing participants: UCLA (where Kleinrock taught), Stanford Research Institute (where Engelbart was), the University of California at Santa Barbara, and the University of Utah (where Ivan Sutherland, Sketchpad graphics inventor and Bob Taylor's predecessor, was now installed). Neither the Pentagon itself nor MIT would be one of the first four "nodes," as they were called. It might not be Licklider's intergalactic network, but even intercity or interstate would be a huge step. The network experiment that Larry Roberts himself had conducted between Santa Monica, California, and Lincoln, Massachusetts, had demonstrated that phone lines could be used to connect computers. But Roberts got advice from the British researchers that led him to decide upon broader band lines—50-kilobit-per-second lines—than he was considering. Perhaps as a result, the geographical limitations of the first four nodes was an advantage.

Larry Roberts explains that "We didn't want to run lines for the network all across the country too early because we knew that was just extremely expensive for experimentation. We didn't need to do that to get it operating. We needed that for operations but not for experimentation, to see how the network worked. So we wanted to be on one coast to start with. UCLA was very critical because they were the measurement center and they were the most interested and cooperative node in terms of getting that working."

Each site was already ARPA-funded, with particular research specialties or network functions planned. UCLA would be home to Kleinrock's Network Measurement Center (NMC). UCSB specialized in interactive graphics. Stanford Research Institute had Engelbart. Under another ARPA contract, he was developing something he called oNLine System, or NLS, to foster computer-literate communities; Engelbart offered to make SRI the Network Information Center (NIC).

By definition, each site had a mainframe computer, or several. But in part thanks to federal purchasing policy, the Pentagon had deliberately bought different computers that used different languages, had different operating systems, and were often understood by exclusive and separate groups of people. The solution to this huge incompatibility obstacle was proposed by Wesley Clark. He had left Lincoln Lab (like Ken Olsen) to build nonmilitary computers and applications. Severo Ornstein had gone with him to St. Louis, before returning to BBN.

Wesley Clark was himself not enthusiastic about putting his Washington University mainframe on the network. But he figured out a solution for the mainframe-to-mainframe connection. He proposed that a smaller computer (a minicomputer, such as a PDP-6 or PDP-8) should stand in front of every mainframe to be connected to the network. Each of these minicomputers would be the "interface" between the network and the mainframe nodes. All the minicomputers would be able to "speak" to one another, and run on the same operating systems and language. But each mainframe would speak only to its local interface. Because the job of the interface computers was to process messages, and because nerds love acronyms, the minicomputers were dubbed IMPs—Interface Message Processors. Clark's idea became a core component of Larry Roberts' plan.

Wes Clark—regarded as a mentor and inspiration by Kleinrock, Roberts, and many of the networking pioneers—made another prophetic intervention when he recommended Frank Heart, whom he knew from MIT and Lincoln Lab, as the only person who could actually manage the building of the network. That also would come to pass. Frank Heart heard about the proposed network relatively late in the day: around May 1, 1968, at the Spring Joint Computer Conference in Atlantic City. On the boardwalk, Larry Roberts mentioned the forthcoming ARPAnet plans, and suggested to Frank Heart that BBN might want to consider bidding.

Technologically, the proposed network would depend on subdividing, transmitting, and reassembling digitized messages, a process that became known as "packet switching." It was founded upon Kleinrock's research, behaved like Baran's "store-

and-forward" model, and took its Anglicized name (it isn't called "package switching," which would be more American) from Donald Davies' network. The pioneers who have been trying to explain it for almost thirty years have polished the analogies that help the layman glimpse how the thing actually works. Part of the secret is in how packet switching works differently than circuit switching, the latter behaving like the phone system.

At the time of writing, Vint Cerf is a senior Internet executive with the telephone company MCI. As Cerf explains, the role of the telephone network has always been integral to networking: "We use the same transmission circuits. The same circuits that connect telephone switches connected the computers together. In a circuit switching environment, you make telephone calls and what you hear are dial tones. You push the buttons or you use a rotary dial. And you tell the immediate central office switch that you're connected to, what number you want. After it finds out what number you want, it then begins to build a circuit through the network until it gets to the destination switch, and then that rings the phone. So that means there is an electrical linkage, an electromagnetic linkage between your telephone and the other one, which stays up fully connected until the conversation is over and one of you hangs up."

Len Kleinrock compares "the magic of packet switching" to the "resource sharing" of a commercial airline. Nobody owns a seat, because it would be empty most of the time. When you need a seat, you rent it for the efficient, brief period needed: "By sharing, we get enormous efficiencies. Packet switching adds the feature that when one sends a long block of data (say this book), the block is broken up into smaller pieces called packets, and each packet makes its way through the network, to be put back together at the destination. Packet switching can deliver the entire book more quickly, but the key idea is to let go of the circuits when you don't need them."

Frank Heart offers this analogy: "When you make a phone call to your mother-in-law, and then talk to her on that phone line, whether you talk fast or *slow* or halt . . . in . . . the . . . middle, you tie up the phone line the whole time. But computers tend to talk in little bursts when they talk to each other. So packet switching was a technique for intermixing bits of message all together with other people's messages and using a phone line efficiently so that you could transmit many, many, many different conversations all intertwined."

The technical challenge was to merge the way computers work with the existing infrastructure, as Cerf explains: "Another alternative is to say, look, let's accept the fact that computers send bursts of data out and then they're silent. What if we label the data as to where it wants to go and hand it to the first switch in the chain and, instead of having a continuous connection, just have it look at where the data's supposed to go, forward it over the next link, but then the link becomes free for the next packet of data to go. Possibly to go someplace else. That's packet switching as opposed to circuit switching."

Bob Kahn points out that efficiency in using resources was the key:

> Back in the 1960s, as today, you know, to dial up a circuit from one location to another took a few seconds. Well, if you're only trying to send a very small amount of data so much that it could go in a fraction of a second, there's a lot of overhead to dial up for a few seconds worth to just send a fraction of data and then shut the line down. It's a very inefficient use of a line as well. It would be the equivalent in order to drive from, let's say, Washington, D.C., to Los Angeles, having to reserve the whole road for you to make the trip and it's not a very efficient use of the road space. A lot of people could share it by having dedicated lines that were always in place that could be multiplexed, shared that is, by lots of users' traffic.

Bob Taylor explains packet switching thus:

> Packet switching contrasts with normal switching technology, which is called line switching, where in order to move from one destination to another you actually unplug and plug in. But with packet switching you encode the message that you're sending with addresses for the destination. And with other codes that enable the destination to send back to the sender information that says, "I got it." And each

of those pieces will have this stuff at the beginning and this stuff at the end with a little piece in the middle. So it all comes to you, and your computer then knows what order to put these pieces back together in. The fifth piece may come to you before the first piece does. But your computer doesn't care because it will sort them out for you. That's packet switching in a nutshell.

Vint Cerf elaborates with an analogy: "The best way to describe packet switching technology and the way it behaves is to just remind you that packets are just like postcards. You know, they've got 'to' and 'from' addresses and they've got a finite amount of content on them. And like a postcard, you know, you put it into the post box. If you put two in, you don't know what order they're going to come out. They might not even come out on the same day. Some of them get lost. That's true of packets. They don't necessarily follow the same paths to get to the destination. That's also true of electronic packets. The only difference is an electronic packet goes about a hundred million times faster than a postcard."

By the summer of 1968, Larry Roberts had prepared the official ARPA Request for Quotations (RFQ) which was to be sent out to 140 interested parties. After a decade, ARPA was on the brink of creating a new technology that would have profound and lasting consequences for technology, society, culture, employment, even the global economy. Alongside ARPA, NASA was accelerating its efforts to meet the end-of-decade lunar landing deadline. The Apollo program succeeded Gemini, and the lunar missions began. Separate but parallel, the two ventures would both deliver the goods in the summer of 1969. Oddly, the Moon landing would come to seem the end of an exciting era of adventure, while the ARPA effort would be just the beginning of a massive technological and economic boom.

One of the 140 technology companies that received the RFQ in August 1968 was BBN in Cambridge. Having been involved in the consultation process, and having half a dozen of the best people in the field on the payroll, they had already done some thinking, and a lot of testing, of the ARPAnet concept. Bob Kahn summarizes how the task ahead of them was understood:

The basic idea in this network was that of packet switching, whereby what the computer actually communicates are
chunks of information. We call them packets, some finite set
of bits, with an address at the front of the packet which says
where the packet is supposed to go. Then that packet would
get routed through the network by going from one computer
inside the net to another computer inside the net in a kind
of a store-and-forward fashion until it finally got from the
source to the final destination. That round trip, if the lines
were sufficiently high-speed, could be done in a fraction of
a second. So we were actually able to test that hypothesis
and show that it could work using state-of-the-art minicomputers as the nodes of the network.

The challenge was to invent the first-ever digital computer network, with packet-switching technology, a half-second response
time, sophisticated measurement capability, and continuous operation, with no downtime for servicing. The inner ring of IMPs,
while existing to prevent the host mainframes from being overloaded with message processing, also had to be effectively invisible. As the ARPA specifications stated, "Each transmitting host
looks into the network through its adjacent IMP and sees itself
connected to the receiving host."

It may not be surprising, in light of the Pentagon parentage of
ARPA, and the original work of Paul Baran, that the idea has taken
hold that the ARPAnet was designed expressly for the purpose of
maintaining military communications in the event of catastrophic
nuclear attack on the United States. The technological theory was
first proposed by Paul Baran for that very purpose, and much early
computer research, at Lincoln Lab and elsewhere, was intimately
connected with defense communications applications.

As Larry Roberts says, "Recently, people have been taking
what Paul Baran wrote about a secure nuclear defense network,
his concept of what the network was, and applying it to the
ARPAnet. Of course, they had nothing to do with each other. I
went to Congress and defended it. And what I told Congress was
that this was for the future of science in the world—the civilian
world as well as the military—and the military would benefit just
as much as the rest of the world. It was worthwhile being done

under government and military sponsorship, but it clearly wasn't for military purposes. And I didn't mention nuclear war."

As Bob Taylor learned, there are occasions when the facts can't be allowed to spoil a good story. "*Time* said the ARPAnet was built to enable Defense Department scientists to connect to one another in the event of a nuclear war. I wrote a letter to *Time* pointing out they were mistaken, and they wrote a letter back to me assuring me that their sources were correct."

In August 1968, computer science stood on the eve of a new era. Ideas and ideals that had been floated and debated, then turned into theory and experiment, were on the brink of becoming a physical reality, and opening a new chapter in technological history. It may not have been an intergalactic network, in Licklider's adventurous phrase, but within a year the ARPAnet would be real, and would thus establish the first foundation for the networked computing and distributed communications environment that we now call, simply, "the Net."

Chapter Three
Not So Hard

It has become a truism of the computer industry that the leader or leaders of one technical generation rarely if ever succeed in transferring that leadership to the next wave. Existing leaders tend to discount new trends, or to stay focused on their existing business. In either case, opportunities are created for new, unexpected, energetic players to emerge suddenly and gain a position of prominence. It may be no surprise today, with thirty years' history of this trend to review, that neither IBM nor AT&T bid for a government contract to build a network of mainframes connected by telephone lines. But it was a surprise at the time.

In the summer of 1968 the Defense Department issued an RFQ* based on the proposals Larry Roberts had been circulating and discussing informally for a year or more, themselves based on the technology of Kleinrock's theory and simulations. The successful applicant would receive an ARPA contract to build a network of (initially) four "nodes," expanding later to nineteen. The method of transmitting messages and data would be "packet switching." At each node (simply meaning each separate location), there would be one IMP. For this crucial piece of computer hardware, which today would be called a router, Roberts proposed the Digital Equipment Corporation PDP-8 minicomputer, which was first released commercially in 1965. When "ruggedized," each PDP-8 would cost $80,000.

Responses to the Pentagon's RFQ, from both IBM and Control Data Corporation, said the network could not be built. According to Larry Roberts, speaking at the 1989 UCLA Act One conference, "This concept was so foreign to the maxi-computer

---

* Although the document was officially a Request for Quotations—ARPA was proposing all the technical details—it is widely referred to as a Request for Proposals, or RFP.

people that IBM and CDC no-bid this RFP. They said it was impossible; we couldn't possibly get the cost down to anything reasonable, because you'd have to use a Model-50 (mainframe) to do this job."

The reluctance of established computer companies was matched, or exceeded, by a thoroughly negative attitude towards Roberts' plan from both AT&T, the long-distance telephone monopoly of the time, and more conventionally minded engineers. Larry Roberts began to feel like a pariah. At the Act One conference, he remembered, "I gave speeches about this in the 1967-to-1969 time frame in the Pentagon and around there. The same agency that Paul [Baran] talked about, Defense Communications Agency; and AT&T; and the other people around had all these engineers who actually booed and hissed . . . 'Everything would go wrong, and it couldn't possibly work.'" He adds, "AT&T and DCA laughed at me. In fact, they more than laughed. They actually were very nasty. I felt like people were throwing rotten eggs at me when I was giving speeches as we were preparing for this, because they basically thought we were crazy."

As Dave Walden points out, Larry Roberts wasn't the only one giving speeches. The telephone companies' representatives were doing so too. "The telephone companies seemed to me to be working pretty hard to discredit packet switching. They would go give speeches. They'd talk to their customers and say this isn't a good idea. This can't be. The telephony attitude is not very compatible with packet switching—I hope my phone doesn't get cut off!—the telephony attitude is about guaranteed levels of service and capacity. It's about investments that you make that you get back over decades. And the world is simply moving much faster than that. The ARPAnet started something which is a very speedy way of developing new standards."

As Roberts says, the phone companies had close to a hundred years of experience of doing the same thing—circuit switching—and had allowed familiarity and repetition to create technical assumptions about what was and was not possible. "They thought they were facts, but they were actually assumptions. They were from history."

Len Kleinrock recalls participating in a number of industry panels in which the computer researchers would face off with the telephone industry: "I would say, 'Please give us good data communications,' and they would reply, 'The United States is a copper mine—we have phone lines everywhere so use the telephone network.' I would counter, 'But you don't understand, it takes twenty-five seconds to set up a call, you charge me for a minimum three minutes, and all I want is to send a millisecond of data.' Their reply was, 'Go away, children, the revenue stream from data transmission is dwarfed by that of our voice traffic.' So the children went away and created the Internet!"

Bob Taylor also tried to talk to AT&T about the venture. "When I asked AT&T to participate in the ARPAnet, they assured me that packet switching wouldn't work. So that didn't go very far."

To be fair to Ma Bell, Big Blue, and the technological establishment skeptics, the proposed new network did indeed depend upon a technology that existed largely, if not exclusively, in Len Kleinrock's Ph.D. thesis. But Roberts' own Q-32/TX-2 experiment, and Kleinrock's simulations, had satisfied a significant number of researchers that packet switching *would* work. It was a technological compromise between speed and efficiency, using existing hardware and principles in a new application.

Data was already being sent along phone lines from terminals to mainframes and from terminal to terminal, using a device called a *mod*ulator/*dem*odulator, or *modem*. Because a computer is digital, and works with distinct electrical signals representing 1 and 0, but a phone line is analog, carrying a large range of signal variations, the modem is needed to convert from binary to analog at the input end, and from analog to binary at the output end of the line. The fax machine works the same way. Both involve annoying whistling and beeping noises.

Before packet switching, sending data by phone could be immediate but inefficient in using resources, or delayed but efficient. In the first instance, a phone connection would be established (by circuit switching) and maintained for the whole duration of the exchange. Each person, typing slowly, would get their message across immediately, but for the great majority of time the line is effectively empty. As Dave Walden explains, "We're using very little of the capacity. This is an approach which is very low latency. Every message I send to you gets to you immediately because we've got a dedicated circuit."

Another alternative, message switching, concentrates on improving the utilization of the expensive phone lines by saving the material that is to be sent on a hard disk, then dialing up, making the connection, delivering all the information quickly, and hanging up.

Dave Walden observes, "The first example is very slow. The other is very efficient. Packet switching is a compromise between those two, which gets probably the best two-thirds or three-fourths of each. It's got some delay, but the delay is measured in milliseconds, rather than hours. It's got not as good utilization perhaps as if we buffer whole files, but almost as good utilization."

Kleinrock's untested, but theoretically ideal formula for packet switching was at the heart of the RFQ. And among the applicants to ARPA was Bolt, Beranek & Newman, in Cambridge, Massachusetts—where half the staff already knew Larry Roberts from working together at MIT Lincoln Labs. Frank Heart was appointed to manage the application process: "I think it was very clear that it was going to be a very tricky business. I think everybody that looked at it was concerned and worried, as was BBN. We had some people, people like Will Crowther—who was a really quite extraordinary programmer—and others like Severo Ornstein who looked at it, and we concluded that we thought we knew how to build it. We even said in the proposal that we thought it was going to be hard to build."

Severo Ornstein felt they started out with serious disadvantages: "BBN was a very small outfit, and it seemed that it would not win the competition unless it submitted a really outstanding proposal. And furthermore, the fact that many of us knew Larry Roberts, who was a honcho at ARPA at that time, I thought that was a considerable disadvantage because Larry did not want to be seen passing a contract out to his old buddies."

Dave Walden thought their team had some positive assets: "BBN was aware for some time before that a request for a proposal was coming. Bob Kahn, in particular, who was one of our team, was aware of that. BBN put together a team of people to get ready to bid. So, in fact, we were working on the bid before the request for proposal came out. Planning, thinking, doing designs. So when the actual request for proposal came out, in some sense it was like doing the design a second time."

Severo Ornstein sealed his reputation as a skeptic early in the process:

> I talked to Frank about it one night and he said, "Well, here's this RFQ, from ARPA. They want to build a network and so why don't you take it home and look at it?" And I did and I thought about it a little bit overnight and it seemed as though this was a fairly straightforward thing to do. It was fairly well described in the RFQ. And so it seemed we could build it. And I went in and told Frank in words that I guess have become somewhat immortalized that sure, we could build it, "But I had no idea why anybody would want such a thing." Which I still say was, at that time, a valid observation. Hindsight is easier than foresight, and people had all sorts of ideas about what the network would be about and for that had not really come to pass. I think they've all been surprised by what's happened.

Frank Heart's BBN team developed their proposal for a cost of about $100,000. In doing so, they concluded they could process data ten times faster than the RFQ required. BBN submitted its proposal, with significant disclaimers about the feasibility of the venture, on both technological and schedule grounds, on September 6, 1968.

The proposal summarized the description of the ARPA network and its technical requirements; proposed a number of hardware and software details, with diagrams; described the partnership BBN had struck with Honeywell to reengineer their minicomputer into the IMP; and expressed considerable caution about the venture. It also rejected the hot-potato routing technique originally and unsuccessfully proposed by Paul Baran, in favor of a very different technique. The document is worthy of extended quotation, for both technical and historical reasons: It describes the major features of the system ARPA requested, which became the fundamental basis for the global Internet and Web of today. The non-technological reader, however, may choose to skip the undiluted engineering jargon to read on where the story resumes.

PROPOSAL: INTERFACE MESSAGE PROCESSORS FOR THE ARPA COMPUTER NETWORK

RFQ NO. DAHC15 69 Q 0002
BBN Proposal No. IMP P69-IST-5

6 September 1968

BBN has obtained the interested cooperation of the Computer Control Division of Honeywell for the provision of hardware and technical assistance on a subcontract basis. Honeywell will provide DDP-516 computers, specialized interface hardware, maintenance, systems engineering assistance, and field engineering assistance.

Because of its experimental nature, the ARPA network must be viewed as a growing and evolutionary system. The first two stages of its development are discussed in the RFQ: (1) a 4-node initial net followed by expansion to (2) a 19-node net.

We take the position that it will be difficult to make the system work. As a consequence we have devoted considerable attention to techniques for simplification, for improving reliability, and for testing the state and performance of system elements for correcting or recovering from failures of many different kinds.

This network is envisioned as an interconnected communication facility that will allow researchers at ARPA-supported facilities to utilize capabilities available at other ARPA sites. The network will provide a link between user(s) programs at one site, and programs and data at remote sites. A typical use might involve a question-answering program at BBN working on extracts from a database available at SDC.

To simplify the problem of communication between nodes of the network, each site is to be provided with a small computer, an Interface Message Processor (IMP). *The ARPA network could have been constructed without any IMPs.* That is to say, each Host could have been forced to deal with line disciplines and errors entirely without an in-

terface machine. The decision to include IMPs, and to produce a subnet, implies a strong desire to save each Host
some of this time and trouble and to concentrate it in one
standardized place, namely the IMP.

Despite changing times and changing views about "foreign attachments" to the phone system, the rigid position
that customers may not tamper with telephone equipment
has contributed to the reliability of the phone network. Similarly, if customers initially avoid IMP programming, the reliability of the net will be enhanced.

IMP-to-IMP communication will be substantively different from communication between an IMP and its Host in either direction.

As a packet is transmitted from one IMP to the next, it remains stored in the sending IMP until acknowledged by the
receiving IMP. Thus, the way is clear for a receiving IMP to
discard incoming packets, if the occasion demands, by not
acknowledging them. Retransmissions are instituted if acknowledgments are not forthcoming within a suitable time
period. Negative acknowledgments are insufficient, unnec-
essary, and not proposed.

The network will be a very difficult system to operate, at
least initially. It is a complex interconnection of sizable
quantities of equipment distributed over much of the continental U.S. . . . Reliability is a primary problem. . . . Moreover,
the IMPs are expected to operate unattended for long periods, without marginal checking or daily preventive maintenance. . . . Many features usually only included in the design
of militarized hardware will enhance the reliability performance. . . . Even in laboratory environments, people do
accidently [sic] push up against, bang, kick, drop, shake, vi-
brate, heat and cool equipment and subject it to dust, unusual humidity conditions, power-line transients of various
sorts, and electromagnetic interference. . . . We therefore propose the use of a computer for which standard ruggedized
options have been designed and delivered.

An IMP must be able to test itself, but, even more importantly, an IMP must be able to test all of the surrounding digital hardware to which it is connected.

> We do not think that we can accomplish all of the work required within the very short time scale specified in the RFQ even though we have done much of the hardware and software design already. Instead, we propose a slightly longer time period for the performance of the contract.

BBN was one of only two finalists for the ARPA network contract. The other was the Raytheon Corporation. Despite the caution BBN expressed in their proposal, individual team members and their manager Frank Heart had a high level of confidence that what was required (a) could be done and (b) could be done *by them*: "I think it was partly because we had a set of people who had followed me from Lincoln, who knew a great deal about how to connect computers to real-time systems and to phone lines, and to make very clever little computer programs that dealt with data coming along."

It was Larry Roberts who made the decision, whether despite or because of his close professional links with the BBN team. "BBN had a superior [technical] proposal, but probably ranked almost equal with Raytheon when we got all through. The thing I saw as different was that the team was a lot stronger. Frank Heart had a very flat team without a lot of hierarchy and a lot of superstructure, and had a bunch of bright people working on it under him, and they had good ideas, as the proposal showed. I just felt the management structure was a lot sounder and was going to work a lot faster."

Frank Heart had the pleasure of managing the winning proposal, and the responsibility to deliver on the promises. It was a daunting task for a company that was dwarfed by many of its competitors. "I was essentially responsible for trying to get that RFP answered, and I put together the team that wrote the proposal; and then I ran the project for many years. It was a very exciting time, because we certainly didn't know we were going to win. We were very concerned that we weren't big enough. We vacillated between thinking we had written the best proposal since we knew the most, to thinking it was impossible for the government to give the job to a small company when there were other large organizations bidding. So it was certainly a very pleasant surprise to have won."

Roberts believed BBN would work faster. Speed was undoubtedly a major element of the assignment, but unlike their distant
federal relatives at NASA, the ARPA pioneers, as they were about
to become, were not operating under a presidential deadline to
ship packets across the country by decade's end. Yet the RFQ had
specified a deadline all the same: Labor Day (September 1) 1969.
Less than a year from the date BBN submitted their proposal; and
only nine months—an apt gestation period for the birth of a new
communications medium—from when BBN actually won the bid.
After thirty years, no one can precisely remember the reason for all
the urgency. It may have been arbitrary, or budgetary. Heart prefers
the first interpretation: "The government sometimes picks dates for
the hell of it. I mean there was no reason. Truth be known, it was
an artificial date picked by the government and picked by Larry
Roberts. I don't know how the devil they picked it. I think there
was certainly no basis that we ever knew why it had to be on that
particular day. But that's what it was. That was the RFP's stated
goal and everybody felt that was an absolutely critical thing to do.
Our reputation was on the line. As well as our next contract."

Larry Roberts no longer remembers the true reason—if there was
one: "I know that my funding had to go back to Congress at that
point, at the end of the year, to get my next budget approved and I
needed this project to have made some progress. It had something
to do with the whole process of keeping the funding going and getting the next year approved. But I'm not quite sure why it had to
be nine months, which seems to be extremely rapid."

BBN learned of their success from ARPA at about the time the
astronauts on Apollo 8 were sending their Christmas message to
earth. But BBN received another special message, with an ecu-
menical flavor, to mark their success, from the office of Senator
Edward Kennedy.

Frank Heart received that obsolete message format, a telegram:
"There is a habit that when one wins a big federal contract you first
hear about it from your congressional delegation calling you up or
sending you a telegram to congratulate you on winning the contract. Our particular telegram was an interesting one. It was maybe
more prophetic than it knew, because we were 'to be congratulated
on winning the contract for the inter*faith* message processor.'"

Work began in earnest at BBN around New Year's 1969. The

tasks ahead of the team were far from routine. First, packet switching in practice had to be made to work; a minicomputer from Honeywell had to be reinvented to become the IMP; software had to be written to operate the IMPs; fifty-kilobit telephone lines had to be leased and installed from the skeptical phone companies. Four node locations—in Los Angeles, Santa Barbara, and Menlo Park (all California), and in Utah—had to establish local teams to develop software to operate between their host mainframe computer and their IMP.

Frank Heart says his team members "were afraid that we wouldn't get the hardware built in time. That was a critical problem because we had to design it. We had to get Honeywell to then understand the design. We had to get Honeywell to construct it. It had to be delivered and tested. I mean, that was a critical path through the whole system. We had to get the software written. That was very difficult. We had to invent the algorithms for routing and congestion control. So that wasn't anything which felt easy, it really wasn't. We were worried that AT&T wouldn't be able to deliver the long lines. They had to put in special lines to get fifty-kilobit lines to these sites and usually it took a terribly long time to get special lines put in anywhere."

Despite these significant challenges, what is perhaps most remarkable is that the trailblazers are so unassuming about what they achieved. Bob Kahn, for example: "It took a lot of expertise that we actually had in the group—expertise in hardware, software, system design, architecture, communications, computing, the whole panoply of stuff. Armed with that expertise, I thought the task was not only very doable, but one that we were all convinced was just going to happen on schedule."

As Dave Walden points out, "We were engineers. We turned in a full-blown design. So, when we actually implemented, it was like doing yet another design. I think none of us had any doubt that we could do it in nine months. It was an engineering task. It was a fun one. Yes, we were going to have to work day and night, weekends, but not so hard."

Severo Ornstein thought "the hardware and software both seemed like a fairly straightforward thing to do. I saw no reason why we couldn't do that. There seemed no insurmountable problems. It was straightforward engineering....We had our heads

down in the bits. I still consider the ARPAnet to have been a relatively easy thing to start off with. The initial system just to build
a half dozen computers and connect them together and enable
them to pass messages around in a network is really a relatively
straightforward task. Genius? No, this is engineering work. This
is an evolutionary process. Occasionally someone has an insight
and you move more of a step. But genius is a rather strong word."

Frank Heart is equally modest: "I don't think there was anything like inventing a new second law of thermodynamics. It
wasn't that kind of thing. So there were a lot of very difficult, detailed technical problems, but *breakthrough* would not be how I
would describe any of that. You know, I tend to think of *breakthroughs* as inventing DNA. There was none of that really."

The BBN team did not invent packet switching. As we have
learned, it was invented, in theoretical form, by Len Kleinrock,
and further investigated by Paul Baran and Donald Davies in
three separate, but largely contemporaneous research ventures.
What BBN did invent was *doing* packet switching, rather than
proposing and hypothesizing packet switching. Few on the team
other than Bob Kahn had any direct experience; Kahn's experience was also, by definition, theoretical. Nevertheless, the confidence of Roberts and Kleinrock in the technology carried the
BBN team along. As Dave Walden recalls, "Packet switching was
sort of in the wind, but in terms of our particular engineering
team, none of us really knew anything about it."

The IMPs were to be the hardware backbone of the ARPAnet.
Each IMP would sit in front of its mainframe "host," communicating with the host in one direction, and other network IMPs outside. The IMPs had to run the software that "packetized" outgoing
data, and reassembled incoming packets into coherent, ordered
messages. The IMPs were connected to each other by leased 50-
kilobit telephone lines. An IMP would be in constant touch with
the traffic patterns on the network, and make a continuously
changing assessment of the most efficient available route to send
packets to their final destination. Individual packets—different
parts of the same message—might travel by any number of different route permutations. The IMP at the receiving end would confirm that it had received all the packets, read the labels on the
individual packets, and reconstitute them into the right order. One

of the first tasks, which Frank Heart identified, was how the IMPs would connect to their hosts. Severo Ornstein had drawn diagrams of the peripheral hardware required, for the BBN proposal. Now he was assigned the task of designing it for real.

In 1969, it was not an option to buy an IMP the way its descendant, the router, can be ordered from an 800-number hardware catalog or the World Wide Web. The IMP had to be designed from scratch, or some existing hardware had to be adapted. BBN's proposal indicated that they had already identified a hardware supplier, though it was not Digital Equipment Corporation, which manufactured the PDP-8, originally recommended by the ARPA brief. Frank Heart chose the Honeywell DDP-516 minicomputer instead, in his determination to pursue reliability above all. Other respondents to the RFQ also proposed this reliable Honeywell machine. This was a robust computer, which could be "ruggedized" for an additional 10 percent cost. Heart had visions of rampaging students on university campuses, and he wanted a machine that would be indestructible.

This was an image Honeywell had gone out of its way to foster. Len Kleinrock recalls a computer convention demonstration of the DDP-516 that had nothing to do with its processing power: "It was first announced at a Joint Computer Conference in 1968. Those were these big gala affairs like Comdex these days, with all the showgirls and the glitz. And they had this machine running. It was a military version, hardened version with big hooks on the top, and it was hoisted up in the air. And it was swinging in the air. And there was a big brute there, stripped down to the waist with a sledge hammer, and he was whacking on this machine to show it would survive that kind of beat-up."

In February 1969, Honeywell delivered a standard 516 to BBN's offices on Moulton Street in Cambridge, as a "development" machine. This was not an IMP. It was the machine that would be taken apart by Ornstein and the hardware team so they could figure out how to change it, and what to attach to it, so that it could grow up to be an IMP someday—someday soon.

Reliability was a primary consideration because the IMPs were supposed to operate unattended for long periods and keep running in the face of power failures, downed phone lines, host computer failures, or any other predictable or unforeseeable crisis. As Frank Heart recalls, "It wasn't actually mil-spec [military specification], but it was very close. It was a battleship-gray cabinet with eye-hooks on the top so that the helicopter could lift it, a refrigerator-sized object with a computer in it, a Honeywell 516. With special interfaces that had been designed by Ornstein, built by Honeywell in that cabinet so that it would then connect to host computers at each site. And inside was a program which had been written at BBN."

The program inside was Bob Kahn's bailiwick. It had to provide the mathematical instructions, or algorithms, that would route the packets to the right places. It was, in effect, the traffic manager. The ARPA RFQ had not specified how it should be done, or what algorithms were to be used. The BBN software design team had to write this program, while the hardware people were inventing the IMP. Kahn, who had helped write the proposal, found himself getting more and more involved in the project itself. So he jumped on board, and played a major role in the system's design.

Reliability was not just a hardware issue. Rampaging students beating on a grey metallic cabinet were probably not the primary threat to the success of the ARPA network. Its value would be measured by successfully delivering whole messages, arranged in the right order, to the right places. In order to ensure this kind of reliability, the IMPs had to have a series of internal checks—to make sure that all packets of a message were delivered, to request retransmission of missing packets, to acknowledge messages received, to redirect stray packets, and more. The rules they would all obey are known in the trade as a protocol.

If packets are like ultra-high-speed postcards, Vint Cerf asks us to imagine an attempt to send an entire book, cut up into paragraphs, on postcards. The assumption of unreliability—that some postcards will go astray, that they must be numbered, that they will arrive out of order, and that the recipient needs to know how many to expect—requires a set of rules for how to monitor the progress of the undertaking. With packet-switching, the first networking protocol was put in place. As Cerf describes:

> I would number each one of the postcards so that you could put them back together in order. Then I'd remember that some of them were going to get lost, and so I'd keep

copies so I could send you duplicates if necessary. Then I'd wonder how would I know if I should send a duplicate? The answer is, you should tell me, by sending me postcards, how many you got. So periodically you could say I got everything up through 402 or 430. But the postcard you send me could get lost. So we have to have a timeout that says if I haven't heard anything from you for a while, I will start sending you duplicates of the things that you haven't acknowledged yet. Eventually I'll get one of your postcards telling me how much you've received and I can throw away the copies. Then you and I should have an agreement that I won't send more than a hundred postcards at a time without getting an acknowledgment back from you. That's an example of a protocol.

By the spring of 1969, despite some prolonged struggles with Honeywell to get what they actually wanted in the DDP-516 prototype IMP, BBN had hardware and software working in their own building. With little fanfare (in fact, with no fanfare), the ARPA network was passing its first test. To the layman, it might seem that a bench-test under controlled circumstances might be of limited relevance to what would happen when the real test was for the technology to operate between two IMPs in Los Angeles and Palo Alto, about 415 miles apart. The leased fifty-kilobit telephone lines had about twenty-five times the carrying capacity of a typical domestic phone line of the time, which would vastly exceed the traffic needs of the network for years to come. Capacity was not an issue. And to BBN's Severo Ornstein, distance was of no consequence either. "We had two machines operating in the same room together at BBN, and the difference between a foot of wire and a few hundred miles of wire was not important as far as we were concerned. The phone company assured us that the length of the cable didn't matter. So at some level, we knew it was going to work. There were really no particular surprises."

The BBN team had the advantage of having a core of people who had worked closely together, first at MIT, then at Lincoln Lab. They were of much the same age, either side of thirty; they were first generation Nerds. They describe themselves and each other thus:

Ornstein points out that "we [BBN] had stellar engineers.

Frank Heart was really a very experienced system designer at that point—an MIT-trained electrical engineer with a management and computer systems background."

Dave Walden says that "Frank was an excellent project manager. He had a defensive attitude in the sense of 'I want to build the program, write the system so it can't be broken. I want to control things.' It was sort of amusing at times, the degree to which he wanted to control things, but in fact, it led to a good design."

Severo Ornstein, a hardware perfectionist with music, geology, and rock-climbing in his resumé: "We were building IMPs but we were working closely in conjunction with the programming people. We had all worked together, Frank and Will Crowther and I had all worked together at Lincoln for years prior to this. So we really knew how to speak to one another, which was important."

Bob Kahn was a specialist in communications theory, and one of the team's best writers. "Bob Kahn was a very smart information theory person, communications theory person. He tended to work all day and all night," which was more unusual then than it is in today's Silicon Valley startups.

Dave Walden was a younger, outgoing Californian—"a very, very proficient, hardworking, hard-driving programmer." Walden is credited with bringing juggling to the ARPAnet community. "After I'd learned to do a little bit of juggling, I rushed in and was all excited. People would bring their passions to work, show them to other people, and everybody would take on that passion. So there was a period of time, several years, when everybody in BBN, in our development group, was learning to juggle. We were doing club passing at lunch hour. I would take my juggling balls to a meeting at ARPA, and I remember Vint Cerf had his juggling balls at one point. Certainly I spread the culture of juggling around the ARPAnet. But I wouldn't say it actually had anything to do with the ARPAnet."

The software group included Will Crowther—a somewhat shy programmer described by Frank Heart as "extraordinarily clever—an expert rock climber and a caver who has drawn cave maps for the Cave Foundation of the United States." Crowther also invented Adventure, the first computer game. Walden regards him as "really my mentor, a brilliant fellow. Crowther and Kahn used to argue theory versus practice: that was fun to watch."

Bernie Cosell was a resource required by every technology team working on a deadline. He could find and fix problems. "Cosell was a brilliant debugger. Absolutely stunning debugger. We used to think of him sort of as our insurance policy that whatever happens, Bernie can somehow make it work."

The BBN team reported to, and was mentored by, Larry Roberts in Washington. Larry was "quite an amazing manager of people in research labs. Giving us a lot of freedom but keeping in touch. A person who seemed to work day and night, because he would do his management all day and then he would do calculations at night and send memos out, write technical reports; really quite an impressive fellow."

Roberts was not only monitoring the development work at BBN. Out West, at the four locations chosen for the first nodes, work also had to be done, on a crash schedule, to meet the deadline and to marry local installations to the systems BBN was developing. At each site, the host was a mainframe, not a minicomputer, manufactured by IBM, Digital, or SDS (Scientific Data Systems); and used either as a time sharing machine or, in some cases, for batch-mode serial computation. In each case, the individual machine had to be connected to the IMP. But Frank Heart realized that each set of connections would be different: "The question was, just exactly how do they connect? How do they connect electrically? How do they connect logically? How does the software connect? That's a very difficult problem. And it had to be solved very, very, very quickly because not only did we at BBN have to build special hardware into the Honeywell machine to be our end of that connection, but, in addition, all the poor host sites had to also build specialized hardware for their big computers and write special programs for their big computers to match our connection."

Within the total time frame of nine months, the host site teams had even less time than BBN to define the interconnection. Kleinrock's host team at UCLA was forced to begin its host-to-IMP design before the specifications were actually released. In due course, a numbered BBN technical document was issued: Document 1822. As Kleinrock insists, "Anybody who was involved in the ARPAnet work will never forget that number because it was the defining spec for how the things would mate."

The ARPA definition of the network had been quite clear: one host per IMP. Each location would connect a single large computer to its IMP. But this elegant plan was at odds with the reality: the host sites all had multiple large computers and, as Len Kleinrock recalls, they told BBN they all had to be hooked up. "The minute the project started and all the host organizations got involved, they said, 'Wait, wait! We've got more than one computer! We want to connect two or three computers to your IMP, please.'"

As the ARPA contract was cost-based, it was relatively painless for ARPA to ask BBN, as they did, to change the plan to serve multiple hosts at each site. Once again, the technological challenge was to standardize a protocol for communication among varying makes and models of hardware.

Frank Heart's team found themselves accidentally creating a solution to a problem they had not been asked to solve: "Even at one site they were different. There might be two or three computers at one site, each of which was from a different manufacturer. But the IMP provided a standard way to connect, so, curiously, many of the sites had been unable to interconnect even their local computers until the IMPs came along, and they then found that was a very convenient standard way to connect their local computers as well as to connect the computers across the country."

Len Kleinrock was at the University of California, Los Angeles. As the theory pioneer of packet switching, he was best able to take charge of the measurement of real traffic, once there was some, on the proposed network. Larry Roberts awarded an ARPA contract to UCLA to set up the Network Measurement Center, and thus to be the first node on the network. The fact that he was funding the host sites as well as the network itself helped to overcome any residual reluctance on the part of the participants, as did Roberts' personal expertise in the technology.

Frank Heart would talk to Larry Roberts frequently: "Once a week, maybe oftener in some cases. There would be a constant involvement with the host sites, and meetings of the host sites with the government. So it was a very steady involvement. They were not just funding agencies: the people there were as smart as we were, if not smarter. And they were as knowledgeable and involved."

At UCLA, Len Kleinrock put Steve Crocker in charge of the programming effort, and he assigned Crocker's high-school buddy Vint Cerf, also a graduate student, as well as Jon Postel and Charlie Kline. With the others, Cerf was assigned to develop the software to connect the host computers to the IMPs. As he recalls, "It was a little funny because we were just graduate students. We kept expecting that professional managers would show up and tell us what to do. But they never did, so we just went on our merry way."

Another legacy of the graduate students' caution is the Internet tradition of documents known as RFCs—requests for comment—which Steve Crocker initiated. The idea was to solicit comments and suggestions as people began to use the network, in order to improve it. Another UCLA graduate student of 1969, Jonathan Postel, has edited the RFCs ever since. Cerf says, "Steve Crocker chose the most diffident language he could possibly compose to keep from appearing to step on anybody's toes. What's truly interesting is that that set of documents continues to this day to document the development of what is now the Internet. And the guy that edited that series is still editing the series, Jonathan Postel out at USCISI, who has had this role literally for his entire career."

Obstetricians often tell expectant mothers that nine months is "a month too long" for pregnancy. Certainly most mothers feel that way. But to develop, test, and install a new high-tech communications medium, the gestation period from January 1 to September 1 was far too short. Inevitably, there were both surprises and compromises. BBN's policy, defined by Frank Heart, was to make the system good enough. "Bob Kahn regretted that we didn't do a better job on the routing algorithm. He was always convinced it was going to fail, and he was right. It eventually failed. To have listened to him would have meant not meeting the deadline. So I don't regret for a minute having gone forward with an imperfect system, but it was certainly the case that there were things wrong with it. We got surprises and the network broke in smaller and larger ways a little bit over the next few years and then those problems were fixed."

Len Kleinrock would later complain that BBN wouldn't listen when problems were brought to their attention. "We'd tell BBN, 'There's a problem here. Fix it.' And the standard reply would be, 'It's going to take us six months to fix it.' The way they were structured they had a sequence of things they needed to do. They had a set of tasks, and the management there just was very rigid. Now, in defense of that style, they had a network to keep up. And some hotshot comes by and says, 'Try this,' they're going to stiff them and make sure the network is up and running and at least providing a minimal degree of service."

As Dave Walden observes of Kleinrock, the UCLA hotshot, "It wasn't so much we were having an argument with Len as we were trying to get something going and good enough, working in the field, running. That was what we were concentrating on."

As the intensity of the work increased at BBN, and the weeks and days to the deadline were counting down, the far more public drama of the Apollo program had captured the world's imagination. By one of those curious coincidences of history, the ARPA-sponsored geeks designed the blueprint, wrote the software, and built the computers of the world's first digital network at exactly the same time as NASA's Apollo program reached its lunar zenith. In early 1969, the *Apollo IX* and *X* missions orbited the Moon, rehearsed the Moon landing, and prepared for the fulfillment of Kennedy's promise: the Sputnik-inspired challenge of a Cold War Space Race. On July 16, 1969, Neil Armstrong stepped onto the Sea of Tranquillity and uttered his immortal soundbite. NASA and its multibillion-dollar budget beat ARPA's one-million-dollar program to the payoff. Two visions of science and technology, one begun in 1958 and the other in 1960, were to succeed within a few weeks of each other. The irony is that from the perspective of the late 1990s, the unheralded, low-budget, obscure venture of wires and bits seems more significant and universal in its impact upon our daily lives than the heroic, but perhaps inconsequential, adventures in space.

At BBN that summer, there wasn't much time to watch the drama and spectacle of *Apollo XI*. For the BBN team and their host-site colleagues, the last month before the first IMP's delivery to Los Angeles was a mixture of excitement, competitiveness, and exhaustion. The lab at UCLA wasn't quite ready; rumors flew that BBN was running late. And there was very little history of shipping computers across the country and having them work right away.

Severo Ornstein knew this was tricky: "First of all, the ability to ship a machine across the country and have it be plugged in at the far end and have it work was important. Today you carry machines around and you expect to plug them in and you just expect it all to work. But not many years before that, machines were built into the walls, and if you shook the room a little bit, it was days before you could get the machine to work again."

Dave Walden enjoyed the drama of meeting the deadline: "Delivering the first machine in nine months was pretty exciting. It did get shipped on time. When we heard that the UCLA people weren't expecting it because they were running a little bit behind and they were hoping we were behind, too, that made us, of course, feel pretty good."

Vint Cerf was at UCLA: "Our software wasn't quite ready when the hardware showed up, and it was Labor Day weekend and we were sort of hoping it might be delayed. We scrambled to get the hardware interface between the IMP and the SDS-7 that we were using as our main host to work. That was the very first BBN 1822 interface that was built."

Bob Kahn was back in Cambridge: "We had done quite a bit of testing of the ARPAnet IMPs right at BBN before we ever shipped them. But the first IMP was shipped to UCLA at the end of August of 1969. A few days short of the nine-month delivery period, which I think astounded the folks at UCLA because they were expecting it to be late."

Vint Cerf was one of those astounded: "BBN delivered the product on time. First of September. Actually a little earlier than the guys at UCLA hoped. They air-shipped it. So the machine shows up. They get it on a forklift. It goes into the UCLA facility and they turned it on and it picks up where it left off. Very impressive."

On schedule, on budget: it was hard to believe this was a government project. The whole job had been completed in nine months. As the UCLA IMP was the only one on the network, and its host was the only host, the first tests ran software that masqueraded as other hosts to send packets between IMP and host, or between host and "fake hosts." That first IMP, the most historic (ruggedized) machine in the history of networking, stands today in Len Kleinrock's computer-science laboratory at UCLA: "My laboratory was the place where the Internet came to life. It was then called the ARPAnet. We had the first switch, called an IMP, which was wheeled into my laboratory over the Labor Day weekend in 1969. And on Tuesday of that next week we had bits moving back and forth between that switch and my host computer."

To witness this historic event, there was no shortage of interested parties. On the day following Labor Day, September 2, as Len Kleinrock recalls:

> We had messages moving back and forth. Everybody was there. BBN was there. The computer science department was there. The school of engineering. UCLA administration. GTE was there. We were using their local lines. Honeywell was there. It was their machine. AT&T was there. It was their long lines network. Scientific Data Systems was there because our host machine was an SDS. Everybody was there and they were all ready to point the finger, right? If it didn't work. Fortunately, everybody had done their jobs very well. It worked beautifully. And there was a big celebration. But nobody had a camera. Nobody thought to memorialize this event. It just didn't seem like that big a deal. You know, two machines talking to each other.

Until a second node was connected, a true network test could not occur. But in the meantime, the UCLA team sent local messages to test the packet-switching technology, which seemed to be working correctly. A month later, on October 1, 1969, the second IMP was installed at Stanford Research Institute. The lines were connected, both IMPs were prepared, Stanford's PDP host and UCLA's SDS Sigma-7 were set, and the fledgling network was ready to be blitzed with bits. With the historic examples of Alexander Graham Bell's "Come here, Mr Watson" and Neil Armstrong's recent "One giant leap for mankind" as prototypes, what memorable message did the ARPA pioneers compose? Kleinrock confesses:

> What was the first message? "What hath God wrought?" Or, "Great step for mankind?" No. All we tried to do was log on from our host to their host. Remember—we're engineers. So I had one of my guys, Charley Kline, set this up and we also had a voice line in parallel over the data line. He had a pair of headphones and a speaker and so did the other guy at the other end. You want to type in LOG and the rest

would span out: "LOG IN." And so we typed in L. And we said, "Did you get the L?" And he said, "I got the L." Typed the O. "You get the O?" "I got the O." "You get the G?" Crash! The system failed on the G. A couple hours later we successfully logged in, did some minimal things, and logged off. That was the first message on the Internet. "Log in, crash." Or, as I like to phrase it, the first message was "Hello" which is the way the two letters L, O sound.

The message may not have been of much consequence, but the event was. Despite the theoretical, experimental, and local testing which meant that the ARPA network *should* work, the first connection between UCLA and SRI meant that it *did* work. As Ornstein says, "The first two were the really crucial ones. That was really the first time that remote machines had actually, in our experience, talked to one another."

The ARPA contract had called for four initial nodes, and BBN continued to meet the scheduled delivery dates. IMP #3 was installed at the University of California at Santa Barbara on November 1, 1969, on schedule; IMP #4 was installed at the University of Utah on December 1, 1969, on schedule. The impeccable execution of the contract requires some explanation, not least for people who have had less happy experiences of government contracting.

Frank Heart says, "It's an example of what can be done with reasonably bright, dedicated management both on the government's side and on the contractor's side. What can be done with small groups of people, all of whom talk to each other, where there's no communication problems. For a government project and a Defense Department project, it was amazingly free of the usual kinds of bureaucratic nonsense that afflicts so many government projects."

The entire ARPAnet project was unclassified, despite being run by the Department of Defense. It was also provided to its users as a free good. There were no access charges or service charges. There was also an absence of concern over who gained access to the network, though the project was entirely government funded. Because it was a brand-new technology, it did not have to be "backwards compatible" with any preexisting hardware or software; there was no legacy to incorporate. And the cost-based contract meant that plans could be changed quickly without wholesale renegotiations of contracts and budgets. Those were the days.

On the twentieth anniversary of the first IMP's going into service at UCLA, Len Kleinrock composed six stanzas of doggerel—to recall the romance of IMPs, nodes, and technical specifications that only nerds could love—or make rhyme.

It was back in '67 that the clan agreed to meet.
The gangsters and the planners were a breed damned
　　hard to beat.
The goal we set was honest and the need was clear to
　　all.
Connect those big old mainframes and the minis lest
　　they fall.

The spec was set quite rigid, it must work without a
　　hitch.
It should stand a single failure with an unattended
　　switch.
We decided UCLA would be the first node on the net.
As the best researchers out there, we would be the
　　perfect bet.

I suspect, you might be asking, what means "first
　　node on the net"?
Well, frankly it meant trouble, especially since no
　　specs were set.
For you see, the interface between nascent IMP and host
Was a confidential secret from us folks on the West
　　Coast.

BBN had promised that the IMP was running late.
We welcomed any slippage in the deadly scheduled
　　date.
But one day after Labor Day it was plopped down at
　　our gate.
Those dirty rotten scoundrels sent the damn thing out
　　air freight.

As I recall that Tuesday, it makes me want to cry.
Everybody's brother came to blame the other guy.
Folks were there from ARPA, BBN, and Honeywell,
UCLA and ATT, and all were scared as hell.

We cautiously connected, and the bits began to flow.
The pieces really functioned, just why I still don't
  know.
Messages were moving pretty well by Wednesday morn.
All the rest is history. Packet switching had been born.

Bob Taylor had proposed the ARPA network to provide interactive access between ARPA-funded computer resources around
the country, and to save money that ARPA would otherwise have
to spend on buying more and more computers. Larry Roberts, appointed by Taylor to execute the plan, believes both goals were
met: "By 1973, I had cut our computer budget to 30 percent of
what it would have been if I hadn't had the network. And saved
more money than the network cost. Because I could share computers all across the world and not have to buy computers for
every research group that wanted one."

Even skeptics who had resisted the very idea of the network
began to recognize the value once it came into existence, as Roberts
found: "After it came up, they found that they could exchange papers between Stanford and MIT very easily, and write papers
jointly, which was great; and they suddenly found that this was a
tremendous benefit rather than a tremendous harm. And they
didn't lose any computer power. They actually probably gained because there were other computers that they could access."

Bob Taylor, the originator of the ARPA network idea, left ARPA
almost as soon as it had come online. He left partly because he
had done what he set out to achieve; partly from a sense that it
was time; and partly because he grew increasingly uncomfortable
in the Vietnam-era Pentagon. "The ARPAnet was my objective
when I became head of the IPTO office. That's the project that I
really wanted to see carried off. It was sort of my baby. And in
1969, when we had those four nodes up and running, okay, we
know it's going to work. We know it's going to grow from there.
So I felt like I'd done what I wanted to do."

Taylor doesn't believe in having a job for life, especially in government. But his tours of duty to sort out data processing for the war effort in Vietnam gave him an additional motivation for moving on. "My first trip to Vietnam I thought, 'Well, it's a good thing we're over here because these people are getting downtrodden by folks who don't care about human rights and liberties and so on.' But about the third trip over there I thought, 'This is a civil war. We've got no business here.' And I began to get really down about our involvement in Vietnam. I wanted to get out of not just the Defense Department, but the whole government and Washington scene."

Bob Taylor left ARPA in October 1969 for a position at one of the network nodes, the University of Utah. He left the management of the ARPAnet to Larry Roberts, who succeeded him as director of IPTO. But Taylor did not rest on his laurels, or retire into decent academic obscurity. Within a year, he was approached to consult for, then join, the newly established Xerox Palo Alto Research Center. As a result, he would witness, and manage, several further milestones in computing and networking history.

Part Two

The 1970s: Networking the Nerds

Chapter Four
Kind of a Happening

ONE OF THE PASTIMES THAT BRINGS the greatest joy to hardcore nerds is pushing a system to its limit, and beyond, then tinkering until the limit is revised. Then they start pushing all over again. In the first weeks and months of the ARPAnet, Bob Kahn, Dave Walden, Vint Cerf, and Len Kleinrock all participated in this engaging activity, thereby better understanding and improving the growing network.

Once UCLA and Stanford were connected, Kahn and Walden spent a pleasant time in California, to measure how the net was working and how it would function under different loads of traffic. They worked with Len Kleinrock, Steve Crocker, and Vint Cerf at the UCLA Network Measurement Center, which generated real and artificial traffic to test the network. The UCLA team saw it as their job to experiment with the network. Kleinrock says, "Indeed it was our job to break the network, and break it we did, at will. We found one problem after another over the next few years, including serious deadlocks and lockups, such as 'Christmas lockup' and 'Piggyback lockup.'" Kleinrock put Holger Opderbeck in charge of the Network Measurement Center in the early 1970s, and together they had "a terrific time attacking the net."

UCLA's pride at being able to lock up the network was matched by BBN's determination to prevent it: the BBN engineers went home to Boston to fix the software. It took more than six months to fix and upgrade the software. But one of the more fateful encounters in networking history took place as a result. Bob Kahn, then at BBN, met Vint Cerf, then at UCLA, for the first time. In due course, they would be responsible for the evolution of the Internet. Cerf recalls: "I first met Bob Kahn when he came out to UCLA with Dave Walden to run tests on this thing. Bob would ask me to do a battery of tests and I would run them and we would knock the net over. I almost got to the point where I wanted to put little

pictures of networks up on the side of the computer like they used
to do in World War II for shooting down airplanes. Because we
knocked ARPAnet down pretty regularly. But it was a terrific experience because it exposed a lot of the deficiencies in the design,
in the early design, by pressing it to the limits of its behavior."

President Kennedy was dead, but NASA had put his men on
the Moon, and returned them safely to earth, by the end of the
decade. ARPAnet had packets flowing among IMPs and hosts by
the same deadline. As the decade turned, the secret achievement
of the ARPA geeks was destined to remain largely secret for years
to come. But the network quietly grew, more IMPs were manufactured and installed, more nodes were added.

In March 1970, the fifth node on the ARPAnet was installed at
BBN headquarters in Cambridge, Massachusetts. There was still
no connection to ARPA itself in Washington. But the ARPAnet
was connected from its four nodes in the West to its fifth, in Massachusetts. Within a couple more years, it was sending packet traffic across the Atlantic, and across the Pacific to Hawaii, by radio,
satellite, and telephone line. One radio packet network was established in a panel truck that drove up and down Highway 101 on
the peninsula south of San Francisco. Kleinrock could control and
measure the behavior of the ARPAnet Atlantic Satellite Network
from his Network Measurement Center on the Pacific coast using
the land-based ARPAnet to cross the continent. The experimental
network became operational, and grew steadily.

Frank Heart found himself managing an increasingly large
federal research contract: "The government was incredibly ec-
static about that. The contract was extended to go build more
sites and put more sites in to keep running the network and to
keep improving the software. So BBN's contract just grew. From
BBN's point of view, it was a big success. From ARPA's point of
view, it was a big success."

Connecting BBN to the ARPAnet made other technological innovations possible. The IMPs had been designed by BBN to provide a constant monitoring of the state of the network—its
message traffic load, the telephone connections, its power load.
As Heart points out: "This was the first time computers had ever
sat on phone lines really watching them carefully. A phone line
between UCLA and Santa Barbara would begin to cause trouble.

The IMPs on the West Coast would notify us in Cambridge this was happening. So somebody in our Network Management Center would pick up a phone and call California and say, 'Your line from Santa Barbara to UCLA is in trouble. You better go and check on it.' They'd say, 'Okay, which end are you on?' We'd say, 'Well, we're in Cambridge, Mass.'"

With the connection to BBN in place, the design team was able to provide software upgrades directly over the network. They could release an entire program to the entire set of IMPs in the space of a few hours. For the first six months of the network's life, software upgrades were supplied by Dave Walden, who flew from node to node with paper tapes in his briefcase.

Remote management of the IMPs, debugging tools, and reloading of machines across long distances were all technological innovations special to the ARPAnet. Ten years later, in the 1980s, software distribution via bulletin boards would become a hugely successful business; in the 1990s, it would become something close to the norm.

Another by-product of the IMP technology was the creation of the first local area networks (or LANs). The ARPAnet was designed and built to be a wide area network (WAN)—a widely dispersed network of identical machines, in this case the IMPs, working on the same operating system and hardware platform. But with the decision, mid-contract, to allow more than one host computer to be attached to each IMP, a new computing arrangement was enabled: multiple different mainframes, connected to each other by their shared IMP. Frank Heart explained the origins of this additional breakthrough at the Act One conference: "An interesting surprise was that when you put an IMP into some place, people had more than one computer there that couldn't communicate. The fact that the IMP created a standard for interconnecting meant that the people at the sites promptly began using the IMP as a way to communicate among their local machines. In some cases, that was as big a benefit to them as being able to get out to anybody else in the network, because they hadn't been able to do that before."

It was accidental, but the reason it was so useful was the repeated lesson of networking history—overcoming incompatibility always represents an advance. The same story at Stanford University, a decade later, would represent the foundation of

Cisco Systems, a company that today is climbing towards a market valuation of $100 billion. But the pioneers of the ARPAnet were people with little interest in, or expectation of, either fame or fortune. They were academics, even those who had wandered into the private sector, and their ambitions focused on interesting problems, tenure, and an agreeable lifestyle. Norm Abramson, a Ph.D. engineer who was teaching at Stanford in 1969, went looking for a job with tenure; allowed himself to fall in love with surfing; and wound up living, teaching, and adding a chapter to the history of packet switching in Hawaii.

Pearl Harbor had underlined Hawaii's military importance. Norm Abramson brought to the University of Hawaii his electrical engineering skills and a belief that packet switching would work as well over a radio network as along telephone lines. A community separated physically into islands, and dotted with mountains, has obvious uses for transmitting information and sharing resources by radio waves. But it wasn't the topographical challenges that drew Norm Abramson to Hawaii—it was the surf: "I was teaching at Stanford, when I first saw Hawaii. And I decided to move there. It took me about a year to find a university position there—and moved to Hawaii to go surfing."

Abramson inevitably persuaded Larry Roberts at ARPA to fund the experiment. Packet switching by radio had never been done. In due course, the Alohanet, as Abramson called it, was the first network that transmitted data into a computer by means of radio waves, rather than telephone lines or conventional wires. It was the first "wireless" networking system. The important protocol at the heart of the Alohanet was one that allowed each terminal to transmit at any time. If and when one transmission collided with another, thus garbling both, the terminal would retransmit after a random interval. Messages received were acknowledged. Messages unacknowledged were deemed to have gone astray, and were thus resent.

Bob Kahn saw the incontrovertible value of testing a theory: "In Hawaii, they showed that you could communicate sending packets over the radio, not that I think any serious engineer would have doubted it. Sometimes just showing that it works is worth everything. They were able to show that it worked and able to actually use it." Engineering landmarks aside, Abramson's motivation for the Hawaii venture remained resolute: "Frankly, I was doing it because of the surf."

In 1970, the Alohanet had packets flowing by radio, and it was connected to the ARPAnet on the mainland. With a link to Hawaii, the network had proved it could function not just over long distances on land, but across the oceans. And with networking conducted by radio, it was, in practice, both international and mobile.

In 1970, Norm Abramson was in Washington, in Larry Roberts' office at the Pentagon. According to Abramson, he tricked Roberts into allocating funding to provide a Terminal Interface Processor, or TIP, to connect the Alohanet to the ARPAnet:

> I noticed he had a list on the blackboard of various universities where he was planning to put in a TIP, or a node in the ARPAnet at that time. The Aloha system and University of Hawaii was not on that list. As we were talking, Larry was called out for an emergency, which often happens with the people in DoD. So Larry went out for about five minutes and I was left in his office. So I went over to the board and took the chalk and wrote in on the list, "Aloha networks," and I put a date, chosen at random—I think it was January 22—on the list. When Larry came back into the office, he had the same list there with one addition that I had made. But about five days before that date that I put in just at random on his board back in Washington, we got a call from the people at BBN that they were shipping an ARPAnet TIP out to us and were going to install it for us.

Abramson confessed; Roberts authorized the TIP anyway. Despite the steady growth of the network, its uses and usefulness remained largely invisible. The original goal of resource sharing was barely met. Files and data were exchanged between sites, and colleagues at different locations became able to work together, remotely. According to Len Kleinrock: "Resource sharing hardly happened, and here's the reason: far too difficult. The main use of resource sharing is if I had my machine and I moved to your facility, changed jobs, and wanted to use the old machine, then I knew exactly how to do all of that."

Making it easier for their principal investigators to change jobs was not one of the intended outcomes of ARPA's computer network; nor was the sudden vogue for playing computerized role playing games, like Will Crowther's Adventure. The original budget-saving, shared resources of the ARPAnet—while effective in fact—were not the "killer application." The killer app of the ARPAnet was e-mail.

Every new information technology needs a feature that makes people just have to buy it—a killer app. For the Apple II and the IBM PC, it would prove to be the spreadsheet; for the Macintosh, it would be desktop publishing. The ARPAnet was no exception. It was a communications network—so the killer app was a way of communicating.

Ray Tomlinson of BBN was the first person to send e-mail on the ARPAnet. In 1972, he devised an experimental program for sending files. Time sharing systems had mail systems inside a single computer, where twenty or thirty different users might have a mailbox. People could leave messages for each other within that one computer. But there was no such thing as electronic mail between computers. One day, with access to two separate minicomputers at BBN, Tomlinson wrote a simple file-transfer program, to open a connection, send a file from one machine to another, and then confirm that the file had transferred. As each minicomputer had user mailboxes, which were no different from files, Tomlinson decided he could modify the file-transfer program to carry a mail message from one machine and drop it into the file of the other. As this quiet pioneer states: "E-mail was the next step. Once we had the ability to transfer a file from one machine to the other, it became fairly clear that one thing you could do was just write the file across the network and send mail to somebody else. I also happened to be working on a piece of software to be used to compose and send mail, called 'send message.' And it seemed like an interesting hack to tie those two together to use the file-transfer program to send the mail to the other machine. So that's what I did. I spent not a whole lot of time, maybe two or three weeks, putting that together and it worked."

As Frank Heart explains, Ray Tomlinson "just did what is called in the computer trade a hack, just put that together and it worked quite nicely, and that became known to people and it began to be implemented in other machines around the network."

Tomlinson himself admits: "It was just a hack. And the next step was to get other people to try using it, because so far I'd only sent mail to myself first and then to the other people in my group. The actual communication was from one machine in one part of the building to another machine in an adjacent room. It was going through the network, but it really wasn't going out through telephone lines or to other sites, like Utah or UCLA or the other places that had ARPAnet nodes at that time. The next release we sent out of our operating system software, we included this 'send message' software and started sending the messages."

The e-mail experience spread rapidly. Not least because everyone using the ARPAnet automatically had a mailbox, by virtue of having access to the network at an ARPA node. Ray Tomlinson was just the first: "That was clearly an advantage because you didn't have to do anything special to start sending e-mail to somebody. They already had a mailbox. In fact, all of the operating systems being run on computers connected to the ARPAnet, had at least some kind of local mail facility, and everybody in charge of those operating systems was out there trying to figure out how to connect their mail system to the electronic medium across the network."

Len Kleinrock was struck by how rapidly e-mail proliferated: "One of the first applications we put on the system was Ray Tomlinson's network e-mail. As soon as e-mail came on, it took over the network. We said, 'Wow, that's interesting.' We should have noticed there was something going on here. There was a social phenomenon that was happening."

Severo Ornstein, the skeptical engineer, found it hard to believe that e-mail was going to be a major use of the network. "It really was. That was not what had been touted in the first place, that sending messages back and forth, from person to person, was going to be a large use of the network. It was hard to believe for a long time."

Bob Kahn observes that ARPA "would never have funded a computer network in order to facilitate e-mail. The telephone was a quite serviceable device for person-to-person communication. But once it came into existence, it had tremendous benefits: overcoming the obstacles of time zones, messaging multiple recipients, transferring materials with messages, simple collegial and friendly contacts."

Larry Roberts argues that the *original* purpose of the ARPAnet is in fact the *actual* use of today's Internet and World Wide Web: "People all over, going after resources all over the world. What it was used for to begin with was, heavily, electronic mail and we had no idea that that was going to happen. The electronic mail was just sort of a new thing that happened. It was a communications use of this computer resource-sharing network that we had created."

Len Kleinrock quickly learned what the whole history of the Internet has repeatedly demonstrated: "People-to-people communications was what excited people. You know, machine-to-machine or human-to-machine was not all that exciting. At that point, we perhaps should have been able to predict the kind of phenomena we see today. And some of us began to see, this is bigger than what we created. That was the first glimpse."

Every single e-mail address has Ray Tomlinson's personal stamp on it, because he decided how to identify the e-mail user with his/her location or institution. The upper-case 2 key, standard on the QWERTY typewriter keyboard since the 1940s: the @ sign.

Ray Tomlinson looked at his keyboard on a Model-33 teletype: "The one that was most obvious was the '@' sign, because this person was @ this other computer, or, in some sense, he was @ it. He was in the same room with it anyway. And so it seemed fairly obvious and I just chose it. There were, at the time, there was nobody with an '@' sign in their name that I was aware of. I'm not so sure that's true any longer because there are a lot of strangely spelled names out there now."

By 1972, the same year Tomlinson hatched his hack and changed the world of communications at least somewhat, the ARPAnet had grown to include dozens of locations, including MIT. BBN was continuing to manage and extend the network rather than creating it. The production line of Honeywell IMPs was known at BBN as "the factory." But still hardly anyone knew about the network, so Larry Roberts at the Pentagon decided that the ARPAnet was ready for primetime. ARPA had seen the future of computing—and it mostly worked.

The International Conference on Computer Communications (ICCC) was scheduled to take place at the Washington Hilton in Washington, D.C., on October 24–26, 1972. After three years, Washington still did not have a node on the ARPAnet, and the event coincided with ARPA's being moved out of the Pentagon to the "Siberian" suburbs. Bob Kahn had suggested to Larry Roberts that a first public demonstration of the network would be timely. Roberts accordingly asked Kahn, still at BBN, to organize it. On the eve of Richard Nixon's reelection as president of the United States, an event with profound repercussions for global communications was taking place in the ballroom of the Hilton.

It was not until 1972 that the ARPAnet had a number of machines functioning fully every single day, and the public demonstration was designed to galvanize and focus energies on proving that it really worked, with multiple terminals connected, performing a variety of functions. Roberts picked the date, and announced that the ICCC would see the first public demonstration of the network.

A temporary 50-kilobit line was run into the Hilton ballroom under a false floor, and BBN set up an IMP on site—a temporary node on the ARPAnet. Bob Kahn was the chief organizer: "We actually got donations of some forty or fifty computer terminals from different manufacturers, and then we orchestrated with a variety of different research places to put applications up on their system and make them work. It was a 'who's who' of everybody in the field and it was just very eye-opening to a lot of people who did not know this was possible—and it was just very self-satisfying to those people who knew all along that it was."

Bob Kahn recruited Al Vezza from the MIT time sharing venture Project MAC to assist with the technical set-up. By the time of the ICCC meeting, twenty-nine nodes were connected to the ARPAnet. Larry Roberts had a small, but growing population around the country actually using the technology: "Everybody brought in all their stuff and got their computers online. The show really pushed them to complete that and make that happen, and everybody around the world, then, realized what was happening at the show. The show showed everybody in the communications world that this worked."

The technical performance was no small matter. From a terminal in Washington, Len Kleinrock would log on to a host at MIT. From MIT, he called up a program from UCLA, whose job it was to execute, run, and send the data to a printer right next to him in Washington. It put the system to a real test. People had brought chess-playing programs, and a group from MIT had "Turtle"—a robot that could be programmed to navigate a room full of obstacles. (Turtle is now retired, in the basement of the Museum of Science, in Cambridge.) Len Kleinrock explains: "We logged on to MIT, pulled up the file from UCLA, ran it, executed it, sent the data—and nothing came out on the printer. And we wondered what happened. Then we looked around and we saw Turtle was jumping around. Someone had wired the printer to Turtle accidentally and that was the output, the dancing movements of Turtle was the output."

A dancing Turtle was not the only thing to go wrong. Bob Metcalfe was a Harvard graduate student working at MIT at the time of the ICCC. Metcalfe was responsible for drawing up a user's guide for visitors to the show, on how to use twenty or so different applications on the ARPAnet. His graduation photograph shows a red-bearded giant, towering over his proud parents, and not necessarily the ideal choice for the job of escorting the perennially skeptical AT&T delegation around the show. As Vint Cerf recalls, "They were fully anticipating that it would be a miserable flop. And just as Bob brings them up for one of the first demonstrations, the network crashed and they were all very happy about this, except for Bob. If they'd hung around for a little longer, they would have discovered that it popped back up again."

It was the only time the network crashed in three full days. But it confirmed AT&T's view that circuit switching had nothing to fear from the upstart packet-switching technology. Indeed, a year later, AT&T rejected an ARPA invitation to take the network off the government's hands entirely. As Larry Roberts says:

> They wouldn't buy it when we were done. We had decided that it was best if industry ran it, because the government had done its experiment and didn't need to run it anymore. I went to AT&T and I made an official offer to them to buy the network from us and take it over. We'd give it to them basically. Let them take it over and they could continue to expand it commercially and sell the service back to the government. So they would have a huge contract to buy service back. And they had a huge meeting and they went through Bell Labs and they made a serious decision and they said it was incompat-

ible with their network. They couldn't possibly consider it. It was not something they could use. Or sell.

Despite the cold shoulder from Ma Bell, the network's boosters were delighted with their public presentation. Bob Kahn, the prime organizer, describes it in aptly sixties language: "I think the public reaction varied from delight that we had so many people in one place doing all this stuff and it all worked, to astonishment that it was even possible. Apart from the people who just did not know and weren't exposed to this before. It was a real, real event. It was kind of a happening. You know, like happens once in your lifetime."

With the ICCC behind him, Bob Kahn was able to make the career move that he had delayed for the show—to go to work at ARPA, where in due course he would succeed Larry Roberts as IPTO director, joining the progression of pioneers that began with Licklider and ran through Ivan Sutherland and Bob Taylor before Roberts and Kahn.

Through the seventies, the ARPAnet grew, adding more and more IMPs and nodes to the network. But soon ARPAnet was not the only network switching packets around the country. Other small, local networks, and overlapping, big networks started to be established within academia, federal agencies, and research establishments. But they weren't able to inter-network. Each of them had their own "protocols" that defined how one network would organize communication among its own nodes.

The reason the ARPAnet worked so well was that it was a single network of uniform IMPs, all engineered at the same place, by the same people, running the same software and the same hardware interfaces to their host computers. The protocols in the computers connected by the ARPAnet made assumptions about how the network functioned because there were no other alternatives in that system. Technically, the ARPAnet worked as designed. In terms of use, things were different. The resource-sharing objectives were only modestly fulfilled, but a 1973 ARPA report showed that three-quarters of all use was e-mail.

But by the early 1970s, other networks were being created too. Now there was a problem. Each network was different, working exclusively within its own protocols, hardware, and software. A user could not send packets from one network to another, let alone through another to a third. They had vastly different technical characteristics. The Alohanet had different protocols from the ARPAnet, as did the satellite packet-switching Atlantic Packet Satellite Network, or SatNet. Another example was the Mobile Radio Network in the San Francisco Bay area, whose topology and reliability kept changing as the vehicles moved. All of these were separate wide area networks that overlapped geographically, but were otherwise quite unalike.

This may explain why for a long time the network was operating at only a fraction—one estimate was 2 percent—of its technical capacity. The problem of incompatibility among disparate networks began to make the success of the ARPAnet look like a modest achievement, even in the eyes of one of its own creators, Severo Ornstein: "That was a relatively straightforward, small piece of work, compared to dealing with this great diversity of languages and machines that existed out there in the world that were going to try and use this thing. And it did take a number of years. It took a lot longer to try to start to work that out so that all these multiple machines could talk to one another."

Not least because of government purchasing rules, every location seemed to be running different machines, operating in different technological media. One place had IBM machines, another Digital machines, a third a Burroughs machine. Larry Roberts saw this as a throwback to the communications difficulties of tribal societies: "They were all different. They couldn't talk to each other. There was no common language, no common way to communicate, and no way to get a program from one to the other. So we basically had a serious problem in transporting anything in terms of knowledge. We had no way for language, for civilization to grow. And we were stuck back like man before he had language."

The incompatibility problem demanded a new solution. It was to be provided by two thirtyish scions of the ARPAnet community: Bob Kahn, now at ARPA in Washington, and Vint Cerf, now at Stanford. As program manager at ARPA, Bob Kahn became involved in new applications of packet switching, packet radio, mobile packet radio, and packet satellite. One of the sites where packet radio was being developed was Stanford Research Institute. On one of his visits to the Bay Area, Bob Kahn stopped in to see Cerf at Stanford, and described these other packet-switching networks; and pointed out that he needed to find a way of interconnecting them, because they did not behave as the uniform ARPAnet did. Thus Kahn and Cerf began to think about protocols that would allow such an amalgam of networks to inter-work.

Their solution was a cross-network protocol, a technological midwife that facilitated the birth of the Internet. The essence of the idea was to replicate the role of the IMPs as a set of boxes that communicated outwards only to other IMPs, and inwards only to their own hosts. The Internet plan was to create what Bob Kahn called a "gateway" as the entrance to each different network: "The idea of the Internet was that you would have multiple networks all under autonomous control. By putting this box in the middle, which we eventually called a gateway, it would allow for the federation of arbitrary numbers of networks without the need for any change made to any particular network. So if BBN had one network and AT&T had another, it would be possible to just plug the two together with a [gateway] box in the middle, and they wouldn't have to do anything to make that work other than to agree to let their networks be plugged in."

To Vint Cerf, the fundamental thing that protocols allowed was "the interconnection of packet-switching networks that weren't all identical. Different packet sizes, different transmission bandwidths; the satellite takes a lot longer. So all of the parameters of operation varied. The whole system couldn't work if there wasn't a way to interconnect everything and hide the fact that there was this nonhomogeneity throughout the system. So it's absolutely vital to have a set of protocols that smooth out the differences and, essentially, are network independent."

The protocol they invented is known by its initials, TCP/IP—standing for the mouthful Transmission Control Protocol/Internet Protocol. It is significant historically for originating the use of the term Internet, in about 1973, as a handy abbreviation for the "inter-networking of networks." In simple terms, the Internet Protocol was like an envelope enclosing one of Vint Cerf's postcards. It allowed a message to leave one network, be enclosed inside an IP-addressed envelope to travel from one gateway to another, be removed from the IP envelope at the destination gateway, and be sent on its way as raw packets into the network it was destined to reach. The Internet Protocol did the routing of packets. It never operated inside a network, only in the space between networks.

The Transmission Control Protocol was more complex, yet almost self-explanatory. It had the effect of controlling and counteracting the much-higher risk of losing packets when they made the arduous journey from one network through the thickets of 50-kilobit lines to another. Information is packetized by TCP on departure, "controlled" during the journey, and reassembled by TCP on arrival. Although Cerf and Kahn began by seeing the protocol as a single approach, it was later split into its two halves, TCP and IP, which functioned separately.

The ARPAnet had addresses that only ARPAnet IMPs could understand, so when a message popped out at the other end of the ARPAnet, only that machine could get it. By contrast, for a journey across the Internet, a message originating in the ARPAnet would have an Internet header on it, containing an Internet address for the end destination that would be interpreted in the gateway. The most important feature of the TCP/IP is the one that is the easiest to grasp: It worked.

Bob Kahn and Vint Cerf published the academic paper that launched a thousand networks in the May 1974 edition of the journal *IEEE Transactions on Communications Technology*. They called it "A Protocol for Packet Network Intercommunication." While its title is sober and scholarly, its impact over the following quarter-century has been spectacular. The Internet pioneers have seen their scientific approach hold up over twenty-five years of growth in networking. But they somewhat underestimated the scale of that growth, as Bob Kahn admits: "When we did the original design of the Internet, we only allowed eight bits for network field, thinking that 256 networks, which is all you can address with eight bits, would be more than enough in the foreseeable future. Of course, it didn't take very long before that whole theory went out with the wash."*

The TCP/IP protocol, which still operates at the time of writing throughout the Internet, was devised before the personal computer and workstations, before the explosion of local area networks in business, before the World Wide Web. What Cerf and

---

* A footnote for the non-digital reader: with 8 bits, each of which can be in an on/off position, there are 2 to the eighth power, or 256 permutations.

Kahn did was to anticipate all these later developments, allowing any network and any computer to fit in and operate compatibly.

Besides different networks, there was an increasing variety of users. Legend has it that in 1976, to mark her Royal Jubilee—the twenty-fifth anniversary of her coronation—the Queen of England was sending e-mail to her loyal subjects. At the time, probably only a few thousand could receive it. But it showed that the Royal Family was up to date.

In 1976, Len Kleinrock published the first book describing the design and performance of the ARPAnet. For the first time, the technology of packet switching was available to a broad audience across the world. The book won the 1976 Lanchester Prize, and Kleinrock multiplied the prize money at a blackjack game in Las Vegas to the extent that he was able to buy an original of the book's cover photo (M.C. Escher's famous "Ascending and Descending" lithograph).

Although the non-homogeneity of the networks in use was what propelled the Internet protocol, it was not until 1977 that Cerf and Kahn demonstrated an inter-networking experiment that featured the ARPAnet, the Atlantic SatNet, and the Mobile Radio Network. Data was being transmitted from the Mobile Radio Net's unmarked panel truck somewhere on the Bay Shore Freeway near Stanford. The data passed through an Internet gateway, carrying its IP address (or travelling in its envelope) and traveled into and through the ARPAnet. Next, the data traveled across a point-to-point satellite hop, first to Norway, then down a land line to London. London sent it back over the packet-switch satellite network, across the United States to a PDP-10 computer at the University of Southern California Information Sciences Institute in Marina Del Rey. To travel about 400 real miles, the data was transmitted approximately 95,000 miles. As Vint Cerf recalls (encouragingly, for the non-technologists among us): "It worked. I'm always amazed when anything like this works, especially if you know how complicated it all is. I'm even surprised when you make a phone call that works. So that was really the first dramatic demonstration of all three networks interworking together."

Oddly enough, the development of new networks, especially mobile radio networks, reintroduced the theme of survivable, flexible command-and-control functions for the military. The

ARPAnet, being fixed, didn't satisfy all the needs of the military. In 1976, Vint Cerf became the next networking expert to move from academia to ARPA, and upon his arrival, he became immersed in more directly military applications for the agency, which still belonged to the Pentagon, though it no longer was located at the Pentagon. Cerf says that "ARPA was very much focused on how this technology could be used to build a highly reliable and resistant command-and-control system. That meant it had to work over the ocean for ships at sea. It certainly had to work for tactical environments on land, and we wanted the continental U.S. wireline network to be embedded in a system as well. So a lot of my time at ARPA was spent helping to move the technology in directions that would provide this kind of resistance and robustness."

By the end of the 1970s, ARPAnet had expanded to connect over a hundred nodes, with at least twice as many host computers attached. At each location, there were perhaps two hundred new users per year. After ten years, it was still being used almost exclusively by people in universities who had access to terminals and nodes. So in the first decade of networking, maybe half a million people had had access of some kind; many fewer had used the networks regularly. How useful was it really? As Len Kleinrock observes, it was growing, and full of potential. "The people-to-people part of it was natural. It's what caught people's imagination and attention. And the way the network evolved, of course, nodes were added, it began to grow, we got cross country links, e-mail began to thrive. It still remained a computer scientist's and a computer researcher's private dream network."

Trends in the computer industry have proved, over forty years, notoriously difficult to predict. J.C.R. Licklider was probably the first to express impatience with the fact that it was easier to predict the uptake of technology twenty years out than five. People who were present at the creation of the ARPAnet are excellent forecasters of the technological advances, and poor judges of the timescales required.

In 1972, as e-mail started to take off, Dave Walden says, "I became very aware of where it could go. So from '72 on I couldn't quite understand why we all weren't communicating by e-mail. If you think about what we've got today with the World Wide Web, with the exception of the point-and-click interface, there's nothing that hasn't been there for the better part of fifteen or twenty years. So my surprise today is that it's taken so long to get there."

Bob Taylor describes himself as "a very poor prophet of what's going to happen in the future, because in 1969–70, I could see that we were going to move away from time sharing and into personal computing. But personal computing, in my view, that was connected; not a PC that stands by itself. And so by the early seventies, I thought that within maybe ten years we would be where we are today with regard to the Internet. Because I saw a lot of the pieces falling into place."

On the other hand, Len Kleinrock was able to foresee the magnitude of what he had helped to create and anticipate its future impact. On July 3, 1969, fully two months before the birth of the Internet in his laboratory, Kleinrock published the following statement: "As of now, computer networks are still in their infancy. But as they grow up and become more sophisticated, we will probably see the spread of 'computer utilities,' which, like present electric and telephone utilities, will service individual homes and offices across the country." It has only taken about twenty-five years to come true.

As Kleinrock has observed, the creation of these "computer utilities" has been a very uncertain process, and along the way large sums of money have been lost. In 1975, Telenet Corporation began to offer a public packet-switching service. In 1979, they were rescued from near-bankruptcy when GTE bought the company and infused an enormous amount of cash into it. It was not until the early 1980s that Telenet became profitable, almost fifteen years after the technology had been proven by the ARPAnet. AT&T had an even harder time. After a prolonged period of reluctance, they announced they would deploy a data network called the Bell Data Network in April 1978; it never happened. They announced they would roll out the Advanced Communication Service in 1979, and then unannounced it. Early in the 1980s, they announced the Bell Packet Switching Service, ran into trouble with the FCC, changed the name to Basic Packet Switching Service, and got it approved.

What was the problem with this remarkable and successful new technology of communications? Why did it take so long to become popular? Kleinrock analyzes it thus: "Packet switching was a new technology. Telenet was an unknown company. Networking is unique in that its benefits come only when a sufficiently large number of others are connected (as with telephones, Federal Express locations, etc.), and this takes many years to achieve. But at long last, AT&T finally came out with their premier packet-switching service, Net 1000, in 1983. The sad story is that they closed down Net 1000 in 1986 with a $1 billion loss! No, packet switching did not have an easy birth."

The first decade of networking was distinguished by one strikingly different feature compared to later eras of the computer industry. Not only was the original technology designed to save money, but few attempted to exploit the technology for profit. In the mid-to-late 1970s, that would change. Networking would ultimately become a hugely profitable business, as one generation of digital geeks after another would continue to overcome incompatibility and technical obstacles. But for those profits to become feasible, and for networking truly to change the face of global communications, another revolution would be required.

Chapter Five
Suits, Hippies, and Hackers

THE TERM "PERSONAL COMPUTER" WAS first used, or so it is claimed, by Stewart Brand, that perennial trailblazer of cultural and technological ideas. In 1968, he founded and published *The Whole Earth Catalog*, the sourcebook for the alternative lifestyle—and for the generation that shaped and influenced the emerging computer industry and its applications. By the time the final installment of the series, the two-volume *Whole Earth Epilog*, was published, "personal" computer equipment was being listed, along with books to be read and classes to be taken that would demystify computers and subject them to the *Whole Earth Catalog* mantra (and subtitle): "Access to Tools." As Stewart Brand explains, "*The Whole Earth Catalog* was thought of as 'back to the land,' but actually it was 'back to any technology that would work for you.' So we were pushing computers from the very start. In our magazine *CoEvolution Quarterly*, we had a whole section called 'personal computers' that existed before personal computers did."

In the late 1960s, the ARPAnet had been established, primarily in California, on campuses that were also in the thrall of hippy fashions, Flower Power, student uprisings, antiwar protests, women's liberation, and other causes, real or imagined. The hippies and the hackers coexisted amid the turmoil. In retrospect, Brand concludes, "Hackers succeeded and hippies failed. Same group of people. Same length of hair. Only instead of drugs, it was computers. I think the main difference there is that drugs never got any better, and computers just kept getting better and better and better. The kind of money you could make with drugs was problematic, and the kind of money you could make with computers was fabulous."

It's important to remember the wider social and industrial context in which technological advances in computing were taking place. To the vast majority of Americans in the 1960s, if computers meant anything, they meant IBM. The International Business Machines Corporation *was* computers in the sixties, and everything about IBM and its corporate leadership, first under Thomas J. Watson, Sr., and then his son Thomas J. Watson, Jr., personified twentieth-century American business and technological confidence.

IBM was, and remains, an American business icon. Over the course of sixty years, the Watsons built what their workers called Big Blue into the top computer company in the world. IBM never fired anyone, requiring only an undying loyalty to the company and a strict dress code. IBM hired conservative hardworkers straight from school. Few IBM staff participated in the Summer of Love or showed up at Woodstock. It was big, paternalistic, and rule-bound. IBM was not the only big corporation to have a company songbook; but surely no other company can have had the same penchant for such numbingly hagiographic lyrics. To the tune of "Pack Up Your Troubles in Your Old Kit Bag," IBMers would sing:

> Pack up your troubles, Mr. Watson's here
> And smile, smile, smile.
> He is the genius in our IBM
> He's the man worth while.
> He's inspiring all the time
> And very versatile—oh!
> He is our strong and able President!
> His smile's worth while.
>
> "Great organizer and a friend so true."
> Say all we boys.
> Ever he thinks of things to say and do
> To increase our joys.
> He is building every day
> In his outstanding style—so
> Pack up your troubles, Mr Watson's here
> And smile, smile, smile.

IBM had been a contractor on government projects like those at Lincoln Laboratory, and was synonymous with both computing and reliability. While there were other computer companies, such as Computer Corporation of America and the upstart mini-computer company Digital Equipment, the saying "No one ever got fired for buying IBM" became a cliché because it was true. Sam Albert spent forty years working at IBM, from 1959 to 1989. When he retired, he owned thirty-five white dress shirts. "When I started at IBM, there was a dress code. You couldn't wear anything but a white shirt, generally with a separate, starched collar. I remember attending my first class, and a gentleman said to me as we were entering the building, 'Are you an IBMer?' and I said, 'Yes.' He had a three-piece suit on, vests were in vogue, and he said, 'Could you just lift your pants leg please?' I said, 'What?!' And before I knew it he had lifted my pants leg and he said, 'You're not wearing any garters.' I said, 'What?!' He said, 'Your socks, they're not pulled tight to the top, you need garters.' And sure enough, I had to go get garters."

Sam Albert was one of those who had a copy of the "Songs of the I.B.M." in his attaché case. At Christmastime, to the tune of "Jingle Bells," the sales force sang:

> IBM, happy men,
> Smiling all the way.
> Oh, what fun it is to sell
> Our products night and day.
>
> IBM, Watson men,
> Partners of TJ,
> In his service to mankind
> That's why we are so gay.

Conformity and loyalty were expected at IBM. The workforce was rewarded with de facto jobs for life, and an enviable association with one of the icons of American capitalism. For those who attempted not to conform, intervention was swift. As it was for Rich Seidner, a programmer who put an early indiscretion behind him and lasted twenty-five years at Big Blue: "In 1967, I had just gotten out of the basic programmer training at IBM. I had seen Sammy Davis, Jr., perform down in New York, and he had this really beautiful mohair jacket with this incredibly gorgeous medallion. So I went and had something tailored just like that. Medallion and all. I went in on a Monday morning. I was so excited, I thought I looked great but within half an hour of showing up in my office three levels of management—my manager, *his* manager, and *his* manager—had come by and told me to go home and change. Now I was working in the development laboratory, I wasn't working with customers, so I didn't think that the dress code quite applied to me. But I went home and I changed." In later years, Sam Albert saw the unthinkable: "Slowly but surely some executives decided to wear tassle shoes. That was a day that I will remember. Or somebody might wear a double-breasted checked suit."

Big Blue was in some ways too powerful, too successful. The company ran into trouble with both anti-trust regulators and its competitors for being so dominant in the marketplace. But IBM was identified with the national interest. According to Rich Seidner, it was known that if you were of draft age and had a job at IBM, the company would send a letter to the local draft board stating that the company was working on "national security" matters. The draft board was allowed to conclude that the individual in question was involved in national security, though the company did not say so explicitly, and those potential draftees got to stay home.

This reliable, solid enterprise was the antithesis of the new spirit entering into the ranks of computer science. Computers were beginning to be available enough—thanks to ARPA's funding and networking, as well as substantial university endowments—for younger, more liberal people, mostly students, to be both aware of and competent in computer science. At BBN itself, there had been some discomfort among team members about working for the Pentagon in the height of the Vietnam War era. As computer science became more widely taught and accessible to people beyond the white-coated priesthood of the batch-processing mainframes, a far wider range of attitudes crept into the computer-science community. Hackers and hippies did overlap.

Both Rich Seidner, the IBM programmer in the Sammy Davis outfit, and Larry Tesler, who was ultimately to become chief scientist at Apple Computer, spent part of their teenage years in a basement computer room at Columbia University in New York. In 1960, Larry Tesler was a high school student: "I went to the Bronx High School of Science and I was in the cafeteria one day reading a programming manual that the teacher had gotten me, and another student came along and said 'Where did you get that? What do you know about computers?' And it turned out that he was a computer programmer who had somehow gotten time on a computer at Columbia University. He arranged so I could get time also. I got a half hour every other Saturday morning on a 650 in the basement of the Watson Computer Lab at Columbia."

In 1960, you couldn't do much in half an hour on an IBM 650. But Rich Seidner liked it just as much as Larry Tesler: "I liked math, I was a math geek at the time and my school wasn't that far from Columbia University. Through some association we had access, so kids who showed an interest were able to do some small amount of programming on those computers. I worked on IBM 650s, big old machines that took up a huge amount of space and had a two thousand-word memory on a storage drum."

The drum would spin until the machine was shut down. There was one firm rule: Do not turn the machine back on while the drum is still spinning. Larry Tesler forgot the rule, flipped the switch back on, and broke the drum belt. He was banned from the Columbia basement. "When I got to Stanford a few months later to start college, I found the computer center on the first or second day I was there and got permission to use the computers there too, and after a few months decided to stay around for the summer so I could do a lot of programming and managed to get a job as a computer operator during the summer. That led to some jobs doing programming for various professors and graduate students, and soon I had a business. I incorporated it actually, in 1963, and I did contract programming mostly for Stanford clients. I was about eighteen."

Bob Metcalfe, the graduate student who escorted AT&T through the ICCC demonstration of the ARPAnet in October 1972, had a similar introduction to computer programming—as a summer vacation job. "I took computer programming courses because my fraternity brothers told me that if I took 6251, which was Systems Programming, I could get a job in the summer for appreciably more than I was then getting during the summers as a cabana boy. In the summers I worked at the Brightwaters Beach and Cabana Club as a cabana boy until the fall of '65, the beginning of my sophomore year, when I actually got a job as a computer programmer, thanks to the courses I took at MIT."

Metcalfe is a major figure in networking who owes a good deal to his impeccable knack for being in the right place at the right time. But he also had a knack for computing, from a very early age. In 1959, in the eighth grade, he built what his science teacher assured him was "a computer." "I built a calculator that could add any number between 1 and 3 to any other number between 1 and 3 and display the result by lighting one light among the lights labeled 2, 3, 4, 5, and 6. It was built out of relays and toggle switches and neon lights. And my science teacher called it a computer."

Metcalfe scarcely looked back, apart from his spells patrolling the lounge chairs at Brightwaters Beach. He accumulated Bachelors degrees in electrical engineering and business from MIT, and a Master's in applied mathematics from Harvard in 1970, then embarked on a Ph.D. in computer science. He soon secured himself an interesting assignment, back along the river at MIT working on the time sharing computers of Project MAC. "As a graduate student, I was at Harvard, miserable and unhappy, looking for research, and I ran into opportunities to work on the ARPAnet. Those opportunities took me to MIT, where I was much happier. So while remaining a student at Harvard, I worked on the ARPAnet at MIT."

Moreover, Metcalfe was working in a research group run by J.C.R. Licklider, who had completed his own circular tour from MIT to ARPA and back. His new research project was called the Dynamic Modeling System. In 1970, once BBN had been wired to the network it had built, MIT came next. Metcalfe was one of the three or four people who wired IMP #6 to Licklider's host, on the ninth floor of MIT's computer laboratory in Technology Square. "It was very exciting. Not that I understood what was going on, but it was the most exciting thing, I thought, being able to deal with people in faraway places, to send them bits. Like this bit that I had right here on my screen or my piece of paper, this bit would appear in Santa Barbara or Los Angeles seconds later. And then bits would come back—and that was intoxicating."

There are many ways of defining the difference between the solid, professional aura of IBM computing and what excited smart kids like Bob Metcalfe and Larry Tesler. IBM made its money by leasing and servicing computers, ensuring that IBM staff, rather than the clients, maintained the expertise. What ARPAnet allowed its users was a glimpse of Licklider's vision:

the "Man-Computer Symbiosis," which made the user able to instruct and control the machine. While Metcalfe was intoxicated by shipping bits from Cambridge, Larry Tesler found his way to ARPA's IMP #2, at Stanford's artificial intelligence lab—where he was equally enchanted. "One day somebody said, 'You can now transfer your files to people at MIT, not just here at Stanford.' And I thought, how can that be? They showed me this little program, FTP [file transfer program], and I'm sending files back and forth. I was really amazed. And became very attached to it. I developed what's called a markup program right after that, it was something we used at Stanford for students to write their theses and then transfer them to all the other universities on the net. By 1971, they all were using this program to print their dissertations. It was really amazing. I never had to send a tape anywhere."

For his Ph.D. thesis, Bob Metcalfe undertook to investigate how the ARPAnet and the Alohanet—the only two packet networks of the time—worked, and how they worked differently. In the ARPA network, each IMP would send packets to the next IMP on a store-and-forward basis, and while there might be errors on the telephone lines leading to loss of data, the IMPs themselves would not send packets in such a way that they would collide. The Alohanet experimented with terminals using a radio channel, which meant that many more users were able to transmit data than had been possible with telephone lines. Norm Abramson describes the technology as "a supercharged telephone party line, but it's not just two or three users that can share the line. It's hundreds, thousands, even hundreds of thousands of users can share a single Aloha channel."

With so many potential users, Abramson and his University of Hawaii colleagues needed to overcome the problem of transmissions coinciding, colliding, and crashing. They created the novel signature of the Aloha network: random retransmission as a remedy for interruptions and collisions. This simple idea stuck in Bob Metcalfe's mind until his own Eureka! moment in 1973, which led to his invention of Ethernet—the breakthrough method for networking personal computers, though it occurred slightly before personal computers existed.

Although Harvard was not initially impressed with the thesis (it was accepted later) Metcalfe had again given himself a rare and valuable qualification for a move to the hotbed of computer-science innovation. "In 1972, since the ARPAnet was such a hot topic in academia and research, being a Ph.D. in ARPAnet made me a hot property—just because people wanted to hire such people so they could attract research funds from ARPA. So I had lots of job offers. The one I wanted was to be a professor at MIT. They would not have me so they forced me to take much more money to move to Palo Alto, California, to be surrounded by some of the world's *best* computer scientists with no students to deal with and no teaching load and an infinite budget for capital equipment. . . . It was *horrible.*"

Both Bob Metcalfe and Larry Tesler were recruited by the recently established Xerox Palo Alto Research Center (it had opened in June 1970), which would prove to be the single most important facility for the development of both personal computing *and* networking before long. Bob Taylor was already there, and Severo Ornstein would join later. The move from east to west, despite the Pentagon and MIT parentage of the ARPAnet, was irresistible.

ARPAnet had sprung to life amid the social and artistic ferment of the sixties. While Big Blue represented one version of computer science, Yankee and conservative, it was the polar opposite of an entirely different ethos of computer use and exploration, largely associated with California. This was embodied by organizations like the People's Computer Company in Berkeley (which was both a company and a newspaper), the People's Computer Center in Menlo Park (where children were taught simple programming on programmable calculators donated by Hewlett-Packard), Community Memory (founded by Lee Felsenstein from Berkeley), and Resource One (an activists' group using computers to campaign for social change). It was "Computer Power to the People."

It was a conscious movement, Stewart Brand recalls:

> That's how it started, turning a mainframe into a "personal computer." They just found various ways, first with time sharing, and then with actually making these things, to make personal computers. The idea was power to the people. Straight sixties doctrine. Kennedy had said, "Ask not what your country can do for you. Ask rather what you can do for your country." And he was shot. Basically we were

saying, "Ask not what your country can do for you. Do it yourself." And really what a lot of the sixties was about was reinventing civilization in our own terms. We had the money to do that. We had the time to do that. We were taking the drugs that gave us weird notions to try out doing that. And it was what you did. You just tried stuff and you did it yourself. You didn't ask permission.

Stewart Brand is a lifelong ringmaster of new thinking, whose early career did not foreshadow the blue-chip hipness of his resumé. As posted on his Web site, Brand's curriculum vitae takes in Phillips Academy and Stanford (a degree in biology) before the U.S. Army, Airborne Division, and a stint as a Pentagon photojournalist. He began to attract notice in the Bay Area in that quintessentially sixties role of multimedia performance impresario. In 1966, he made and distributed buttons asking the rhetorical question of NASA: "Why Haven't We Seen A Photograph of the Whole Earth Yet?" NASA's breathtaking photographs of the home planet, duly published, are at least in part credited with the rise of the global ecology movement.

In the same year that the *Whole Earth Catalog* was launched, Brand also played a peripheral role in one of the keynote events of computing history. It has entered legend as "the mother of all demos," staged by a neglected genius, Doug Engelbart. If a Computing Hall of Fame is ever built, Engelbart will be among the first half-dozen honorees. For in 1968, Engelbart, a Stanford researcher regarded from time to time as both eccentric and difficult, demonstrated the future of personal, interactive computing. The occasion was the Fall Joint Computer Conference, held that Flower Power year in San Francisco. Stewart Brand was moonlighting as one of the backstage team from his real endeavors as a biology student. "There *weren't* any computers at the time that we were starting the [*Whole Earth Catalog*] back in 1968, but I did get involved with Doug Englebart, over at SRI. He was doing what turned out to be the mother of all demos, showing what the mouse was going to do, what Windows was going to do, all that stuff. I was helping with television cameras for the multiple screens at the demo. One of those shots you see on there of, like, the hands down in Menlo Park. Stuff like that, that was me."

Stewart Brand is frank about the role of mind-altering sub-
stances in the culture of the time, and one might wonder, as he
refers to the mouse and windows in 1968, what had he been
smoking? Indeed, the Engelbart demo made many people question Engelbart's sanity and/or his honesty as he demonstrated
technologies that looked like science fiction. Inevitably, Engelbart too was pursuing "Man-Machine Symbiosis." Stewart Brand
recalls that "Engelbart's whole idea was that the human took
over, that what was interesting to a computer was not interesting. What the computer should do is become interested in what
the human was interested in. And he started creating tools like
the mouse and windows and online text and so on, to make that
happen. Part of that assumption—and it was there in the demo
that we did—was people communicating at a distance by text.
So from at least 1969, I was seeing up close and personal how
good it would be to have a Net."

Engelbart used his invention, the computer "mouse," and live,
interactive TV pictures and sound fed down leased video lines
between computer terminals in Stanford (at his SRI lab) and San
Francisco (at the Fall Joint Computer Conference). The demo was
"an online session" that showed the linkage between two terminals, with video pictures of both. On the screens, Engelbart gave
the audience a preview of a variety of word-processing, document display, editing, and viewing formats, including "hypertext" and "hypermedia," (which would become the graphical
bedrock of eighties and nineties personal computing and Web-
browsing), on-screen cursors from users at both locations, and
split-screen live pictures of himself as he led the astounded audience towards the future. "I had thought if we show this to the
world, within a matter of months the research community in IBM
and all would be shifting to say, 'Let's go after this kind of online
flexible work.' What happened? Nothing. One guy thought it was
a hoax, and got very upset and angry, came storming up. We sent
him down the next day to talk to our software architects."

Doug Engelbart is a self-described Depression kid who served
in World War II, joined NACA (the predecessor of NASA), and at
age twenty-five had achieved both his two life goals: he was happily married and had a good job. So, feeling "slightly ridiculous,"
he started looking for new goals—what he settled on was to cre-

ate personal computing, interactive distributed computing, inter-networking, and resource sharing in a single package. Having aimed too low at first, but succeeded, he has spent the better part of fifty years trying to achieve near-impossible dreams.

At the time he got his Ph.D. from Berkeley, the nearest computer was on the East Coast. His "far-out ideas," as even he calls them, were less unwelcome at Stanford Research Institute than they were at Berkeley, but he quickly realized that his research interests, in word processing for example, were being taken no more seriously than others' quest for extra terrestrial intelligence—though both did get some funding from a small air force research office. Engelbart also received some funding from ARPA under Licklider, and some from Bob Taylor while the latter was at NASA. Under the NASA grant, Engelbart's lab experimented with different pointing devices to be used with computer terminals, and the mouse was born.

In 1967, when Larry Roberts was soliciting interest for the proposed ARPAnet, Engelbart was at Stanford Research Institute. Naturally, he was hugely enthusiastic for the network, and SRI was slated to become both the second node on the net, and the Network Information Center. Engelbart's NLS (oNLine System) was based here, and he wanted a wider audience of users to see it and use it. As Larry Roberts recalls, "Engelbart at SRI had a hypertext system that he was using at SRI and we all used it. We arranged with him to be the document center for the network so all of the documentation, all of the publications would be online at SRI. That was, in fact, a very valuable addition to the network to have the documentation online. And in 1971, that became a publishing center for all of the research on packet switching."

In subsequent years, Doug Engelbart attracted a small, loyal following and a serious lack of interest in funding his remarkably prescient ventures. It would be fifteen years before the mouse was fully adopted (by the Apple Macintosh in 1984), and twenty-five or more before interactive video conferencing would work fully.

Larry Tesler had graduated from Stanford in 1965, and came as a graduate student to the Stanford artificial intelligence lab, where he had close contact with Engelbart: "The wonderful thing about Engelbart's group was that a lot of people that he mentored understood the importance of human interaction with

computers and the potential there, and they thought about it in
a different way from the rest of the industry. They thought about
it as a way that the computer could amplify human capabilities.
There was also a sense of drama."

The drama in Engelbart's ground-breaking demo was its emphasis upon interactivity, linking users, their materials, and their
technologies. In his own view, "From the first, having other people with whom you can exchange and share and codevelop
knowledge, that's where the leverage comes from." This ethos fit
nicely with the place and the times. *Whole Earth Catalog* founder
Stewart Brand, somewhat inevitably, became a consultant in 1972
to Engelbart's "Augmented Human Intellect Program," and from
that experience, and with his highly tuned antennae for both social movements and technological innovation, wrote a renowned
magazine article. On December 7, 1972, *Rolling Stone* published
"Fanatic Life and Symbolic Death Among the Computer Bums."

Billed as "Stone Sport Reporter," Brand wrote these opening
lines: "Ready or not, computers are coming to the people. That's
good news, maybe the best since psychedelics." As Brand observes, a quarter-century later, "It was pretty much foretelling
what came to pass, which was that computers had been liberated
from the IBM mainframe approach to life." The article reads like
a time capsule of hip 1970s cultural stereotypes. Words that have
fallen into disuse, like "freaks" and "heads" are used to describe
hip, drug-tinged computer fans on the cutting edge. "These are
heads, most of them. Half or more of computer science is heads.
But that's not it. The rest of the counterculture is laid low and
back these days, showing none of this kind of zeal." Words that
have now entered everyday language from computer science, in
1972 needed to be explained:

> The hackers are the technicians of this science—it's a
> term of derision and also the ultimate compliment. They are
> the ones who translate human demands into code that the
> machines can understand and act on.
>
> "Glitch"—a kink, a less-than-fatal but irritating fuck-up.
>
> "Up" around computers means working, the opposite of
> "down" or crashed.

Brand's article mainly focused on the growing campus passion for computer games. But it reported on the status of the ARPAnet, giving credit where it was due. "At present some twenty major computer centers are linked on the two-year-old ARPA Net. Traffic on the Net has been very slow, due to delays and difficulties of translation between different computers and divergent projects.... The trend owes its health to an odd array of influences: The youthful fervor and firm dis-Establishmentarianism of the freaks who design computer science; an astonishingly enlightened research program from the very top of the Defense Department..."

Seeing the Pentagon thus complimented in *Rolling Stone* must surely have been a unique occurrence. Brand did indeed foresee uses for networks that have barely been achieved today: "Since huge quantities of information can be computer-digitized and transmitted, music researchers could, for example, swap records over the Net with 'essentially perfect fidelity.' So much for record stores (in present form)."

He also reported on a classic political-action effort, Resource One. Led by Pam Hart, it was located in a five-story warehouse south of Market Street in San Francisco—the very hip location that in the nineties has become the center of the Website and Web publishing industries.

The activities of Resource One have a political period flavor: databases to coordinate "all of the actions on campus" during Cambodia invasion protests; investigative work on major corporations; research on foundations; statistical systems for the city's free clinics (for free) and other health centers (for a fee); and political analysis of assessor's tapes and census tapes, city records, and education records. This was the social movement devoted to "Computer Liberation."

Stewart Brand and others were applying the *Whole Earth* slogan "Access to Tools" to explore making computers what today we know they should be: user-friendly, timesaving devices to access information, provide cheap communication, and make information a less protected commodity. Somewhat inevitably, the base of operations was Sausalito, the hippest of hippy communities, in a variety of derelict—or charmingly renovated—tugboats and sloops.

Another of these liberators was Theodor "Ted" Nelson, another disappointed disciple of Engelbart: "The whole point of computers was to enhance the work of the human mind. What Doug Engelbart calls the augmentation of human intellect. [He's a] wonderful, wonderful saint. The augmentation of human intellect [is] helping people think better and deeper thoughts and compare things more deeply. So I had expected a [rise] in the level of human discourse from all this."

The gospel according to Theodor found its expression in his remarkable, reversible book, published in 1974. One front cover was titled *Computer Lib*, and the other (the back) was *Dream Machines*. Nelson, a Harvard-educated fount of hacker energy and hyperactivity, invented a version of the World Wide Web about twenty-four years before it finally took shape. He named it "Xanadu," in romantic tribute to Coleridge's unfinished, drug-enhanced poetic vision. Nelson's Xanadu has failed to materialize as surely as the "person from Porlock" drove Coleridge's dream beyond recall.

Ted Nelson originally invented the word "hypertext" for "nonsequential writing." As a writing and editing device for moving between documents, or between storage locations, it has been at the heart of personal computing, and in its Web incarnation (http, or hypertext transfer protocol) is ubiquitous on the Net.

Reading between the lines of the seventies jargon of hip liberation, one sees that *Computer Lib* provides a startlingly simple, digestible account of what computers do, how they work, and why their mystique can (and should) be challenged. The book is printed in broadsheet, newsprint fashion. The first column begins thus:

Computer Lib
'You Can and Must Understand Computers Now'
© 1974 Theodor H. Nelson
Additional copies are $7 postpaid...

Any nitwit can understand computers, and many do. Unfortunately, due to ridiculous historical circumstances, computers have been made a mystery to most of the world....

This book is a measure of desperation, so serious and abysmal is the public sense of confusion and ignorance...

This book is therefore devoted to the premise that EVERYBODY SHOULD UNDERSTAND COMPUTERS. It is intended to fill a crying need.

In the *Computer Lib* half of the book, Nelson lists his "author's credentials"—B.A. in Philosophy from Swarthmore, graduate study at the University of Chicago, M.A. in Sociology from Harvard, listed in the New York Times *Who's Who in Computers*. On the corresponding page of *Dream Machines*, one finds the "counter-culture credentials"—"Writer, showman, generalist. Gemini, moon in Libra, Gemini rising. Author of what may have been the world's first rock musical.... Photographer for a year at Dr. Lilly's dolphin lab, Miami. Attendee of the Great Woodstock Festival." This is a seventies polymath, whose range of interests and experience presaged the technological, social, and artistic integration of the nineties Internet world. This is indeed what Nelson had in mind when he wrote *Computer Lib*:

> I have an axe to grind: I want to see computers useful to individuals, and the sooner the better, without necessary complication or human servility being required. Anyone who agrees with these principles is on my side, and anyone who does not, is not. THIS BOOK IS FOR PERSONAL FREEDOM, AND AGAINST RESTRICTION AND COERCION...
>
> A chant you can take to the streets: COMPUTER POWER TO THE PEOPLE! DOWN WITH CYBERCRUD!

Nelson's "discovery," hypertext, is explained, along with the differences between big and minicomputers, basic programming, the history of IBM, and computer languages:

> By hypertext I mean non-sequential writing. Ordinary writing is sequential for two reasons. First, it grew out of speech and speech-making, which have to be sequential; and second, because books are not convenient to read except in sequence. But the *structures of ideas* are not sequential. They tie together every which way.
>
> And the pity of it is that (like the man in the French play who was surprised to learn that he had been "speaking prose all his life and never known it") we've been speaking *hypertext* all our lives and never known it.

Like Stewart Brand in *Rolling Stone*, Nelson foresees a new

dawn of digital hope, as computers all have screen displays and
memory becomes cheaper (another accurate prediction):

> Computers offer an interesting daydream: that we may be
> able to store things *digitally* instead of *physically*. In other
> words, turn the libraries to digital storage; digitize paintings
> and photographs; even digitize the genetic codes of animals,
> so that species can be restored at future dates.

It may be that as a philosopher, sociologist, writer, showman,
photographer, lecturer in art, and consultant to CBS Laboratories,
Ted Nelson's vision is too broad, too globally ambitious, to actually get anything done. (He is also a masterful punner: "Where are
the shows of yesteryear?," a pun in translation; "Does the name
Pavlov ring a bell?"; "Hardening of the artistries"; "Thinkertoys";
and "Crazy Leica Fox.") But since 1960 he has been planning
Xanadu, a global network of literature libraries that allows text retrieval, hypertext links, and a copyright and royalty micropayment structure. It is still, at the time of writing, a plan:

> Now the idea is this:
> To give you a screen in your home from which you can
> see into the world's hypertext libraries. (The fact that the
> world doesn't yet *have* any hypertext libraries—yet—is a
> minor point.)
> To give you a screen system that will offer high-performance
> graphics and text services at a price anyone can afford. To
> allow you to send and receive written messages at the Engel-
> bart level. To allow you to explore diagrams. To eliminate the
> absurd distinction between "teacher" and "pupil."
> To make you a part of a new electronic literature and art,
> where you can get all your questions answered and nobody
> will put you down.

Ted proposed franchised "Mom-and-Pop Xanadu Shops." He
drew plans for the layout of such venues, with a reception and
snackbar area, an equipment pit, and carrels for users to sit in
and log on. Today we would call them cybercafés, or the rapidly
expanding Cybersmith chain. Where McDonalds' Golden

Arches attract one type of traffic, "The Golden X's welcome the mind-hungry traveller."

Ted was even wooed by the CIA. "They told me they would be glad to set me up in business as a hypertext company, but I would have to have a corporation, because that was the way they always did things. And so it came to pass that The Nelson Organization, Inc. was founded at the express request of the United States Central Intelligence Agency. I wouldn't have had it any other way. If life can't be pleasant it can at least be surrealistic."

In the final paragraph of the book, Nelson makes an important realization: "That reminds me. Nowhere in the book have I defined the phrase 'computer lib.' By Computer Lib I mean simply: making people freer through computers. That's all."

Howard Rheingold was another member of the Sausalito circle, a *Whole Earth Catalog* writer who felt, in 1968, that "conforming to the program" of church, government, or corporation (even IBM) was a dead end. "You have to try to build a life that's meaningful for you and try to think for yourself. That's not easy to do. The *Whole Earth Catalog* was a great pointer to tools for that, and computers were nowhere in that picture. Computers were the tool of the bureaucracies. They were trying to fit us into pigeonholes. The idea that computers could really be used for extending our intellects and communicating with each other was something that didn't emerge for a while."

But with the work of Engelbart, the emergence of the ARPAnet, the buzz that Stewart Brand and *Rolling Stone* and Resource One were all building, Rheingold and thousands of others began to understand that computers could take on a socially and politically liberating and liberated role: "We're very fortunate that the administrators of ARPA were visionary and saw that this research tool that the Defense Department had funded was, in fact, a new communication medium. In fact, many of the people in Doug Engelbart's outfit and in ARPA were counterculture kind of people, and I think that it's not so much anti-establishment as empowerment of the individual. The belief that if you can give people tools, they can do things. They can make the new, better society. And that doing some crusade to create some great cause has failed."

It is one of the greater ironies of computer history that the vision of the hippies had to be married to the technology funded and fostered by the Pentagon, before a world of integrated information and communication became possible. From Vannevar Bush, to Licklider, to Engelbart, to Nelson, the goals were relatively clear; but half a century has elapsed while they have been reached. As Ted Nelson told Howard Rheingold in 1983, quoted in the latter's *Tools for Thought*, "It seemed so simple and clear to me then. It still does. But like so many beginning computerists, I mistook a clear view for a short distance."

While futuristic thinking was generally outpacing the technology, there was one location where well-paid computer scientists were already "living in the future." Since 1970, the Xerox Palo Alto Research Center had been pushing at the limits of computer technology. One of those who signed up early was Bill English, Doug Engelbart's partner at the landmark demo, who quit ARC (Augmentation Research Center) with others in 1970 to join PARC. He was soon followed by Larry Tesler, the kid who broke the drum belt at Columbia, incorporated his consulting firm at age eighteen, and shocked Xerox by turning down their first offer for him to join PARC. Their second offer was better. Tesler joined a research group named POLOS, or PARC On-Line Office System, which was led by Bill English. The computer science laboratory was managed by Bob Taylor, who had moved on from Utah after just a year.

This was the hothouse of research opportunity to which MIT sentenced Bob Metcalfe when they decided not to give him a faculty job in 1972. Xerox offered Metcalfe a job, and he took it after striking a deal. His freshly minted Ph.D. thesis had analyzed Alohanet in Hawaii; now he wanted to make a research trip to study it firsthand, for an extended period. As his host, Norm Abramson, recalls: "Bob had just finished his Ph.D., and he had taken a job at Xerox PARC. Bob is a consummate salesman. Imagine this: if you had just gone into a new job, before you showed up for work, you get your boss to send you to Hawaii for three months. Bob did that. He spent that time with us, looked at what we were doing, did some stuff on his own, and went back and took some of the ideas that we had and changed them in very significant ways to come up with Ethernet."

In 1973, at Xerox PARC, Bob Metcalfe and his colleagues would develop Ethernet, the next big advance in networking computers. In fact, it was the first technology to network personal computers.

Remember what Stewart Brand said—that "Computers are coming to the People...the best thing since psychedelics." But Xerox PARC's staff of computer wizards, largely hand-picked by Bob Taylor, was not tripping. Personal computers didn't exist yet, with one exception: at Xerox PARC they'd already built them. Living in the future had its advantages. And Bob Metcalfe would later leverage that opportunity, using his talent for both engineering and entrepreneurship, into a hugely successful networking company. But to Norm Abramson, Metcalfe's engineering wizardry was ultimately less striking than his chutzpah: "The most impressive thing for me was convincing his boss to send him to Hawaii for three months before he showed up for work."

Chapter Six
A Human Could Use It

As COMPUTER LIBERATIONISTS ARGUED, until a network was available to a mass market it would remain a technological curiosity or an elite academic tool. Since most Internet use today occurs through personal computers, it seems ironic that the PC was actually invented and developed long after networking. But PCs gave networking the massive parallel application it needed to be both widely accessible and thoroughly useful.

In 1973, Xerox PARC had its Alto computers running on many desktops. But they were about a decade ahead of reality, almost nobody knew about PARC's work on the techno-frontier, and the machines were not for sale. So the personal computer would have to be invented elsewhere. Despite the variety of candidates, both people and locations, that might have been the Wright Brothers and Kittyhawk of personal computing, "elsewhere" turned out to be a very unlikely place indeed. Albuquerque, New Mexico, had no track record as a high-technology center, no obvious pool of appropriate talent, and no economic or educational advantages. But the electronic device that is now generally accepted as the first "personal computer" appeared as a mail-order product from Albuquerque.

The computer-science community was very much split, in the 1970s, between the technological haves, working on high-altitude scientific computing problems in ARPA-funded university research programs, and the have-nots, average Joe Nerd garage tinkerers who found computers fascinating not least because they could *not* get their hands on one. Mainframe computers were far from "personal." They were remote in both a practical and a political sense, sitting in big air-conditioned rooms at insurance companies, phone companies, and banks, the institutions that generally controlled the lives and communications of ordinary citizens. But computer terminals had filtered down from university departments and had begun to appear in schools. Most of us ignored this development completely. But there was always a handful of despised kids who fell in love with the digital delights of computing. It included Rich Seidner and Larry Tesler, in the basement at Columbia; Bob Metcalfe in the eighth-grade science fair; Vint Cerf climbing up the walls at UCLA; Bill Gates and Paul Allen (later to found Microsoft) at Lakeside School in Seattle; Steve Wozniak and Steve Jobs (later to found Apple Computer), fooling around with long-distance phone "blue boxes"; and Ed Roberts, an ex–air force officer with a passion for medicine and electronics.

These were the nerds. Some were kids, others were adults with real jobs in technology companies. They were CB radio enthusiasts, model train club members, and hippy/hackers partly motivated by political ideas about information liberation, and partly by the overwhelming desire to flip toggle switches until light bulbs danced before their eyes. Steve Wozniak and Steve Jobs, who graduated from Homestead High School in Cupertino four years apart, were captivated at an early age. Jobs, demonstrating his forceful style at an early age, introduced himself to a Silicon Valley titan: "When I was twelve I called up Bill Hewlett. This dates me, but there was no such thing as an unlisted telephone number then, so I could just look in the book and look his name up. And he answered the phone and I said, 'Hi, my name's Steve Jobs, you don't know me, but I'm twelve years old and I'm building a frequency counter, and I'd like some spare parts.' And so he talked to me for about twenty minutes—I'll never forget it as long as I live—and he gave me the parts, but he also gave me a job working at Hewlett Packard that summer, and I was twelve years old."

Steve Wozniak was shy, with the typical nerdly passions for wires, valves, and technical manuals. He developed an unusual taste in reading materials: "I took this book home that described the PDP-8 computer, and it was just like a bible to me. I mean, all these things that for some reason I'd fallen in love with, like you might fall in love with doing crossword puzzles or playing a musical instrument, I fell in love with these little descriptions of computers and their insides. It was a little [bit of] mathematics, I could work out some problems on paper and see how it's done, I could come up with my own solutions and feel good inside."

Steve Jobs had started doing some basic programming in school, and the impact of this relatively simple experience would govern his life's ambitions: "So you would keyboard these commands in and then you would wait for a while and then the thing would go dadadadadada and it would tell you something. It was still re-markable—especially for a ten-year-old—that you could write a program in Basic, let's say, or Fortran, and this machine would take your idea and it would execute your idea and give you back some results. If they were the results that you predicted, your program really worked. It was an incredibly thrilling experience."

Nerds wanted their own computers, but it took a technological breakthrough to make that possible. Until the invention of the microprocessor, or "chip," computers had thousands of vacuum tubes, three times the size of a regular lightbulb, as their switches. The invention of the transistor reduced the scale considerably. But what enables us to have a mainframe computer on the desk is the chip—a single piece of silicon (made from sand), etched with thousands of transistors. The people who invented the microprocessor worked at Intel, a company founded in 1968 when Robert Noyce and Gordon Moore wanted to leave their former company, Fairchild Semiconductor.

Intel's corporate pedigree owes a great deal to pioneers of earlier generations, and its own innovations have helped define the Silicon Valley ways of doing business. These owe a great deal to the vision of Frederick Terman, Stanford's dean of engineering in the late 1930s, who encouraged Stanford engineers to get businesses going, even while continuing to teach part time on the faculty. With a judicious mixture of encouragement and the use of Fellowship grants, he got David Packard and Bill Hewlett together. Hewlett and Packard held their first business meeting on August 23, 1937. They planned to call the venture "The Engineering Service Company." David Packard and his wife lived in a pretty house on tree-lined Addison Avenue, Palo Alto; for a time, Bill Hewlett lived in the guest house out back. Setting a pattern for generations, they started the business in the wooden garage at the side of the house. Now wisteria-laden, the garage was in 1989 designated a California Historical Landmark—"the birthplace of Silicon Valley."

When the founders of Fairchild Semiconductor attempted to raise venture capital to start the company, they found Arthur Rock, a man who is now principally credited with establishing the venture-capital model for the Valley. Rock was a New York investment banker who came out to California to examine the deal, and saw that the area around Stanford University was full of imaginative engineers trying to start companies. The funding for the new venture came from Sherman Fairchild, the only son of Thomas J. Watson's original partner in the company that became IBM. As Watson had more children, and the inheritance of his stock was subdivided, Sherman Fairchild became IBM's single largest shareholder, with plenty of funds to invest.

Though Fairchild was successful, after eleven years Robert Noyce and Gordon Moore had a business philosophy they wanted to pursue: to run a company in a more democratic, open fashion, and to reward people not just with pay, but with ownership. So Intel, like so many Valley successors, became a company that made stock options a core element of the reward structure. To start Intel, Arthur Rock raised $2.5 million in "the time it took to make ten or fifteen telephone calls."

Intel may not have invented the Silicon Valley style of doorless offices and shared company ownership through stock options. But as founder Gordon Moore describes it, the company set out to run itself in a way that got the most out of everyone: "We decided that a rather collegial way of operating was most appropriate. In a business like this, the people with the power are the ones that have the understanding of what's going on, not necessarily the ones on top. And it's very important that those people that have the knowledge are the ones that make the decisions. So we set up something where everyone who had the knowledge had an equal say in what was going on."

The original markets for Intel's chips were in electronic calculators and elevator and traffic-light controls rather than computers. There's a wry reference to this in the fact that a traffic light is included in the Intel corporate museum in their headquarters building in Santa Clara. Chips were used in electronic timers, controllers in domestic appliances, "embedded applications." It became apparent to Gordon Moore early on that the technology for putting processing power on a chip was improving steadily, and without any apparent limit. As he recalled thirty years later, he first described what has become known as "Moore's Law" in 1965: "I published an article trying to project the future of semiconduc-

tor components for the next ten years, and taking the little bit of
data then based on the first few generations of integrated circuits,
I postulated that the complexity of integrated circuits was going to
double every year for the next ten years. I didn't predict the price
specifically, but certainly projected that the cost of doing things
electronically was going to continue to decrease dramatically."

Moore's Law is usually summarized to say that the performance doubles, *and* the price halves, every year. Certainly Intel's
microprocessors kept getting more powerful. By 1974, the company came out with the 8080, which had enough horsepower to
run a whole computer. Intel itself didn't appreciate the brilliance
of its own product, still thinking mainly about calculators and
traffic lights. Intel had all the technology, and brainpower, necessary to invent the PC business, but the management just didn't
see it, according to Moore: "Looking back, I know of one opportunity where an engineer came to me with an idea for a computer
that would be used in the home. Of course, it wasn't yet called a
personal computer. And while he felt very strongly about it, the
only example of what it was good for that he could come up with
was the housewife could keep her recipes on it. And I couldn't
imagine my wife with her recipes on a computer in the kitchen.
It just didn't seem like it had any practical application at all, so
Intel didn't pursue that idea."

But someone did. In 1975, the first glimpse of a truly personal
computer occurred: not in Silicon Valley, certainly not in the research divisions at IBM or Bell Labs, and not at Intel. (We'll return to Xerox PARC later.) It was a last-gasp defense against
bankruptcy by an ex–air force engineer from Georgia, who really
wanted to be a doctor. But Ed Roberts, who ran MITS (Micro Instrumentation Telemetry Systems) in Albuquerque, New Mexico,
speculated that he could build a kit computer, based on the Intel
8080 microprocessor. In January 1975, *Popular Electronics* magazine featured what it announced as the world's first personal
computer—the Altair 8800, brainchild of the ambitious, and desperate, Ed Roberts: "If you look at it, it was a kind of grandiose—
almost megalomaniac kind of a scheme—and now I couldn't do
it because I could see right off there's no way you could do this.
There isn't any way you could do this. But at that time, we just
lacked the benefits of age and experience. We didn't know we

couldn't do it. There were some of us that lusted after computers really at that time. All the computers in the world tended to be in big centers and you had to get permission to get close to them, and you know, nobody had access to computers. And the idea that you could have your own computer and do whatever you wanted to with it, whenever you wanted to, was fantastic."

Out in the desert near the airport in Albuquerque, New Mexico, Ed Roberts ran his small electronic kits company. When hand-held calculators from Hewlett-Packard cost $395, MITS brought out a kit for less than a hundred dollars. Almost immediately, Texas Instruments and Commodore entered the market, and drove the price down to far below the MITS kit price. So MITS was going bankrupt. Nobody was buying their calculators, and the rest of the business, which sold kits and components to people who wanted to play at being NASA, firing off miniature rockets, wasn't going to keep them afloat. Ed needed $65,000 just to stay afloat. So he persuaded himself that he could build a "computer" around the Intel 8080 chip, and went to explain it all to the bank manager: "We went to the bank, we had a late-night meeting, and the issue was whether we closed MITS down or they loaned us an additional $65,000. I was asked how many machines did I think we would sell in the next year after it was introduced, and I said 800, and was considered a wild-eyed optimist at that—I couldn't really think of anyone who would buy one. Within a month after it was introduced, we were getting 250 orders *a day*."

The front cover of *Popular Electronics*, January 1975, is a real milestone in the story of personal computers. It announced to all those frustrated hackers that maybe the dream of owning and using a computer of their own wasn't impossible. The Altair attracted passionate interest. One of the technical writers at MITS was David Bunnell, who went on to make his own fortune as founder-publisher of *PC Magazine, PCWorld,* and *MacWorld* magazines: "There were actually people that came to MITS, a couple of people with camper trailers, and camped out in the parking lot waiting for their machines. I mean, they were so eager. This is what really amazed me was that there was a sort of pent-up demand for having your own computer."

Eddie Currie was a childhood friend of Ed Roberts, who had watched Ed go through high school in Georgia as a medical science prodigy. While both were in college, or the service, and too broke to make long-distance phone calls, they would send each other "letters" on audiocassette tapes. On one of these, to Eddie Currie's astonishment, Ed announced he had figured out how to develop a personal computer. Eddie Currie recalls, "I think everybody had sort of a daydream. Ed Roberts had 'Walter Mittyed' about owning a computer. The surprise was that it would be possible for the average college student, for example, who was living on bare subsistence, to actually buy a computer. And if it could be that cheap, what a wonderful thing."

Altair serial #1 was sent off to be photographed for the *Popular Electronics* cover, and was never seen again, lost in the mail. At this point, legend has it, the computer-to-be had no name. The problem was discussed at the home of Les Solomon, technical editor of the magazine, whose family was watching a *Star Trek* episode that referred to the (real) Altair constellation. The consensus was: Why not? So the Altair 8800 was named.

The oldest personal computer in the world—Altair serial #2— is owned by Roger Melen, a veteran computer scientist who has been working at Stanford and in Silicon Valley companies for thirty years: "I had the good experience to see the Altair before it was sold. I made a special trip to New Mexico. I bought two on the spot. Actually, they were bought built. We felt it was best that way. I think it was $495 built and $360 in kit form."

Built or not, this was a computer that bore almost no relationship to the personal computer of today. It had a front panel with switches for programming, one bit at a time, and lights that could turn on and off, but it had no place to connect a keyboard, or a monitor, or a printer. There was no software, minimal memory, and no games. But in 1975, the people who had one were thrilled. Despite its shortcomings, more expensive, industrial machines had less performance, according to Roger Melen: "We had used machines like this in research labs, but they were much, much more expensive, and they were actually in some cases much slower than this machine. So this machine was not only more than ten times cheaper, but sometimes up to ten times faster than what we were used to. A typical machine you might use in a research lab at the time cost $50,000."

The other great asset of the Altair was that it had expansion options. Memory boards could be added, and peripheral devices which would—at a price—allow screens, cameras, paper-tape loaders, and more memory to be added to the basic system. Harry Garland, who has been Roger Melen's friend and business partner for decades, remembers: "It created an opportunity because of the expandability of the system, the fact that you could add cards to increase memory or add interfaces."

Garland and Melen invented a digital camera, called Cyclops, and a color television interface they called Dazzler, as accessories to the Altair 8800. Another enthusiast went overboard on memory. Harry Garland recalls "a gentleman named Ed Hull in the Homebrew Computer Club had 12K of memory in his Altair, and that was considered on the lunatic fringe end of things, to have 12K of memory."

As Roger Melen points out, "That was three expensive memory boards, $3,000 in memory, in his $500 computer."

While MITS had started producing a "personal computer" in New Mexico, the Homebrew Computer Club was the meeting place for computer hobbyists in and around what was becoming Silicon Valley. Bright students from local high schools rubbed shoulders with professors of electrical engineering (like Garland and Melen) from Stanford; and in the democratic spirit of the times, and of a true hobbyists' community, the older, more experienced participants could learn from the younger. The Homebrew was by legend founded by Gordon French, a professional engineer, and its first meeting took place in his garage. The second meeting was held in a disused school building, the Peninsula School, in Menlo Park, but as interest grew the club had to move out to more spacious premises. Every Wednesday evening, the Homebrew met in the large, raked lecture theater of the Stanford Linear Accelerator Center complex (SLAC).

Larry Tesler was one of the first few people to turn up:

My next door neighbor said, "Come to our meeting— we're having a meeting of the Home Brew Computer Club," and I said, "What's that?" He said, "We're all going to make computers at home, we're going to get everybody to get a computer kit. Everyone will make their own computers, we'll drive all the manufacturers out of business. IBM,

Honeywell, they'll all go out of business, Digital Equipment, because everyone will make their own computer at home and it's a revolutionary movement." I went to one of the very early meetings. I think fifteen people showed up. After about a half hour, I got extremely bored because these people were showing all these boxes that had wires hanging out all over them, and they got very excited if a light would turn on, and I thought this is ridiculous, this isn't personal computing, and I don't think I went to another meeting for a year.

Larry Tesler, immersed in real (if futuristic) personal computing in his office at Xerox PARC, was a difficult audience for the baby steps in personal computing that the Altair 8800 represented. Meetings at SLAC were "moderated" by Lee Felsenstein, a Berkeley-born-and-bred computer engineer with a devotion to populist, liberationist causes. Felsenstein's principal tool for maintaining order amid the anarchy was a big stick. Home movies show Felsenstein flourishing the stick from his position in front of the chalkboards: "I would start the meeting by making a horrendous loud noise because everyone was talking and I had to get some attention somehow. And I would use it to call upon the person in question. I'd make threatening gestures with it. Most of us were in the electronics industry to a certain extent, there was also a stratum of physicians and there were a lot radio amateurs, finding a new technology that wasn't stale. But most of us were at a sort of middle level or downwards. We saw ourselves as crazed, ignored geniuses or possibly geniuses but at least we could each hope to get our hands on a computer of our own."

The very awkwardness of the Altair is what brought the hobbyists together. Some of them would prove, like Roger Melen and Harry Garland, to be entrepreneurs. They started an early computer company named Cromemco—after the dorm they had lived in at Stanford.

The Altair was tedious to use. At first, the only way that data and instructions could be given to the computer was by flipping switches. To do a simple addition, one digit needed eight different switches to be flipped, then a ninth switch flipped to load that in the memory. And so on. Harry Garland explains further: "You would put in the code for each byte to be loaded in the memory and you would enter that code on these front panel switches marked *Data*, so you might enter a 11001100 for instance, and once you had that in there you hit the switch to deposit that in the memory. That was displayed on the lights. You would then go to the next memory location and would load each byte of memory, byte by byte."

For a program a hundred bytes long, one had to follow this procedure a hundred times to load it into the memory. Garland and Melen came here to meet others, to display their switch-flipping skills, and figure out what, if anything, could be done with this new toy. At the second meeting of the Homebrew, one Steve Dompier used his Altair for a demo that amazed everyone. Lee Felsenstein describes one of the watershed moments of Homebrew history: "Steve Dompier set up an Altair, laboriously keyed a program into it. Somebody knocked a plug out of the wall and he had to do that all over again. Nobody knew what this was about. After all, was it just going to sit and flash its lights? No."

Dompier had developed software that could create music as a by-product. He placed a transistor radio next to his Altair, and by manipulating the length of loops in the software—by repeating instructions—he could create a signal to play tunes through the radio. Felsenstein, like the others present, was transported: "The radio began playing 'Fool on the Hill.' Da da da daah, da da da da daaaah...and the tinny little tunes that you could hear were coming from the noise that the computer generated, being picked up by the radio. Everybody rose and applauded. I proposed that he receive the Stripped Philips Screw Award for finding a use for something previously thought useless. But I think everybody was too busy applauding to even hear me."

Turning the Altair into a useful tool rather than a five hundred dollar curiosity required a number of major improvements, not least a programming language so users could enter their programs from a terminal interface, or some kind of keyboard, rather than flipping switches. What it needed was a computer language like Basic, modified for the small memory capacity of the fledgling PC. This was called a Basic interpreter, but no one thought that Basic was basic enough to fit inside the tiny Altair memory. But in January 1975, two friends in Cambridge, Massachusetts, looked at the front cover story of *Popular Electronics* and realized that their time had come. As teenagers, they had hung around the computer room at school, and had started a company to analyze traffic patterns (Traf-o-Data). They would have fit right in among the disheveled members of the Homebrew Club. But Bill Gates was at Harvard, and Paul Allen had a real job as a programmer with Honeywell. Paul Allen remembers the occasion thus: "One day in Boston, I was in Harvard Square and saw a cover of *Popular Electronics* with this thing on the cover that looked like what I had been imagining, so I grabbed it off the shelf, and I ran back to Bill's dorm. I think he was probably playing poker that night and usually losing money at that point. One of the few times when that's been the case."

Gates and Allen had watched the arrival of the Intel 8080 chip, wondering what might be made of it, and this was the development that they believed was the start of a major opportunity. But they could see things were moving fast. Bill Gates broke off from his poker hand: "Paul showed that to me and here was a company that would be needing software. We realized that things were starting to happen, and just because we'd had a vision for a long time of where this chip could go, didn't mean the industry was going to wait for us while I stayed and finished my degree at Harvard."

Paul Allen was designated to make the momentous phone call to New Mexico: "Bill said, 'OK, we gotta call these guys up and see if this thing's for real.' So we called up Ed [Roberts], we told him, 'We've got this Basic and it's just for your machine, and it's not *that far* from being done, and we'd like to come out and show it to you.'"

Having announced the Basic interpreter, and full of the confidence of youth and brainpower, they sat down to create it. They had first established that an Altair could be loaded with a punched paper tape. As they didn't have enough money for two plane tickets, Paul Allen headed for Albuquerque alone. Bill Gates stayed at Harvard: "So we created this Basic interpreter. Paul took the paper tape and flew out. The night before, he got some sleep while I double-checked everything to make sure that we had it all right."

If Albuquerque and Ed Roberts were, respectively, the birthplace and the founding father of the personal computer industry, neither much looked the part. At the airport, Allen was met by Roberts, driving a battered pick-up. They headed straight for the wrong side of the tracks, where MITS was based. Paul Allen (himself an exceedingly shy Honeywell junior engineer) had been expecting to encounter a captain of industry, not another (older) disheveled engineer keeping his creditors at arm's length.

What was worse, Gates and Allen had no idea what it would really be like to run the software: it had never been run on an actual computer before. David Bunnell was one of those who witnessed the event: "He was very nervous about whether this would actually work. He got to the office and we all gathered around him and he put his fingers on the switches and he loaded Basic with paper tape into the Altair." Allen agrees: "I was so nervous, I felt this is just not going to work—and it worked!" As Bunnell and others watched, "It came up, and it could do a few little simple things." Gates heard the news back in Cambridge: "It was amazing, when Paul called me up and said the thing had worked the first time. And of course, it was incredibly fast. That was unbelievable. The fact that it really worked was a breakthrough."

MITS is long gone, but these two opportunists realized that even a *micro*computer would need *soft*ware, just like big and huge computers did. So they called themselves *Microsoft*. They were hardly titans of industry. But such was their commitment to the new venture that Gates quit Harvard, and Allen his job; Microsoft was founded in Albuquerque too.

David Bunnell remembers the less palmy days of the Microsoft founders: "They lived across the street from MITS in the Sundowner Motel, with the prostitutes and the drug dealers out on the corner, and they were writing Basic for the Altair computer, and gradually they actually started Microsoft here in Albuquerque. Maybe there wouldn't be a Microsoft if that screen hadn't come alive. Who knows? It might all be quite different."

Twenty years after finishing the first microcomputer Basic, Paul Allen returned to Albuquerque for a MITS reunion in 1995. Some of the pioneers were still driving pickups around the dusty streets of Albuquerque, but Allen arrived in his $15 million private jet. But the excitement and comradeship of the pioneering days seemed to be fresh for many of those who came, including Allen himself: "We hired some of our high school friends basically to come down and stay with us in our apartment, which became very crowded. Sometimes it would be Bill and these two other guys all sitting on tables around the apartment with stacks and stacks of paper writing, converting the Basic for the 8080. We'd usually go out, eat pizzas, and then . . . watch action movies."

As David Bunnell remembers: "They worked really hard. They listened to really loud music. I could hardly stand to go to the software room sometimes because the music would be banging off the walls, mostly acid rock. They would work all night long, and there were days when Bill Gates would be sleeping on the floor in the software lab." Bill Gates was in his element: "We were pretty young. We started when I was nineteen and so we just had a lot of energy. I still know the source code by heart, and that was a work of love; we just kept tuning and tuning that thing. And so that kind of craftsmanship paid off."

Bill Gates did not make it to the MITS Altair reunion in 1995. The timing wasn't good, coming just two months before the launch of Windows 95, the software product that would emphatically, definitively seal Microsoft's status as the dominant software provider worldwide for the personal computer. Had he made it to the reunion, he would have witnessed a comic scene: at around midnight, after all the speeches had been made and the rubber chicken long digested, three of the group felt a little peckish. Paul Allen had dismissed his limo for the night, so Eddie Currie, David Bunnell, and their billionaire ex-colleague all walked through the drive-up lane of FatBurger for a late-night snack.

Ed Roberts took some persuading to leave his home in Georgia, where he now has a practice as an M.D., to celebrate the twentieth anniversary of an inspiration that did create a revolution, but mostly benefited and enriched others. MITS was ultimately taken over, and Roberts went out of the computer business entirely, resuming his first love of medicine. "*We* created an industry and I think that goes completely unnoticed. I mean there was nothing—every aspect of the industry when you talk about software, hardware, application stuff, dealerships, you name it."

The Altair—and its users, its vendors, its imitators, and its suppliers—spearheaded a small revolution. Finally, individuals could imagine owning and using a computer. Not only was this an intriguing product for hobbyists, but its very existence enabled both academic computer scientists (like those who built the ARPAnet) and technological idealists (like Doug Engelbart, Stewart Brand, and Ted Nelson) to think creatively about how big-computer technology could be adapted to run on small computers, how small computers might be linked to share costs or functions, and how recreation and education might be enhanced.

Bill Gates confirms the excitement and the novelty of the industry that began to evolve around MITS and its clunky Altair computer: "It was a wild time. It was a very exciting time. At the first [Altair] user convention, we got people to come in and tell us what they were doing, what they were excited about. Other companies like Processor Technology or Imsai or Cromemco got going as add-on companies. These companies are long-forgotten, but they were the humble beginnings of the PC industry."

Not everyone thought the Altair was such a big deal. Gordon Moore, whose Intel company manufactured the chip that made the Altair possible, didn't see the appeal at all. In this regard, he was typical of the traditional thinking of the computer industry: "One of our sales people brought in a kit that had been glued together by the New Mexico group actually, using one of our microprocessors, where the program was put in by flipping a bunch of switches, rather than using a keyboard or a disk drive or anything we do today. The program actually had to be put in in ones and zeros, depending on if a switch was up or down. Not very useful for practical applications, but enough that hobbyists could play with a computer, where they could program it themselves. Not very much, frankly, [like a computer]. At that time a computer to me was something that sat in a large room with glass windows you couldn't get in to without a special access card."

However, "computer" dealerships began to spring up, selling Altairs and add-on products. The very idea of retail computers was laughable until 1975. But the Altair made the computer a consumer product of sorts. Although Albuquerque was its geographical birthplace, Silicon Valley was the spiritual center of this revolution. Hobbyists alone might have been necessary, but could never be sufficient to bring the personal computer to the shopping mall. To reach the wider market required a different type of vision, and better, smarter engineering, too. At the Homebrew Computer Club, there was a young pair who had these qualities in ample supply: a true nerd and a true visionary.

Steve Wozniak was a prodigiously talented engineer who treated each engineering problem as a game and a challenge: "I wound up with so few chips, when I was done I said, 'Hey, a computer that you can program to generate colored patterns on a screen, or data or words or play games or anything!' It was just the computer I wanted for myself, pretty much, but it had turned out so good."

Steve Jobs was a visionary with abundant self-confidence and a philosophical streak: "Remember that the sixties happened in the early seventies, and that's when I came of age. To me the spark of that was, it's the same thing that causes people to want to be poets instead of bankers. I think that's a wonderful thing. I think that same spirit can be put into products, and those products can be manufactured and given to people, and they can sense that spirit. There was something beyond what you see every day."

At the Homebrew, there was more than just the presentations and Q&A sessions moderated by Lee Felsenstein. In the hall outside the auditorium, hackers would bring in the boxes of wires, transistors, and paper tape to demonstrate what they had achieved. There was criticism, suggestions, competition to outdo each other. And out of this creative show-and-tell came Apple Computer, the first mass-market, legitimate consumer PC manufacturer.

The Apple founders, both recent graduates from Homestead High School, were regulars at Homebrew meetings. Steve Wozniak, known everywhere as "Woz," was almost mute with shyness, so he would let his technical prowess do the talking. The first Apple computer was primitive. It was cobbled together by Woz to impress his friends at the Homebrew meetings. "I started getting a crowd around me. Even though I was too shy to raise my hand and say anything in a club meeting, after the meetings I would put out my computer that I had built, and every week it had a little bit more working on it, too. I would set it down and let people type on the keyboard and I would explain what's in it."

Steve Jobs was not a hotshot technology geek, but his talent search ended with "Woz." Steve Jobs was the visionary who saw microcomputers as a potential business beyond the ranks of Homebrewers: "It was very clear to me that...there were a bunch of hardware hobbyists that could assemble their own computers, or at least take our board and add the transformers for the power supply, and the case, the keyboard, and go get the rest of the stuff. [But] for every one of those there were a thousand people that couldn't do that, but wanted to mess around with programming—software hobbyists. Just like I had been when I was ten, discovering that computer."

Apple Computer wasn't their first business, but it was their first *legal* business. Woz and Jobs had once built a device to cheat the phone company—as Wozniak recalls, it was known as a "blue box": "Blue boxes were devices that could put tones into your phone and direct the phone company to switch your calls anywhere in the world for free. It was weird for people to imagine that: how could this worldwide phone system let you put a few little tones into your phone just like punching a touchtone phone, put the right tones in and it would direct your call anywhere in the world for free?"

Steve Jobs says that it was thanks to the Homebrew's meeting venue that they figured out the technical specifications they needed: "We were at Stanford Linear Accelerator Center one night, and way in the bowels of their technical library, way down at the last bookshelf in the corner bottom rack, we found an AT&T technical journal that laid out the whole thing. That's another moment I'll never forget: we saw this journal, we thought 'My God, it's all real!' So we set out to build a device to make these tones."

Wozniak and Jobs were not primarily seeking to deprive the phone giant AT&T of long-distance revenue, though this was, given the counter-cultural atmosphere around Silicon Valley, perfectly acceptable to most of the radicals who used their blue boxes. There was a major element of sheer pranksterism (another surviving Silicon Valley subculture, especially on April 1 each year). They would use a reel-to-reel tape recorder as an amplifier, and connect a telephone to it with alligator clips so that everyone in the room could hear the phone conversations. Woz would start by demonstrating how well the blue box worked: calling "Dial-A-Joke" in Sydney, making dinner reservations at the Ritz in London. "So one time I said I could call the Pope. I called into Italy and asked for the number of the Vatican and eventually got the call in to the Vatican. And I said, 'This is Henry Kissinger and I'd like to speak to the Pope about the summit trip'—he was on a summit trip. And they said, 'Oh, wait, wait a minute, we'll have to wake him up.' It was like 4:30 in the morning there. And I hung on the line and they said, 'We're waking him up.' Finally the highest Bishop up, who was going to be the translator for the Pope, came on and he said, 'You're not Henry Kissinger.' And I went into a little accent and said, 'Oh, yes, I am. You can call me back at this number.' They never called back—but I woke him up."

Aside from the amusement of dorm-room residents, and some real long-distance service for free, the Blue Box taught Steve Jobs an important lesson about the way technology was changing: "What we learned was that we could build something ourselves that could control billions of dollars worth of infrastructure in the world—that us two, we're not much, but we could build a little thing that could control a giant thing. That was an incredible lesson. I don't think there would ever have been an Apple computer had there not been blue boxes."

The other new component in the mix, a world away from the academic environment of the ARPAnet, was the presence of entrepreneurs. True, they were mostly hippy entrepreneurs, but whether their intention was to get rich or to buy more dope, some of the players in the Homebrew and hacker worlds had an instinct for making a buck. Not unlike Bill Graham, whose Fillmore rock concerts defined the music of the Bay Area for decades, these were people who were turning their passion into public performance and, sometimes, profits. Stewart Brand was a typical product of these times, the "Multimedia Performance Entrepreneur."

Another was the larger-than-life figure Jim Warren. A former mathematics teacher at a Catholic girls' school, Jim was immediately fascinated by the PC, like many Bay Area hippies. He was founder-editor of a serious, but absurdly-titled, computer magazine: *Dr. Dobbs' Journal of Computer Calisthenics and Orthodonture: Running Light Without Overbite*. As Warren says, California counterculture was crucial to the PC's development: "The whole spirit there was working together, was sharing. You shared your dope, you shared your bed, you shared your life, you shared your hopes. A whole bunch of us had the same community spirit, and that permeated the whole Homebrew Computer Club. As soon as somebody would solve a problem they'd come running down to the Homebrew's next meeting and say, 'Hey everybody! You know that problem that all of us have been trying to solve, here's the solution, isn't this wonderful? Aren't I a great guy?' It's my contention that that is a major component of why Silicon Valley was able to develop the technology as rapidly as it did, because we were all sharing—everybody won."

Chris Espinosa, who had established a friendly rapport with Steve Wozniak at the Homebrew meetings, was only fourteen years old when he joined the fledgling Apple Computer, working on the afternoons when he had early release from high school: "Impressing one's friends, especially impressing one's circle of technical friends, is crucially important. It's part of the 'demo or die' mentality. You are judged by how cool what you've created is, and while impressing yourself is important, impressing astute friends is *really* important."

Steve Wozniak built the "Apple I" computer in and around the Homebrew Club. The Apple I was even less of a computer than the Altair—a single circuit board with neither a case nor a keyboard. At the time, he was a junior technician at Hewlett-Packard, and had every intention of staying there for life. According to Jim Warren, once Woz started fooling around with "personal computers" in his spare time, he did the obvious and right thing regarding his employer: "He went to Hewlett-Packard and said 'I would very much like to work on a microcomputer project, would you set up one?' And Hewlett-Packard said 'Ha, ha, ha!'—essentially, 'There's no future in that.' And Woz said, 'Well, would you sign a release so I can work on it as my own hobby?' And they said, 'Sure, it's not going anywhere, there is no business potential there.' Great industrial insight. They signed a release."

Steve Jobs demonstrated both insight and a singular talent in sales by managing to sell fifty of them. Part of the motivation was to recover some cherished personal possessions: "I sold my Volkswagen bus and Steve sold his calculator and we got enough money to pay a friend of ours to make the artwork to make a printed circuit board, and we made some printed circuit boards and we sold some to our friends. I was trying to sell the rest of them so that we could get our microbus and calculator back."

Business acumen was largely lacking from the first Apple venture. In what has become a mantra of the early personal computer industry, Jobs admits "We didn't know what we were doing." The plan was to buy a hundred sets of parts, build fifty Apple I boards, and sell them to the Byte Shop on El Camino Real (possibly the world's first personal computer store) for twice what it cost to build them. This would cover the cost of all the parts, thus allowing the partners to build the other fifty boards for their profit.

As Jobs explains, this venture provided an early lesson in the cruel world of profit and loss, liquidity and inventory control: "We convinced these distributors to give us the parts on 'net thirty days credit'—we had no idea what that meant, but sure, sign here. So we had thirty days to pay them. We bought the parts, we built the products, and we sold fifty of them to the Byte Shop and got paid in twenty-nine days and then paid the parts people in thirty days, and so we were in business. But we had the classic Marxian profit realization crisis in that our profit wasn't in a liquid currency, our profit was in fifty computers sitting in the corner."

Nevertheless, that experience showed Jobs that there was a market for a "real" personal computer. Something better than the Apple I, something better than the Altair, something that didn't exist: "So my dream for the Apple II was to sell the first real packaged computer."

Steve Jobs' dream was impossible. It needed too many chips, making the product too complicated and expensive to build. But (as Ed Roberts said of making the Altair) Jobs' partner Wozniak didn't know it was impossible: "Why have memory for your TV screen *and* memory for your computer, make them one. That shrunk the chips down. And all these timing circuits—I looked through manuals and found a chip that did it in one chip instead of five, and reduced that. One thing after another after another happened."

This was the computer Woz "wanted for myself." And it turned out to be a computer that Jobs believed could sell in mass. Or so he told Woz. "He said, 'I think we have a computer we could sell a thousand a month of.' How can you sell a thousand a month, you know?"

Jim Warren, a.k.a. Dr. Dobbs, a powerful hybrid of hippie and hacker, conceived the remarkable idea of a trade show for an industry and product line that barely existed yet. But enough little companies had spun out of the Homebrew Club to raise hopes that there might be enough vendors and enough customers for Jim not to have to return to teaching math. The First West Coast Computer Faire (its final "e" a hip, neighborly reference to the

Renaissance Faire, a grand annual hippy gathering in Marin County) took place in San Francisco's Civic Auditorium, in 1978.

Jobs had a clear vision of the Apple II: it should look not like a piece of laboratory equipment, or a hobbyist's lash-up of wires and bulbs; rather, it should look like a domestic appliance. The Apple II was launched at the Faire. The show drew thousands of attendees and dozens of exhibitors, setting Jim Warren on the way to a fortune as a convention entrepreneur. But there was only one company showing something that looked like a modern personal computer. Right by the entrance, in a prime spot negotiated by Steve Jobs, sat the Apple II. As Jim Warren says, "Unlike all the rest of these techno-gadgets that looked like computers, that had the flashing lights and the switch registers and all that stuff, this looked like a human could use it. That was really neat. It simply had a keyboard and a monitor. "

Steve Jobs remembers the event with his trademark confidence: "My recollection is we stole the show, and a lot of dealers and distributors started lining up and we were off and running. I was twenty-one."

Jim Warren claims that Jobs personally, and the Faire in general, "precipitated a whole other viewpoint, in that business people said, 'Ho, ho, that's a pretty interesting consumer product, maybe this could be a business.' Jobs was a stellar entrepreneur and promoter. He saw the opportunity."

The opportunity to mass-market a consumer product was entering a new league for the Apple duo. Selling "a thousand a month" required real manufacturing, which required real money. Jobs persuaded a venture-capital investor, Don Valentine, to come by the Apple HQ (the Jobs family garage) and evaluate the business opportunity. Valentine, who described Jobs at the time as resembling "a renegade from the human race," declined to invest at first, but put the two enthusiasts in touch with Mike Markkula, a former Intel executive who had retired early (and rich) thanks to that company's enormous success. Markkula, in turn, contacted Arthur Rock, who had himself invested in Intel. But at least the Intel team had graduated from university and owned suits. Arthur Rock now faced a quite different prospect: "Jobs wore sandals and he had very long hair and a beard and a mustache, and was kind of unkempt . . . but very articulate. He was at one time in his life, and it was probably when I first met him, eating nothing but fruit. He'd just come back from spending a long period of time in India with a guru." To the sober venture capitalist: "This is not the norm. This is *not* the norm."

Jobs and Mike Markkula persuaded Arthur Rock to visit another computer show, in San Jose, to judge for himself the nature of the market and the enthusiasm that Apple was generating. "I think it was called the Home Brew Computer Show. It was a commercial show, where all the companies attended, wanted to show all their products. No one was at any of the other booths—everybody was at the Apple booth, and you couldn't get next to the Apple. It was the first time I'd ever seen anything like it, the first and last time I think it's ever happened. I said to myself 'Gee, this has got to be something.'"

Arthur Rock invested "less than $100,000 in Apple" but his investment was crucial to the growth of the company. It also solidified his reputation as a flawless judge of investment opportunities. Apple in due course raised money also from Venrock (the Rockefeller investment vehicle) and from Valentine's Sequoia, for a combined total of around $600,000. Following the West Coast Computer Faire, the next two years saw explosive growth for Apple, with thousands of customers literally arriving on the doorstep of their tiny office in Cupertino, California. Sales and profits grew so quickly that Apple had more money than it could spend. The company and its workforce were very young. The founders were still in their early twenties and some employees were even younger, like fourteen-year-old Chris Espinosa, who never left. He was still working at Apple twenty years later. "There would be public demonstrations of our product every Tuesday and Thursday afternoon at three o'clock. That was good because it was after school. So I would get out of my sophomore or junior year of high school, I would ride my little moped down to the Apple offices and at three o'clock I'd give the demonstrations of the Apple II. And some of the people that I did original demos to came up to me years later and said, 'You know, I founded a hundred-million-dollar chain of computer stores based on the demo you showed me one Tuesday afternoon at Apple.' It was really fun."

Steve Wozniak's life abruptly changed: "It went so successfully that all of a sudden Steve [Jobs] and I wouldn't have to worry about work for the rest of our lives. Then it got even more successful and more successful after that, and it was sort of a shock."

The Apple II set a new standard for personal computers and showed there was some real money to be made. It vindicated the venture-capital investors, and encouraged them and others to invest in companies like Apple. The Apple offices were informal, even anarchic, yet these unlikely pioneers launched an industry sector that made an indispensable contribution to the ultimate networking of the world's computers and computer users. First, this industry made possible the spread of ownership. Now, instead of having to negotiate access to time sharing terminals (whether run by university managers or hippy radicals), individuals could own and control their personal computing. Networking without ownership existed for the old-style mainframes and terminals; ownership and convenience had arrived for the stand-alone personal computer users—but they weren't connected. They would be, soon.

Chapter Seven
Copierheads

ENTER BOB METCALFE IN 1973 WITH his freshly minted Harvard Ph.D. and a Hawaiian tan. He also has a notebook full of packet radio networking ideas from Hawaii. In this happy state, he arrives for work at Xerox Palo Alto Research Center, and steps into the "time machine," the "economics-free zone," where ideas are the preferred currency.

Until 1958, Xerox was known as the Haloid Company, then for three years Haloid-Xerox, Inc. The company became Xerox Corporation with the introduction of the Xerox 914, the first really effective modern photocopying machine. From $32 million of sales in 1959, the company saw their sales increase between 30 and 50 percent every year through the 1960s, until in 1968 sales exceeded $1.1 billion, and profits $138 million. This was a blue-chip company that dominated its sector, and had the funds available to pursue new product avenues. The Xerox Research Center was the idea of Peter McColough, then CEO of the company, who had a vision of a Bell Labs–style institution for Xerox, a place where pure research could be conducted, by the brightest minds in the country, without regard to short-term profit.

PARC's first director, George Pake, had just resigned from a career as a university administrator when Xerox approached him. Once he was in place, Pake approached Bob Taylor to consult on the planning and hiring for the research facility. Taylor had left the Pentagon in 1969, and spent a year or so at the University of Utah. Having recruited and managed the talent that created the ARPAnet, Taylor had firm views about whom to hire and how to attract them to this new institution. He argued that it needed to be close by a major university with impeccable computer-science credentials, and it should be in California, because it was easier to get people to move there than anywhere else. The choice was simple: Xerox PARC was built in the Stanford Research Park, which had been established in 1951 by Fred Terman. Jerry Elkind was hired, at Taylor's recommendation, after leaving Bolt, Beranek and Newman in 1971. He was a highly regarded acquaintance of Taylor's from NASA days, and later a recipient of some of Taylor's ARPA research dollars. Elkind was named manager of the computer science laboratory, and Taylor (who thus recruited his boss) associate manager of computer science. Unlike Elkind, Taylor was not a trained computer scientist, and it would be eight years before he became the official manager. But his managerial and recruitment skills helped to define PARC as a frontier territory in computer science.

Bob Taylor's hand-picked computer scientists had an extraordinary degree of freedom to pursue their intellectual hunches or obsessions, and spend generous research budgets. In return, he got their total loyalty, according to Bob Metcalfe: "Bob Taylor was the spiritual leader of the computer science lab. He hired us all and took care of us. He wasn't himself a computer scientist. He has a knack for judging and attracting and motivating and taking care of research scientists and protecting them from the outside world. So it was a privilege to work in his lab."

Xerox had a strong motivation to research the future of office "information systems." It was widely held that computers could create "the paperless office"—a bad place to be selling photocopying machines. But if Xerox could be at the forefront of that technology, it could stay ahead of the competition. The intention was to use computer technology in the office, making it a better, more productive, more enjoyable place to work.

Larry Tesler joined Xerox PARC in 1973, where "The management said 'Go create the new world. We don't understand it.' Here are people who have a lot of ideas and tremendous talent, [they're] young, energetic. We really thought we were changing the world, and that at the end of this project or this set of projects personal computing would burst on the scene exactly the way we had envisioned it, and take everybody by total surprise. We were looking into distributed computing, personal computing, what we now call imaging, laser printers, things like that. It was going to be completely from left field. And that's what we felt we were doing, so we were very excited about it."

Bob Metcalfe was equally excited by the opportunities: "We were working in what Doug Engelbart might call an outpost or a time machine, where, in order to conduct research, you create a completely artificial environment which is an approximation in some dimensions of the remote future, and then you plop your scientists down in it, and they develop things as if the world is going to be the way it's not yet, and you learn things."

Another of the PARC alumni is John Warnock, who later left to found Adobe Systems: "PARC was a magnificent place. From a researcher's point of view it was almost ideal. For all practical purposes, they gave you very large resources to work with in terms of computing equipment and in terms of intellectual freedom and in terms of ability to pursue your own creative bents. It was an amazing place. A huge amount of creative activity came out of it, a huge number of product ideas came out of it. The atmosphere was electric, there was total intellectual freedom. There was no conventional wisdom: almost every idea was up for challenge and got challenged regularly."

Bob Metcalfe admits that modesty was in short supply: "We were really proud of ourselves and we lived in this really posh research center. We were frequently told and *believed* that we were the world's best computer scientists. So we were really elitist swine basically. We really liked ourselves a lot."

Adele Goldberg was one of the few women computer scientists at Xerox PARC. Inevitably, she also left to found a software company, Parc Place Systems: "As far as I could tell, when I first got there, there was no dictation from the corporation that you were working on anything in particular. People came there specifically to work on five-year programs that were their dreams."

Larry Tesler recalls that beneath the glamour and privilege of a well-funded research lab, there was a hint of anxiety about where it was all leading: "There was this sort of heady feeling that you were doing this momentous thing, this historic thing actually. You were creating a future that was kind of semi-secret and you were very grateful that the Xerox Corporation was taking all their copier profits and investing them into this venture. At the same time, it was very frustrating because it wasn't at all clear how any of this was going to ever come to market."

In April 1973, just about the time Bob Metcalfe arrived, a personal computer called the Alto was created at PARC. It was designed principally by Butler Lampson and Chuck Thacker, two of the half-dozen people Bob Taylor recruited in 1971 when their start-up company, Berkeley Computer Corporation, was heading downhill fast. By the end of 1973, there were ten Altos around PARC, and a year later, forty. It was the first ever embodiment of what we now call a personal computer, intended to serve a single person, sit on every desk in an office building—and be connected to all the other Altos. It had a keyboard, a mouse, and a screen. They called it "personal distributed computing," echoing Licklider's notion of "distributing" computer resources for the sake of economy and efficiency. By making it personal, they also achieved the "Man-Machine Symbiosis" requirement.

The Alto was born a year before the feeble, complicated Altair. The real world wouldn't see the IBM PC until 1981, or the Macintosh, the first computer with built-in networking, until 1984. So the Alto—which would have cost $20,000 or more, had it been marketed—was a vision of the future, according to Bob Metcalfe: "We worked in an economics-free zone. Even though it was unaffordable and we had no clear idea what they were going to be used for, we built computers to sit on everyone's desk and then watched what happened. We knew as a fact what the world was going to look like in ten years, because we had already built it and we saw that it worked. So we knew what to do. First you do this, then you do this—because we did it already."

John Warnock confirms the futuristic aspects of PARC: "Everyone lived in an environment that in many cases *today's* environment doesn't duplicate. We had reliable electronic mail systems. We had reliable electronic printers that were very, very fast and effective. We had color monitors and equipment that no one else had."

Having created the technology of the mid-eighties a decade early, the PARC researchers proceeded to create a network of PCs, or what Metcalfe calls "an internet of PCs." Ten years ahead of the rest of the world, PARC built their own Internet.

When Metcalfe arrived, Xerox PARC already had some experimental personal computers based on Nova minicomputers about the size of a microwave oven, and they even had a crude local area network that connected them together. Up to fifteen of them could be connected in this LAN by cable. The resident networking researcher was one Charles Simonyi, who had begun his computing career as a teenage night watchman in a computer center in his native Hungary before graduating to learning programming, by programming for free. As Metcalfe recalls: "He was designing an ARPAnet that would run a thousand times faster than the real ARPAnet, only it would run locally and connect all these PCs together. When I arrived, they gave me that project so Charles could go off and write a text editor called Bravo, which became Microsoft Word. I immediately, of course, threw away all of his work which he had called SIGNet: Simonyi's Infinitely Glorious Network."

How Bravo "became" Microsoft Word is an exemplar of the core problem at Xerox PARC. In almost every meaningful respect, the technological roots of the personal computers we use today can be traced to Xerox PARC. It is the Rome, the Jerusalem, the Mecca, the Lord's Cricket Ground of personal computing technology and imagination. Yet with the exception of a decent market share in laser printers, none of the technologies or products are associated with Xerox. The story is eloquently captured in the title of a book about Xerox PARC—*Fumbling the Future*.

Bravo was a highly original word-processing program, developed at Xerox PARC with Xerox funds by Xerox staff, but it was not marketed by Xerox. Xerox was not in the software business. Ultimately, when Charles Simonyi was hired by Microsoft, the ideas went with him—and Microsoft Word emerged.

One of the novel technologies developed for the Alto, and key to the success of its innovations, is known as bitmapping. Bitmapping is a technique for relating on-screen images to memory. Each bit of memory is a binary on/off switch; and each pixel (abbreviated from picture/pix element, a single dot on the screen) corresponds to a single bit. By mapping the memory bits on screen, an image is created out of thousands of dots, whether it is text or graphical material. The use of a bitmap display is central to the use of computers with a mouse, and to create images as well as text on the screen. But above all, with one bit of memory per pixel or dot, it was hugely expensive in memory cost. As Severo Ornstein, the ARPA veteran who came to PARC in 1976, points out, the use of so much memory was bold. But everyone here knew Moore's Law: "It took a certain amount of courage. Often more courage than genius is required in the computer field. In that case, the realization that the cost of memory was going to come way, way down and that you could afford to spend it in this spendthrift fashion—because it would be so cheap eventually—at the time that they first did that, it was an act of some bravery."

The first overlapping windows on screen were developed by another PARC researcher named Dan Inglis in 1976. According to Adele Goldberg, he invented a procedure for the movement of whole blocks of bits on the screen which he called "Bit Flit." The movement of blocks of bits in turn allows overlapping windows to be shuffled on screen—the basis of both the Macintosh user interface and Microsoft Windows. But this was in 1976!

With the development of the laser printer, and post-script software, bitmapping and bit images went one further step. As Charles Simonyi recalls, PARC researchers created WYSIWYG—by which the printer delivers almost exactly what the screen shows: "We fed a transparency stock to the laser printer, printed the transparent stock, and held it up against the screen to show that they are identical. In fact, they were just similar. On *Rowan and Martin's Laugh-In*, Flip Wilson had a tag line, 'What you see is what you get,' and one of the visitors, when presented with this demo, said, 'I see, what you see is what you get.'"

The same story is repeated for one product after another until, most notably, the Xerox graphical user interface, windows, and bitmap displays were hijacked wholesale to create the Apple Macintosh.

Promotional film made in the mid-seventies to publicize Xerox PARC research, shows how revolutionary the Alto was. Unlike its near-contemporary, the Altair, it was user-friendly above all. But of all the innovative features it had, perhaps the most remarkable was the core concept: as Metcalfe says, "to put one on every desk. In 1971 or 1972, you were lucky to have a computer in your city, let alone your building. If it was in your building there would be *one*. We were talking about putting them on every desk, and this required a new kind of network."

Until the mid-1970s, the world of networked or distributed computing was confined technologically to the "big iron" of mainframes, and sociologically to academic/government ranks. Personal computers barely existed, and aside from PARC were a gleam in the eyes of entirely different people: failing businessman Ed Roberts, fruit-eating hippie Steve Jobs, multimedia impresario Stewart

Brand, and company. PARC was the only place that had members and influences from both constituencies. Bob Metcalfe and his colleagues added the component that would begin the slow convergence of the stand-alone PC and the networked computer.

Metcalfe understood the packet switching of ARPAnet from his experience in helping to connect IMP #6 in Licklider's lab at MIT. (IMPs #9, 10, and 11 wound up at Harvard, Lincoln Laboratory, and Stanford University, respectively.) He had studied and written about the randomized retransmission protocol of the Alohanet packet radio network before arriving at PARC. Drawing on these two technologies, and with Alto computers in place thanks to Xerox PARC's Thacker, Lampson, and others, Metcalfe invented Ethernet and made networking a building or a company full of PCs possible: "I used the ideas that I had collected from the ARPAnet and the Aloha network to, on May 22, 1973, invent Ethernet."

Given the futuristic assumption that there would be a computer on every desk, Metcalfe and his collaborators (Thacker, Lampson, and David Boggs) aimed to create a network for "hundreds of computers at hundreds of kilobytes per second at hundreds of meters of separation." The specification that emerged was a network of 2.94-megabits-per-second capacity, linking up to 256 computers separated by up to a mile. The high-speed requirement was imposed by another advantage of the PARC environment: they were inventing the laser printer at the same time.

Unlike the ARPAnet, which connected the IMPs with 50-kilobit telephone lines, and unlike the Alohanet, which transmitted radio waves, the Ethernet used coaxial cable, a solid wire that is shielded by insulating material to prevent interference. The wire (the same kind that connects cable boxes to television sets) was connected to each Alto by cable TV taps and connectors. The name "Ethernet" is Metcalfe's obscure joke, referring to the outmoded notion of "the ether" as a "passive, omnipresent medium for the propagation of electromagnetic waves. We began to call our coaxial cable—that ran up and down every corridor to which all these computers tapped in—the ether. And they would send their packets up into the ether." Metcalfe likes to tell people how his mother has the New York license plate ETHERNET. "Most people think that she's a dentist."

Like the ARPAnet, the Ethernet sent packets. There was software installed in the Altos to control transmission, ordering, and reassembly of packets, like the IMPs of the ARPAnet. It sent messages at will, and in case of collision and corruption of the packets, it used the Alohanet idea of randomized retransmission for packets that went unacknowledged. The store-and-forward ("hot-potato") method of the ARPAnet required expensive IMPs, or something similar. But it was too expensive to build more Altos to function as IMPs. The general transmission of messages by the Alohanet via radio caused messages to collide and get scrambled, like two phone conversations on one line. This is why we have the busy signal.

For the Ethernet, Metcalfe and David Boggs didn't "insist on success." All messages went along the line, but only got delivered to their addressed destinations. Interference did happen, but could be detected. That would halt the transmission, briefly and for a random delay, before it would be retried, much as a conversation among half a dozen people involves a lot of false starts, interruptions, and repetitions.

This access procedure has a heavyweight acronym, CSMA/CD, standing for Carrier Sense Multiple Access with Collision Detection. Larry Tesler was present at the creation of Ethernet, inside PARC: "Metcalfe and Boggs were working on getting their two machines to talk to each other through the Ethernet. We had a lot of late nights at PARC where they were working on their Ethernet stuff. I'd sometimes take a break and go over there and see what they were doing. It was an exciting time. It came up a little bit at a time. First they were able to get, you know, a little bit across and a little more across, and then at one point they said, you know, we can all use it now, and we started building Ethernet boards and installing them in all the machines and, after a while, everybody in PARC was able to communicate through the Ethernet."

Everyone was also, in due course, able to print documents via Ethernet from their Alto, via another PARC invention, the Research Character Generator, on yet another, the Scanned Laser Output Terminal (SLOT), which we would now call a laser printer. For this procedure, they came up with another laborious acronym: Ethernet-Alto-RCG-SLOT, or EARS.

Like a team of tunnelers breaking through to meet another team coming from the other side of the mountain, the network of personal computers at PARC (a very local area network) was quickly connected to the wide area network that was ARPA. By 1974, there were sixty-four nodes on the ARPAnet, all over the United States. One was at PARC. Two trends in networking had met halfway. Bob Metcalfe recalls that "almost the first thing we did with the Ethernet was to hook it up to the ARPAnet at Xerox. So from your personal computer at your desk, you would go through the Ethernet out through the IMP into the ARPAnet. With what we built at the Xerox Research Center we did a lot to transform the notion of the ARPAnet from a wide area network of hosts to an Internet of LANs (Local Area Networks) and personal computers."

Of course, this transformation could not take place until personal computers existed in the real world. Ethernet was a technology that was now waiting for its market application. Like so many of the technologies developed at PARC, it wasn't a commercial product, because the company neglected to commercialize it. Larry Tesler, like many others, was frustrated that a company with both technological and marketing muscle was doing so little with it all. "Everybody who came there thought Xerox could be the company that pushed IBM aside and shot past them and had enough marketing prowess in corporations to actually displace IBM."

John Warnock suggests that Xerox management had never fantasized about what the future of the office was going to be: "When it was presented to them, they had no mechanisms for turning those ideas into real-life products. That was really the frustrating part of it because you were talking to people who didn't understand the vision, yet the vision was getting created every day within PARC: and there was no one to receive that vision."

Somewhat belatedly, in 1975, Xerox's head office approved the formation of a Systems Development Division, intended to engineer PARC inventions into products: operating across the street from PARC, the new division recruited several of the pioneering technologists to become product managers, including Bob Metcalfe (Ethernet), Charles Simonyi (Bravo), and Chuck Thacker (the Alto). Unfortunately, this new direction coincided with a very significant downturn in Xerox's overall fortunes and profitability.

First, they were hit with an antitrust suit by the Federal Trade Commission. Outstanding success had allegedly tipped over the line into monopoly. Profits suffered as Xerox defended itself not only against the federal suit but against numerous private suits brought against it by disgruntled competitors kicking a corporate giant while it was down. There was a general recession in 1974, which hit the bottom line. And Xerox's infamous acquisition of Scientific Data Systems—an effort to acquire a computer business at a stroke—was finally written off at a total estimated cost in excess of $1 billion. This was not a good time for Xerox to commit itself to a whole new departure—to market the office of the future. So they put it all aside.

The central paradox of the Xerox PARC phenomenon was that the company literally synonymous with copying had invested heavily in technologies that might replace the central, profitable role of copying in the office. Despite this excursion into the future, Xerox management were, in Steve Jobs' opinion, stuck in their successful existing technology: "The people at Xerox PARC used to call the people that ran Xerox toner-heads, and these toner-heads would come out to Xerox PARC and they just had no clue about what they were seeing."

Adele Goldberg tells the story of how, on one occasion, Charles Simonyi was asked to give a demonstration of Bravo to the chairman of the board. "Peter McColough came for the demo and was very attentive." Some weeks later, one of Goldberg's colleagues from Xerox PARC went back to corporate headquarters in Stamford, Connecticut, for a dinner where McColough was present, and asked what he had made of the demo. "And Peter said, 'I've never seen a man type so fast.'"

Goldberg and company knew their vision of the future was in trouble if that was all he saw. On the other hand, McColough had been CEO of Xerox for about a dozen years, in which time the company's revenues grew tenfold. It is easy to understand why Xerox management just didn't see the need to go after an entirely new, so far non-existent business. Like many others at PARC, Bob Metcalfe came to a realization: "We were in a research center of a copier company. At the time, we didn't realize what a fatal situation that was. We thought we were in an information-technology research center, in an information-technology company, and that just as Xerox had been able to build a humongous and successful copier business, as soon as we got the computer thing right, they

would do that too. And it took a long time before we realized that
we and Xerox and those ideas were somehow immiscible."

Nevertheless, entrepreneurial instincts were not absent from
Xerox PARC. Frustration and the pervasive culture of entrepreneurship fostered by Stanford University, venture capital, and
Californian spirit led a procession of PARC researchers to seek
their fortunes outside. They already had the considerable benefit
of theorizing, experimenting with, and testing their ideas at
PARC's expense, over years.

John Warnock and Chuck Geschke (one of the first PARC
computer-science researchers, who arrived in 1972) quit in 1982
to start up Adobe Systems, the prime software venture in laser
printing and key to the desktop publishing revolution that the
Apple Macintosh ultimately fostered. Many others followed in
their footsteps: people like Adele Goldberg, who founded Parc
Place Systems; John Ellenby, who founded GRiD Systems; and
Charles Simonyi, who wrote Wordstar for Xerox, and rewrote it
as Microsoft Word farther north, becoming a centi-millionaire
and scientific philanthropist along the way. The modern Darwin,
Professor Richard Dawkins, holds the Simonyi Chair in the Public Understanding of Science at Oxford University.

Despite the ease with which Xerox can be (and is) criticized for
letting so many hugely profitable products slip through its fingers, it is worth remembering, as Bob Taylor points out, that
Xerox did exploit the laser printer, the product from PARC that
was closest of all to its core business: "We built the first laser
printer and the Xerox people can say correctly that taking advantage of that one piece of work more than paid for all of their research investment, time and time again because they built up a
billion-dollar business out of just that one piece of work. The argument has two sides. You can talk about the stuff they took advantage of—or you can talk about the stuff they dropped on the
floor—which Sun, Apple, Apollo, Digital, Microsoft have all
taken advantage of."

Yet in due course even Bob Taylor was to move on. Digital
Equipment Corporation established a systems research center in
the heart of Palo Alto, and Taylor concluded that a research center in a computer company was a better place to do computer research than the research center of a copier (and printer) company.

Among the PARC alumni who followed Taylor down the hill were Chuck Thacker, Butler Lampson, and David Boggs.

Among the smarter commercial decisions Xerox made was to invest modestly, through its ventures division, in Apple Computer. As a consequence of this privileged relationship, and of the buzz reaching from PARC to Apple headquarters in Cupertino, Steve Jobs was invited in to see the futuristic computing ideas Xerox researchers were turning into reality.

Steve Jobs had cofounded Apple Computer in 1976. The first popular personal computer, the Apple II, was a hit—and made Jobs one of the biggest names of a brand-new industry. At the height of Apple's early success in December 1979, Jobs, then all of twenty-four, had a privileged invitation to visit Xerox PARC, to see a demonstration of the Alto and all its innovations. Larry Tesler was one of those present: "Because of the investment that Xerox had made, one promise was that the Apple people could come and see what was going on at PARC. A lot of people were very irritated about that, that we would let in these people who were kind of competing with us, so they had trouble finding people willing to do the demo."

Steve Jobs had been urged by several people at Apple "to get my rear over to Xerox PARC and see what they were doing." He made an initial visit, then returned with the Xerox Ventures partner and his Apple development team, which was then working on the Lisa computer, the planned high-end office system successor to the Apple II. But the second demo was delayed by a prolonged argument about whether it should happen or not. Adele Goldberg was designated to present the demo, and demurred: "The way you really could influence what Steve was doing of course was to show his own programmers. Steve—I almost said *asked*, but the truth is—*demanded* that his entire programming team get a demo of the Smalltalk System. The then head of the science center asked me to give the demo because Steve specifically asked for me to give the demo and I said, 'No way.' I had a big argument with these Xerox executives telling them that they were about to give away the kitchen sink. I said that I would only do it if I were ordered to do it, because then of course it would be their responsibility, and that's what they did. So I gave them a full Smalltalk demo. One of the members of their team, who is someone I've known a long time, has since told me that they went back and completely re-designed how they were going to build their product."

Smalltalk pioneered a whole array of language and development techniques, not least the on-screen icons that were first seen commercially in the "graphical user interface," or GUI, of the Apple Macintosh. As Steve Jobs remembers the occasion: "They showed me really three things. But I was so blinded by the first one I didn't even really see the other two. They showed me object-oriented programming, but I didn't even see that. They showed me a networked computer system—they had over a hundred Alto computers all networked using e-mail etc., etc. I didn't even see that. I was so blinded by the first thing, which was the graphical user interface. I thought it was the best thing I'd ever seen in my life, and within ten minutes it was obvious to me that all computers would work like this some day."

Bill Atkinson, one of the members of the Lisa design team, and later of the Macintosh, recalls that "mostly what what we got in that hour-and-a-half was inspiration, and basically a bolstering of our convictions that a more graphical way to do things would make this business computer more accessible."

To Larry Tesler, it was apparent that the young founder of Apple was definitely not cut from the same cloth as Xerox executives: "Steve Jobs himself was a most impressive character. I had met him before at an Apple company picnic but I hadn't ever felt the power of his personality until this demo. After an hour looking at demos, they understood our technology and what it meant, more than any Xerox executive understood it after years of showing it to them. And right then and there, I thought 'I'm in the wrong company' and I needed to go to a place like Apple."

A few months later, Larry Tesler did go precisely to Apple, where he became chief scientist and stayed for seventeen years. The Damascene conversion of Jobs to the GUI has now taken on the aura of nerdly scripture. Jobs' "insanely great" Macintosh computer, dogged by many early missteps, but ultimately launched in a blaze of publicity in 1984, was the result and the direct descendant of the Alto, a computer Xerox never marketed or popularized. As Steve Jobs says, "Basically they were copier heads that just had no clue about a computer or what it could do. They just grabbed defeat from the greatest victory in the computer industry. Xerox could have owned the entire computer industry today. Could have been a company ten times its size. Could have been the IBM of the nineties. Could have been the Microsoft of the nineties."

Perhaps Xerox was fatally restrained by the burden of antitrust legislation from becoming bigger, or equally dominant in a new field. And although their profitability did not benefit from the technologies invented at PARC (other than the laser printer), the personal computer industry put them all into service. Steve Jobs likes to quote Pablo Picasso on *homage*: "Picasso had a saying, 'Good artists copy, great artists steal.'* We have always been shameless about stealing great ideas, and I think part of what made the Macintosh great was that the people working on it were musicians and poets and artists and zoologists and historians, who also happened to be the best computer scientists in the world. They brought with them to this effort a very liberal arts air, that we wanted to pull in the best that we saw in these other fields into this field."

Not least among the innovations of the Macintosh computer— unlike the IBM PC, which would precede it by three years—was built-in networking.

Charles Simonyi left PARC, like so many others, because the pleasure of research experimentation, without pressure, was replaced by the frustration of a scenario in which the product could never be successful. He began to look outside for opportunities, and Bob Metcalfe recommended a number of people for him to talk to, starting with Bill Gates. In January 1981, this was not quite such an obvious idea as it now seems. Microsoft had fewer than forty employees, and had so far confined its activities to languages and more recently the IBM DOS operating system. Microsoft had no experience in applications, which was Charles' specialty. But that meant that Charles Simonyi got to start Microsoft's applications business: "It took only a few minutes of conversation with Bill to see his commitment to all of these ideas."

Not everyone is in a position to become employee #40 at Microsoft, with stock options that represent a license to print money. Many members of the Xerox staff set out to to seek their fortunes in the venture-capital market, starting new companies to

---

* Did Picasso steal this, too, for T. S. Eliot wrote, "Immature poets imitate; mature poets steal."

"productize" the ideas they had already explored inside PARC.
Bob Metcalfe was no exception.

People once dreamed of finding El Dorado, a city whose
streets were paved with gold. Sandhill Road, in Palo Alto, is Silicon Valley's answer to that dream—home today to half of all the
venture-capital funds in the entire world. From tastefully low-
key cedar-and-glass office buildings, about $35 billion is being
invested in people, ideas, and products that exist because of the
personal computer and the microprocessor, and increasingly because of networks. In exchange for the money required to get a
business up and running, venture capitalists (VCs) also make
certain demands of the entrepreneurs with start-up companies.
It's often summarized as "adult supervision." They will insist on
bringing in professional management, marketing consultants,
and board members from related business areas to build strategic alliances, and will generally shift the growing company from
being an embodiment of wild and youthful enthusiasm into a
more mature, focused enterprise.

All of this Bob Metcalfe was to learn as he embarked on his career as an entrepreneur. Metcalfe saw Ethernet going unexploited
as a commercial product by the Xerox Systems Development Division, and saw his opportunity. He had already, while at Xerox,
succeeded in forging an alliance between Xerox, Digital, and Intel
to establish Ethernet as a 10-megabit-per-second (mbps) standard,
ratified by the IEEE. Somewhere in there, as costs fell and engineering improved, he felt there was a business opportunity. So he
employed his most basic research skills: looking under V for venture capital in the Yellow Pages. In fact, he got a copy of the
Western Association of Venture Capitalists directory, and started
his research: "Starting in November 1978, I started going through
that directory having breakfast, lunch, and dinner with everybody I could find in that directory. Not to raise money. I just
asked them how to start a company. I did this for three years,
while doing lots of other things. And I boiled that all down to
three lessons, the three ways in which companies fail most often.
Number one, the uncontrollable ego of the founder. Number two,
a lack of money. Number three, a lack of focus."

After three years, Metcalfe was offering these three lessons
back to the VCs, who were naturally impressed by his insight:

"I would tell them that I'm going to make a lot of mistakes when I get around to starting a company, but I'm not going to make any of those three mistakes."

The business opportunity Metcalfe identified was again a repetition of the same core insight that has driven every advance in networking: overcoming incompatibility. The advance of information technology was being held back. In local area networks, and wide area networks like the ARPAnet, technologies were incompatible: printers and drivers and software would not connect together. "If we could somehow get compatibility under control, the rate of progress would accelerate. That was my grand idea. That, incidentally, is how 3Com got its name. In June of 1979, I sat down to name my company and ended up calling it Computer Communication Compatibility—3Com—to pursue that grand idea."

Technological difficulty was not the issue for 3Com. Using twenty or more Altos as "gateways," PARC researchers by the summer of 1979 had connected several hundred computers, on twenty-five or more Ether-networks in a "Xerox internet service." Metcalfe had built network interfaces for the ARPAnet back at MIT, and with colleagues had built Ethernet interfaces at PARC: "We had done it before—two, three, four, five times. The challenge wasn't building it, so much as getting it to be cheap and reliable and small. So the first Ethernet cards we built cost $5,000 per connection. The personal computers in those days cost $2,000, or $3,000 or $4,000, but the cards were completely inappropriate for personal computers. So we built them for minicomputers, which were much more expensive."

The breakthrough that made Ethernet a universal standard, and 3Com a huge success, was a combination of technology and timing. Metcalfe worked with a semiconductor company to move the Ethernet onto a chip, instead of a board: "So what we achieved was a card, called the Etherlink, that plugged into the IBM PC, which in 1982 was brand new, the IBM PC having been announced in August of '81."

The arrival of the IBM PC in 1981 was a milestone for networking in every way. While networked Alto personal computers had been created, nobody had them. Networking the IBM PC, the computer that allowed American business to take the personal computer seriously, was a huge new market. It would allow many

new businesses to be created and thrive, before being overtaken
by the next technology. In the meantime, 3Com and Bob Metcalfe
did nicely: "A thousand dollars could put your PC on the Ethernet. Of course, we had to build a network operating system to
make it useful, which we did. And we shipped all that in September of 1982 and people started buying it. And by 1983, we
were growing 50 to 80 percent per quarter sequentially. And by
March of 1984, we were public with about $12 million in rev-
enue. By the time I left in 1990, we were $400 million a year with
two thousand people. And in 1997, 3Com is a $5 billion company
with twelve thousand people. Incredible."

Today Bob Metcalfe enjoys an enviable lifestyle: he is a youthful industry elder statesman, with a farm in Maine devoted to
preserving rare breeds, a majestic townhouse in Boston's Back
Bay, and an unassailable reputation as a networking Hall of
Famer. The transformation from cabana boy to gentleman farmer
has taken him just about thirty years. He attributes his success
not to inventing Ethernet, but to a long career of selling, travel-
ing, jetlag, hiring, firing, managing people and compensating
them fairly, and more selling. After all, he is the man who sold
Xerox PARC on the idea of a research trip to Hawaii in 1972. "It
helps to have good parents, and it helps to work really hard for a
long period of time and go to school forever, and it helps to drop
quite by accident into the middle of Silicon Valley, where you're
swept up into an inexorable process of entrepreneurship and
wealth generation, and you pop out the other side with a farm in
Maine. I hate to oversimplify."

Part Three

The 1980s:
Serving
the Suits

Chapter Eight
"OK for Corporate America"

A YEAR AFTER THE INTRODUCTION OF the Apple II, in October 1979, a new software application went on sale in one store in Bedford, Massachusetts. Although VisiCalc was not a network product, and the Apple II was not a networked computer, the event set the stage for the rise of the PC in the 1980s as a serious, useful tool of business. VisiCalc inventor Dan Bricklin remembers the impact it had: "I remember showing it to one accountant around here and he started shaking and said, 'That's what I do all week, I could do it in an hour.' They would take their credit cards and shove them in your face. I meet these people now they come up to me and say, 'I gotta tell you, you changed my life. You made accounting fun.'"

Visicalc made what some dismissed as a toy into a business machine. IBM saw a market they could no longer afford to neglect. Network hardware and software were developed to connect IBM's PCs. The pool of users grew until networking was a desirable activity not just for business but for social contacts, game-playing, and virtual communities. In parallel, on campuses and federal institutions, and increasingly among the largest corporations, networks like ARPAnet were being supplemented and duplicated until they linked themselves into an Internet. If the 1960s was the decade when packet switching was discovered, and the 1970s was the decade when the personal computer and the ARPAnet were first developed, the 1980s was the decade in which the foundations and ground floor of today's wired world were truly built.

It was really a matter of supply and demand. Networking wasn't in commercial demand until there were enough computers to be networked. Until computers became personal, that was an impossibility. Back in the 1960s and 1970s, multiple users could access one mainframe from terminals—either locally or via dial-up service along a phone line. But such time sharing use was limited to perhaps dozens of users at a time, per mainframe; or hundreds of users all told, per installation. By the end of the seventies, ARPAnet had less than 200 host computers. Despite SATnet and Alohanet, probably fewer than 250,000 people had ever used a networked computer or terminal.

The economics of the personal computer revolution created a paradigm shift in thinking about who could use computers and for what. The first, huge change was the fact that non-technologists, non-scientists, even *women and children* could use computers. Networking, especially in the business world, was the second.

The advent of a true personal computer coincided with the widespread deregulation of the financial services industries in the United States and UK. Suddenly there was vigorous competition on Wall Street and in the Square Mile—requiring speed, responsiveness, and ease of use—for services that had been the comfortable private fiefdoms of banks, or insurers, or brokerage houses. The personal computer, whether used "personally," or within a corporate office setting, became a remarkably useful tool in this new environment.

At the start of the eighties, in the boardrooms of corporate America, a computer still meant something the size of a truck that cost at least a hundred thousand dollars. The idea of a $2,000 computer that sat on your desk in a plastic box was laughable. In addition, Apple Computer's hippie corporate tone was well known. (Apple's competitors, such as Atari, Commodore, and Tandy were also tainted with the "toy computer" problem, though with some justification thanks to "Pong" and other early computer games.) But with VisiCalc, even corporate types started to enthuse over the Apple. Marv Goldschmitt was the retailer who sold the first VisiCalcs: "A killer app is the one that just makes everybody sit up and say, 'Wow, now I understand what this thing does.' Every technology has a killer app or it doesn't get accepted into society. The telephone had a killer app, connecting two people together. All of sudden I could talk to my uncle in New Jersey. That's a killer app. The internal combustion engine had a killer app, and that was putting it in an automobile and giving people the ability to drive around on their own. The computer had a killer app and that was VisiCalc."

The Apple II was a product of the hacker and hippie culture of Silicon Valley but its killer application was not. It came straight from the blackboards of the Harvard Business School. Perhaps inevitably, following the pattern of invention and exploitation in the industry, the very first electronic spreadsheet was created by two men whose names are not widely known, and whose invention was imitated and copied widely, to the great financial benefit of others. Invented by a Harvard University graduate student, Dan Bricklin, the code for VisiCalc was written by his programmer friend Bob Frankston.

A spreadsheet is a tool for financial planning. Dan Bricklin's professor at Harvard's Graduate School of Business showed how company accountants used a grid of numbers on a blackboard to project expenses and profits. The trick to a spreadsheet is that all the values in the table are related to the others. So changes in one year or column would ripple through the table, changing cost and profit estimates for subsequent years. Students were asked to calculate how future profits would be affected by various business scenarios. It was called "running the numbers" and even with hand-held calculators it was laborious drudgery. As each value was linked to others, one mistake could mean disaster.

Dan Bricklin had worked as a programmer and started daydreaming about how he could use a computer to replace the tedious hand calculations: "I imagined that there was this magic blackboard that worked like word processing does word wrapping—if you make a change to a word it automatically pulls everything back. Well, why not recalculate in the same way? So that if I change a number, if I should have used 10 percent instead of 12 percent, I could just put it in and it would recalculate everything. That would be this idea of an electronic spreadsheet."

Dan Bricklin designed the program, and enlisted his friend Bob Frankston to write the actual computer code. After months of programming late at night when computer time was cheaper, the Harvard Business School blackboard came to life. His partner Bob Frankston points out: "You have to remember, in those days we did not use the word spreadsheet because nobody knew what a spreadsheet was. I came up with the name 'visible calculator' or VisiCalc, because we wanted to emphasize that aspect."

VisiCalc appeared in October 1979, priced at $100. After a slow start, VisiCalc took off. Marv Goldschmitt sold the first ones: "It gave people who were obsessed with numbers, whether they were in business or at home—how much am I worth today? what's my stock portfolio worth? how am I doing against budget on this project?—it gave them an ability to play with scenarios and say 'Well, what if I do this.' It put people in a sense in control of the thing that lots of people feel is driving them, and that's numbers."

It is an irony that the first serious business application for the Apple II, and for the eighties, was developed by two software entrepreneurs who had a somewhat unbusinesslike, sixties outlook. It is very difficult to patent software, and Dan Bricklin decided not to patent his spreadsheet idea. The conceptual basis of software cannot be patented, nor can the software's performance, only the code. Thus, a new application can be written that precisely imitates a previous application, but as long as the code is different, there's no way for the originator to claim paternity of the offspring. There are startling similarities between VisiCalc and Lotus 1-2-3 (which fueled the IBM PC), and between VisiCalc and Microsoft Excel. Though tens of millions of spreadsheets have been sold since 1979, Bricklin and Frankston haven't earned VisiCalc royalties in years.

Dan Bricklin is sanguine about their achievement: "Looking back at how successful a lot of other people have been, it's kind of sad that we weren't as successful. We're kids of the sixties and what did you want to do? You wanted to make the world better, and you wanted to make your mark on the world and improve things, and we did it. So by the mark of what we would measure ourselves by, we're very successful."

Bob Frankston has the same accepting attitude: "It would be very nice to be gazillionaires, but you can also understand that part of the reason was that that's not what we're trying to be."

Given the pedigree of personal computers, from MITS in Albuquerque to Apple in Cupertino, it might seem absurd that the next milestone would be a competing product embossed with the three letters that guaranteed quality, reliability, and conservatism in the American corporate mind. Such was the enthusiasm and buzz about personal computers that IBM ultimately had no choice but to pay attention. Apple's Steve Wozniak remembers the heady days of Apple's apogee: "Everybody you talked to just seemed excited talking about what we were doing. There was this huge media explosion, like the Internet is receiving today, of 'This is the happening thing.' You read about it over and over and over, and every time you took an airplane flight you read about it, in every newspaper every week you'd read something about small computers coming, and Apple was one of the highlight companies. We were being portrayed as a leader of a revolution, and we really felt that we *were* a leader of a revolution. We were going to change life a lot."

Big Blue made and serviced "Big Iron"—mainframe computers for large, blue-chip American companies. IBM ran its business by having committees to verify each decision. It was designed to ensure that good decisions were made, bad decisions were weeded out; and the chain of command ran from bottom to top throughout the enormous company. The ultimate decision forum was the CMC, the Corporate Management Committee, chaired in 1980 by Frank Carey. Recalls twenty-five-year IBM veteran Rich Seidner: "IBM had created this process and it absolutely made sure that quality would be preserved throughout the process, that you actually were doing what you set out to do and what you thought the customer wanted. At one point, somebody kind of looked at the process to see well, you know, what's it doing and what's the overhead built into it, what they found is that it would take at least nine months to ship an empty box."

This was not a nimble, passionate venture like the upstart start-ups of California. But by 1979, IBM had to take notice of the explosive growth of personal computer companies like Apple. For the company synonymous with computers, it was galling at least to observe a growing computer business they didn't control. In 1980, IBM decided they wanted a piece of this action. Jack Sams was a senior IBM executive at the time, observing Apple computers making inroads: "There were suddenly tens of thousands of people buying machines of that class and they loved them. They were very happy with them, and they were showing up in the engineering departments of our clients as machines that were brought in because 'You can't do the job on your mainframe.' The people who had gotten it were religious fanatics about them. So the concern was we were losing the hearts and minds."

The solution to IBM's problem was far from the boardroom where the CMC met. In August 1979, Bill Lowe ran a small IBM research laboratory in Boca Raton, Florida. He knew the company was in a quandary, and he thought he had a solution. Unlike every IBM product ever made, designed, and engineered in-house, Lowe proposed to buy off-the-shelf technologies to create an IBM PC in one year flat.

If it took nine months to prepare and ship an empty box, they would have to work very fast. Lowe pitched his idea to Chairman Frank Carey: "He said, 'Well, what should we do?' and I said, 'We think we know what we would like to do if we are going to proceed with our own product.' He said, 'No, at IBM it would take four years and three hundred people to do anything, I mean it's just a fact of life.' And I said, 'No sir, we can provide you with product in a year.' He abruptly ended the meeting; he said, 'You're on, Lowe, come back in two weeks and tell me what you need.'"

The IBM Personal Computer would prove to be the second important product in the story of networking (the first was Ethernet) that advanced the cause of networking by espousing "open architecture." As defined by the Microsoft Press Computer Dictionary, Third Edition, open architecture is "Any computer or peripheral design that has published specifications...[that let] third parties develop add-on hardware for a computer or device." IBM had no time to build the processors, hardware, operating system, or applications themselves, and contracted with others to supply them all. Neither IBM sales nor IBM service departments had anything to do with the PC, either. As Bill Lowe understates it, "This was a new concept for IBM at that point. Mr Carey bought it. And as result of him buying it, we got through."

For the operating system, IBM ultimately contracted with the tiny Microsoft company, which had decamped from Albuquerque to Seattle, Bill Gates and Paul Allen's home town. In 1980, IBM was three thousand times the size of Microsoft in market capitalization. In a moment of earthshaking opportunism, Microsoft seized the opportunity to retool and resell an operating system they acquired from a local competitor for $50,000 as the PC-DOS operating system inside *not only* every IBM PC, but also every other IBM-like PC manufactured for the next ten years or more. Bill Gates could scarcely believe his own luck: "IBM was the dominant force in computing. At a lot of these computer fairs, discussions would get around to how people thought the big computer companies wouldn't recognize the small computers, and it might be their downfall. But now to have one of the big computer companies coming in and saying, at least the people who were visiting with us, that they were going to invest in it, that was amazing."

The story of Microsoft's coup has been exhaustively told elsewhere, and will not be repeated here. The most important consequence of that opportunity was that it created a continuous flow of revenues to Microsoft, which enabled it to ride and take advantage of every successive software, applications, and networking opportunity. Without the IBM PC's success, Microsoft might today be unknown.

When they launched the PC, IBM forecast sales of half a million computers by 1984. In those three years, they sold two million. Members of the PC management team, like Jack Sams, felt vindicated, or at least relieved: "Euphoric, I guess, is the right word. At that point, with two million or three million, they were now thinking in terms of a hundred million, and they were probably off the scale in the other direction."

Sparky Sparks was another IBM manager who had invested his energy and reputation in the PC project: "What IBM said was 'It's okay, corporate America, for you to now start buying and using PCs.' And if it's okay for corporate America, it's got to be okay for everybody."

The IBM PC not only transformed the personal computer market, it also transformed IBM itself. In the words of Rich Seidner: "IBM was an extraordinarily successful company. It was a company of around two hundred thousand people when I joined. Probably closer to four hundred thousand when I left. IBM went from being a company where it had thousands of customers to which it sold million-dollar machines to a company where it had millions of customers that were sold thousand-dollar machines."

With the IBM logo and the IBM imprimatur, the personal computer became accepted as a serious business tool, and many of the pioneering PC users in the business world were on Wall Street. Oddly enough, the entrance of this huge competitor greatly *benefited* Apple's sales, as Chris Espinosa, the former fourteen-year-old product demonstrator observed: "We had been struggling to establish personal computers as a credible alternative to institutional computing. [It was felt] personal computers had no place in business. They were things that weirdos in the lab use, but certainly an accountant or a designer or an executive would not use a personal computer. No, they'd use the company mainframe. Only when IBM endorsed the idea that personal computers belonged as part of a company's information system, and only when IBM endorsed the idea that it wasn't abnormal to have a computer at home, our sales went up. If you look at Apple's sales after the introduction of the IBM personal computer they continued to rise steadily."

IBM helped the sales of many competitors, and even facilitated the creation of new competitors. Thanks to the published specifications of the IBM PC, anyone could examine how it worked, and copy its performance by "reverse engineering." One such venture broke all records for new business revenues. The Compaq company was founded by ex–Texas Instruments executives, including Rod Canion: "In our first year of sales, Compaq set an American business record. I guess maybe a world business record. Largest first year sales in history. It was $111 million."

American corporations bought vast numbers of PCs, even though they often already had mainframes with terminals. It quickly became apparent that these smaller computers, useful as they were, would be still more productive—lowering overhead, increasing efficiency, and improving competitiveness—if they would behave more like the mainframe terminals. And there indeed was Bob Metcalfe's 3Com company, ready in 1982 to sell Ethernet connections at $1,000 per unit, to begin the next major era of networking: connecting "the suits" and the desktop computers of corporate America, together.

1. Bob Taylor, the Pentagon bureaucrat who devised the ARPA network.

REQUEST FOR QUOTATIONS	PAGE	OF
(THIS IS NOT AN ORDER)	1	6

1. REQUEST NO.	2. DATE ISSUED	3. REQUISITION/PURCHASE REQUEST NO.	4. CERTIFIED FOR NATIONAL DEFENSE UNDER BDSA REG. 2 AND/OR DMS REG. 1 RATING:
DAHC15.69 Q.0002	1968 July 29	1001/2 (C–69–515)	

5. ISSUED BY

DEFENSE SUPPLY SERVICE-WASHINGTON
Room 1D 245, The Pentagon
Washington, D. C. 20310
Mr. Daniel B. Dawkins

FOR INFORMATION CALL *(Name and tel. no.) (No collect calls)* OXford 5-0494

6. DELIVER BY *(Date)*

See sample Contract

7. DELIVERY

[X] FOB DESTINATION

[ ] OTHER *(See Schedule)*

8. TO NAME AND ADDRESS

(Street, City, State and ZIP Code)

9. DESTINATION *(Consignee and address including ZIP code)*

See Sample Contract

10. PLEASE FURNISH QUOTATIONS TO THE ISSUING OFFICE ON OR BEFORE 4:30 p.m. Local time 9/9/68 SUPPLIES ARE OF DOMESTIC ORIGIN UNLESS
(Date)

OTHERWISE INDICATED BY QUOTER. THIS IS A REQUEST FOR INFORMATION, AND QUOTATIONS FURNISHED ARE NOT OFFERS. IF YOU ARE UNABLE TO QUOTE, PLEASE SO INDICATE ON THIS FORM AND RETURN IT. THIS REQUEST DOES NOT COMMIT THE GOVERNMENT TO PAY ANY COSTS INCURRED IN THE PREPARATION OR THE SUBMISSION OF THIS QUOTATION, OR TO PROCURE OR CONTRACT FOR SUPPLIES OR SERVICES.

SCHEDULE

11. ITEM NO.	12. SUPPLIES/SERVICES	13. QUANTITY	14. UNIT	15. UNIT PRICE	16. AMOUNT
	SERVICES NECESSARY TO COMPLETE THE WORK DESCRIBED IN THE SAMPLE CONTRACT, ATTACHED.				
	Total Estimated Cost				$
	Fixed Fee				
	Total Estimated Cost Plus Fixed Fee				$

NOTE THE CERTIFICATION OF NONSEGREGATED FACILITIES IN THIS SOLICITATION. Bidders, offerors and applicants are cautioned to note the "Certification of Non-Segregated Facilities" in the solicitation. The certification provides that if the amount of the bid or proposal exceeds $10,000, the bidder, offeror or applicant, by signing this bid or offer certifies that he does not and will not maintain or provide for his employees facilities which are segregated on a basis of race, creed, color or national origin, whether such facilities are segregated by directive or on a de facto basis. Failure of a bidder or offeror to agree to the certification will render his bid or offer nonresponsive to the terms of solicitations involving awards of contracts exceeding $10,000 which are not exempt from the provisions of the Equal Opportunity clause. (Mar. 68)

17. PRICES QUOTED INCLUDE APPLICABLE FEDERAL, STATE, AND LOCAL TAXES.

DISCOUNT FOR PROMPT PAYMENT _____ % 10 CALENDAR DAYS; _____ % 20 CALENDAR DAYS; _____ % 30 CALENDAR DAYS; _____ % _____ CALENDAR DAYS.

NOTE: Reverse must also be completed by the quoter.

18. NAME AND ADDRESS OF QUOTER *(Street, city, county, State, including ZIP Code)*	19. SIGNATURE OF PERSON AUTHORIZED TO SIGN QUOTATION	20. DATE OF QUOTATION
	21. SIGNER'S NAME AND TITLE *(Type or print)*	22. TELEPHONE NO. *(Include area code)*

18-105-01   5

2. The Pentagon's ARPAnet Request for Quotations, 1968.

3. The Bolt, Beranek & Newman (BBN) team, including Dave Walden
(third from left), Bob Kahn (fifth from left), Frank Heart (sixth from left),
and Severo Ornstein (far right).

Frank Heart (signature)

PROPOSAL: INTERFACE MESSAGE PROCESSORS FOR THE ARPA
             COMPUTER NETWORK

RFQ No. DAHC15 69 Q 0002
BBN Proposal No. IMP P69-IST-5

6 September 1968

Submitted to:

Department of the Army
Defense Supply Service-Washington
The Pentagon, Room 1D 245
Washington, D.C.   20310

BOLT BERANEK AND NEWMAN INC.
50 Moulton Street
Cambridge, Massachusetts   02138

4. BBN's proposal to build the ARPAnet, 1968 (Frank Heart's copy).

5. Frank Heart, with Interface Message Processor (IMP).

6. The pioneers at BBN who built the IMPs and created the ARPAnet, including Dave Walden (front center), Frank Heart (standing center, with tie), Severo Ornstein (second from right), and Bob Kahn (far right).

7. Len Kleinrock at UCLA's Computer Science Lab.

8. The pioneers of Bolt, Beranek & Newman in Cambridge, Massachusetts, including Frank Heart (top, left) and Severo Ornstein (top, right).

9. Norm Abramson developed a radio packet-switching network, named Alohanet, at the University of Hawaii.

10. Norm Abramson on his trademark surfboard.

11. Bob Metcalfe, coinventor of Ethernet and founder of 3Com.

12. *Computer Lib/Dream Machines*, Ted Nelson's 1974 hacker bible.

13. Ted Nelson, foreground, in a towel at the First Hackers' Conference.

14. Ted Nelson, inventor/discoverer of Hypertext, creator of Xanadu.

15. Bob Taylor in a beanbag chair at Xerox PARC.

16. Bob Taylor in the corridors at Xerox PARC.

17. An IMP or Interface Message Processor, part of the ICCC demo of the ARPAnet, October 1972.

18. Vint Cerf, coinventor of the Internet protocol TCP/IP, at his terminal.

Whole Earth Epilog

access to tools

U.S.A. $4
Canada $5
United Kingdom £1.75
Australia $4 (recommended)
New Zealand $4

Second Edition
October 1974

19. Stewart Brand's *Whole Earth Catalog*.

20. Howard Rheingold, hippie savant.

21. Bill Gates: "A personal computer in every home and in every office, running Microsoft software...."

22. Cofounders of Sun Microsystems (left to right): Scott McNealy, Andy Bechtolsheim, Bill Joy, and Vinod Khosla.

23. Andy Bechtolsheim, cofounder of Sun Microsystems.

24. Andy Bechtolsheim's Sun staff pass.

25. Bill Joy's Sun staff pass.

26. Scott McNealy's Sun staff pass.

27. The Sausalito-based server of the WELL, or Whole Earth 'Lectronic Link.

28. Sandy Lerner and Len Bosack, founders of Cisco Systems.

29. Cisco's first router, from Sandy Lerner's hand-colored scrapbook: Kirk Lougheed (left), Len Bosack (center), and Sandy Lerner (right).

30. The Cisco headquarters (the living room), 1985.

31. Sandy Lerner, the Annie Hall look.

32. Len Bosack, as interpreted by Sandy Lerner.

33. The original team at Cisco Systems: Len Bosack (front left) and Sandy Lerner (front right).

34. Sandy Lerner, showing her own logo design for Cisco.

May 1990

Upside

U.S. Edition   For Executives and Investors in Technology Companies

$6⁵⁰ Per Issue

Who Cares?

Don Valentine Might Give You Money If He Likes Your Answer

Why Digital F/X Has Patient Friends

Talking Back To The Japan That Can Say No

35. *Upside* magazine, featuring Don Valentine of Sequoia Capital.

36. Microsoft former President & CEO Jon Shirley (left) with Bill Gates.

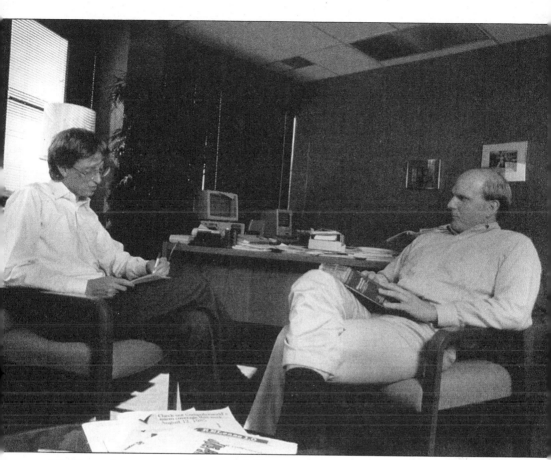
37. Harvard roommates, Microsoft billionaires: Chairman Bill Gates (left) and President & CEO Steve Ballmer (right).

Information Management: A Proposal

Abstract

This proposal concerns the management of general information about accelerators and experiments at CERN. It discusses the problems of loss of information about complex evolving systems and derives a solution based on a distributed hypertext sytstem.

Keywords: Hypertext, Computer conferencing, Document retrieval, Information management, Project control

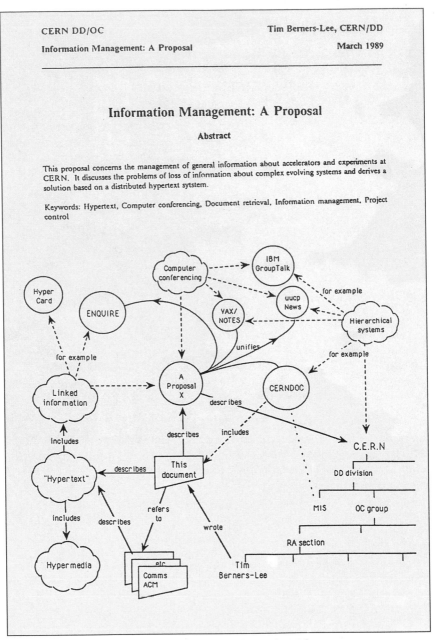

38. Tim Berners-Lee's diagram of the World Wide Web.

39. Tim Berners-Lee, inventor of the World Wide Web.

40. Cofounders of Netscape Communications: Jim Clark (left) and Marc
Andreessen (right).

41. The founders of Architext, later known as Excite: (left to right, from top) Joe Kraus, Mark van Haren, Ben Lutch, (bottom) Graham Spencer, Martin Reinfried, and Ryan McIntyre.

Chapter Nine
Close to the Silicon

THE COMPANY THAT WOULD DOMINATE networking software through the 1980s was in tough shape in the summer of 1982. As a consultant saw it: "The company was really in trouble. They were shopping around for new venture capitalists. They'd run out of money. And actually at the eleventh hour, we actually had a little auction at the company and we were selling desks and chairs and equipment so we could make the payroll the next week."

This corporate corpse was the remains of a computer hardware company, Novell Data Systems, based in Orem, Utah—nowhere near the power centers of Silicon Valley or IBM's New York. Not only was it distant in geographical terms: nothing could be further from the free-wheeling social attitudes of California or the corporate grandeur of Big Blue than the straitlaced Mormon culture of Utah. The people of Utah *are* different—godfearing, hardworking, highly educated. Mormon values of hard work, children, and a family focus could not have been more different from the often-bizarre workplace style of the Silicon Valley industry.

David Bradford, general counsel of Novell, is a lawyer who has the distinction of having once practiced Hollywood law alongside Judge Lance Ito, of Simpson trial fame. He graduated from the Mormon Brigham Young University Law School in Salt Lake City, and after working for other computer companies in California, returned to Utah: "The workforce, because there's not a lot of places to go, remains very loyal. There's pioneer stock here, Brigham Young crossing the plains and so forth. It's 150 years ago that Brigham Young came and said, 'This is the place.' It's that heritage of hard-working, loyal, moral people that form a good workforce foundation."

3Com, Bob Metcalfe's Ethernet company, was the standard-bearer of a new breed of ventures, which from the early 1980s emerged as a huge second wave of start-up businesses, company formation, venture-capital investment, and wealth creation, rivaling that of the PC and software industry that preceded and facilitated it. These companies created both hardware and software to meet the needs of local and long-range networking in business, manufacturing, design, architecture, engineering, and media. Novell, relaunched in 1983, was another. In 1983, it managed revenues of $3.8 million. In 1995, revenue of more than $2 billion made Novell the fourth-largest software company in the world.

Today, fifteen years since networking took off, 60 million Americans work in networked offices. That multibillion-dollar business has been generated and divided by 3Com, Novell, Sun Microsystems, and Cisco Systems (and many other competitors) in turn. Each company was created to address one particular piece of the networking puzzle, and oddly, the founders of each acknowledge that had they looked at the whole market more broadly, they might have precluded their successors from entering onto the stage. Each company tended to stick to its knitting, stay focused, and miss cashing in on the next wave—from Ethernet to the network operating system, to workstations to gateways and routers.

Novell Data Systems was a start-up that failed. The silhouette of its name can still be made out on the high brick wall of the building where it expired. In a grimy industrial neighborhood, close to a noisy and foul-smelling steelworks, it's easy to imagine the depression that set in as the company sold off the furniture. But this start-up was not destined to die. It would be rescued and refocused, thanks to a remarkable combination of luck and vision. It wasn't the U.S. Cavalry that came riding up over the hill at the eleventh hour, but the next best thing: Raymond J. Noorda, a veteran businessman, turnaround wizard, and venture capitalist.

Ray Noorda was called in by the investors in Novell Data Systems to see if he could rescue the company. It's said that for a few hundred thousand dollars he took it off their hands. Noorda grew up in a Dutch Mormon family in Ogden, Utah, during the Depression. He had a variety of arduous and unrewarding jobs as bartender, bowling-alley pinsetter, and railroad cargo hauler. The frugal habits imposed by that experience have lasted a lifetime, according to his staff and associates: he always flies coach, eschews limousines, and doesn't believe in raises—he always makes the staff take stock options to enhance their commitment to the company's growth and their shared success.

Noorda served in the navy in World War II, got an engineering degree from the University of Utah, and worked for General Electric for twenty years before going independent, as a company doctor. When he saw Novell, in 1982, the patient was in terminal condition. One of those present at the time—and still working there as chief scientist and vice president of advanced development—was Drew Major: "Noorda had a great knack for turning companies around, identified companies that had potential but had some business problems. He'd done it two or three times in the past. The day we walked into Novell Data Systems, which was the predecessor to Novell, we knew they were going to probably go under. His wife told me he kind of felt sorry for us. He saw us working really hard. Ray Noorda literally came at the eleventh hour and rescued us."

If Ray Noorda was to prove to be Novell's new battle commander, Drew Major was the secret weapon. According to Brian Sparks, a former colleague who ran a development group at Novell: "I think Drew Major is a man that lives right above the Silicon. I don't know anybody on the planet who lives so close to the Silicon but actually doesn't get involved in the Silicon. He knows the Intel chips as well as Intel does, and how to utilize them and grab all of the performance out of them."

At the time Noorda arrived, Drew Major and three ex–Brigham Young University colleagues, Kyle Powell, Dale Neibaur, and Mark Hurst (a consulting group known as SuperSet), had been working on a six-week contract for Novell Data Systems, to build a network of computers running the CP/M operating system of Digital Research. (CP/M stands for Control Program/Monitor, and the CPM-80 was an operating system designed for the Intel 8080 processor in the Altair era. Digital Research famously lost out to Microsoft when IBM went looking for an operating system for their PC.)

As Drew Major recalls, their jobs weren't at risk as Novell Data Systems fell apart, because they didn't have jobs. As contractors, they had dreamed up another project while they were there: "We knew that the industry was going to need file servers and they were going to need to share data. Though the company was falling apart, we just kept cranking on it because for example, if the company had gone bankrupt, we were contractors. We would have had at least some right to what we'd developed. So that kept us going, even though the company itself, business-wise, was in real trouble. Ray [Noorda] saw that enthusiasm. I think he got a glimpse of how big it was."

According to Willie Donahoo, a Novell executive from 1990 to 1998, Ray Noorda was the antithesis of the expansive Wall Street CEO whose caricature tended to define business in the eighties. "Ray was an older gentleman in an industry of young people. He brought wisdom and maturity but also a simple-mindedness in a very complex eighties. The eighties was 'Buy low, sell high' and 'Greed is good' and all this stuff, and Ray had simple principles— Plan, make, sell. Ship, cash, fast. His four-letter business plans. He also had the five E's rule: *Enthusiasm, excitement, exuberance, entrepreneurism.* But when you got *euphoric*, the next E was *extinction.*"

The gold dust that Ray spotted in this near-extinct company was four weeks of work on a software program called Netware. It was a "network operating system" aimed at the just-announced IBM Personal Computer.

In December 1982, the SuperSet quartet saw the first IBM PC in Utah, and concluded that it was going to succeed. Major saw this was the direction to focus on their networking idea: "IBM had done a lot of stuff right. And so we thought, 'Well, hey! We could network that.' And so we bought the first IBM PC in Utah. We were the first guys to network the IBM PC."

As Bob Metcalfe points out (and no one knows better than he): "Personal computers are not really built to be on networks. They're built to be personal. A network operating system is software that you add to the personal computer to put it on the network. Now, in the future, the notion of a network operating system will fade because all operating systems will be networked. But in 1982, a network operating system was the software that you added to retrofit the personal computer to put it on a network."

Novell's "Netware" concept was first demonstrated at a computer conference in Houston, Texas, in June 1983. By this time, Novell Data Systems was disappearing: that same year, Novell Incorporated rose from the ashes. Noorda's commitment was not just to the hard-working consultants and their product idea: it was to a wider vision of what networking would mean across the industry. According to Major: "Ray caught the vision of what networking really meant. The fact that you had networking meant that *all* the computers could be connected together. It meant that the different proprietary barriers of older systems were going to get broken down. He had this philosophy of 'coopetition' where we would work with our competitors because customers wanted that. If they connected two or three things on the same wire, they wanted it to talk. In the old world, the old way of doing things, they wouldn't."

This was indeed what networking meant, and had meant since the ARPAnet first inserted IMPs between incompatible hosts to create a compatible packet-switching network. Once again, compatibility is key to the advance of networking technology. But Ethernet had already achieved the physical interconnection of desktop computers: what did Netware add?

To understand, we need to undertake a brief, simplified technical digression. The core difference between Ethernet (developed for the Alto, but promptly launched to serve the IBM PC) is that it was primarily hardware providing "access" rather than "sharing." An Ethernet pipe connected to a PC allowed that PC to send e-mail messages, or any kind of data packets, to a central laser printer, or a hard-disk drive. It also allowed users to retrieve material stored on a common (expensive) disk drive. Incidentally, there were competitors to Ethernet, also developed in the 1970s.

Thus Ethernet allowed disk-sharing; but in Drew Major's view that was of limited value, segmenting a big hard-disk into the storage equivalent of separate users' floppy disks: "We said, 'Hey, that's stupid.' You'd really want to be sharing it. Instead of a disk server, splitting it up into a bunch of floppy disks, you want to make it into a file server and have everyone share the same files. We caught that there ought to be a file server instead of a disk server. In a time-share system, you take a big machine, you slice it up into a whole bunch of little pieces. What we wanted to do instead is take a whole bunch of little computers and combine them together in a system and have something equivalent."

Replicating a time-share system with multiple personal computers might seem like a step backwards; but it had another value that has more to do with office politics than technology itself, or so thinks Dave Walden, who helped create the ARPAnet from BBN: "Desktop computing caused local area networking to happen. This is where Ethernet came from. You had to hook these computers together. Now, the reason people wanted to hook those computers together, I believe, is that people in branch offices, people in departments wanted to escape the central control of their corporate computer center who was making them do things exactly this way."

Novell was not selling an alternative to the PC, or to Ethernet: their product (first ShareNet, then Netware) was software that ran on the PCs IBM made, connected by the Ethernet cards 3Com made, to create a network operating system, which suddenly every business that had bought multiple PCs wanted. (Every PC had its own internal operating system inside the box, supplied by Microsoft.)

As David Bradford describes it: "Netware provides the road map to allow a series of personal computers to talk to one another, and share files and share hard-disk storage. That's what a PC LAN operating system is. LAN stands for local area network. So the Netware operating system links all of that together and acts as a traffic cop. In one Netware operating system, you can link up to a thousand users and do so pretty efficiently."

3Com also sold a network operating system to run on top of Ethernet hardware. But Novell's product (and legendary marketing skills) gave them a running start in the network software sector. As Drew Major says: "We just built software that delivered the solution on top of these other components that other people were developing. This was the second wave after the PC wave. PCs added so much power and then we came in and made them work together as a group. Sharing the resources was just a very natural second wave."

The second wave made Novell into high-speed surfers. The company grew rapidly, and gained a high profile in both the software industry and the corporate world. Brian Sparks was one of those who worked 100-hour weeks helping Novell cope with success: "When I started at Novell, we were in the Ogden carpet building up in North Orem. There was a bunch of us in the bottom floor and there was another company upstairs, and it was chaos. Every month, we would rewire the whole company because we were adding people so fast that the network just became total chaos. And the testing process of Novell was, if it compiled you shipped it."

Since Novell's software needed other people's hardware (like Ethernet) to run, Ray Noorda realized that the more connections there were in the world, the more Novell Netware he would sell. So he came up with the idea of Novell's selling Ethernet (and another competing product, ARCnet) adapters, at a heavily discounted price, to "grow the market." This was a highly unusual practice, in that Noorda was selling the product of a competitor, for less, to the very people 3Com would otherwise have hoped to sell to at full price. Then Novell sold Netware to sit on top of the Ethernet hardware. Inevitably, the result was that Novell succeeded in reducing the cost of getting PCs connected, and increased the size of the market for their Netware.

This caused 3Com a most peculiar dilemma. At one time, Novell was their single biggest customer, at the same time as being a competitor to Bob Metcalfe's company: "Novell succeeded famously. 3Com fought them tooth and nail. At one point, we discovered that Novell was our largest customer. They were buying adapters and reselling them to their customers. We immediately, stupidly I think, shut them off. We called up Novell and said, 'We're not going to sell you adapters anymore,' which only added to our problems."

Drew Major was on the other side of the fence: "3Com thought we were their competitors. We were selling some of their adapters. We were like 25 percent of their business. And most of the people that were buying their adapters were running our software with it."

In the annals of missed opportunities, an encounter at Comdex between Bob Metcalfe and Ray Noorda has to rank highly. Instead of competing, the two companies could have cooperated from the start. But things didn't work out that way. 3Com had their own network operating system, sold with Ethernet since 1982, and Metcalfe wasn't interested in Noorda's coopetition. "Ray Noorda came into our booth at Comdex. 3Com, tiny little company. At Comdex, tiny little booth. In shuffles this guy, saying that he wanted us to use his network operating system. But we had a network operating system and it was selling like hotcakes, so I threw him out of the booth. Because you don't have a booth to talk to competitors. You have it to talk to customers. So I literally asked him to leave."

Drew Major recalls that when Noorda and his colleague, Kyle Powell, showed up, "Metcalfe was very anxious. He thought, first of all, that his disk-sharing was as good as file-sharing, and we were competitors. We thought he would get it, that this would sell more networking hardware."

Metcalfe's other concern was that if the two companies joined forces they would risk attracting an antitrust action from the government. That fear now seems misplaced, but it prevented Metcalfe from appropriating much of Novell's later success for 3Com: "There's been a lot of chuckling about this since. Noorda went on to sell a better operating system than we had, called Netware. Had we been on the ball, built a better operating system or licensed one from Mr. Noorda, there wouldn't *be* a Novell. But there *is* a Novell."

By networking the personal computer effectively, Novell clearly helped to increase demand for the PC—which also benefited Microsoft. As Major expresses it: "We sold a lot of MS-DOS. We helped Microsoft take the PC beyond just being a standalone personal productivity thing into a real genuine business tool. Because networking was so fundamental."

Bill Gates, whose Microsoft company developed MS-DOS as the operating system for the PC and its clones, doesn't disagree: "Starting in probably 1984, every year people are saying this is the year of the network. And that meant inside the business, that 100 percent of the PCs would be connected up. Novell became the high-volume provider of the file-sharing software in the late '80s and that helped grow the market, grow the distribution channels. So networking was a feature that we thought was very important in the operating system."

Despite the impact of networking on the PCs that businesses bought, there was relatively little effective competition for Novell's increasing dominance of the network operating system market in the 1980s, created by Drew Major and his SuperSet team: "The thing that's amazed me the most is other people, for a number of years, didn't get it. They were focusing on other things, the sexy things. This was plumbing. Who wants to write a file server, file systems? But it was very strategic and very fundamentally valuable for us."

As Larry Ellison, founder of the huge database company Oracle, points out, Novell had provided a timely and cost-effective solution to a real, if limited demand: "They had figured out the most cost-effective way to link a bunch of personal computers together. They had taken a very small part of the problem: to let you share files off disks, to attach all these computers in a network, to share printers and maybe send e-mail back and forth. That's pretty much it, and virtually everyone wanted to do that with their PC network. And they came to utterly dominate the PC network world. That red box, at their height, was as common as any logo I can think of. It was the equal, certainly the equal of Microsoft in those days."

Microsoft themselves were not (yet) a player in this field. But the business model of grabbing and building market share is one that Chairman Bill Gates recognizes readily: "In the computer market, when the first person comes along and does something very well, if they get over a certain threshold then it really develops momentum because the distribution channel doesn't want to learn a lot of products. Once you get a customer base, they start talking to you about 'Why don't you fix this, why don't you improve that?' We've seen many, many products like that in the history of personal computing. Some Microsoft products, some non-Microsoft products. Netware's a great example of that where it got good enough that the customers got interested and the refinement process took place."

In due course, Microsoft was bound to get involved in this market. At the time, in say 1984, Microsoft was a far smaller company, with almost no applications business and none of the omnipotent aura it enjoys, or suffers, today. One of the people who was recruited to Microsoft, and was thrown into the front line of the company's effort to get into the networking business was Rob Glaser.

Glaser was another computer-mad kid from New York, who was programming in the fourth grade. He went to Yale, where he switched from mathematics to a dual major in computer science and economics. At the age of twenty-one he started a computer games company with friends from Yale, and spent the summer of 1981 working at IBM, at the very moment of the launch of the IBM PC: "In the spring of 1983, Paul Allen and Steve Ballmer came to Yale to recruit. Microsoft was doing college recruiting even back then when the company was about 200 to 250 people. I met Paul on campus, and I guess Paul thought that some kid that started a software company while I was still in school must know a little bit about PCs. I didn't flunk the IQ test."

Glaser is today the founder and CEO of Progressive Networks, the Seattle company that makes Real Audio and Real Video Internet media products. He's been networking since fourth grade, one way or another. He was able to observe, from close at hand, the impact upon Microsoft and Bill Gates of Novell's unfettered rise to dominate the PC network market: "A thing that's always been true of Bill is whenever someone builds a big business—some people say that this is a bad thing, some people say it's a good thing, but it's clearly a thing—Bill looks at how does that business relate to the businesses we're in? If that's a good business, on a standalone basis, let's get into it, and certainly, if it's a good business, and it's adjacent or linked to our business, we had better get into it."

In the mid-1980s, Novell Netware was dominant. Their red box and logo were ubiquitous. Their stock price rose and rose. But staff pay did not rise in the same way. Ray Noorda is legendary for his policy on salary raises, as Brian Sparks recalls: "It came up once at a board meeting and Ray's mentality was, 'You know, we don't give raises. If you want more money, we'll give you more equity in the company. And you just grow your company.' That's his mentality and there was a fair amount of shared wealth there at Novell. There was a lot of people who had a lot of stock options and I was grateful to be one of them that did quite well riding the stock."

The value of the stock accurately reflected the growing success of Novell. As Rob Glaser recalls: "By 1985, Netware was reaching critical mass. Microsoft felt really like there was a huge missed opportunity. In fact, I remember some memos Bill wrote, in '84, '85, '86, where he said, 'One of the biggest disasters for the company is that we have no assets in networking, or very weak assets in networking.'"

As we shall see ten years later, the point at which Bill Gates writes memos to the troops is when things really start to happen. But throughout the eighties, no one could catch Novell. Drew Major's timing proved to be impeccable, and the fire sale was soon forgotten: "Novell Netware was a gigantic accident. We happened to be at the right place at the right time, and had the experience of knowing that just disk-sharing wasn't enough. We caught the vision that network and sharing resources was going to be very fundamentally valuable to the industry. We just tried to ride it from then on. You just had to grab it. You just had to build it. Fortunately, we saw that vision a few years before anyone else did, and then we also decided not to quit. We kept going and that was good. Because Microsoft was always coming."

This was the beginning of Microsoft's major effort to acquire market share for LAN software. Ironically, Microsoft would prove to be handicapped by their greatest asset: the relationship with IBM.

Although Novell, 3Com, and other companies were forging an entirely new business in networking the PC and compatible machines for business, the original networking trend begun by ARPA had meanwhile spun off a variety of new, larger, faster networks in universities, corporations, and research institutions. The number of nodes on the ARPAnet doubled in two years from 213 in September 1981 to 562 in September 1983; doubled again in one year to 1,024 by October 1984; and doubled again, to over 2000, by the end of 1985. Growth and use was accelerating everywhere.

Ever since the beginnings of ARPAnet, other institutions, both private and public, had been building networks for research or communications purposes. The more there were, the more it made sense to hook more people in. As we have learned, overcoming incompatibility with the Internet protocol TCP/IP made all the difference in enabling the interconnection of different networks.

A wider range of scientific and research interests became connected: networking of the research community was no longer confined to computer scientists. As Len Kleinrock of UCLA observes: "Now we had physicists, meteorologists, geologists, oceanographers. Once research opened up, then other research labs could join, like IBM research labs, and AT&T research, and Xerox PARC, and Honeywell research. These research labs were affiliated with commercial companies. And so they had their foot in the door and began to experience what it meant to be on this network."

The government origins of the ARPAnet were also replicated,

starting around 1980, as the ARPAnet became more visible to the wider academic research community. Other agencies began to sponsor networks, including NASA, the Department of Energy, and most particularly the National Science Foundation (NSF). In the 1980s, the NSF had created supercomputer centers around the country, and in order to provide connectivity among the supercomputers, a new network backbone, a kind of Super-ARPAnet, was funded and built by the NSF.

The NSF Net had its own origins in the ARPAnet. In 1982–83, at the University of Maryland, a proposal was drafted to connect its computers with those of other universities and with other organizations that could help the universities and the commercial world connect together. Glen Ricart, now a Novell executive, was at Maryland, and was instrumental in planning this new network: "The important thing was we wanted to connect together a diversity of these different computers. How could we do that? The main protocol we could find that was available on all these computers was implemented by the ARPAnet. So we adopted the ARPAnet protocols and decided that we could try to band together all the computers at major universities and research centers in the Southeast using these ARPAnet protocols. That became SURANet, the first network that was a part of the Internet apart from the ARPAnet."

When the University of Maryland approached the NSF for funding, it is said the NSF had never heard of networking. In response to the SURAnet proposal, the NSF created a new Division of Networking and Computing Research Infrastructure, and many more regional networks were established: an alphabet soup of acronymous and punning names proliferated. The SURAnet example will suffice to demonstrate how inexorably networking was tying together the different computer-using communities. As Ricart describes events: "About a year or year-and-a-half in, we connected the first commercial [entity] that hadn't been part of the ARPAnet. That was IBM in Raleigh-Durham, North Carolina. We were already connecting the three universities in that triangle research area so it made sense to connect them. Then we were faced with an additional question. Should we bring on additional commercial organizations or leave them to be a separate network?"

The lesson of networking's decade-long history was already

clear: one network is better than several. So SURAnet embraced commercial partners—even though Ricart's expectation was that "eventually the university community would lose control of that Internet network because eventually the commercial organizations would vastly outnumber us."

Len Kleinrock, on the other side of the country at UCLA, saw the expansion to the commercial world as an endorsement of networking itself: "So it became easy for certain kinds of commercial activity to take place. E-mail was now reaching beyond the research community and organizations to managers, to the chief technology officer, to people who were building product. And so the commercial world began to get some interest and realization this is a very interesting thing to do."

In due course, the NSF Net would swallow the ARPAnet. Starting more than ten years later, it had the advantage of faster technology, wider pipes, hugely more memory. The original ARPA IMPs were ultimately retired in 1989.

While figuring out the SURAnet at the University of Maryland, Ricart and his colleagues also polished off another piece of the puzzle. At the time, the IBM PC had just been launched: "We found that although we had implementations from the Department of Defense [ARPA] for the big computers, for the DEC computers, for the IBM computers, there was no implementation for the personal computer. So we took it upon ourselves at the University of Maryland to create the first implementation of the Internet protocols for the IBM personal computer."

We have already learned that the next ground-breaking personal computer, the Apple Macintosh, owes much of its design and performance to some Picassoesque thievery from Xerox PARC. Although 3Com and Novell *turned* the IBM PC into a networked computer, Apple *built* the Macintosh as a networked computer. This was no accident. Another of the hires Steve Jobs made from Xerox PARC, to be head of engineering on the Macintosh project, was Bob Bellville. He had worked for Bob Metcalfe, who is proud to claim indirect paternity: "Lo and behold, out comes the Macintosh with—if you step way back from it—a very cheap version of the Ethernet. He used off-the-shelf chips to achieve this local inter-network. One of the beauties of the Macintosh has always been that the local area network, a descendant of Ethernet through Bob Bellville, was built in. Frankly, the notion of building LANs into computers should have been adopted much earlier."

The inclusion in the design of "AppleShare" and "AppleTalk" was intended to have the Macintosh leap over the functionality standard of the IBM, providing multiple users with the ability to share each other's files, and storage, and—perhaps most important—the laser printer.

In one of his most notorious and visionary moves, Steve Jobs had Apple invest $2.5 million in Adobe, the print software company that emerged from Xerox PARC. He persuaded John Warnock to write the PostScript software (the interface between computer and printer) and let Apple build the laser printer (the Apple Laser Writer)—all of which would deliver laser-quality printing of WYSIWYG desktop-publishing. In fact, the only way it made any sense to sell a $6,000 or $7,000 printer with a $2,000 computer, was if multiple computer users could share. But it worked, and at one time in the mid-1980s, Apple Computer was the world's largest manufacturer of laser printers.

The early 1980s saw a quantum leap in the utility of computing devices and computing activities. Networking across mainframes was interesting, but hardly easy. The Alto was a wonderful, but unsaleable product. In the 1980s, the IBM PC legitimized personal computers, networking software made them much more useful, and the Macintosh had an inspirational quality ("insanely great") that lifted the whole field another notch or two in public acceptance and operational value.

Steve Jobs likes to recall the article he read, as a child, in *Scientific American*. This compared the efficiency of locomotion for various species, according to how many kilocalories per kilometer they consumed. In this study, of bears, birds, human beings, and other animals, the condor was the most efficient. People appeared well down the list. But, as Steve Jobs remembers: "Somebody there had the brilliance to test a human riding a bicycle. It blew away the condor, all the way off the charts. I remember this really had an impact on me. Humans are tool-builders, and we build tools that can dramatically amplify our innate human abilities. We actually ran an ad like this very early at Apple, that the personal computer was 'the bicycle of the mind.' I believe that with every bone in my body—that of all the inventions of humans, the computer is going to rank near, if not at, the top as history unfolds and we look back. And it is the most awesome tool that we have ever invented."

Chapter Ten
Earthquakes and Vulcans

THERE IS NOTHING QUITE LIKE THE intensity of the true nerd: the ability to exclude all external influences, work hundreds of hours apparently without sleep, and memorize mathematical formulae or pages of code. In the 1980s, while Novell had shifted the center of gravity in the networking business away from Silicon Valley, the researchers and entrepreneurs of California were far from idle. In the space of about a year, two huge new enterprises were established out of the very same building at Stanford University, by people with all the intellectual firepower and unworldliness of the authentic nerd.

One of these ventures was to become Sun Microsystems: a company that intended, in the words of founder Scott McNealy, to "shoot for the moon." But the fireworks really began when the two engineering wizards, Andy Bechtolsheim and Bill Joy, first met: "The first time they met, they did a Vulcan mind meld. One of these things where they weren't even talking. They were just holding each other's forehead. You could just see that stuff was happening. You couldn't get too near them because of the sparks and the smoke and the flame and all the rest of it."

The second was Cisco Systems, and the people who established Cisco, in a nutshell, solved Stanford's networking incompatibility problems with an updated 1983-vintage IMP, which they called a *router*. The powers of concentration required to figure out, build, market, and refine this technology were amply illustrated in 1989. Company founders Len Bosack and Sandy Lerner were recording a video tutorial when the walls (and the video camera) began to shake, and both threw themselves to the floor. "Well, that was very interesting," says Len as the tape continues. "That wasn't the Wellfleet marketing department (a competing router company) bombing the Cisco premises, that was a genuine San Francisco earthquake, looks like over Richter 5. But we're back."

Then they resumed the talk. It shows just how single-minded computer-scientist entrepreneurs can be. Not even an earthquake could divert their attention from the glorious business of routers, bridges, and building a $60 billion company.

While Novell might have the advantage of the Mormon work ethic, Sun, Cisco, and others around the Stanford campus had the benefit of operating in a hothouse atmosphere of constant problem-solving, innovation, and regular infusions of research grants and venture capital to provide an incentive. It had been this way for a couple of generations. Stanford Research Institute had the second node on the ARPAnet, and the university got one of the next dozen. One of the most successful companies in Silicon Valley history was born right there. Stanford's active encouragement of start-up companies, since Fred Terman's fostering of Bill Hewlett and David Packard in the 1930s, enabled students and employees of Stanford to develop and exploit ideas they had developed in research labs on campus. Where Hewlett-Packard led, literally hundreds of later companies have followed, commercializing the intellectual property developed at Stanford University.

Sun Microsystems was another classic Stanford start-up, in which three Stanford graduates (and an outsider, Bill Joy from across the Bay at Berkeley) brought different skills to found a computer workstation company to embody their slogan "The Network Is The Computer." The Sun workstation has become an $8 billion a year business.

When the personal computer was little more than a high-powered typewriter, workstations offered the processing power to meet the needs of Wall Street, NASA, and even Hollywood. It was a product that embodied perfect timing. In 1982, when Sun was launched, it was too late to start competing for market share in personal computers, but it was early enough to build on the value of networking and open standards—which had been demonstrated most clearly by the Alto's Ethernet network. The Sun workstation began as a solution to a problem in the Stanford computer science department, with the expensive, unprogrammable Alto as a role model. Sun founder Andy Bechtolsheim wanted to create something that would massively outperform the toylike PCs: "We had this crazy idea that if we build a 32-bit microcomputer with a big screen display and the Ethernet connection running the UNIX operating system, we would have the perfect product for, you know, the researchers and the scientists and the students at Stanford. And sure enough, once we started the company, we had the perfect product for the researchers and the scientists and the engineers."

The personal computer was not the perfect product for heavyduty, memory-intensive operations that serious researchers needed. While the PC of the time was a 16-bit machine, Andy's was 32-bit. While PCs did not have virtual memory (a way of using more memory than the machine physically has), Andy's had virtual memory. And the PC of 1982 did not have an Ethernet connection (though it could be added on) while Andy's machine had Ethernet built in. The workstation had muscle, and was designed to be networked from the beginning.

Andreas Bechtolsheim came to Stanford from Germany: "I was actually quite frustrated with the German university program at the time because I truly felt I was wasting my time. So the first thing, when I went to a German university in the middle 1970s, was I applied to come here. It was very boring. Simple things like we had to sign up for terminals to use a computer and then you could only get one hour of terminal time per week. I mean, how could you even learn programming in this way?"

Until Vinod Khosla arrived, Andy had no intention of starting a business with his workstation—he had a Ph.D. to finish. But the persuasive Vinod—a Stanford MBA who had already started one successful company, Daisy Systems—was determined to pursue his Silicon Valley dreams: "Ever since I was sixteen going to high school in India, I dreamed of coming to Silicon Valley to start a company. I was a technology geek. And it was very much a dream of mine to start a company. In fact, in 1976 when I graduated from engineering school in India, I tried to start a technology company in India, which was a hopeless task."

Because he was a penniless graduate student, Andy Bechtolsheim had, in designing the workstation, used standard parts like the Motorola 68000 processor, the Intel multi-bus, and standard software like the UNIX operating system. From the fourth floor of Margaret Jacks Hall, Andy Bechtolsheim built a modest licensing business for his workstation. Anyone who wanted to license his design could do so, and he anticipated that soon someone would build the workstation commercially: "I had licensed about seven or eight companies, prior to Sun starting. The problem was they didn't see the opportunity in the workstation space. I tried to explain it to them, but they just didn't do it. They all could have done Sun, but none of them did."

Vinod Khosla did not want to buy a license. He wanted to buy Andy: "Andy was developing the Sun technology at Stanford. He had complete rights to it. He said he didn't want to start a company but he would license all of the Sun technology to me for $10,000. I said, 'I don't want to do that.' He said he didn't want to quit his Ph.D. and he said he had already licensed it to about five other players. And I said, 'I want the goose that lays the golden egg. I don't want the golden egg.'"

Vinod made Andy an offer that was too good to refuse—half of his share in the proposed company. The next person Vinod Khosla recruited was his best friend and former roommate, Scott McNealy. Another Stanford MBA, with a background in the automobile business—and a fanatical Detroit Red Wings fan—McNealy already had a job at a company called Onyx Computer. Over a power McLunch at McDonalds, Khosla persuaded McNealy that they could do something big. "We used to say we own a great rocket ship but it doesn't matter how high it goes if it doesn't reach orbital velocity. If we're going to fail, we'll be a big splash. We'll go high and shoot for the moon and be the biggest belly flop ever, but our goal is truly to get in orbit."

McNealy caught the enthusiasm, and has been cheerleading for Sun ever since: "We said there were not going to be any small computer companies, in the same way there are no small car companies. We said scale matters. We're going to grow big, grow fast, grow like crazy and if we're going to do a belly flop, we want to empty the pool out. That was our strategy: Go big, early."

By odd coincidence, Bechtolsheim at the time had turned down an offer to join Microsoft. The person who tried to recruit him, Steve Ballmer, had known Scott McNealy since they were in high school together in Detroit.

Among the three founders, there were two MBAs and a nearly Ph.D. hardware specialist. They needed a software guru to add to the team, and the best candidate was an obvious choice. The core concept of the Sun workstation was its network capability; what provided this was the operating system Andy had chosen, Berkeley UNIX, developed at U.C. Berkeley and licensed to anyone for about one hundred dollars. UNIX had been originally developed at Bell Laboratories for use on minicomputers, and is more "portable" (less machine-specific) than other operating systems. Berkeley UNIX, most importantly, included the Internet protocols that would enable the Sun workstation to be truly connected. The legendary programmer who had written the Berkeley UNIX was Bill Joy, often referred to (by people who should know) as "the best computer scientist of his generation." So he was the man that Andy, Scott, and Vinod went across the Bay Bridge to recruit, all crammed into a VW Beetle. "They showed up in my office, and I thought they didn't look old enough to be in charge of anything so I kept them waiting till the rest of the people showed up."

Bill Joy had some experience with ARPA-funded research, when Berkeley had received funding to "put inter-networking in a portable system." The virtues of the network were thus already clear to him. In addition, he was unimpressed by the lack of power available in the PCs of the time: "My background was in scientific computing, so I was more interested in making bigger computers, in doing interactive graphics, these 'Star Trek' machines, not in spreadsheets and word processors. I didn't really get interested in that."

According to Eric Schmidt, who worked alongside Bill Joy at Berkeley, spent fourteen years at Sun, and in 1997 became chairman and CEO of Novell, Joy's capacity to write and evaluate computer code is prodigious: "At Berkeley, Bill would simply take the UNIX system, and rewrite it over the weekend. No human on the planet could do this except for Bill. And you'd come in in the following week and say, 'What has Bill changed now?' Every once in a while, he'd decide to do a new release and he would personally rewrite all of the code in the system including all the applications. Inconceivable today and amazing at the time."

Bob Kahn, who with Vint Cerf published the TCP/IP protocol that allowed the ARPAnet to expand and grow into the Internet, attributes great importance to Bill Joy's decision to incorporate the Internet protocol into Berkeley UNIX: "The mechanism by which the Internet really came to be was, I think, through the work that Bill Joy had done, by embedding TCP/IP into the

Berkeley UNIX system, which was widely used in the research community. People got it for free without having to figure out how to roll their own, so to speak."

Furthermore, the decision to use Berkeley UNIX in the Sun system meant that for the first time the Internet protocol would become available and widespread through the commercial world, rather than merely the academic research community. As Bob Kahn explains: "It happened on a major scale because here was now a major computer company, Sun Microsystems, that essentially made this part of their normal product service offerings. You could buy it from commercial folks."

It took several months for the trio to persuade Bill Joy to make Sun a quartet. According to Vinod Khosla, what convinced Bill Joy was the opportunity to work with Andy Bechtolsheim. Joy shared Andy's desire to create a workstation capable of serious engineering, design, and communications applications: "I was very frustrated in 1982 that there was better graphics on video games than was available to scientists, and I felt that we needed good computers for scientists. Some of the problems that we'd created with growth could only be solved with an intelligent investment after understanding how things worked with simulation and visualization."

Whether it was going to be a "Star Trek" computer or not, this was the Vulcan mind-meld of Andy and Bill's hardware and software objectives, which underpinned the design and execution of the Sun workstation. Now it was time to create the company. Though Vinod Khosla had done a start-up before, he offered McNealy to pick his role: "He said, 'What job do you want?' And I go, 'I don't know. I don't know anything about this stuff.' And he said, 'Well, why don't you be CEO?' And I said, 'No, no. I don't know anything about it. You be it.' So we had an argument and he finally agreed to be CEO."

So far this was a start-up out of a textbook. It had a technology entirely based on open standards. It had a three-page business plan. Now this quartet from America's melting pot had to cross another hurdle—financial backing for their idea. The founders, all twenty-seven years old, went looking for money. They found it almost immediately, first from Robert Sackman, a general partner at U.S. Venture Partners, who provided an initial $300,000.

Another investor who was in the right place at this time was John Doerr, of the venture-capital firm Kleiner, Perkins, Caufield & Byers, whose investing insights have always been combined with an impeccable capacity for being in the right place at the right time: "I was a wise thirty-year-old venture capitalist and there were these four twenty-seven-year-old kids, and none of us knew what we were doing. We all thought that UNIX was a big idea and that building a computer out of standard parts was the way it ought to be done. I'll never forget first seeing Andy Bechtolsheim in Margaret Jacks Hall at Stanford when he had developed the first Sun motherboard. The team said, 'Well, we need some money and some help,' and I'd been hanging around with them so they asked us to invest."

Andy Bechtolsheim recalls that the initial trio (*sans* Joy) got together in late January 1982: "We wrote a five-page business plan. A week or two later, we showed it to some venture people. They said, 'Oh, this is great. Here's a check for you.' Basically we showed them the plan on Thursday, Friday. On Tuesday, we had a check in the hand and we started the company."

Bill Joy remembers the moment the company began its existence: "We got our first load of furniture for the new office and got asset tags for it, and we put a tag on a chair and took a picture of Andy holding all the motherboards in a box on his lap, so that was the first picture at Sun Microsystems, of employee #1 sitting in asset #1, with all the intellectual property of the company in the box."

Sadly, no one can now find the picture they snapped that day.

As the ARPAnet had demonstrated with mainframes and minis, and as Ethernet tried to replicate with PCs, a network of computers allows efficiencies, cost savings, convenience, and computing power. Vinod Khosla explains that the concept was first facilitated by Ethernet: "You could share the disk drives, which were thousands of dollars, and not share the microprocessors, which were getting very, very cheap. The magic was Bob Metcalfe had invented Ethernet that let you separate those two physically. So we put the memory and the CPU [central processing unit, i.e., the hardware] and the display [the monitor] on people's desks and put the disk drives [the storage], etc. in the back end. Now the notion of a computer was spread over a network."

Sun targeted a new market sector—more expensive than PCs, less costly than minicomputers—with the networking gospel. McNealy says the slogan and the strategy are one: "The whole concept of 'The network is the computer' we started at Sun based on the fact that every computer should be hooked to every other computing device on the planet. And that's been our strategy and our goal from day one."

At some stage in the early life of Sun, Bob Metcalfe of 3Com, and his partners, Bill Crouse and Howard Charney, had the opportunity to put their belief in "focus" to the test. Metcalfe, we recall, had learned that "lack of focus" was one of the three ways start-ups most often fail. "We had focus on the brain. When Bechtolsheim came and said, 'There's this Sun workstation, and here's 3Com with a factory, why don't you build it, build workstations?' And we, by the way, were specializing in UNIX and Ethernet at the time, and TCP/IP. Andy said, 'You should really make this workstation.' We said, 'Focus.' So we promised Andy that we would sell him Ethernet cards for his workstations, and we did. Of course, we then began to notice how many cards they were buying and what an opportunity we had passed up."

Sun was not the inventor of networked computing. Scott McNealy gives credit for that to a Boston company founded in 1980, Apollo, which also adopted many lessons from Xerox PARC. But unlike the Apollo, which was a proprietary system, the Sun workstation was based on open standards. Because Andy had used off-the-shelf hardware and software for his workstation, Sun made a virtue of necessity. It made them different from companies like Apollo, or Apple, or Microsoft, as Scott McNealy pointedly observes: "We had openness. In other words, nobody should own the written and spoken language of computing. In the same way, nobody owns English, French, or German. Now, Microsoft might disagree and think that they ought to own the written and spoken language of computing and charge us all a $250 right-to-use license to speak English or Windows or whatever they happen to own."

Sun Microsystems, based in "rent-by-the-hour" office space in Santa Clara, was profitable from its first quarter. This was no surprise to Andy Bechtolsheim, who had designed the workstation to meet the requirements and preferences of engineers all over the country. He had done all his market research, via the Internet, and received hundreds or thousands of e-mail messages indicating what the workstation should be able to do. He and Bill Joy gave the customers what they wanted. McNealy recalls their initial collaboration: "Bill Joy was extroverted, very, very outgoing and very seventy-thousand-foot level. Didn't do a lot of prototyping. Wrote some code. But mainly it was helping on the strategy side and very software oriented. Andy Bechtolsheim was in the lab. Totally focused on building prototype after prototype after prototype—he would crank the products out and Bill would make sure of the strategy direction."

From 1982, the first year of business, every Sun employee had e-mail. Networked communications, by computer, was the way of life at Sun. But the company's name was not always Sun. The business plan was originally entitled "VLSI Systems." It became Sun for two reasons: one, to poke fun at Apollo, the then-leader in workstations; and two, as an acronym for Stanford University Network, where Andy's prototype workstations were running a real network already. The fact that Sun Microsystems is not a wholly owned subsidiary of Stanford may seem surprising. The explanation is a mixture of enlightened policy, and perhaps, missed opportunity.

Most networking advances have in fact been funded by federal government grants and developed in university research centers, yet it's the individual scientist-entrepreneurs who have exploited the research commercially and reaped the financial rewards. Stanford especially has encouraged this trend. It is not a commercial, manufacturing enterprise; and there is a well-founded belief that fostering successful business efforts of alumni will ultimately benefit the school in the form of endowments, donations, and intellectual cross-fertilization. In any case, as Vinod Khosla recalls, "Stanford never owned a piece of Sun. They did not want any piece of it. In fact, the funny story is Prime Computer and Digital Equipment both looked at the technology, evaluated it, and said they didn't want it. On that basis, I think Stanford decided it wasn't of much value and they let Andy own it."

Indeed, the pre-launch development of the Sun technology was a major advantage in the effort to shoot for the moon. Andy contrasts the Sun experience with that of truly independent start-ups: "It was a very unusual setting because we had the product pretty much developed at Stanford and at Berkeley, in terms of the software and the hardware, and we simply launched it to the market. Most of the companies that start from scratch have one or two development cycles, and while you're doing that your market can change. Whereas, our whole mission, you know, was defined from day one in terms of what we had."

Scott McNealy sees Stanford's hands-off attitude as being both sophisticated *and* ultimately beneficial to the university. "Stanford and Berkeley had a very enlightened technology perspective, and still do. That is, the student developed it, they could take the intellectual property. So Andy, when he created the Stanford University Network under government grants as well as help from Stanford, was allowed to walk out with the intellectual property, and start a company with that. Many companies have been able to spin out of the university environment. It's helped Stanford a lot, because obviously we give a lot back. We certainly paid back Stanford with huge amounts of donations. So you know, I think there's been a really synergistic relationship."

Sun's timing was perfect. Between the modest PC and the expensive minicomputer there was a market niche, and Sun offered a low-cost, high-end computer that used the collective processing power of a network to tackle heavy-duty tasks in architecture, engineering, air-traffic control, movie special effects, and especially financial data. "The network is the computer" provided a solution for another growing need. This was the 1980s, and Wall Street was crunching numbers faster than ever for junk bond issues, arbitrage deals, and other financial smoke and mirrors. Sun workstations filled the trading rooms of banks, brokerages, and perhaps minimum-security prisons. As Andy says, "The thing with Wall Street is it's extremely competitive. In other words, if somebody can compute something or figure something out faster than the guy next door, it doesn't matter what the equipment costs—that's what they want. So each trader wanted the faster, highest-powered workstation right at their tables so they could do better trading. And Sun eventually became the dominant standard on Wall Street for trading workstations. Not just on Wall Street, actually. Worldwide."

Sun did attain what founder Vinod Khosla called "orbital veloc-ity." They became the second-fastest computer company ever to reach $1 billion in annual sales (in 1988), and maintained the ARPA/Stanford practice of juggling Indian clubs, while also gener-ating a renowned tradition for truly spectacular April Fool's pranks. In 1986, Eric Schmidt found an entire Volkswagen Bug, dismantled and reassembled, in his office. (He still has the driver's door, as a souvenir.) In 1987, Bill Joy's Ferrari was winched onto a platform constructed inches below the surface of a campus pond. He paddled out to the car in a rubber dinghy, and called for help from his car phone. In 1991, the pranksters transported the entire office of a scuba-diving executive, Wayne Rosing, to a fish tank at the San Francisco Aquarium. And in 1988, Scott McNealy discov-ered that his office, and his neighbor's, had been converted into a miniaturized golf course, with tee, green, pond, and sandtraps.

The jollity could not deflect Vinod Khosla from his original ambition: to retire at thirty, build a Frank Lloyd Wright house, and raise nine children. He did the first, has yet to do the sec-ond, and stopped at four offspring, before acquiring a small reg-iment of dogs: "I left an operating role late 1984, early 1985. I left the board in 1987. When I left Sun, I had no plans of ever working again. My plans were to do some things I really wanted to do. Top of my list was running the ten hardest rafting rivers in the world."

Despite these plans, Vinod Khosla was drafted into the start-up world in another capacity: as venture capitalist. He is a partner at Kleiner, Perkins, Caufield & Byers, where John Doerr, one of Sun's first investors, enjoys the reputation as Silicon Valley's sharpest VC. Venture capitalists, almost invariably, are indispensable to the initiation and growth of the average start-up. A company can be started (as we are about to learn) on dedication and credit cards, but the ramping-up of manufacturing, sales, and market-ing, and then grabbing a share of the market require one thing above all: money.

John Doerr controls a lot of money on behalf of Kleiner, Perkins, and he has distilled his experience of mostly successful investments and a few failures into simple rules. Doerr is a man who likes to make lists. Lists of risks, lists for success:

Caesar said all of Gaul was divided into three parts. All of risk is divided into four parts. The first is people risk; that is, how the team is going to work together, because, invariably, one of the founders doesn't work out and falls out, which is why you want their options or equity to vest. The second risk is market risk and that's an incredibly expensive risk to remove. That's about whether or not the dogs are going to eat the dog food. Is there a market for this product? And by the time you get the product to market, you may have expenses of a million dollars a month. You don't want to be wrong about market risk. The third risk that we're quite willing to take on is technical risk. That's about whether or not we can make a pen computer that works or be the first to commercialize a Web browser or to split the atom, if you will. That technical risk is one we're comfortable trying to eliminate and take on. The fourth and final risk is financial risk. If you have all of the preceding three right, can you then get to the capital that you need to go grow the business? And typically you can. There's plenty of capital to finance rapidly growing new technologies that are addressing large markets.

The four parts of risk are accompanied by the five factors for success, in Doerr's taxonomy:

Technical excellence, whether or not there's a technical genius inside that company. An attitude that we're going to be the very, very best. The second is outstanding management. Usually a venture doesn't possess that at the start. You've got to add it over time. The third key success factor is strategic focus on a rapidly growing, very large new market. And there's no better advantage to have than being first or second in a large new market. The fourth success factor for a new venture is a reasonable financing strategy. I've seen ventures raise too much money as well as too little. The fifth factor, what really sets the best companies apart and you can sense it when you walk in the door, is this sense of urgency; that time is the most precious advantage a new venture has.

It's a Valley tradition to start new ventures in garages. But the biggest networking company of all, Cisco Systems, was founded in 1983 in the living room of the house where Stanford academics Len Bosack and Sandy Lerner used to live. The technological foundations were laid in the basement of the same Stanford building, Margaret Jacks Hall, where Sun sprang to life. Andy Bechtolsheim witnessed the beginnings of Cisco: "Len was really in charge of networking and running the computer operations, so part of his job was to hook up all of these computers with these networks. He started with the problem that he had to solve right here. Running the wire, getting interfaces in machines, getting the protocols to work. And that's how Cisco started."

Len Bosack was director of Stanford's computer science department. He has degrees in electrical engineering from the University of Pennsylvania and a Masters in computer science from Stanford. His wife, Sandy Lerner, was director of computer facilities for Stanford Graduate School of Business. She has degrees in econometrics from Claremont Graduate School, and Masters in statistics and computer science (which she refers to as "sadistics and confusing science") from Stanford.

Legend has it that as they worked in different departments, they were unable to send e-mail messages to each other, so they invented the router. The reality is more complicated. But the company they created in 1983, Cisco Systems, has a market valuation of tens of billions of dollars, and created great wealth for the founders. Their story is an entrepreneurial saga that began largely by accident and ended in a drama that many founders, from Steve Jobs to Bob Metcalfe, have experienced to their cost.

In the late 1970s, Sandy Lerner was one of very few women who spent time at the LOTSS building—the Low Overhead Time Sharing System—where computer-science nerds gathered to get access to computer facilities. Sandy's recollection is of a somewhat unappetizing sample of the male gender, those who eat three meals a day from vending machines and those who are strangers to the laundromat: "When I got to Stanford, I found out that there were ways in which male nerds did compete in front of the female nerd cohort, which most of the time was me. One of which was to flame each other out with ridiculously hot Chinese food. They would be sitting there with perspiration pouring down their foreheads, saying how great all of this stuff was. Well, they couldn't really speak. So that was my first introduction to the nerd testosterone games."

Yet Sandy is a self-confessed female nerd, and proud of it: "*Nerd* to me is a very complimentary term. It's just someone who cares enough about something to study it very thoroughly and really apply themselves. There are dirt nerds (geophysicists) and music nerds and horse nerds and electronic nerds."

Her nerd credentials are genuine: "I remember there being moments of ecstasy when something would run, the compiler would actually do what you asked it to, and those were moments of great joy. Once you got a terminal, you stayed on it for like ten or twelve hours. I think my longest non-stop terminal session covered three days."

Len Bosack was running the department of computer science's computer facilities during this time. And he struck Sandy as being unusually clean: "I'll just have to tell you something that's so bizarre you'll just have to assume that it's true. Len's mother had done this miraculous job and Len actually knew how to bathe and eat with silverware, and I was absolutely enchanted. If you've been around LOTSS, you understand that statement. He used to take Wisk and wash his collars and cuffs, which was way more than I ever did and I just didn't think that a more perfect man could exist."

Len was not only the perfect nerd, he was also a brilliant network technologist, who arrived at Stanford after a spell at Digital Equipment, helping to design the PDP-10 memory management architecture.

Ralph Gorin was the manager of LOTSS, and recalls that computers and terminals were scattered all over the campus; and students would say, "Well, I have to do my homework here, but I do my research there, and I can't get them to talk to each other."

Sandy Lerner remembers that the crying need was "to promote electronic transfer of course work. Certainly, there was a secondary agenda, which was the ARPAnet tradition of shared research communication. The big thing we were really trying to do was to make it easy for the kids to get their homework in and the teachers to look at it."

The Cisco Systems Employee Handbook explains that in the

late 1970s, Stanford was desperate for hacker graduate students to make its computers work. The Stanford University network, where Andy Bechtolsheim's workstations were running, was a research effort among multiple departments of Stanford and two nearby neighbors, Xerox PARC and Hewlett-Packard Laboratories. As the handbook states, "Microcomputers, minicomputers and terminals/mainframes were gaining ground, but there were no large integrated network systems."

By 1980, this local area network covered about fifteen square miles, and included about 5000 computers of various types. Those computers were linked in building-size networks by Ethernet. But there was no campus-wide network. They were like islands. What was needed were causeways, or bridges, to connect them together—which Len Bosack devised: "We first built some bridges, and then we built some crude routers, and then we built better routers. We solved the problem of how to get terminal access to all of the computers on campus by producing things that we called ether TIPs. And that solved, for Stanford, the same sort of problem that it solved ten years earlier for ARPA of how to use a computer anywhere you want it."

At this time, the Xerox Corporation had made a grant to Stanford of Alto computers and Ethernet network devices. There was also a machine known as the Dover, which was the forerunner of all laser printers. Ralph Gorin had access to the grant equipment: "With considerable effort and initiative on our own part, we started solving the problem. We went and invented—I guess that's the proper word for it—the interface by which we could connect the DEC System 20s to the network. And we started snaking little wires here and there throughout the campus."

Stanford had meanwhile been building an ambitious broadband network, which according to Sandy Lerner largely failed to function, after three years' work and millions of dollars. In the meantime, Sandy, Len and others were hacking together a network of their own, as Sandy Lerner recalls: "Len and I and Ralph Gorin from the student computer center, and Kirk Lougheed from electrical engineering had put together this extralegal network that basically connected the DEC-20 sites on campus. We basically pulled wire through manholes. We pulled wire through disused sewer pipe. We built a lot of things by ourselves. I mean, it was very, very much, at that point, a guerrilla action. We had no money and we certainly didn't have any official sanction." Len Bosack calls it "do-it-yourself networking. If you wanted it, you had better do it yourself because no one else was going to do it for you. You couldn't buy it."

But as Sandy Lerner points out, the guerrilla network did work: "At the end of three years, it was pretty embarrassing to the Stanford University Network, SUN, that everybody was on this bootleg Ethernet thing, including the business school. And anybody else that had a 36-bit machine on campus. And so—poof! One day *it* became the Stanford University Network."

As the Cisco Employee Handbook reports, Cisco's goal, from the very beginning, was "to link widely diverse computers & technologies... The Cisco router prototype was built to connect the LANs into a multi-protocol, campus-wide internet, which grew to include over 100 Ethernets (computers on a single coaxial cable) and thousands of terminals, PCs, workstations and mainframe systems."

Networking history was repeating itself. As Bosack pointed out, the router solved the problem of the ARPAnet all over again; indeed the router was largely an updated IMP. The need for the router existed because networking was half-done in many places And as soon as word got out, largely by e-mail around the ARPAnet, that Stanford's SUNet had fixed this problem, computer scientists and managers from other universities were clamoring to buy or license the technology. The router was a potential business, just like the Sun workstation. But whose business was it to be? Stanford's Office of Technology Licensing (OTL) had allowed Andy Bechtolsheim to leave with his "intellectual property." This time they were more cautious, as Sandy Lerner says: "They'd let Andy out with this really charming letter kind of disclaiming any financial interest in Sun whatsoever. Unfortunately, a number of other companies had also all spun out of Stanford. I think OTL felt very embarrassed and the Stanford board of directors was unhappy."

Lerner and Bosack asked Stanford for permission to manufacture and sell (or even donate) the technology to colleagues at other universities, and at Xerox and Hewlett-Packard. Sandy Lerner was horrified when "Stanford just said no. And we just didn't think that you could just say no. I mean, this was a very academic network. It had happened over the ARPAnet. It was paid for by government money."

If Stanford was not going to permit the technology to be exploited, was Stanford itself going to exploit it? No again. Ralph Gorin was clear that that was not a function of the school: "I was buying the engineering that went into forming the Sun I. And we also bought the engineering that subsequently became the foundation of the Cisco routers. We viewed the establishment of Sun and Cisco with glee because we didn't perceive ourselves in the business of building computing equipment and selling it to people. And as soon as you had one of these gadgets, why, you know, your friends at Carnegie or MIT or God knows where, they all wanted them. And we weren't set up to be in that business, and apparently we found some people who wanted to be in that business."

Len Bosack concluded that Stanford, as an academic institution, is not in the business of manufacturing and sales. Although it would have been good to share the technology with other academic colleagues, "There really wasn't a mechanism in the university to do that. So it was clear that, ultimately, there had to be a company that did it. Because that's what companies do."

Len and Sandy were "scandalized" that Stanford "just said no." They decided not to take no for an answer, and in late 1984 incorporated the company in their living room anyway. As Sandy admits: "Len and I did not invent the router. No way. We did not invent terminal servers and we did not invent Ethernet interfaces and we did not invent Ethernet. Or TCP/IP or any of the rest of that. That was a community effort that was born of that original group of network nerds. It was the fruits of their labor that Stanford was basically holding hostage, and that's why we started that company. So with tears in our eyes we took our $5 up to the secretary of state's office in San Francisco and made Cisco Systems anyway."

The name, Cisco, was Sandy's choice: the last half of San Fran. . . . She designed the company logo (her impression of the Golden Gate Bridge), and for a long time everything about the company was handmade and home based. Corporate headquarters was the living room at 199 Oak Grove Avenue, Atherton; the technology was either borrowed or hijacked from Stanford; and the corporate finance was in the form of credit cards.

Len Bosack sees this as being in the familiar pattern of start-up life: "The same tradition as anyone else in the gulch. You go out and buy a bunch of parts and try to make the stuff, and then go sell it and solve the problems that come up."

For two years, the house in Atherton was Cisco's only home. For three years, Sandy and Len (and their coworkers Kirk Lougheed, Richard Troiano, and Greg Satz) worked unpaid by Cisco, with consulting day jobs to keep the wolf from the door. At nights, they worked on network servers. Mitten and Clutter were the company cats. Sandy's Cisco scrapbook includes a hand-colored photograph of herself, Bosack, and Lougheed, proudly displaying the first Cisco router to be shipped, in 1987.

The early days of Cisco resembled psychological crowding experiments designed to test subjects' patience to the point of violence. The endless hours of work were also seen by Len Bosack as a kind of test: "Sincerity begins at a little over 100 hours a week. You can probably get to 110 on a sustained basis, but it's hard. You have to get down to eating once a day and showering every other day, things of that sort, to really get your life organized to work 110 hours." Beyond 110 hours a week is the level Len calls "Commitment."

Len and Sandy's commitment was never in question. The 1989 instructional video shows the single-minded founders describing Cisco technology, pausing only briefly for the earthquake that levelled the Embarcadero Freeway and caused massive destruction in San Francisco's Marina district. In Silicon Valley, the demo must go on. Nothing could divert their attention from the glorious business of routers and bridges.

The house was no place for entertaining. One bedroom was the lab. Another bedroom was an office. When it was time to build and test a design, the living room was the only space left. As the Cisco routers began to sell, mostly by word of mouth on e-mail, the team bought parts on their credit cards and tried to stay ahead of the bills as checks came in from customers. As to pricing, Len Bosack admits, "We guessed."

In fact, they stayed well ahead. By the time Cisco opened its first office, at 1360 Willow Road, Menlo Park, in November 1986, revenues had reached $250,000 a month—a business funded on plastic and with no venture capital—though not for want of trying. They had been turned down by seventy or more venture capitalists.

Finally a venture capitalist listened to this strange story, with a half-million-dollar-a-month punchline. The seventy-sixth VC was something of a Silicon Valley legend: Don Valentine of Sequoia Capital. Valentine had been a founder of National Semiconductor, and a marketing executive with Fairchild Semiconductor. He set up Sequoia in 1972, and began his enviable track record by investing in Nolan Bushnell's Atari company. There was a brief hesitation over whether the distribution of coin-operated games was Mafia controlled. But Sequoia was satisfied that it was in fact controlled by Jewish businessmen with roots in Tel Aviv, and the investment went ahead. Most famously, Valentine recommended Mike Markkula, the ex-Intel executive, to Steve Jobs, and Markkula became the founding President, alongside Jobs and Wozniak, of Apple Computer. In due course, Sequoia also invested in Apple.

Valentine had also funded 3Com, so he had good instincts for the potential of networking technology. Sequoia's other investments include Tandem; Oracle; Electronic Arts; Cypress; LSI Logic; various biotech companies; and a fancy Palo Alto watering hole, Il Fornaio. In December 1987, Sequoia invested $2 million, in exchange for one-third of Cisco. As always, the venture capitalists began to recruit experienced management, financial, marketing, and sales people. Len Bosack, uninterested in management, became chief scientist, while Sandy Lerner was appointed vice president of customer services.

By May 1988, sales were at $500,000 per month. In August, $1 million per month. In November, sales hit $3.5 million per month. By the end of the 1988/89 fiscal year, sales had reached $27 million, and were flying upwards. Cisco celebrated with their first company holiday party in 1988, but in the same year Sandy Lerner and Len Bosack separated. When Cisco went public, in February 1990, the company was valued by the market at just under $300 million. In just over two years, Sequoia's investment had gained in value thirtyfold. Len and Sandy were each worth about $40 million. A year later, those numbers had all trebled again.

One of the many ironies of the Cisco story is that Len Bosack does not claim to have actually invented anything: "The only thing I actually did with regard to Internet technology was make it economic to build a large, fast Internet. People had surely built routers before me and people had built fast networks. The question was how to do it economically. By taking a functional computing approach where we built very specialized computing devices to actually solve the problem, we were able to drive the cost per function down to the point where you might care to own one of these devices."

Almost a decade later, so many people have cared to own these devices that Cisco is worth $60 billion. On the tenth anniversary of Cisco's founding, Len and Sandy endowed the Leonard Bosack and Sandy Lerner Professorship in Information Systems Technology at the Stanford University School of Engineering. And in other respects, Stanford did not entirely miss out on the wealth creation opportunities of Cisco Systems. As Ralph Gorin recalls: "I understand the athletics department was advised by their financial adviser to buy stock in the company. And they made out very well. I think the computer science department was offered stock in the company and wanted cash instead."

The stock would have been a far better bet.

Chapter Eleven
It Takes Two to Sign a Contract

THESE VARIEGATED COMPANIES, IN Utah and California, shared many of the classic attributes of the Silicon Valley model. They started with nothing, they demonstrated a passion for a single idea, and they grew at remarkable speed. But the networking market was somewhat different from the market for new PC consumer software—games, accounting programs, or word-processing programs. The customers for networking were businesses rather than individuals, and that gave one company a big potential edge. But IBM, which had both mainframe networking products and its new PC selling like hot cakes, largely missed the market—despite the fact that its junior partner, Microsoft, was convinced that networking PCs would be essential.

Steve Ballmer and Bill Gates—who then, as now, drove the strategic and sales vision for Microsoft, were already convinced that networking computers would enhance the product itself. Bill Gates saw it as part of the corporate mantra: "The whole vision of why personal computers would be a great thing on every desktop and every home had to do with using them as a communications tool, had to have them connected together . . . Starting in probably 1984, every year people are saying, 'This is the year of the network.' And that meant, inside the business, that 100 percent of the PCs would be connected up."

Steve Ballmer is emphatic that Microsoft saw the value of local area networks for business relatively early:

> It was clear, clear, clear to us way back then that networking would be a key to really getting people to love and accept computers. The notion that people could communicate with one other on these machines, not just do some of their own thinking and planning, that's a big idea. That was always a big idea. And to customers it clearly adds so much

value. So we were starting to build networking into our DOS operating system. There was a lot of the ARPAnet even back in '81–'82. Product development was clearly focused initially on the local area network. We said, look, if we get these companies to just hook themselves up, let alone connect to the mother of all networks, that would really be something important in terms of PC development.

Microsoft had created the original operating system DOS for the IBM PC. IBM, "the everything company," still of course did far more mainframe business than PC business. But IBM PCs and clones were selling well, creating a market for PC networking that 3Com and Novell were exploiting, with dominant products like Ethernet and Netware. The fact that Microsoft did not have a stake in this lucrative and growing market was a major irritant to Microsoft chairman Bill Gates. But their partnership with IBM kept Microsoft largely out of networking while they focused on working with IBM. But Microsoft was ready to push IBM to add networking to the next PC generation and, ultimately, to work with others to get into the field. It would become a civil war — which sometimes became very uncivil.

By 1984, with the advent of the Apple Macintosh, IBM was getting ready to bring out the second-generation PC. Microsoft and IBM were jointly developing OS/2, the next operating system for the PC. Microsoft was now trying to persuade a reluctant IBM to include networking in the OS/2. According to Ballmer: "Bill [Gates] kept saying to IBM management, 'Please, oh, please, oh, please. This thing will fail without networking.' So we had what I'll call a reluctant partner as the lead partner."

IBM management was neither blind nor asleep in lacking enthusiasm for the idea of adding networking capabilities to the OS/2. Although the PC division might have thought it was a good idea, another part of the company—the mainframe division, responsible for most of IBM's profitability—had its own networking products. As long as IBM saw the corporate market for networking in mainframes, it would be reluctant to compete with itself by introducing networking for the PC—despite the fact that competitors were successfully selling products to do exactly that.

As Ballmer remembers these events, the majority view at IBM

was that networking would be delivered via SNA (Systems Network Architecture): "We had to run these huge SNA protocol stacks on every machine. It was lunacy. It's the old networking technology that hooks up big IBM mainframe computers. And they wanted to stick that basically at every PC. That was corporate strategy. Anyway, they got kind of all bollixed up."

Drew Major of Novell realized that IBM was actually enabling Novell's success: "I remember one day realizing how good a position we were in because I knew that IBM *couldn't* do a really great job with their software. Because, of course, we were focusing on trying to replace minicomputers and low-end mainframes with networks of PCs around, you know, shared data. So we were in the best of both worlds. IBM was pushing the technology and helping us break down the barriers in getting networking into companies, and then they couldn't come in and exploit it like we could."

Jon Shirley joined Microsoft (from Tandy) as president and chief operating officer in 1983 and witnessed the internal contradictions of IBM's position: "There were many groups within IBM that didn't want to see PCs become highly successful and certainly not to the extent that they cannibalized any other business. Their idea was 'Why should we bother to make networking software available?' Of course, the answer was 'Because our customers want us to make it available.' But there were some people that rightfully felt that this was a challenge to some of the other businesses that they had."

Microsoft veterans of the OS/2 era have difficulty finding kind words for OS/2 today: the most common terms are "boat anchor" and "albatross." Meanwhile, Novell took advantage of this absence of competition. As former Novell executive Willy Donahoo reflects, "Novell grew up with a gun to its head. When Novell started, there were two companies. They were Microsoft and IBM. They were creating the next generation of operating systems, Operating System 2—OS/2. Right? Novell was an accident in their minds. A 'should-not-have-been,' and I guess we challenged that. We're an underdog."

Steve Ballmer admits that Microsoft itself wasn't very sure how to make money from networking, as they saw it as being ideally incorporated into operating systems—clearly a forerunner of the debate about "bundling" that has led Microsoft into conflict with the regulators. Ballmer's word for this corporate hesitancy is "jimmyjanging." They were slow out of the gate.

It is not surprising that Microsoft would hesitate to confront IBM over what should be in OS/2. The Seattle company was booming thanks to the sales of DOS to IBM and the clone-makers. IBM was the superpower in the PC world, and Microsoft's fortunes were intimately tied to their ongoing relationship. Gates and his senior managers, like Steve Ballmer, would do whatever it took to keep the OS/2 joint venture on track. Around Microsoft it was known as riding the bear: "You just had to try to stay on the bear's back and the bear would twist and turn and try to buck you and throw you, but darn, we were going to ride the bear because the bear was the biggest, the most important, you just had to be with the bear, otherwise you would be *under* the bear in the computer industry. IBM was the bear, and we were going to ride the back of the bear."

As Bill Gates points out: "It's easy for people to forget how pervasive IBM's influence over this industry was. When you talk to people who've come in to the industry recently there's no way you can get that into their head, that was the environment."

Cultural differences between IBM's managerial style and Microsoft's super-smart hacker culture began to show. Steve Ballmer was always bemused by IBM's standard practice for measuring—and paying for—software development: "In IBM there's a religion that says you have to count K-locs. A K-loc is a thousand lines of code. How big a project is it? 'Oh, it's a ten K-loc project. This is a twenty K-locker.' IBM wanted to make it the religion about how we got paid. We kept trying to convince them, if a developer's got a good idea and he can get something done in four K-locs instead of twenty K-locs, should we make less money? Smaller and faster, less K-locs. That always makes my back just crinkle up at the thought of the whole thing."

Battling IBM over OS/2 wasted years of Microsoft's time and gave the competition in network software a huge head start. Novell's market share rose continuously. In due course, Microsoft embarked on its own networking development program, creating server and client software intended to integrate with OS/2 and create OS/2 LAN Manager anyway.

Despite IBM's lack of interest, Rob Glaser recalls that it was a characteristically thorough Microsoft venture: "It was a very broad, ambitious strategy characteristic of how Microsoft does things. When it rolls the tanks, it rolls the tanks. It was quite an education. It got a lot of things right strategically, technologically. It had one fundamental thing wrong strategically: the operating system it was based on didn't become the mainstream operating system. The Holy Grail strategic operating system was OS/2. It wasn't just some plot that Bill dreamed up to confuse his competitors."

Rob Glaser is a philosophical man. After more than a decade at Microsoft, immersed in the intensity of engineering development and a largely unsuccessful strategy, he went to Egypt. Staring at the 5,000 year-old pyramids, he reflected that for 4,980 years of their existence there had been no Microsoft Corporation. It gave him a sense of perspective. He needed one, after the frustrations of the Microsoft networking effort: "It was a very interesting experience because I was there for two-and-a-half years and it was the least successful thing I've ever been involved in—in some sense, I think [the thing] I learned the most from. Because we had a great strategy except for one minor detail called OS/2. It's one of these things where if you have a great strategy and concept and you've got a fundamental Achilles heel, you lose."

Microsoft managed to get some market share in networking, but was decidedly in third place. It tried to catch up with this elusive market another way—by forging alliances or acquisitions—with the two companies that were ahead of it in networking, 3Com and Novell. With Novell leading the market, the obvious partner was the number two player, Bob Metcalfe's 3Com, which sold Ethernet products with the related operating system and software. Bob Metcalfe recalls: "In the late 1980s, in our frustration with Novell, we, 3Com, threw in with Microsoft to unseat Novell in the networking software business."

It did not prove a marriage made in heaven. Bob Metcalfe ultimately became the ex-CEO of the company he founded, and blames Microsoft's "double-crossing" him for his untimely exit. All now agree that it didn't go well, but they disagree as to why. Scott Oki, the former head of marketing for Microsoft, observes: "We entered into a kind of a strategic relationship with 3Com that ultimately didn't turn out very well. But nevertheless it actually got us bootstrapped and into the networking business."

Takes Two to Sign a Contract

It was clear to Steve Ballmer that 3Com was the natural partner, and he negotiated the partnership: "We both went into it
with a lot of enthusiasm, a lot of energy. I think we wound up
having a business relationship that was cumbersome at best. A
technical relationship that was a little bit difficult."

3Com's product was called 3Plus. Partnering with Microsoft
would enable 3Com to concentrate on the hardware end, leaving
software to a software-only partner. Metcalfe saw the fit between
3Com's networking software technology and Microsoft's operating system. Rob Glaser recalls that 3Com's attitude was "We want
to get out of the software business, and partner with you."

In addition, Bob Metcalfe had scarcely failed to notice that
"Microsoft had a big powerful partner, called IBM, with whom
they were tight and we calculated that the partnership of IBM,
Microsoft and 3Com would be able to overcome Novell, who was
then quite a powerful force."

The role of IBM would prove important, because despite Microsoft's "riding the bear" for half a dozen years, OS/2 was to prove
to be the undoing of the relationship, as Microsoft pursued their
Windows strategy. Metcalfe claims that "what Microsoft failed to
tell us was that their relationship with IBM was falling apart at that
moment. Which came as a big surprise about three days after we
signed the deal.... And that enterprise met a horrible end in the
late '80s—ultimately leading to my departure from 3Com."

The two companies joined forces in 1987, developing networking products around the OS/2 system. The products would
have Microsoft variants and 3Com variants, and each company
would sell its own version to its defined market. Their common
product was known as 3Plus Open LAN Manager. Both parties
committed to sales goals for their versions of the product, and set
about displacing Novell as number one. Rob Glaser, then twenty-
five years old, was exhilarated by the opportunity to create a
high-level alliance aimed at winning a market: "We put together
a relationship that if you hadn't had the problem with the OS/2
boat anchor, might have actually worked."

At this point, versions of history diverge. According to Rob
Glaser, then at Microsoft, 3Com quickly detected the market resistance to OS/2, and neglected the joint venture products to concentrate on their original business instead. "3Com didn't give a

shit about OS/2. It became clear that 3Com did not have an independent reason to push OS/2 against gravitational forces so 3Com ended up deciding, 'Hey, we're in the adapter business. We're in the router business. We're in the hardware and systems integration side of things. We don't want to get squeezed out of that by being theologically tied to an operating system that's a boat anchor.' So the relationship fell apart."

Steve Ballmer also acknowledges that the 3Com-Microsoft joint effort foundered on OS/2: "We had built on good old OS/2, which wound up being an albatross of epic proportion which eventually IBM took and we didn't. That was the real ultimate problem at the end of the day with 3Com. The core technology in which we had built was no longer the technology in which we were going to build on a go-forward basis."

The joint venture was strategically a dead end. But there were sales targets to be met by both parties. Bob Metcalfe claims that 3Com was placed at a great disadvantage by the technicalities of the deal, though he admits that it was "a very stupid deal with Microsoft, where we gave them our technology and then we became a reseller of our technology."

3Com gave their 3Plus technology to Microsoft to be repackaged and licensed back to 3Com for minimum quarterly fees. And Microsoft licensed the technology to other resellers besides 3Com. Although 3Com sold more of the product than other resellers, the sales were not good enough for Microsoft. As Metcalfe describes events, "Microsoft started selling the same product to our customers, which made an impossible deal. The way the contract was set up, they were allowed to do that and we still had to pay them these horrendous fees, quarterly minimums to license our own product back from them while they were selling it around us."

The financial outcome of the deal was bad for 3Com. In one quarter of 1990, the company wrote off more than $80 million in losses, at least partly due to the fiasco of 3Plus Open LAN Manager. The personal outcome for Metcalfe was also negative: "3Com went into a loss situation just long enough for the board of directors of 3Com to decide they needed a change, a new management."

Metcalfe resigned from 3Com, after eleven years in which the company had grown from one employee to two thousand, from zero to $400 million a year in sales. As it turned out, that was just the rehearsal: the growth show was yet to come. But it left Metcalfe with a deep dissatisfaction with how Microsoft does business: "When I complained to Microsoft, the guy involved, whom I will not name, said 'Your mistake was, you trusted us.'"

The Microsoft executives know that Metcalfe was distressed by the outcome. But they also hold firmly to the view that business is tough, and a contract is a contract. Steve Ballmer says this: "I think there was good intent on both companies' part. I, frankly, to this day, think we managed the thing very professionally. I know Metcalfe has some bitterness about it. But we were both properly looking after our business interests and properly, both companies, trying to be good partners."

Jon Shirley retired from Microsoft in 1989, after six years, to polish his collection of vintage Ferraris. According to *Forbes* magazine, those six years made him the twentieth-richest person in technology, with a personal worth of around half a billion dollars. About Metcalfe, he commented: "I don't think he has a reason to be as bitter as he is. We were two grown companies, with grown people operating the companies, and we attempted to do a business deal together. We attempted to make LAN Manager sell and attempted to make their products sell, and they committed to selling a certain amount of it with their products and they weren't able to do that. I think that he felt that we unfairly got them into the contractual situation. But, you know, it takes two people to sign a contract."

In networking as in the operating system business, Microsoft proved the toughest and maybe the most ruthless competitor of all. Meanwhile, Microsoft also considered another way of grasping leadership in the networking market, as expressed in the old adage "If you can't beat 'em, join 'em." If Microsoft, with or without 3Com, could not overtake Novell and their market leadership, then perhaps Microsoft would acquire both.

With Novell, there were two separate, abortive discussions about merging the two companies. Ten years later, the executives involved cannot agree on who initiated the courtship, or why it didn't lead to the altar. But neither proposal worked out. Bill Gates says that one discussion was initiated by Microsoft, the other by Novell. Both happened in the context of IBM's industry dominance, Gates recalls: "One thing that's hard to remember now is that all of us were in fear of IBM, because IBM wasn't just thought of as a hardware company. They were thought of as the everything company. We all thought, hey, maybe if we banded together we'll be able to compete and get some portion of a market in a world that IBM dominates. And so that was a motivating factor of both of the times that we sat down and talked."

The first conversation, according to Novell's David Bradford, was begun by Microsoft in late 1989, the same year that the Microsoft OS/2 LAN Manager was launched. As Bradford reflects: "I can remember reading the headlines: 'OS/2 LAN Manager going to put the Netware operating system out of business.' They predicted by 1991 Microsoft would have 60 percent share of the network operating system market with OS/2 LAN Manager and said that Novell's share of the same market would drop to 25 percent by 1991. Well, by 1991, our share—50 percent that we had in 1989—had grown to 75 percent and they still hadn't made a dent."

With the Microsoft-IBM joint effort to develop OS/2 finally collapsing (as Microsoft launched Windows 3.0) in 1990, Novell found a surprising new collaborator coming their way. As Gates explains, "IBM, actually, as part of not working with us, then went and started working with Novell for a couple of years and gave them a lot of momentum."

Despite Microsoft's wooing, Novell didn't want to be bought, or to merge, though out of the obligation to stockholders it listened carefully. After a while, the conversation ended inconclusively. Bradford says that Steve Ballmer wrote to say that Microsoft had concerns about antitrust issues, and that Bill Gates wasn't comfortable with a geographically divided, merged company. Gates confirms that reservation: "The thing that makes it tough, though, is that you get two different development sites and if you have this vision of a single operating system that's going to do everything, having those multiple sites and those different visions is tough. But I have to say it's surprising that we never got together."

A second discussion took place between the two companies between July 1991 and March 1992, prompted in part by Novell's acquiring Digital Research, and with it, a competing operating system to DOS. Microsoft reacts quickly to perceived or real threats to its dominant position in any market sector. Nevertheless, out of antitrust concerns and lack of momentum, the second conversation ended like the first.

By 1990, Bob Metcalfe had retired from 3Com to tend his stock portfolio, enjoy life, and ultimately assume the role of industry sage with a column in the technology-industry newspaper *InfoWorld*. He and his family moved from an Italianate spread in Silicon Valley's toniest neighborhood, Woodside, to raise rare breeds of sheep, horses, pigs, and goats on Kelmscott Farm in Maine. Metcalfe is still enough of an entrepreneur to take pride in his "scrumptious lamb chops" which fetch $15 a pound at the best butchers' shops in New England. Julia Child is on the waiting list.

Like Rob Glaser at the pyramids, Metcalfe is another philosophical fellow. In 1990, the 3Com board rejected his suggestion that he become CEO of the company. The board appointed Eric Benhamou CEO, and Metcalfe chose to retire, in June 1990, after eleven years with the company: "When he took over I was not optimistic. The company was losing money and going horizontally, which is to say, nowhere. Eric Benhamou [the new CEO] has completely amazed me. He focused the company by cutting back on all sorts of operations we shouldn't have gotten into, and the company has grown from $400 million to $5 billion since I left. So I thank him often for having made me the founder of a $5 billion company."

As for the painful experience of having the board—which he constructed—decline his services, Metcalfe is sanguine: "I take credit for the decision that ejected me from that company." He assembled a group of people smart enough to let him go, in the interests of the greater good of the company. He cheerfully admits that 3Com's multibillion dollar valuation shows they were right.

Bob Metcalfe, let us remember, is the man who was not going to let his company fail through excess of ego, lack of money, or lack of focus. 3Com did maintain focus, as he sheepishly admits; while Sun, Novell, and others built very big businesses: "Had we been on the ball and had we not focused as much as we did, there would be no Sun and there would be no Cisco and there would be no Novell and there would be no Bay [Networks] and there would be no Cabletron, because we would have done it all. Instead, we just focused and ended up with this piddling little $5 billion company."

Metcalfe parted company with 3Com in 1990, and it proved to be a bad year for network industry founders, including the Cisco founders, themselves the beneficiaries of Metcalfe's focus problem.

A paradox of the venture-capital phenomenon is that no sooner have the ambitious founders of a company convinced their investors that their vision of a new product and market will work, than the balance of power shifts to the investors. Their priority is not "the vision" but "the return." Consequently, a company may be shifted rapidly away from one product and toward another, even to an entirely new business area; and if the founders are no longer the best people to have at the helm as circumstances change, they're dispensable.

The fact is that the talents and vision required to work 110-hour weeks and launch a business in a garage or on a dining table—passion, technical excellence, focus, and insomnia—are mostly different from those needed to build a company and make it grow ever larger, create national and international marketing plans, and manage the profit-and-loss accounting of revenues of hundreds of millions—the activities of grown-up technology companies.

Despite the well-understood dangers, there's an almost limitless supply of founders ready to take their chances on fame, fortune, and even firing. Increasingly, they are not just graduates of Stanford and MIT, but graduates of the Moscow State School of Engineering and IIT (the Indian Institute of Technology, in Madras).

Venture capitalists, themselves often experienced managers, frequently decide to step in and hire new CEOs to move the company from the founder era to the multibillion-dollar-revenue era. These are the dangers of "adult supervision."

Like Bob Metcalfe at 3Com, and Steve Jobs at Apple, Sandy Lerner and Len Bosack found themselves no longer working at the company they founded on their credit cards. In the case of Cisco Systems, the founders even by their own admission were unusually naive, and entered into agreements with their venture-capital backer, Don Valentine of Sequoia Capital, that they claim no lawyer would have let them sign. Unfortunately, no lawyer is what they had. The recriminations about Cisco still fly.

For the Cisco founders, Don Valentine was Venture Capitalist #76. And his previous investments show that he knew his business: "We did have an idea of how big the industry was or how big the problem was. We had previously financed 3Com and Bob Metcalfe in the establishment of the Ethernet as the LAN device to connect PCs. Having also financed Apple, we knew that the world was going to be connected."

When Len Bosack and Sandy Lerner pitched Don Valentine, in mid-1987, Cisco was enjoying sales of more than $250,000 a month, with neither a professional sales staff nor marketing campaign. As Bosack says, "It wasn't a bad business just right then. So I think just for the novelty of it, the folks at Sequoia listened to us."

If Cisco was to grow bigger, faster, it needed more than just the receivables income from sales. Monthly sales demonstrated the existence of real demand, but to ramp up to the next level, capital was a requirement. And Sandy Lerner says that the Cisco founders were getting tired of working at Len Bosack's 100-hour-a-week "sincerity" or 110-hour "commitment" level: "You can get a little bit burnt out. So the idea of having some extra money and having some extra people was kind of appealing. We finally did get two firms that thought that we were other than stark raving mad. Of course, when you're selling a half million dollars a month on the Internet, it's not quite such a stretch."

Sequoia Capital's Don Valentine invested promptly: "When we understood the solution that Cisco was advocating, we were quick to commit to the company and we were the only investor. We invested $2.5 million in Cisco, September of 1987. And I joined the board and the rest is history."

But the history comes in different versions. Both the founders, nearly a decade after the events played out, remain upset about the terms of Sequoia's investment. Sandy Lerner admits that she and Len were innocents abroad: "We ended up taking money from Don Valentine and Sequoia Capital, who's a very savvy player, and Len and I were not, and I think that's probably about the best way to put that. We ended up with a four-year vesting agreement and 30 percent of the stock in the company and no employment contract. I would strongly advise anybody [else] not to do it that way. You should certainly get your own lawyer."

Len Bosack agrees: "They essentially dredged out of their word processors the standard agreements and said, 'Here.' Not knowing any better, we signed them. Sandy and I agreed to a forfeiture contract, a type of indentured servitude where if we didn't do what the company asked, they would have the right to repurchase the shares that we *actually already* owned."

Don Valentine sees the Cisco story much differently: "The commitment we jointly made to each other is that we at Sequoia would do a number of things. We would provide the financing, we would find and recruit management, and we would help create a management process. None of which existed in the company when we arrived. We all began with that understanding and a vision of the future."

To Sandy Lerner, this represented a systematic effort to sideline the founders: "We had someone in as a CEO that Don replaced. We had someone in as a CFO that Don replaced. I think we only understood in hindsight that Don was very much afraid that after all the years of grinding in the trenches with all of the very early Cisco people, that Len and I had such a cult of personality in the company that it was going to be very difficult for him to effectively control it. And I think he was probably right. He was certainly much more sagacious about that than we were . . . and just set about systematically replacing enough of the company management to where Len and I would ultimately be expendable. And we were expended."

Soon afterward, two paradoxical dramas played out. On the positive side, Cisco grew in the stereotypical fashion of successful start-ups. The corporate history notes milestones such as "Issues first coffee mug" (1987), and "Holds first company picnic" (1988). In 1990, the company was ready to go public, and at the IPO (initial public offering) on February 4, the company was valued at $288 million. At that point, the founders' shares were worth about $40 million each, and Sequoia's the same.

On the negative side, the founders, by their own admission, grew increasingly uncomfortable with the requirements of corporate life as Cisco grew ever larger. Nor did the investors feel comfortable with them as managers, though Don Valentine emphasizes that each was maintained and encouraged in the most appropriate roles: "Both were very critical and helpful people to launching Cisco. No question about it. Len is a very, very good technician and recognizes that he has little interest or little ability in management, and positions himself accordingly. So in the company he was the chief technical officer. Sandy is very acutely sensitive to how well the customers were treated. So, as a consequence, the company started what may have been the first customer advocacy program any company has evolved and [kept] intact, as Cisco now races towards $10 billion in revenue."

Yet six months after the IPO, Sandy Lerner discovered what many entrepreneurs before her have experienced—that the company she founded was no longer the place she worked: "It was August 28, 1990, but who's counting? Quite simply, I got fired."

Len Bosack admits that this was not a surprise; in Silicon Valley, it's never a surprise: "We had discussed this event and that sooner or later the venture capitalists always want to get rid of the founders. That's just part of Don's formula."

Don Valentine does not accept that firing founders is part of the formula, or that there is a formula. But the kind of tension that existed between these founders and this investor made it perhaps an inevitable outcome. According to Sandy Lerner: "Don's opening words to me, the first time I ever met that man—I wouldn't have known him from the man on the Moon—were, 'I hear you're everything that's wrong with Cisco.' I'm also the reason why there *is* a Cisco."

Len Bosack was still a board member, but with Sandy Lerner's departure, he became an ex-board member. "When they decided that they wanted to get rid of Sandy, what they hadn't anticipated was that it was time for me to go as well. And so I did."

Don Valentine had rarely spoken about these events until this interview—and he put on the record the event that precipitated the final split. "What went wrong back at the ranch? Well, the end of the story is that one day, with President John Morgridge's prior approval, seven vice presidents of Cisco Systems showed up in my office. We had a reasonably civil meeting in our conference room, the outcome of which was a very simple alternative. Either I relented and allowed the president to fire Sandy Lerner; or they, all seven, would quit, because they found it impossible and intolerable to work with Sandy and the nature of her then-behavior."

The behavior, which Valentine will only describe as "conduct unbecoming," was perhaps the most persuasive symptom of the need for the founders to move on and out. As Sandy admits, "It was probably time for Len and me to go. In that Len and I do not have company personalities, and I think that we were finding it difficult to work in a larger organization. I think that the way that this happened was wrong."

Despite the bitterness engendered by their departure, and the manner of their departure, most people would count Sandy Lerner and Len Bosack fortunate, though certainly they earned their success. In their disgust at the conclusion to their Cisco careers, they sold their holdings in the company. Don Valentine remarks: "They lost perspective and urgently sold their shares in Cisco at a time when the valuation of the company was a mere $1 billion or so. Had they somehow or other suffered this outrage with a little more financial wisdom, they might have sold when the company's market value was $10 billion or $20 billion, or maybe even now at $56 billion." Since he said that, the number has continued to rise.

Nevertheless, the pain of not having a $10 billion fortune can be compensated by the pleasure of having $100 million to your name. And Len and Sandy have followed another Silicon Valley pattern, by embarking on philanthropy, as well as new business and technological ventures. In 1992, Sandy Lerner acquired the manor house in Chawton, Hampshire, the English village where Jane Austen wrote her novels. She had discovered that it was for sale at the same time that she learned that there are hundreds of "lost" women novelists who pre-date Jane Austen: "This came up for sale in 1992 and I, for some very illogical reason, bought it thinking that it would be just a wonderful place for the Center for the Study of Early English Women's Writing."

Today Sandy is also the proprietor of a cosmetics empire, Urban Decay—launched with her own money, not venture capital: "We do lips, eye shadow, eye liner, mascara, a really awesome line of temporary tattoos. Some stuff called Body Haze. Basically, alternative makeup and alternative colors."

The company glories in its selection of post-punk colors with names like Frostbite, Bruise, Shattered, Mildew, and Acid Rain. Whatever would Jane Austen have thought? Sense and Sensibility? Or Pride and Prejudice?

Meanwhile Len Bosack runs a Seattle technology company, and his charitable donations support the search for extra-terrestrial intelligence. Far from being a whimsical notion, Bosack treats this venture with a typical philosophical intensity: "It's one of the most important questions that a sentient being can ever formulate, and that is: Are we alone? Either answer, if you could obtain it, is of tremendous import. But you surely do not expect little green men to come and present you with a message. On the other hand, if you don't listen, if you don't in any organized way ask the question of the universe, what if it has an answer waiting for you? Think of what you've missed."

Both founders earned from Cisco a level of wealth that most people, like Len Bosack, would regard as sufficient: "Well, you sort of wonder what's going to become of all that, but then you go look and add up what it is all worth and say, well, that's enough. But most of the money that I've made is destined to be given away. I certainly hope to give a billion dollars to charity before I'm all done."

It's hard to know whether to regard the Cisco story as a fairytale or a cautionary tale. In reality, it is both. Like 3Com, Cisco has accelerated its growth since the founders fell away. In March 1997, the company had a market capitalization greater than its six closest competitors combined. In another year, that value had doubled again. But despite this breathtaking success, Sandy Lerner expresses the wish that growth, success, and experienced management can still find better ways of working with the nerds who get things started: "I think it would have been good for the company and good for the people in the company not to have quite such a sudden, jarring transition. I just wish that as this whole industry gets better, older people would learn how to behave better. You don't have to do that to founders and inventors and little nerdy people who don't know any better."

Chapter Twelve
Steal My Software

In the 1980s, far from the high-stakes gambling of venture capital and new networking technologies, the grassroots of the Internet were steadily growing too, and in unconventional directions. It was still only fifteen years since networking began, and enthusiasts like John McAfee were figuring out what to do with their skills. McAfee deserves at least a footnote in the history of networking, because he was the first person to use the Internet to create a business—by giving away his software. The technological feasibility of doing so has existed since BBN used the ARPAnet to send out new software releases for the ARPA protocols, saving BBN's Dave Walden a lot of jetlag in the era before frequent-flyer programs.

On the other hand, the commercial desirability of distributing software freely, and for free, over the Net has been a matter of some debate. There is a hierarchy of freeness in software, aside from what one buys by mail order or in a computer store. There is *freeware* (users are not usually free to copy or distribute it further), *free software* (with source code, which users may modify and redistribute, with credit), *fringeware* (unreliable freeware), *public domain software* (as free as can be, not covered by copyright, for copying and distribution), *shareware* (try-before-you-buy) and even *shelfware* (unsold or unused software). The Free Software Foundation was founded by Richard Stallman, an MIT pioneer for the practice, whose advocacy was recognized by a MacArthur Foundation "genius" grant. None of these classifications of software, however, would have pleased the earliest software creators in the Altair community, Bill Gates and Paul Allen.

At the time of writing, the U.S. Justice Department is preparing its case to confront Microsoft's de facto monopoly of the operating system business, and its use of that monopoly to build a new de facto monopoly over Internet access via the Windows operating system. The principal tool for this maneuver has been the "bundling" in new personal computers—or giving away for free, by other means—of Microsoft's Internet Explorer Web browser. As we will learn, Microsoft disputes whether or not it can be considered free, when it is "bundled" with a product people pay for. Semantics aside, there's an irony in this tale, for the first person ever to make a fuss about software's being shared and copied for free was Bill Gates himself.

Among Altair users, and in the early days of the Homebrew Computer Club, nerds copied paper tapes and cassette tapes—carrying the first usable programs—in a spirit of collegiality, friendship, and shared enthusiasm. There is little doubt that it was illegal to do so and that it deprived those who wrote the software of legitimate expectations of income, not to mention great wealth. But it was Bill Gates, the then-twentyish founder of Microsoft, who in the earliest days of the Altair, in New Mexico, objected in an open letter to hobbyists that copying the paper tape of the Microsoft Basic for the Altair was "stealing." Nor was he wrong.

Bill Gates' first battle as a software entrepreneur pitted him against those who can only be regarded as his own customers. In the period when the Altair was still experimental, and a van was touring the country to demonstrate it, bootleg copies would proliferate. This was not the way Gates had planned it: "People took the paper type of Basic from the van and copied it, and so there were literally hundreds of copies out there before we could actually officially release the Basic, because we still had it in testing."

Single copies would multiply into hundreds. Paul Allen points out that the Microsoft business *was* those tapes: "Well, you had to realize that Bill and I were getting a royalty for each one of those tapes. We put a lot of blood, sweat, and tears into making that Basic; a lot of late nights, you know, a lot of hard work went into those."

The hippie attitude around Jim Warren's hot tub was that Bill Gates "wasn't making as much money as his greed and avarice desired. That's some people's interpretation of it."

But Gates had no intention of seeing his vision of corporate success blown off course by people who thought "sharing" was cool. Bill Gates saw that "the whole question of 'Should people pay for the software or not pay for the software?' was a hot topic. And I had a clear point of view."

Gates decided to express his point of view, so he approached David Bunnell, and asked for his assistance in writing and publishing, in the fledgling *PC Magazine*, "An Open Letter To Computer Hobbyists"—"where I said, 'Come on, I think it'd be better if people paid for software.' And it was run in a number of other publications."

Jim Warren remembers the impact on the hobbyists' ranks: "'These hobbyists are all a bunch of thieves, they're stealing our life's work,' and all this stuff. And called them all, I don't remember, 'thieves' and 'stealing valuable property' and everything else. And—it was *true*."

Gates' partner, Paul Allen, was no less concerned about their potential losses from the sharing of their software: "We had very strong feelings about it. I guess we were a little bit surprised with the reaction, but we still believe we were 100 percent right in our position."

David Bunnell, Boswell to Gates' Johnson, admits that "It created a firestorm. And the basic problem was, in my opinion anyway, that in the letter he said, 'You are all thieves.' And the problem with that was that they weren't actually *all* thieves, just most of them. It was really the first time that, at least in the personal computing industry, where software piracy became a big issue. And so, that was a lot of fun."

With the determination that would become Gates' professional hallmark, and despite much grumbling from the hackers, Gates established the model of charging users for every copy of a software program. The willingness to confront a problem and win has not deserted him for more than twenty years, while his personal fortune has grown to uncountable size. The original paper tape that he and Paul Allen created for the Altair is now behind glass in the Computer Museum in Boston, Massachusetts.

Although today Gates is most renowned for his extraordinary business skills, they are undoubtedly built on a foundation of outstanding technical ability. In Albuquerque, he and Paul Allen were scheduled to deliver a disk-based version of Basic for the Altair; but Bill was also scheduled to return to Harvard to continue his studies. His parents were very concerned about this extracurricular business in New Mexico. But Paul Allen was concerned that the extra-curricular business wasn't getting done: "He kept postponing and postponing actually writing the code. He said, 'I know how to write it, I have a design in my head, I'll get it done, don't worry about it, Paul.' Four days before he was due to go back to Harvard he checked into a hotel and he was incommunicado for three days. Bill came back three or four days later with this huge sheet of paper. He'd written 4K of code in three days, and typed the whole thing in, got it working, and went back to school, just barely. It was really one of the most amazing displays of programming I've ever seen."

To the non-nerd, the idea of spending days on end chewing over computer instructions holds few charms. But to men like Gates and Allen, and women like Sandy Lerner, the fascination is genuine. John McAfee, founder of McAfee Associates and later of PowWow/Tribal Voice, is a lifelong software engineer who loves his work the way others love solving crossword puzzles or excavating prehistoric bones. His career began as the ARPAnet was born. In 1968, he left graduate school and started his romance with software with General Electric, as a programmer trainee: "That's all I've ever done. It's been my whole life and my real love. It's like unraveling a mystery. There's something that you know you want to do, and the technology of software can solve the problem. It's how? How can you do it? How do you structure it? What will the architecture look like? And the challenge is so spectacular and seductive that I've stayed with it all my life."

McAfee's great innovation would come at the very end of the 1980s, and it occurred in the grassroots of the networking industry rather than the high-powered corporate world of the civil war between IBM, Microsoft, Novell, 3Com, Cisco, and others. Generally, those companies were catering to the business world—serving the suits—while the millions of individual PC buyers were using standalone machines. But there was an undercurrent of networking for individual users nevertheless. The first significant trend was the creation of bulletin board systems (BBS). A BBS was, as it sounds, a digitized version of the cork-faced bulletin board on an office or dorm-room wall.

Bulletin board systems provided the first glimpse of "virtual communities." These were computers dedicated to providing information; news; gossip; and a forum for exchanging opinions, messages, or sometimes abuse, among a community of like-minded souls whose shared interest drew them to that BBS. It might be devoted to aficionados of one particular software product, or art-form, or sport. Technically, it was a computer, whether personal or mainframe, usually equipped with modems to enable remote users to access information, leave each other messages, and sometimes interact in real time. Usually some form of monthly subscription was required in order to participate. Someone with a personal computer, and a modem, and a good deal of expertise, could hook up to a BBS in the eighties and experience the thrill of networking without being on the staff of Xerox PARC, or having access to an ARPAnet terminal at a university. As John McAfee remembers: "Prior to the Internet, we had bulletin board systems, which were a loose collection of electronic exchange mechanisms where individuals could buy a personal computer, install bulletin board software, and have two thousand users who would dial in and exchange programs and messages and information. The Internet is merely the world's largest bulletin board system."

Len Kleinrock recalls walking into his graduate students' offices looking for a book one of them had borrowed. In the course of chatting with the students, he asked about a particular piece of telephony equipment. "And before I knew it, that student clicked away at his terminal, connected to a newsgroup devoted to telephony, and got a detailed answer for me. I was amazed to find that most of the computer science graduate students were spending hours each day accessing all manner of newsgroups. Here was an underworld alive with activity and energy! These were the precursors to today's bulletin boards."

Another who was brave enough to try this was Steve Case, the founder of America Online. This is a man who should have networking in his blood—born and raised in Hawaii, home of the Alohanet, and educated in Massachusetts, home of BBN and birthplace of the IMPs that created the infrastructure of the ARPAnet: "In 1982, I bought my first computer and wanted to hook it up and be part of this online world, and I went to great lengths to make that happen. It took many months, and hundreds of dollars to get the modem to work with the software to work with the cable to work with the computer to actually connect to this world. So it was very frustrating. At the same time, I found it exhilarating that I actually got it to work, and I was able to access information and talk to people all around the world from my little desktop in Wichita, Kansas, which was where I was living at the time. So I thought the whole thing was really quite magical."

By 1984, as the Macintosh was launched, the hippie origins of networking were once again beginning to show themselves. Part of the impetus came from an electronic version of the Whole Earth Catalog (whose Epilog had come and gone a decade earlier). Inevitably, it was Stewart Brand who originated and branded what he called the "Whole Earth 'Lectronic Link," or WELL. Now more users were able to tune in and turn on to the highs of networking, attracted by the chance to connect with like-minded people—even "Dead" people. One should not underestimate the importance in the history of the Internet of the Grateful Dead.

The WELL was launched in 1984, in full consciousness of the Orwellian, totalitarian implications of that date. But the WELL's server was located on a houseboat in Sausalito, and was presided over by as authentic a collection of blue-chip counter-cultural personalities as one could wish to find, including John Perry Barlow, one of the lyricists for the Grateful Dead. Stewart Brand claims that he created the *Whole Earth Catalog* as a sourcebook for the hippie commune life so that he could avoid actually living on one. The WELL was a natural successor to the trend: "I sense communities worked on places like the WELL because you would have some of that fellow feeling that you might have in a commune, or an 'intentional community' as it was called at the time, or the idealized village that people imagined would be nice to have."

Slowly, the global array of inter-networked computers, both personal and institutional, was becoming a medium of communications, rather than just data transfer. Howard Rheingold is a writer and founder of the Whole Earth brand. He has written the observational books *Tools for Thought* and *Virtual Communities* which have provided a close-up view of the places where hippie attitudes and technological innovation have met. Known for his spectacular Hawaiian and tie-dyed shirts, he has also been a TV pitchman for Kinko's Copy Centers as they branched out into video-conferencing and Internet access. If E. M. Forster were alive today, he would recognize Howard Rheingold as a fellow promoter of the philosophy "Only Connect": "It's vitally important because it's a many-to-many medium. Every desktop, every computer that's connected to the Internet, whether it's through an ordinary telephone line and a modem, is potentially a printing press and a broadcasting station and a place of assembly. This is very important, probably more important in some ways than the fact that people are making billions of dollars on it; that democracy and community and a lot of things that are very important to people may be at stake here."

A sense of community is at the heart of the WELL, and of electronic communities in general. Stewart Brand recalls:

> There was a book called *The Great Good Place* that came along, which is about great pubs and barber shops and beauty shops and coffee shops where people go and they just hang out. It's not work and it's not their house. It's this other, third place that they go to just hang. The WELL became a great good place. You would "see" the same people— in the sense of seeing their ideas flowing by in the conversations, because nobody knew faces. Real interactions were taking place. Real ideas were getting swapped. Real books were being recommended and then talked about. People were generating topics that you would want to talk about. Parenting. Health. Various regions of the Bay Area. Books—the writers wanted their own conference.

The WELL's Bay Area roots and Deadhead pedigree probably made it inevitable that one of the most popular early conferences on the WELL was one devoted to the appreciation of the Grateful Dead and all their works. As David Gans—a musician, Dead art expert, and radio DJ at KPFA in Berkeley—claims, "There are a million ways to appreciate the Grateful Dead, and we found a lot of ways to talk about them."

The Dead, famously, was a ubiquitous, improvisational band. Not only did it have followers and fanatics all over the country, but some of them roamed the land to see as many concerts as possible. A mythology sprang up around the different performances of the huge repertoire of constantly evolving Dead songs. Unlike Bill Gates, with his strict ideas about software piracy, the Dead accepted, then encouraged, the informal recording of live concerts, even reserving a special audience section at the concerts to facilitate it. Tape-trading thus became another reason for Deadheads, as they are known, to want to communicate with each other. It was the ideal "virtual" community to be networked by bulletin board. As Stewart Brand remembers: "You began to get some entities like the 'Deadheads,' people who were basically following the Grateful Dead, who were not a regional phenomenon at all. And where they became regional was on the WELL. *That* was their neighborhood."

Before long, Deadheads on the WELL decided to establish their own sub-community, known as a conference. David Gans was one of those involved: "So why don't we start our little Grateful Dead community over there and see what happens? On March 1, 1986, the Grateful Dead conference opened its doors. Various people from the Net came over and got accounts and even more interestingly, various people went out and bought computers so they could get online and start talking with us."

At the time, the WELL was having a hard time staying in business, and was offering free accounts to people who would start new WELL conferences to attract more subscribers. Even communal activities cost money, and they had to buy their computers, and their disk drives for storage, rent telephone lines, and manage the business. The Deadhead conference created such an influx of users that the WELL was kept alive, says Gans, who remains the cohost of the Deadhead conference: "We're credited with generating sufficient cash flow to keep the WELL going through its early start-up days. It was great to see it. It was really, really fun because we were people who had a lot to talk about.

Stewart Brand confirms that "It probably saved our butt. It just gave us a commercial scale of absolutely dedicated customers all in a couple of months. One fell swoop, suddenly here's a whole bunch of people who want to talk to each other all the time."

The WELL thrived by the peculiar attraction of disembodied communication among like-minded people. David Gans and his wife Rita Hurault met at a musical event, called Sing Thing, which was publicized via the Berkeley conference on the WELL. While they did not meet "in cyberspace," and scorn the notion, their meeting occurred because both "hung out" on the same conference and were introduced thereby. Rita Hurault today cohosts the "Women on the WELL" conference, known as "WoW," where only women may participate. The WELL makes strenuous efforts to exclude virtual female impersonators.

A Boston writer, Fawn Fitter, is cohost—with Mary Elizabeth Williams—of Byline, the WELL's conference for freelance non-fiction writers, which offers a supportive community forum for people pursuing a solitary, often trying profession, and an opportunity to gripe about agents, publishers, and editors. Fawn says that the WELL is a major influence on her life: "I have made friends through the WELL. I have had a romance, very brief but nonetheless. . . through the WELL. I have gotten work through the WELL. I've made professional connections through the WELL. You know, it literally has touched every aspect of my life, personally and professionally."

WELL conferences have sprung up, over the years, to discuss and share ideas about every conceivable topic, especially in areas where self-help or supportive help are needed: for baby-boomer WELL users confronting the problems of sick children, or parents with Alzheimer's seeking information about travel destinations and restaurant recommendations. While no one guarantees the quality of the information (just the same as in a real, physical community), people become passionate about living in the online community. And sometimes they just become passionate.

Fawn Fitter herself knows this phenomenon:

> I will confess that when I first got online, I had a little cyber fling. The thing about online romances is that because you aren't actually with the person, you can project anything you want onto them. Then when reality slaps you in the face, it can either be a real wake-up call or it can work out wonderfully. Any time you're thrown into a new situation and someone starts paying attention to you, it's very seductive, and it's particularly seductive online if the person is a good writer. Of course being a writer myself, that's what happened. I was just blown away by the style and fluency of this person's written communications. Then, when we met in person, it just became apparent that he wasn't quite as fluent with emotional interchange. But I'm not slamming him.

He's a good guy. He's just not the one for me. I don't think of having met him online as being all that very different from having met him at a party or in a bar or through a personals ad or rollerblading down the sidewalk.

Fawn Fitter, like most WELL users, emphasizes that she is not interested in the technology itself, but what can be done with it: "I'm not a geek. I'm not fascinated with technology for its own sake. I basically think of this computer as a very intelligent type-writer, which occasionally, when hooked up to the modem, talks back to me."

Increasingly, virtual communities like the WELL operate on the Internet rather than via Bulletin Boards. In 1989, the WELL gained some public attention by providing instant news coverage of the earthquake—the same one that interrupted Len Bosack and Sandy Lerner—that caused terrible destruction around San Francisco. Stewart Brand recalls that people "raced to their computers to get on and talk about what happened to them. Howard Rheingold was talking about all the earthworms jumping out of the ground in his garden. I was talking about being caught in the marina and then helping rescue people from a burning building. Since we'd invited journalists on from the very beginning with free accounts, which was our entire marketing strategy, there was a guy from the *Wall Street Journal*, who saw this earthquake stuff and just downloaded it, and that was the center column story in the *Wall Street Journal* the next day."

While the personal and social utility of BBS-driven online communities motivated some, the sheer technological beauty of shipping bits along the wire fascinated others. John McAfee also saw a business opportunity in the frictionless, cost-free distribution of digital information. Unlike Bill Gates, who got rich by quashing the idea of free software, John McAfee got rich by doing the opposite: the giveaway style of doing business.

As Frank Heart and Dave Walden of BBN discovered back in 1969, one of the greatest technological assets of a network is that distribution of bits is easy: whether the bits are e-mail messages or software applications. What fascinated John McAfee about software was its very insubstantiality: "The unique thing about software, which I'd thought about, you know, ever since the

mid-seventies, is that software production is unlike any other production that preceded it. No raw materials are required, no time is
required, and no effort is required. You can make a million copies
of a piece of software instantaneously for free. It's a totally new
paradigm of production. If you leverage that zero cost, you can do
magic and that's what we did. My motto was, 'Steal My Software.'"

In the 1980s, as more computers were sold, more computer
viruses began to circulate; and more potential customers were
looking for a solution to virus problems. John McAfee wrote the
best anti-virus software and gave it away to people via dial-up bulletin boards. The application was posted as a downloadable file.
Unlike shareware, where the author hoped for a check if users
were honest and generous, but had no further involvement with
the software or the user, McAfee had a different model in mind: "I
thought if you created a company and supported the software, updated the software, kept it in sync with the changing operating
systems and computer architectures and made it real, then the
standard software developer couldn't compete against that."

John McAfee set up a bulletin board with five telephone lines.
At any time, five people could separately download the anti-virus
software. Up to a thousand people per week would log on, but
any and all of them could reload the software to multiple other
BBS sites, and "within a matter of days, my software would be in
the hands of a million people."

Compared to the traditional software production model, the
efficiency is remarkable. McAfee claims never to have bought a
single stamp in the service of distributing his software: "My first
competitor was Symantec, and just to package the product costs
them $10. You had to shrink wrap it. You had to do the docu-
mentation, duplicate the diskettes, put labels on the diskettes,
ship it around. It didn't cost me a dime. The magic of software is
that once it's developed, duplication is instantaneous and has
zero cost."

Computer viruses continued to emerge, the anti-virus software improved, and word of mouth spread about his product. So
far, no revenue. The first stage of the plan was to ensure customer satisfaction and loyalty, to make the McAfee software the
standard: "You just give it away because it doesn't cost anything.
If it becomes a standard—if people use it, if people like it—they

become habituated to your interface and your way of doing it, then you're in like Flynn."

The second stage, having outmaneuvered the old-fashioned competitors who still expected customers to pay for software, was to "throw the switch." After a certain date, McAfee's customers would be asked to pay for the upgrades: "When it becomes a standard, you simply charge for the update process. You get the copy free. You can use it as long as you want. If you want the updates, we'd be happy to give them to you for a nominal fee. And after we had five or ten million copies out there, it was a very simple process to turn the switch and begin charging for updates. They're used to your interface, your documentation, your way of viewing the world through your product. When you start charging for updates, it's very easy for them to rationalize paying for it rather than going to a competitor. I've been using the software for two years. I like it. They've done it for free. I like the company. Sure. I'll give these guys five bucks a month."

John McAfee was the first person to come up with this uniquely Internet business proposition. It earned him an enviable lifestyle, with a spectacular house on the side of Pikes Peak in Colorado, sports cars, motorcycles, and a lot of money in the bank. This was what the venture capitalists noticed when they took a look at McAfee Associates in 1991. After two years in business, by McAfee's own account, the company consisted of two rooms filled with computers and some grubby people.

The venture capitalists from TA Associates and Summit looked at the bank statements and invoices, and in their puzzlement asked McAfee if they could send in auditors. There was $15 million in the bank and only five employees. The business was only costing $300,000 a year to run, and those five people weren't getting rich. In fact, money was not what McAfee Associates needed: rather, to grow into a bigger business they needed advice, experienced management, sales, and marketing: the adult supervision that often represents such a painful transition.

There was no obvious pain for John McAfee. Each of the VC firms put up $5 million, in exchange for 25 percent of the company. Each of them in due course netted over $100 million on the deal. In July 1998, the company was worth $3 billion. Since the company didn't need money, the $10 million investment went elsewhere: "This is a very unusual deal. The $10 million didn't go into the business. It went into my pocket."

McAfee still owned the other half of the company, valued at $200 million when the VCs cashed out. John sold out later still and has a relatively positive view of venture capitalists as a result: "You know, as much of a bad reputation as VCs have, they are, in fact, sharks. There's no question. But once they're on your side, they're your sharks. So if you struggle with them and if you can come out bleeding as little as possible and survive, then you're in fat city."

In 1984, when the WELL was founded, the ARPAnet/Internet had expanded to include a little over a thousand hosts. By 1986, when the Grateful Dead conference started, it had five thousand. In 1989, when McAfee started distributing free software, there were 150 thousand. And in 1991, the year John McAfee cashed in the venture capitalists' check, it reached half a million.

This acceleration of networking was the result of the cross-fertilization of the various strands discussed to date: government-sponsored research, business wide area networks, academic local area networks, proliferating bulletin board services, and the constantly increasing number of personal computers in individual hands.

Thanks to the TCP/IP protocols of Vint Cerf and Bob Kahn, all these networks began to be connected to each other. They all had their own local protocols, so there was no common interface; but data could be sent to almost anywhere, by navigating cleverly from Ethernet to ARPAnet to Internet (and SatNet, NYSERNET, BITNET, etc. . . .) Little by little, throughout the 1980s, in business, academic, and personal computers, networking became more familiar, more available, and more useful. In 1989, after twenty years, ARPAnet was decommissioned, allowing faster networks and backbones to take over. It then cost just $14 million a year.

Sometime in the 1980s, personal computers had outnumbered all other computers, with the result that for hardware and software there was a huge, profitable consumer market; to this was added a diffident consumer market for network service, in the form of information services such as Compuserve, Prodigy, and America Online. These began as BBS services, but with pretensions to becoming media ventures. With none of the visual quality of today's Internet media sites, they were not yet connected to the Internet, but they offered a simulation of what the Internet could provide, with a far more consumerist, family-oriented style.

The history of personal computing tells us that for every seventeen nerds willing to struggle through baffling commands to connect to another eleven like-minded nerds, there are thousands of people who will use a computer function if it has a user-friendly look and feel. Here was a new way to follow the news, stock prices, and sports scores; to provide community e-mail service, chat rooms, and access to all kinds of data. Rather than catering to smaller, specialized groups (as the WELL's conferences did), these services attempted to offer generalized services of information, entertainment, and interaction.

In 1982, one of these nerds was Steve Case: "I was dabbling. There were local bulletin boards, some national services. The Source was one of the real pioneers. I was primarily using that. A little bit of CompuServe was just coming onto the scene, as well. Back in 1982, the services were really quite primitive in terms of what would then evolve. Nevertheless, you could see that something was happening. Even though it was hard to use and expensive and there wasn't much there that was useful and the interface was just scrolling text, there really was something happening there. And that's really when I kind of felt like I had to get into it."

With Compuserve already in the market, Steve Case and his co-founders launched the ancestor of America Online, a company called Quantum, offering an online service called Q-Link. They started in 1985 with a radical new idea: the same radical new idea that launched the Apple Macintosh one year before. Unlike the text-only competitors, and the arcane protocols ARPAnet/Internet users needed to understand, America Online offered its subscribers the GUI: a graphical user interface.

Quantum arose from the ashes of an effort to add modems to Atari game systems and turn them into interactive game network terminals; it is interesting to note that Len Kleinrock was a Board member of that venture. In 1983, the Atari system market evaporated, so Quantum leapt across to the Commodore 64 platform. Q-Link was based on the Commodore 64 (then the best-selling personal computer in the market) and Quantum established an alliance with Commodore to bundle Q-Link software with Commodore computers and modems, creating a captive subscriber pool. By the fall of 1986, Steve Case had 50,000 Quantum subscribers: "Then we said, 'What do we do next?' And we established partnerships with Apple, Tandy, and IBM to essentially do the same thing, create a private label service. For Apple it was Apple Link Personal Edition, for Tandy it was PC Link, for IBM it was Promenade, to try and move into each of these computer segments with services designed to meet the needs of people who bought those particular computers."

The market for online services was growing, but it was also getting very crowded. When Quantum launched, CompuServe was already operating, as was the Source. Also in 1985, General Electric started a service called Genie, and Knight-Ridder another named Viewtron. Shortly after Quantum started, IBM and Sears launched Prodigy. Among this "hyper-competitive market" of media and industry forces, Steve Case felt "we were kind of the little guy."

Despite the competition, and the capital most of them had to build their services, Quantum (which became America Online in 1989) broke out of the pack. Steve Case attributes their success to luck, to the passion of a start-up business style as opposed to the corporate rivals' corporate attitudes, to their graphical user interface, to their subscription pricing, and to word of mouth—probably the single most important asset for any service or business on the Internet today: "People liked it. They told their friends about it. We tried to make it easy to try the service and built this groundswell, and by the time the big players really figured the market out, we already had a fair amount of momentum."

As technology (like faster modems and cheaper memory) improves, and global access to material is provided by the Internet and the World Wide Web, America Online (AOL) has become more useful and appealing. So have the other online services, but AOL, with about ten million users in 1998, has captured around half of the market.

As Steve Case points out, this may be—and he hopes so—only the early days of the online service industry: "We think of it as just as important as the telephone was a hundred years ago or the television was fifty years ago, but if you look at the history of the telephone or television, they didn't happen overnight. It took decades before they really had mainstream appeal. So we believe we're still in the development of the industry. Maybe it's the third inning. Only 15 percent of households subscribe to anything. Eighty-five percent are saying, what's the fuss?"

Until the Internet became highly accessible, and the World Wide Web made it visual, online services competed with the Internet and were considerably more appealing in design. Today, online services provide their own proprietary content, and also provide access to everything else via the Internet.

While some services, like AOL, are thriving, others have fallen by the wayside. In 1994, for example, Apple Computer created its own online service called "e-world," bundled with new Macintosh computers just like Q-Link, PC Link, and Promenade had been. Typically, Apple gave the service a cute graphical format, which allowed the user to point and click at a cartoonish "world" that seemed borrowed from Dr. Seuss' oeuvre. But e-world didn't last.

Steve Case is optimistic about the growth of online services, and the prospects of companies that serve this market well. In five years, the number of AOL subscribers rose from two hundred thousand to eight million. At that rate, everyone on the planet will have an AOL account by 2007. So it's not unreasonable for Steve Case to aim high in comparing the prospects of America Online with the biggest, most successful companies of the old and new technological eras: "The companies that are leaders in making this happen and popularizing this concept for a mainstream audience, I think, are going to be very, very successful. We'd like AOL to be in this new interactive world what AT&T was in the telephone business, or Microsoft has been, more recently, in the software business. There's a big opportunity here."

Naturally enough, Microsoft has every intention of being the Microsoft of the online market, too. Inevitably, Microsoft launched its own competitive online service, Microsoft Network (MSN), though not until 1995, with Windows 95. It fit well with Bill Gates' original idea of the connected home computer, running Microsoft software and services: "The Microsoft network was our decision to get into the online service business. We thought that for people at home, in particular, this would be explosive, and we very much believe that to this day. Electronic mail, staying in touch with your friends, seeing what's going on in your local community, getting up-to-date news and having that be nicely packaged with chat sessions and neat new software features, we saw a market for that."

Although America Online, as the market leader, has so far outmaneuvered the competition to establish its market leadership, Steve Case does not underestimate Microsoft's capacity to compete with, and overtake, rivals: "A company that's been as effective as they have been in so many markets, that has something like $10 billion in cash sitting in the bank and has very smart, aggressive people: you'd best take that threat seriously." Microsoft did not give away software; and in competitive markets, they never give an inch.

Part Four

The 1990s:
Wiring
the World

Chapter Thirteen
People Just Laughed

IF ANYONE SAW THE FUTURE OF networking—at least the decade that unfolded from 1980 to 1990, as seen from the perspective of 1979—it was Bob Metcalfe. As a researcher, he had enjoyed the opportunity at Xerox PARC to design, create, and observe the future. In business, he created products to exploit that future. All of the developments up to the World Wide Web were largely thought through and planned inside PARC. Metcalfe has thus joined the ranks of scientists like Newton and Einstein (and more recently, Gordon Moore of Intel) who has lent his name to a law. As defined by Netscape founder Marc Andreessen, Metcalfe's Law states: "The power of the network is N squared, where N is the number of nodes. So if you double the number of nodes, you actually double squared or you quadruple the overall value of the network. The reason is that the network gets more valuable to me if you come on it. Even though I'm already there, the network's getting continually more valuable to me as more people come on, as more contact comes on, as important businesses are connected."

It's an eloquent explanation of the extraordinary rates of growth that successive waves of network technology and connectivity have enjoyed since the beginning of the 1990s. After the ARPAnet was built and consolidated in the 1970s, and the business world was networked in the 1980s, the wired world started to reach the consumer. Throughout the 1980s, individual local networks, of universities, businesses, or small communities began to be connected into a network of networks.

Andy Grove was one of the cofounders of the Intel Corporation in 1968, and in 1979 became president of the company. For ten years, from 1987 to 1997, he was also CEO. He has observed the successive eras of networking, as Intel's microprocessors (according to his colleague Gordon Moore's Law) have driven the technology up and prices down: "The first implementations, in terms of cabling and nodes and everything, were like Russian tanks by today's standards. Expensive, over-engineered, and clunky, with these big yellow cables hanging out of the ceiling tiles all over the place."

Grove recalls that Bob Metcalfe made a habit of announcing, year after year, that this was the year of the Ethernet. Each year, he would revise the date by a year. But the local area networks, which Ethernet and other products facilitated, provided the platform for the Internet phenomenon, Grove argues: "The networking that took place in the 1980s was a necessary pedestal on which the Internet phenomenon was built. The way the Internet could take off in terms of numbers of people that access it so rapidly, was that for ten years before, islands of networks were being created. This was taking place in hundreds of places and thousands of places and tens of thousands of places. *All* these computers were networked through, largely, Ethernet technology, local area networks. Then the task was to connect all of these networks together and connect them across companies, across organizations, to the Internet."

Networking had come a long way from the Pentagon's ARPAnet; the next step was the grand goal of linking *all* these computers together. It would happen, as so often, by accident and in an unlikely place. In 1990, an English information technologist named Tim Berners-Lee created the World Wide Web from his cubicle in the information technology unit at the world's premier particle physics laboratory.

Tim Berners-Lee is a shy Englishman who is insistently modest about his achievement. His computing gifts are perhaps inherited; both his parents worked on the first commercial computer built in Britain, the Ferranti Mark 1, and his mother was the first British commercial programmer sent out to program the machine for customers. Tim graduated from Oxford University in physics, and worked for the British telecommunications company Plessey, before cofounding a company named Image Computer Systems. In 1980 he spent six months at CERN, the European particle physics laboratory just outside Geneva, Switzerland. While there, he worked on a project that would be familiar to Frank Heart of Lincoln Laboratory and BBN: "distributed real-time systems for data acquisition and system control"—in lay terms, getting and distributing information instantly.

While at CERN in 1980, Berners-Lee wrote a program he called "Enquire Within," which allowed the user to store information using random associations. Rather than storing a file in a folder, inside another folder, on a tree-shaped directory, this format allowed information to be accessed and cross-referenced by its content. Almost ten years later, he would revive and enhance this notion as "World Wide Web."

There is an apt parallel between the birth of ARPAnet and the creation of the Web. In both cases, they were born of governmental or institutional investments in making difficult, technical research easier and less expensive to do. In the Web's case, it was to solve a simple problem—the same problem from which all previous networks had suffered—incompatibility. But the difference between ARPAnet and the Web illustrates another key theme of the evolution of networks, and the results of that evolution. While the ARPAnet was created because of a top-down decision by government functionaries, the Web was created thanks to a bottom-up effort. Networks, as they decentralize, also often empower and democratize the workforce. Nobody demanded the Web; yet Tim Berners-Lee, overcoming some initial reluctance, was able to create it.

CERN, the European organization for nuclear research, is "a web-like place," as Tim Berners-Lee observes. Research physicists come from all over the world—from their own national or academic research institutes which use different computers, languages, and software—and then try to share and exchange knowledge: "There was always different sorts of people from different countries who brought different sorts of computing equipment. So CERN was at the forefront of making gateways for file transfer exchange so you'd get files from different computers; e-mail exchange so that you could get e-mail from the proprietary systems to cross borders and go into another proprietary system. While I wasn't involved in that, that was the spirit. There was a lot of networking."

Tim Berners-Lee decided to try and fix the problem of incompatible information technologies. The problem was that CERN itself was not an information technology laboratory;

however useful his proposal would be to the scientists there, it was difficult to get their attention: "I wrote a proposal saying that a global hypertext project was going to be really important for the high-energy physics community, and the proposal's on the Web now. That was March 1989 and nobody really knew what to do with it. There was no system to pick it up, and CERN really was not a place where one was suppose to be doing information technology. One was supposed to be doing high-energy physics."

The work evolved thanks to the fortuitous location of CERN's Proton Synchrotron Control Division's coffee shop, between the offices and computer rooms used by the people who needed to share their information: "The only place where you could get this information about this interdependence would be by asking over coffee. As it happened, by luck or judgment, the coffee place was [at the junction of] four corridors. Two of which went to the offices and one of which went to the computer room and the terminal room. So there was a constant flow of all the people involved in computing through the coffee area."

Based on "Enquire," the new proposal was intended to allow CERN's scientists to combine their knowledge in a web of hypertext documents: "I started in October 1989 writing a program which I called World Wide Web. When you were reading something you could, if it's interesting and you've got write-access to it, you could just highlight a phrase, hit a hot key (control shift N) and it would bring up another window."

Tim wrote the software for the first World Wide Web server, and for the first client—a "WYSIWYG" hypertext browser/editor. By December 1990, it was in use inside CERN. In 1991, CERN embraced Tim's achievement and published the code on the Internet, making it available to all users—for free—by the summer of 1991. It very rapidly proliferated—and within four years the World Wide Web was sending more packets on the internet than any other service—because Tim had wanted the particle physicists to know more about what each other was doing.

One of the oddest aspects of this story is that Tim Berners-Lee's idea was not new. More than twenty years earlier Ted Nelson, author of the seminal hacker work *Computer Lib* had proposed something similar—his digital paradise was named

Xanadu, after Coleridge's poem "Kublai Khan," a "magic place of literary memory."

> In Xanadu did Kublai Khan
> A stately pleasure dome decree,
> Where Alph, the sacred river, ran
> Through caverns measureless to man
> Down to a sacred sea.

Xanadu was immensely ambitious, measureless indeed. Today Ted Nelson is based at Keio University in Japan, which happens to be the third international base of the World Wide Web Consortium (W3C). The others are MIT, and the French national computer research institution.

Nelson had his vision of a World Wide Web in 1960—an astonishing leap of the imagination—before computers had terminals, let alone keyboards, mice, and GUIs. Xanadu was not only inspired *by* literature, but it was designed to *store and index* the world's literature, on databases, for reuse, quotation, and micropayment of royalties. As Nelson describes it: "The original intention was to create a generalized electronic networking and publishing system that would take care of stability; allow reuse, deep interconnection, deep annotation; and allow every piece to be quoted virtually. It's a very simple idea. I've had it thirty-six years; it's still a simple idea."

Access to Xanadu would be through electronic links which Ted Nelson called "hypertext." This is defined by the *Microsoft Press Computer Dictionary* as "text linked together in a complex, nonsequential web of associations in which the user can browse through related topics." In theory, instead of linear relationships between passages of text (one reads to the end of one before beginning to read the next), there are dynamic links between texts, driven by ideas and associations. In practice, hypertext is embodied in the highlighted or underlined text on a Web page or document; hypertext links allow the user to jump from one page to another by hitting the "hot button." The button conceals a new instruction ("Go to XYZ...) but all the user sees is the button, and then the new page. Ted Nelson coined the phrase but denies the invention: "Hypertext is obvious. I do not claim to have invented hypertext. I merely discovered it. It's like the telephone. The telephone, at the time, seemed to be an invention. To us, now, it's a discovery because it's obvious. Hypertext is like that. To me, it was simply the obvious next step of literature."

While Tim Berners-Lee was met with skepticism and passivity, Ted Nelson—with his hyper-energetic and eccentric presentation of ideas—received more disparaging responses. This despite the fact that his ambitions were squarely in the mainstream of the Bush-Engelbart-Licklider tradition of computers' making human efforts easier and more efficient: "People always just laughed at what I said. They thought I was spouting gibberish apparently, and I've never uttered gibberish in my life, except plainly marked. The whole point was always getting the same ideas across to people: that we have to multiply human intellect."

Coleridge's vision of Xanadu was dispelled when the person from Porlock knocked at the door of his cottage and banished his possibly opium-induced reverie. Nelson's modern Xanadu has proved to be equally insubstantial. But hypertext has become central to the World Wide Web, as Tim Berners-Lee acknowledges: "The power of a hypertext link is that it can link to absolutely anything. That's the fundamental concept. The fundamental idea was anything which was out there somewhere sitting on a computer disk where that computer was attached to a network you ought to be able to give it an address, you ought to be able to make a link to it."

At the time that Berners-Lee embarked on the Web project, there were about 800 different computer networks attached to the Internet, with about 160,000 computers attached to them, all with files and databases containing information that one might want to access. The World Wide Web program established three core components, all known by their acronyms: URL, the Universal Resource Locator; HTTP, HyperText Transfer Protocol; and HTML, HyperText Markup Language.

In simple terms, the URL is what we might call an address; HTTP is the client/server protocol which defines a universal method for transmitting text and graphics over TCP/IP so that pages appear identical regardless of the computer system used; and HTML is a language that describes how graphics and text should be displayed when they are delivered. The Web works on a client/server model: the individual user is requesting material stored on local or distant computers; and the Web application goes out to find, retrieve, and deliver it. Until the Web existed, it was technically possible to do all this, as Tim Berners-Lee is first to note: "It was basically technically trivial to go and get it. It just happened that you had to be a guru of the highest degree to actually be able to navigate all the networks and figure out all the programs that you would come across on your way and know what commands to give them to actually get the data back. Chances are, when you got it back you wouldn't be able to read it anyway, because of all the incompatibility."

Rohit Khare is a Web wunderkind, whose career has already included a spell as an executive of the World Wide Web Consortium in Cambridge. He has subsequently become a Ph.D. student at the University of California, Irvine, developing new Web protocols and studying the process of Internet standardization. At the age of twenty-two, he has as much hands-on experience of the Web as anyone: "The key insight I credit Tim Berners-Lee with, is the URL. The idea there's a Uniform Resource Locator that says I can point at any particular bit of information on the Internet. If I mean that you should go to this university, look in their FTP [File Transfer Protocol] archive, and download this picture of a Corvette and put it up on the screen, I now have a way of doing that. Whereas before I would have actually had to send you an e-mail telling you use your file transfer client, go to Washington University in St. Louis and go to the graphics directory and get the Corvette."

This is the streamlined, user-friendly procedure that has created the proliferation of http//www. addresses on every billboard, bus, and magazine of the nineties. Every Web site has its unique URL, or Web address, and the growth of sites has been breathtaking. By the end of 1997, there were about 1.5 million "domain names," more than double the number one year earlier. Appropriately enough, the very first United States Web site belonged to the Stanford Linear Accelerator Center. The reason, no doubt, was that SLAC is in the same particle research business as CERN. But SLAC was also the principal venue of the Homebrew Computer Club, that band of pioneer nerds devoted to the personal use of computers *ab initio*. In another apt event, Tim

Berners-Lee left CERN to take on a senior role in the World Wide Web Consortium at MIT, based in Tech Square—where Licklider started (and indeed ended) his years of advocacy for Man-Computer Symbiosis. The Web was undoubtedly a major step along that path.

Ted Nelson admires the method that led to the creation of the Web, but not the result: "Tim Berners-Lee figured out that the key was extreme simplicity, and that's very painful to me because now the websters are trying to grapple with all the issues we were trying to solve in a single design at the beginning. The World Wide Web is pretty awful. I mean, I dearly love Tim Berners-Lee and I think he's a great guy and a wonderful idealist and he just achieves wonderful things. But the unfortunate thing about the World Wide Web is just how messed up it is."

By contrast, Bob Taylor—the man who set the very first phase of networked computing in motion at the Pentagon—argues that the Web's achievement has been in overcoming the mess, and creating something that works in spite of it: "It was a tour de force. The people who did the World Wide Web were really willing to take existing pieces of things, in God-awful condition in some cases, and figure out a way to make it work. Whereas the ARPA people and the Xerox people were trying to create new things that were precious from the beginning, that were right. They were less willing to work with junk, or things that they thought were junk. The World Wide Web people deserve a lot of credit for what they did. What they did was very difficult."

Like the ARPAnet, the World Wide Web is not a commercial product, and no one has made any money by selling the Web application. As a consequence, according to Rohit Khare, it has evolved quickly, and in a collaborative fashion: "The Web is a success precisely because it is not a monolithic new software product. You don't get Web 9.0 in the mail on a CD-ROM. The Web is a collection of a whole bunch of small technologies that fit together because a couple dozen people all thought about how they'd work together cool. They're all being evolved constantly in realtime by thousands of people around the world. There isn't any central release. You can't go anywhere to go buy a copy of Web."

Dave Walden, the ARPAnet software scion from BBN, likes to quote his colleague Dave Clark at MIT on why standards become accepted: "Strong consensus and working code. We don't have to have everybody agree, just if enough agree. And we're not interested in theories about what might be, we're interested in what works. Tim Berners-Lee followed that pattern. He brought out something, he gave it to a few of his friends, they tried it, they saw that it was good, and he gave it away. It went all over the world. That's how the World Wide Web standard came on the world. Strong consensus and working code."

The trends of networking, from the sixties to the eighties, saw a general movement from federally funded, noncommercial research efforts to increasingly commercial motivation, and battles for consumer markets. ARPAnet and Alohanet prepared the ground for Ethernet, Netware, Cisco, and Prodigy. But the World Wide Web reversed the trend, in a way that recalls the idealism of some of the pioneering advocates of networking. Tim Berners-Lee reflects: "I think the main intention was to make the thing fly. When you're really attached to a dream of how things could be, then you pursue that dream and it's very, very satisfying to see it work. The fact that the World Wide Web did work, I find is just exciting for itself. Exciting that you can have an idea and it can take off and it can happen. It means that dreamers all over the world should take off and not stop."

Irving Wladawsky-Berger, who today has the daunting task of directing IBM's company-wide strategy for the Internet and Web environment, has an appropriately literary analogy for Tim Berners-Lee's remarkable innovation: "In *War and Peace* Tolstoy had an appendix where he asked the question: 'If Napoleon hadn't been born, would we still have had the invasion of Russia?' He concluded, yes. There are these historical winds and somebody like Napoleon would have been born. I suspect that if Tim hadn't done his great work at CERN, somebody else would have done something similar to Tim. Maybe not as elegant. Maybe not as quickly, but I think it was inevitable that something like this would happen. So it was an idea whose time had come and it was a matter of time before it happened."

Perhaps it is appropriate to give the last word on the World Wide Web to Ted Nelson—who perhaps had the idea before its time—a man whose perfectionism is only exceeded by his restless evangelism for the interconnection of our Dream Machines:

"On the one hand, the World Wide Web is such an abominable garbage heap compared to what we were trying to build; and on the other hand, when I look at it I say, my God, look what it's done for the world. I think that the Internet has already done more for the human race than all the religions of history in terms of bringing us together and making us feel like one world. The World Wide Web is an astounding resource. It's not what it should be, but considering what it is and the fact that everybody and his uncle is putting stuff out there that is potentially useful and interesting...Gee whiz!"

Chapter Fourteen
An Interesting
Commercial Opportunity

"For years, Bill Joy had been telling me that some day we'd back a twenty-one-year-old kid who would write software that would change the world. And lo and behold, sitting in my office is this twenty-three-year-old. Not a kid. He's a very mature, hulking young executive."

The prediction came true in John Doerr's office at Kleiner, Perkins in 1993. The tall, blond, corn-fed Midwesterner had developed a browser named Mosaic. And he was here to tell John Doerr, the skinny and bespectacled venture-capital geek, as Doerr recalls, "This software's going to change everything. By then there were two million users of his prototype, the NCSA (National Center for Supercomputing Applications) Mosaic, that he'd released from the University of Illinois. So it didn't take a rocket scientist to figure out that there was a big market here."

In quick succession, three events transformed the Internet from a no-go area to a major new market for business and commerce. The first was the World Wide Web; the second, the lifting of commercial restrictions on Internet traffic; and the last, the invention of the browser. In the space of less than three years, everything about the Net did change.

Nobody owns the Internet; it's decentralized and democratic. Above all, no one can turn off the Internet. The original ARPAnet was restricted to research and governmental use. Commerce was forbidden, so commerce built its own networks with proprietary networking products, (both hardware and software) that often emulated the ARPAnet technically. Even personal and recreational use was (officially) frowned upon. Naturally enough, the ARPAnet pioneers prided themselves on breaking those rules to play primitive interactive computer games like *Space War* and *Adventure*, or to send messages that did not relate to work.

Len Kleinrock claims to be the pioneer of illegal personal e-mail. In September 1973, he was attending a conference on computer communications at the University of Sussex in Brighton, England. It was one of the first meetings on computer communications, and all the usual suspects were there. On returning to Los Angeles one day early, he noticed that he had left his electric razor behind.

At about 3 A.M. London time, he logged onto the network, using software called Resource Sharing Executive. Guessing that if any of his colleagues was awake and online, Larry Roberts would be, Kleinrock typed "where Roberts?"—"So after two minutes it came back and said, 'Roberts logged on at BBN.' He was logged on from Sussex through the network to BBN. So I connected with him in a little chat session, explained my problem. He said, 'Don't worry.' Next day I had my razor. This was the first illegal use of the ARPAnet. It was a personal use. It wasn't military. It wasn't research. I simply wanted my razor back."

A decade later, as Sandy Lerner recalls, the initial sales of Cisco routers were to fellow academics at sister institutions over the ARPAnet. She makes the interesting distinction that while they were technically illegal, they were nevertheless legitimate: "The sales channel up until early 1987 was exactly the ARPAnet. Yes, it was illegal. On the other hand, I don't think that anybody buying from us those days was not into government-sponsored research. We were basically dealing only with labs and universities and places like Xerox PARC and HP Labs that were certainly legitimate ARPAnet users with legitimate ARPA connections."

Until 1991, free enterprise over the Net was legally forbidden. The ARPAnet had been supplanted by the NSFNet, which was created in 1986, originally to connect five NSF-funded supercomputing sites, and later to interconnect all other Internet sites. Commercial "backbones"—very high capacity lines, paid for by government agencies like NASA or NSF; or by companies like AT&T, Sprint, MCI, and others—had been built and connected to each other; Internet service providers created local or wide area networks; the online services were building networks and connecting them.

Packet traffic on the Internet, as it was by now widely known, was governed by the U.S. government's "Acceptable Use" policy, enshrined in the National Science Foundation Act of 1950 and subsequent amendments. It was illegal to buy or sell anything—goods, services, pets, or houses—on the Internet. As nobody owned it, nobody profited from it—not directly, at least. Business "intranets" were communicating with each other, with every appearance of doing commercial business. The overlap of commercial research with government research, and business information with pure business, meant that the restriction could not be supported for much longer. A change was overdue.

The World Wide Web application in 1991 had given a huge shot of adrenaline to the Internet, vastly multiplying the reach of the individual user. Companies, institutions, and even families began to create their own home pages, filled with useful or merely narcissistic information for the education and amusement of others. Although the Web's HTML language could translate and deliver both text and graphics from server to client, the on-screen process of searching the Web remained clunky. It was the equivalent of a DOS interface compared to a GUI, and what was needed was a graphical look and feel that would add user-friendliness to the sheer volume of materials that were now available.

All three of the nineties watershed events took place in an *annus mirabilis* beginning in summer 1991 and running through 1992. First, the Web software was posted by CERN on the Internet. Next, the requisite user-friendly interface to the Web *was* invented, and became known as the "browser." Third, in an enlightened but also inevitable concession to commercial forces, Congress passed a bill to permit—though not in quite so many words—commercial activity over the wire. Growth of Internet activity, which had been increasing at a vigorous rate throughout the eighties, shot upwards as these events defined the new priorities of the nineties Net.

User-friendliness is the defining feature of mass adoption of technology. The invention of the Web browser allowed the networked Web of networks, now free to undertake commerce and give full expression to the American (and global) way of business, to be accessible, even pleasing, to the average computer user—henceforth to be identified as the digital shopper. Just as the Macintosh was a personal computer "for the rest of us," the browser opened up the Internet to everyone.

The breakthrough browser was invented not in Silicon Valley, nor in Switzerland, but at the University of Illinois, Champaign-Urbana. By no coincidence, this was the location of the National Center for Supercomputing Applications, one of the five locations originally connected by the NSFNet and funded by the National Science Foundation. In the preceding technological era, the U of I had been home to IMP #12 on the ARPAnet. Marc Andreessen had embarked on his university career by selecting electrical engineering as his major, on the sensible basis that the *U.S. News & World Report* annual survey ranked "double-E" graduates as the highest-paid. However, he claims to have found the workload too great, and thus switched to computer science. For a year he had a job placement with IBM, and on returning to the U of I campus, was hired to work as a low-paid programmer at the supercomputing center, working on software to help scientists use the supercomputers.

As Marc Andreessen explains it: "We ended up, in the middle of night, starting this project that we called Mosaic. What we were trying to do was just put a human face on the Internet. The Internet at that point was a tool for researchers and scientists. You had to be a UNIX hacker if you were to use it. We wanted to take all the graphical user interface things that people were getting used to with word processors and spreadsheets and apply them to the Internet. We were in the right place to do that as it turned out."

Andreessen and colleagues like Eric Bina were not the only people trying to develop tools to make the Internet more accessible. The Web itself was designed to do that, and there were other projects like Gopher which was developed at the University of Minnesota and resembled a bulletin board system layered on the Internet; or WAIS, the UNIX-based Wide Area Information Server; or library search engine, jointly developed by Thinking Machines Corporation, Apple Computer, and Dow Jones.

The Illinois hackers had two purposes in mind: "One was to give users a tool to navigate and to find things. The other was to give content providers an incentive to create content on the Net because, at that point, there really wasn't anything that normal people would want to see anyway."

Marc Andreessen's intent was "to make all the resources on the Internet available with one click." At NCSA, on UNIX-based computers, they made Mosaic work that way. Word around the university-based UNIX community was that Mosaic was hot. Next, other members of the team—Aleks Totic, Jon Mittelhauser, and Chris Wilson—developed Macintosh and PC versions, to allow "the rest of us" to see the virtues of Mosaic.

While these events were taking place in the wholesome academic environs of Illinois, a separate small revolution, in the form of unheralded amendments to already obscure federal laws, was taking place on Capitol Hill. The sponsor was a congressman whose name is not widely known to Americans, yet deserves some recognition for the change he wrought upon the Internet— the Honorable Rick Boucher, who represents Virginia's "Fightin' Ninth" District.

The amendment introduced by Representative Boucher on June 9, 1992, hardly ranks with the Declaration of Independence or the Gettysburg Address, but in the annals of government and commerce, it is legislation of great consequence. For buried in the quaint legislative prose is language that changed the world of networking beyond recognition.

His amendment to the National Science Foundation Act of 1950 read as follows: "The Foundation is authorized to foster and support the development and use of computer networks which may be used substantially for purposes in addition to research and education in the sciences and engineering, if the additional users will tend to increase the overall capabilities of the networks to support such research and education activities."

Rick Boucher explained the meaning of this congressional jargon thus: "The amendment authorizes NSF to support the development and use of computer networks which may carry a substantial volume of traffic that does not conform to the current acceptable use policy." In redefining "acceptable use" of the NSFNet—what Representative Boucher referred to in his speech as "additional flexibility for developing in concert with the private sector"—the Boucher Bill opened the floodgates to digital commerce, and prompted a million home shopping channels to bloom on every desktop. The Bill was signed into law by President Bush on November 23, 1992.

Bob Kahn, cocreator of the TCP/IP protocols that allowed the Internet to get connected in the first place, sees this legislative tweak as an important contributory factor in the accelerated growth of the Net: "The Internet was on a major increase after the Boucher Bill. Commercialization took place. It was growing at a very rapid rate. The introduction of the Web really just changed the rate of acceleration in a way I think we had never seen before. I think the Internet is really a marketplace for information and connectivity and collaboration."

Everyone in high technology likes to debate what is the killer application of a new technology, or platform, or product. Bob Kahn sees the Internet as too large for such a concept to be meaningful: "Is there a killer app in *the economy*? The answer is there just is every possibility of what you can do with human ingenuity. Whether it's at the level of food and agriculture or clothing and goods or whether it's informational."

Undoubtedly the explosive growth of the Internet has provided many people with new, at least potential, business opportunities, with investors ready to bet on promising people, technologies, and products. Kim Polese is a rare Silicon Valley corporate bird: a founder, and a female. As a product manager at Sun Microsystems, she had no background in ARPAnet access, and to her, the Internet was relatively inaccessible and unappealing. But Mosaic changed that: "For me, this whole thing started exploding with the invention of the browser—Mosaic. Suddenly the Internet was accessible to the average person through this rich graphical interface. You didn't have to know these arcane protocols. You didn't have to be a nerd anymore to access the Internet."

Kim Polese left Sun in February 1996 to start up her own Web-specific technology company, Marimba. Similarly, Eric Schmidt left Sun in April 1997, after fourteen years, to head Novell. Schmidt has an enviable networking resumé: he worked on developing UNIX at Bell Labs, worked with and for Bill Joy at Berkeley, went to Xerox PARC, and was then hired by Bill Joy to work at Sun. Schmidt regards Mosaic as a milestone: "Mosaic put a face to the Web. Mosaic, plus the Web, then finally gave us a way to express to the nontechnical person what all of us in computing knew was the tremendous value of having networks interconnected. Now everyone's a Web head and everyone's excited about the Web. Those ideas have been present for twenty years but it took a killer application, clearly Mosaic—as significant as Lotus 1-2-3 was ten years earlier in making the PC happen."

Marc Andreessen, stuck in an NCSA basement in Illinois, was far from the white heat of Silicon Valley's wealth-creation machine. But he would not remain in the digital boondocks for long. He could hardly fail to notice that Mosaic was a success within the first year of its initial circulation: "The number of Mosaic users went from originally twelve to a hundred to a thousand to ten thousand to somewhere in the order of a million by the end of 1993. So it didn't take a whole lot of imagination to figure out that if it kept doubling for the next couple of years that it was going to be a five-, ten-million person environment, which starts to be an interesting commercial opportunity."

Andreessen, then age twenty-one, was exhibiting a precocious talent for commerce. Technological people like Eric Schmidt saw Mosaic and generally realized they were looking at the future. But in 1994, despite the Boucher Bill, the conventional wisdom was that it was not possible to make money on the Internet. The cofounder of Netscape, Jim Clark, did not have a Pauline conversion when he first saw Mosaic; he thought it was "nice." At the time, he was more inclined to start a new company in the interactive television and interactive video games business. But he was concerned that however good his relationship might be with Nintendo, that amounted to a customer base of one.

Jim Clark himself had managed to be in many of the right places at the right time for a network computing career; but he had resolutely resisted those opportunities in favor of different ones, becoming a multimillionaire in the process anyway. He got his Ph.D. from the University of Utah (where the fourth ARPA node was located), not because of his interest in the ARPAnet but because of computer graphics. This was the specialty of Ivan Sutherland, formerly the second director of ARPA's IPTO, who went from MIT to ARPA to Utah. Clark went on to Stanford, where he inherited an ARPA contract to do research in integrated circuits. At the time, he was planning to develop specialized computer graphics systems based on custom integrated circuits. He used the research grant to develop the technology that became Silicon Graphics, and to build his fortune. He worked on the second floor of Margaret Jacks Hall; Andy Bechtolsheim (Sun) was upstairs, Len Bosack (Cisco) downstairs.

Clark made a lot of money from SGI, but in 1994, after twelve years, he had become discouraged about fighting the board to push the company in the direction he favored. He resigned from the SGI board at their February 1994 meeting, and while packing up his office, used Mosaic for the very first time—to find its author Marc Andreessen's e-mail address. The older, experienced entrepreneur and the young technologist debated what kind of company to start up: as Andreessen says, "It took us a couple of months together to really sort of triangulate around an idea of the Internet as a commercial medium."

Jim Clark had started Silicon Graphics with a handful of his Stanford students, and decided to pursue the same strategy: "Marc and I were struggling one night and he suggested that we basically create a "Mosaic killer." I said, 'Look, if you can recruit all the guys, every single guy who helped you write that program, then I'll put my own money in it and we'll just start a company and figure out some way to make a business out of it.' That's exactly what we did. I put three million dollars in. We flew out to the University of Illinois four days later, signed them all up—the same offer to all of them—and we hired them all right then. Six guys."

The Mosaic Gang of Six who joined Andreessen and Clark was: Eric Bina, Chris Houck, Rob McCool, Jon Mittelhauser, Lou Montulli (a University of Kansas interloper), and Aleks Totic. Chris Wilson had already been hired—by Microsoft. Having rejected interactive video games, and hired all the software developers responsible for Mosaic, the two men started a new company they called Mosaic Communications. No prizes for guessing the origins of the name, or the technology they would develop. The name had not been trademarked by the University of Illinois, but the software had been licensed to numerous other companies. As a veteran and beneficiary of Stanford's enlightened intellectual property policy, Clark says that he never considered that the University of Illinois would object to their venture: "I figured, Why not use Mosaic? It never even occurred to me the University of Illinois would care. But they did. They were upset because I gave all these guys jobs and I had essentially stolen them from slave labor from the university, I guess."

Marc Andreessen was equally surprised, and annoyed, by his alma mater's lack of enthusiasm for the venture: "The university had what you might call an allergic reaction to the concept of students actually leaving and then building a company based on the concepts that they'd been working on at the university. Of course, at MIT or Stanford they would have loved it. At Illinois they hated it. So a whole pissing match erupted between the university and our company."

The dispute with the University of Illinois over ownership of Mosaic (both the name and the program) delayed matters for a few months. The programmers rewrote their own work, making it ten times faster, and Mosaic Communications was consigned to the garbage. In April 1994, Netscape Communications rose phoenix-like, and their Mosaic killer product, Navigator, was released in Beta version on the Net in October. At about the same time, Jim Clark raised $5 million of venture funding from John Doerr at Kleiner, Perkins.

The business plan for Netscape at the time defied most conventional wisdom, and relied heavily upon Jim Clark's entrepreneurial gut feelings:

> I was supposed to be a businessman, and here I was starting a business in what everyone knew you couldn't make money on—the Internet. That was what I was being told. But my attitude was if 25 million people are on the Net today, one million of them are using Mosaic (this was April of 1994) and we can displace Mosaic, there's 24 more million people who would like a product like this, presumably. The size of the Net was doubling roughly every year-and-a-half, so that meant that by the time we had our products in the marketplace it would be 50 million people. You got to be able to make money with 50 million people using your product. That was the sum total of the business plan at that time.

Jim's plan for the company was minimalist.

By venture capitalist John Doerr's standards, this investment opportunity was a no-brainer. He was quite able to believe Marc Andreessen's boast that Mosaic (now Navigator) would change everything: "We had one meeting with Jim and Marc. After that, we decided to invest and then set about on a crash program of 120 days, to hire four vice presidents and a world-class CEO, and get the Netscape products shipped. The money was easy. It was knowing the opportunity and recruiting the people."

The statistics of Netscape's immediate and near-vertical climb in market share and profitability have become a Silicon Valley legend. Jim Clark's gut feeling was vindicated more rapidly than any gut feeling in the history of business: "In about a year-and-a-half's time, we had 65 million users—the most rapidly assimilated product in history. No one had ever achieved an installed base of 65 million anything, except perhaps Microsoft."

Netscape's market share rose to 85 percent, and on August 9, 1995, only sixteen months after the company had been founded, the initial public offering of five million shares, priced at $28 each, took place. At seven o'clock that morning, Jim Clark called the stockbroker, and learned that there was a huge imbalance of buy orders to shares available. The stock opened at $70, making the company founders instant multimillionaires. In Jim Clark's case, a repeat multimillionaire with two of two hugely successful start-up companies to his credit.

The Netscape IPO fueled an Internet funding frenzy, in which both inventors and investors reversed the previous received wisdom and convinced themselves that Internet businesses (or their stocks) could make money. Rob Glaser, who founded his Internet-casting company Progressive Networks in 1994 with the proceeds of ten years and stock options from Microsoft, regarded the trend with skepticism: "In 1995 and 1996, if you said you were doing an Internet toaster, I'm sure you could find a venture capitalist to fund it."

Another entrepreneur, Jim Bidzos, has a long management track record as CEO of RSA Data Security, and has benefited both his company and himself by negotiating stock options rather than license fees when new ventures have approached him to include RSA encryption and security software in their systems. In April of 1994, Andreessen and Clark wanted to license RSA technology for Netscape Navigator, and asked how much it would cost them. Bidzos replied: "'Let's not talk about that. Give me stock instead of money in return for a license to use my software.' That was the first time I'd ever even considered that. So I actually made a deal with Netscape in April of 1994, which turned out later to be worth tens of millions of dollars. It was a great stroke of luck in a sense."

As an investor, he watched the hysteria from inside and outside: "In 1995 and 1996, with the craze started by Netscape and the IPO market, if you had a decent idea you could announce that you were forming a company and it was worth $50 million today, and you'd give somebody 20 percent of it for $10 million—and you could probably find somebody to give it to you. Everybody got stars in their eyes and saw what Netscape did and thought, well, we can do the same thing. Reality has set in again. You can't [any longer] take your *aunt* public if you just simply call her a desktop multimedia Internet-based secure interactive electronic commerce widget. In 1995, you could have taken anything public with a prospectus that included all of those buzz words."

Bidzos had secure transaction technology that almost everyone creating Internet businesses wanted, so company after company arrived at his doorstep looking for a license. Repeatedly, he took the stock option instead. Over barely three years, Jim Bidzos seized investment opportunities in the Internet industry that have delivered, by his estimation, a 29,500 percent return: "It's an opportunity I get that nobody else gets. It's not something anybody could go buy. It's a private company that I get to look at. But having a return, you know, of almost 300 times over a couple of years is not bad. You don't have to invest a lot of money in order to realize a good gain. I invested *a lot* of money."

In 1995, Netscape was known as the fastest-growing company in the industry, or any industry, with all the requisite Silicon Valley attributes—shiny low-rise buildings, Generation-X work force, and a parking lot reserved for roller hockey. In the same month that Netscape's IPO set new standards for instant wealth, Microsoft launched their new operating system, Windows 95, with the Microsoft Network, competitor to Prodigy and America Online, built in. It also included Microsoft's first version of their own browser. Steve Ballmer was pragmatic about Netscape's meteoric rise: "The folks in Illinois did some clever work early on. There's always going to be some clever work done some place that's not here. Number two, we had a big thing we had to get done called Windows 95, and while we managed to get our browser done and built in, because we weren't asleep, it didn't get the same kind of passionate, forward, 100 percent focus that we love to give things because we had a lot of that focus already into doing the basic job of Windows 95. So a little bit of cleverness and a little bit of other priority was all it took to create a window—that's how dynamic and competitive this industry is—in which Netscape emerged."

While Ballmer is studiously unimpressed by Netscape, Jim Clark is openly hostile to Microsoft. He describes the Seattle company's attitude towards Netscape in 1995 thus: "About this time, Microsoft was beginning to wake up. They weren't completely awake because they still were trying to force what then was called Microsoft Network down everyone's throat."

Netscape achieved market share by the same elegantly simple method that John McAfee had pioneered five years earlier. Navigator could be downloaded from the Web, used and evaluated, and then paid for, maybe. With Navigator's having attracted tens of millions of users, Jim Clark's assumption that he'd figure out how to make a business of it was proven accurate: " We knew ultimately we had to replace Mosaic because Mosaic had the attention of the world. That's the reason we chose to give [Navigator] away, more or less—free for download, free for use—unless you were a business, and then you had to talk to us about a license, and that was what our license agreement said when you downloaded the product."

The McAfee model and the superior performance of Navigator was the mortal threat Andreessen had planned for Mosaic: "Our goal was to create a Mosaic killer and we killed it. We ate our young. Even though our young didn't belong to us anymore. We put it out there and we watched the download ticker and we took early advantage of the fact—which is not widely understood—that the cost of software distribution goes to zero on the Net, essentially."

Marc Andreessen emphasizes that Navigator was intended to remain free of charge for the traditional ARPAnet, Internet, academic, non-profit community; but that business could pay: "Free for non-profit and educational use; free for evaluation use for ninety days, by businesses in particular. We figured that businesses would be the bulk of our customer base. We'd get most of our money from businesses."

At Illinois, Andreessen's Mosaic had been distributed on much the same terms, with great success: "You had to get a license for commercial use, which was very vaguely defined. We were getting hundreds of phone calls by the time I left at the end of 1993 from people wanting to license Mosaic for business use of different kinds."

The business licenses amounted to huge revenues for Netscape. Jim Clark's sketchy business plan paid off: "That was the way we made money. We made $75 million the first year in revenues and $375 million in the second year. The third year ended up being somewhere north of $500 million in revenues, and we did that by selling licenses for companies to make company-wide use of the browser. Until Microsoft came in and punched us in the face, we were the fastest-growing company in history."

Steve Jobs, the founder of Apple Computer, has had his own experience of seeing Microsoft enter a market and overwhelm the original innovator (the Apple Macintosh) with a similar, competing product (Windows). Jobs regards the Web as "the defining social moment for computing." He foresees all current mail-order commerce (15 percent of the retail economy), and more, shifting to the Web. He approves of the provocative fact that on the Web, the smallest company can look like the largest, and regards the Web as having "breathed a whole new generation of life into personal computing." Steve Jobs is also both a perennial critic and partner of Microsoft and its monolithic tendencies: "The Web is incredibly exciting, because it is the fulfillment of a lot of our dreams, that the computer would ultimately not be primarily a device for computation, but metamorphosize into a device for communication. And with the Web that's finally happening. And secondly, it's exciting because Microsoft doesn't own it, and therefore there is a tremendous amount of innovation happening."

The Netscape-Microsoft drama is unresolved to date, but its consequences may go farther than a mere half-billion dollars a year of revenue here or there. The Department of Justice has become a player, and forces other than those of the market and of smart programmers making good products may define the future direction of the Web browser market. This market may be more important in due course than the PC operating system market, in which Microsoft has what John Doerr regards as "a legal, earned monopoly": "They've got aggressive management, incredible bench strength, and, basically, unlimited financial resources to pursue whatever markets they choose to enter. The Netscape company is far smaller than Microsoft is. It's several thousand people now. Three years old. And they're the rabbit that's running real fast down the road."

By 1997, Netscape had grown in three years to be the same size that Microsoft took eleven years to reach. The widespread skepticism of 1994 has been replaced by a conventional wisdom that the Net, or Web, represents the biggest communications revolution *of all time*. Certainly between 1991 and 1994 the Internet was transformed, thanks to the World Wide Web, the browser, and Congressman Rick Boucher. The technology, politics, and commerce were all in place for a global market to emerge in information, services, and products. All that seemed to be left was the division of the spoils. Somewhat inevitably, Microsoft had a number of ideas about that.

Chapter Fifteen
The Slumbering Giant

"Microsoft's never been accused of not knowing how to make money. It's pretty straightforward. If you can sell volume software, you can do quite well." Bill Gates' manner is still boyish at forty-two—he smirks uncontrollably as he understates the churning billions of dollars that Microsoft's revenues represent.

Until 1992, the noncommercial Internet had barely attracted Microsoft's attention. It did not seem like a business opportunity, for obvious reasons, at least in comparison to the cash cows that Microsoft's MS-DOS and Windows operating systems were. The story of Microsoft's extraordinary growth from a tiny, neophyte software company into one of the most successful companies in the history of world commerce is not to be repeated here. But throughout the 1980s, the attention of the company was focused on making money in two successive ways: by maintaining its symbiotic, synergistic relationship with IBM in order to secure every last dollar available from devising, upgrading, and marketing the operating system for all Intel-based PCs, both IBM and clone; and then, after the strategic decision to split from IBM over OS/2, by marketing the new Windows operating system to the same market of IBM and clone PCs.

The nineties saw more of the same growth in revenues and profits. In the three years, from 1990 to 1993, the number of hosts on the Internet grew roughly tenfold, from over 159,000 in October 1989 to 1,486,000 in April 1993. But Microsoft was booming independent of the Net: in the same three years, the company tripled sales to $3.8 billion a year, and tripled its payroll. Windows 95 would just add to the torrent of profit.

The preparations for the launch of Windows 95 resembled a variety of models, metaphorically. It was a worldwide advertising campaign such as Alexander the Great or Churchill might have recognized. It was a marketing phenomenon that adopted, for a steep price, a Rolling Stones hit song. (When Coca-Cola launched "I'd Like to Teach the World to Sing" as its global marketing theme, it only reached as high as The New Seekers.) It was, too, a sort of self-coronation, like that of Emperor Jean-Bedel Bokassa, who placed the diamond-encrusted crown of the Central African Empire upon his own princely head. Bill Gates had himself introduced to a global, live satellite audience in polo shirt and khakis, with Jay Leno of NBC's *Tonight Show* as his master of ceremonies: "Ladies and gentlemen, welcome to the launch of Windows 95. Yes, welcome Microsoftees—nice to have you all here. But now let's welcome the chairman of Microsoft. Listen to this. This is a man so successful, his chauffeur is Ross Perot, ladies and gentlemen. Please welcome Bill Gates."

August 24, 1995. In Redmond, a suburb of Seattle, this was the biggest, noisiest product launch in the history of the personal computer, and probably in the history of all marketing. Windows 95 software was intended to be installed in every existing PC, by its owner, to upgrade its previous Microsoft operating system; and in every new PC to be manufactured. In either case, Bill Gates' company would reap huge new revenues from an operating system market share now estimated to be in excess of 95 percent. Bill Gates, principal nerd and visionary leader of Microsoft, was the star of the show: "We wanted people to be able to appreciate how Windows 95 makes computing faster, easier and more fun. And for seven years it was a lonely, lonely crusade... This moves the whole PC industry up to a whole new level."

Some might argue that the crusade was not so lonely, given that the Apple Macintosh had offered people most of the same product features since 1984, eleven years earlier; and that those features had in turn been borrowed from Xerox PARC, where they first saw the light of day ten years before that. But the Windows 95 launch extravaganza was not a day for dissent.

With the money to be made from operating systems—as Microsoft had already so convincingly demonstrated—it would have been unexpected perhaps for Microsoft to turn away to the fledgling Internet business realm. But by now, about twenty million people were using the Internet regularly, and they were not using Microsoft software products in doing so. The occasion of Netscape's IPO two weeks earlier did not spoil Microsoft's party.

But the corporate style in Redmond is a marriage of intense focus with paranoia, and Microsoft had shown in their determined efforts to compete in networking software that a good market was always regarded as a potential Microsoft market.

Unlike Bob Metcalfe, who so believed in focus that he allowed, by his own admission, several multibillion-dollar markets to elude him, Bill Gates prides himself on constantly looking over his shoulder. His staff regard this as the most rewarding form of paranoia in the business. Two former lieutenants, Jon Shirley and Scott Oki—both now in retirement thanks to the wealth Microsoft stock options provided—observe that this helps the company to be highly responsive to Gates' instincts. Jon Shirley, former president of Microsoft, has the resources to indulge his passion for collecting vintage Ferraris. As he sees it, "Bill likes to have a general feeling of paranoia throughout the entire company as to who's going to come along with something that's going to destroy one or all of our businesses; and so people are very receptive to an understanding of a sudden direction change."

Scott Oki retired from his position as vice president of sales, marketing and services after ten years at Microsoft and now owns a professional soccer team, the Seattle Sounders; develops golf courses; and runs a personal foundation to support start-up businesses that return all their profits to children's charities. He observed the process whereby Gates begins to see a new industry trend and to pay attention: "When this other thing starts gaining some momentum, when it finally triggers something, usually within Bill, when Bill finally says, 'Boy, we'd better do something about this,' instantly people get it."

But even Gates, occasionally, for a while, overlooks a business he should—or could—get into. It was not until 1995, by which time Netscape had secured an 85 percent market share of internet browsers that Microsoft woke up, paid attention, and really began to compete. As Jon Shirley points out: "Netscape came along and showed us there's a whole other business there and took advantage of the growth of the Net long before we were spending our time on worrying about it. We were worrying about other things. But hopefully, any good company reacts to an opportunity or a potential opportunity that might not be an opportunity unless you move quickly."

Netscape did appear over Bill Gates' shoulder, drawing his attention to a market opportunity: "Netscape's done a very good job, and you always expect new people to come along. I didn't know what their name would be or who they would be. But there will always be, every year, companies that latch onto what the latest thing is and get a lot of visibility and deliver products that relate to that."

Even within Microsoft, a company that owes its entire existence to the technology of personal computers, rather than the mainframes and minicomputers that have driven the creation of the Net, the move towards Internet activity came from the grassroots, not from the leadership. Microsoft campus recruiters like Steven Sinofsky, Bill Gates' technical assistant, found themselves learning, from college students who wanted to get jobs at the company, about the vibrancy and extent of the Internet. In early 1994, both Sinofsky and J. Allard wrote memos to management advocating that more attention be paid to the Net. Some of those campus recruits, once hired, continued to make noise about the Net and Web within the low-rise systems labs of Redmond, Washington. Word of mouth percolated upwards—despite the focus and energy being expended on completing, testing, and shipping Windows 95—as Steve Ballmer acknowledges: "Certainly by 1994 there were the rabble-rousers around here. The guys who were sort of stirring action, saying we've got to invest. We've got to get on top of this Internet phenomenon. [They would] write memos, come to meetings, show stuff, talk about stuff, show enthusiasm, show possibility. They got a lot of attention."

Microsoft was not entirely unaware of the Internet or of the growing utility of the Net as a means of tying together academic, business and personal users. Their first, somewhat hurried steps to embrace the concept in their mass-market consumer products recall several facets of the company's history, and the history of networking.

J. Allard's job was building TCP/IP protocols into Microsoft LAN Manager and Windows for Workgroups (much as Bill Joy had added TCP/IP to Berkeley UNIX). In August 1994, four months after Netscape was founded, Ben Slivka persuaded the senior management that a browser should be part of Windows 95. With less than a year to do it, Microsoft made the same "buy or build" decision that IBM made when licensing the MS-DOS operating system from Microsoft for the IBM PC. In December 1994, Microsoft licensed technology from Spyglass to develop a Web browser for Windows 95; Spyglass was one of the companies that had licensed Mosaic from the University of Illinois— and loudly protested when Clark and Andreessen set up Mosaic Communications.

So Microsoft was pursuing a number of Net directions, but the Net was not yet at the core of the company. The opportunities were impressive, however. In January 1995, Microsoft invested $16.4 million in UUNet Technologies, an Internet service provider that would carry the traffic for Microsoft Network, to be included in Windows 95. As Gates explains: "We did a deal with UUNet, including us getting some stock options there. We've made, at this point, well over $400 million on just that piece, as kind of a sideline. Even for us, the $400 million shows what an amazing space this is."

In the spring of 1995, at the urging of the troops, and even board members, Bill went "surfing." It was an all-nighter that changed Microsoft—and the Internet industry. Jon Shirley recalls the result: "Bill went down to his place on the Hood Canal, with instructions on how to get on or what to go look for; and he got on and started looking around, and started going from site to site, and, I think, eventually, spent the greater part of all night on the Net. He came back and had a meeting and described the experience and said that he was blown away with just how much was really there."

With less than three months to go before the launch of Windows 95, on May 11, 1995, Gates wrote a now-famous memorandum. It demonstrated both his acute business sense of where the opportunities lay; and a remarkable flexibility to turn his attention from the current enormous efforts to think about the future: "I wrote a memo at one point called, 'The Coming Internet Tidal Wave' that very explicitly said, 'I've told you many times in the past, I think the Internet is a priority. I'm now telling you it is *the* priority.' The timing was very good there because we were getting along in terms of Windows 95. We thought we had that all well understood and we could really get a lot of energy focused on the Internet."

These qualities of perspective—by contrast with the performance in the 1980s of the IBM behemoth—win Bob Metcalfe's praise: "Gates is a smart guy. Unlike the management of IBM in the middle '80s, Bill Gates is awake and functioning and he noticed that the Internet was not going to be ignored. He tried to ignore it briefly and then he saw—quickly he saw, in time he saw—that it wasn't going to be ignorable."

Getting energy focused on the Internet meant largely that Microsoft was going to focus on Netscape as a rival. That was Marc Andreessen's expectation, and he was only surprised that it had not come sooner: "We always assumed that Microsoft would be our biggest enemy because they would have to turn their attention to this. We got lucky for a while in that they just weren't paying attention. There were people inside Microsoft who knew what Microsoft should do to respond to us, but the management team at Microsoft was almost willfully ignoring what was happening."

Microsoft executives acknowledge that Netscape's success was part of what prompted the Redmond company to pay attention to the Net. Would Steve Ballmer call this rival a thorn in their side? "Netscape's a competitor, not a thorn. They're a constant challenge, a constant push, a constant opportunity. A thorn? I wouldn't use that word."

Jon Shirley says that Netscape "provided a service of getting us perhaps more energized than we might have [been]. It was much more the weekend that he spent literally online the whole time, that was really the eye opener that caused the sudden shift into really getting onto the Internet."

Bill Gates' personal wealth, staggering though it is, merely reflects the success of his company. On the shores of Seattle's Lake Washington in 1998, teams of architects, high-tech engineers, and interior designers were putting the finishing touches to Gates' legendary new home. The bill for the house had risen to estimates above $50 million. But in the two previous years, his wealth had increased at a rate of $31 million per day. So no matter what it cost, it could not matter. Bill Gates' didn't get to be the richest man in the world, nor Microsoft the dominant power in personal computing, by mere cleverness or luck. It was a combination of both, and a determination both personal and corporate to push every advantage to the limit.

Bill Joy, the cofounder of Sun Microsystems, has observed Gates from the position of both collaborator and competitor: "Bill's very driven. I don't spend as much time with him now as I did ten years ago but you know, he'd sit in meetings and he'd just physically shake all the time. Moving his knees, moving his hands, rocking back and forth. It's just a tempest in there, trying to figure it all out. My rule always was, 'There are a lot of smart people but most of them are elsewhere.' I was just happy if the things got done. I think Bill would rather see them done at Microsoft, and done under his control. That's a big agenda. That's why he's so busy."

Scott Oki argues that Microsoft's greatest advantage over competitors is the cash resources of the company: "So many other companies just can't make strategic decisions and persevere for many years throwing millions of dollars, you know, to make something successful. But Microsoft always had these cash cows, always had MS-DOS, Windows, Microsoft Office. These are huge cash streams that are flowing in. I mean, how many billions of dollars are created every year? They're just throwing off unbelievable amounts of money that now can get directed into things like the Internet and other product spaces that Microsoft thinks is important."

In the six months between the writing of the "Tidal Wave" memo and a public announcement of Microsoft's new vision and direction (and while Windows 95 was actually completed and shipped), Gates redirected the energies of 20,000 people, and a $300 billion company, to compete in the Internet "space." Microsoft had licensed browser technology from Spyglass for its own unfinished, still-in-development browser that became Internet Explorer; and incorporated a first version of their Web browser in Windows 95. But the sheer scale of the Windows 95 launch, and the bundling of the Microsoft Network venture within it, somewhat obscured the modest Internet ambitions of the company at the time. The big guns were yet to be rolled out.

The Microsoft Network was an online service, but not an Internet service provider. In late 1993, Rob Glaser had been charged with analyzing how the Net would affect MSN, and he concluded that it should be retooled, in time for Windows 95, as a part of the Internet. As Steve Ballmer recalls, Microsoft Network missed the boat by failing to be Net-capable: "We started before maybe things hit the knee in the curve of the Internet and we said, 'Jeez, we really got to go Internet with this thing.' On the other hand, we were trying to ship it, and so we didn't fully Internetize it before we shipped it. Then we went back and said, 'Jeez, we probably should have totally Internetized it before we shipped it.'"

Also bundled in Windows 95 was Microsoft's first version of their browser, Internet Explorer. It too was a product that apparently fell short of the customers' growing needs, as Gates recognizes: "We saw that what users expected out of the browser was going to rise so dramatically that we had to put a much, much bigger team on it. We had to really get more Microsoft people involved in the standards processes than any other company would have because the success of the Internet would become the driving factor for demand for our software and everybody else's software."

The recognition that the browser and Internet would drive demand across the board for Microsoft's products did indeed amount to a tidal wave, or a "Sea-Change" (the title of an earlier Gates Net memo). Microsoft revealed their change of direction to the world on a date with a sinister significance for Americans— Pearl Harbor Day. The December 7, 1995, event made the repositioning of Microsoft into front-page news, as Gates remembers: "We did a big event where we, for the first time, showed the world how this had all built up. And they saw, hey, this is pretty dramatic. This company is going to deliver great Internet software. So saying it was an epiphany is a little too much, but saying that it became the centerpiece of our strategy, that's absolutely right."

Acknowledging the date, Gates on stage made a point of quoting the Japanese Admiral Yamamoto, who said that he feared they "had but awakened a sleeping giant." This might indeed have been Netscape's reaction to the development. But Marc Andreessen was skeptical, if not dismissive: "The big break happened at the famous Pearl Harbor Day talk. But Microsoft was doing a bunch of stuff leading up to that and, in fact, they have this thing they do now where every three months they come out and reannounce how hardcore they are about the Internet. They've done that like five or six times now."

Bill Gates announced that the shift was company-wide, and that it ran from top to bottom: "You will hear from us that we're *not* forming an Internet division. To us that's like having an electricity division or a software division. The Internet is pervasive in everything that we're doing."

When the slumbering giant awoke, Microsoft's Internet Explorer—the product designed to compete with Netscape's Navigator—looked awfully familiar. The two were certainly related, through the common parentage or grandparentage of Mosaic. But in 1995 there was one very big difference between the two. Netscape Navigator cost $49 dollars to business users. Internet Explorer came free with Windows.

On stage at the Seattle Center auditorium, before an audience of industry writers and developers, with Microsoft staff watching on closed-circuit television, Gates indulged in some stagy, scripted repartee with his demo man:

> Demonstrator: They're working hard, as you can see here, implementing all the standards we need.
> Gates: And what do you think we'll charge for that?
> Demonstrator: Like all the others, nothing.
> Gates: Okay. Well, that's quite a deal.

Before long, Internet Explorer was downloadable on the Internet, bundled with online services, and accessible to any Internet user, at no charge. For Microsoft to compete by giving away software is indeed a sea change, and an historic irony, since it was Bill Gates who famously protested that software had to be paid for, not shared—thus producing royalties for Microsoft. But the dynamics of the Altair software market and the Internet software market are entirely different.

The results of Microsoft's initiative were just as John McAfee, the first exponent of giveaway software, would have predicted: "If you have two competing products and they are on a par in terms of functionality and usability, the free one is the one that will propagate."

Needless to say, the impact upon Netscape was dramatic. Their market capitalization and revenues both depended upon their dominance of a market that paid for the product. Jim Clark is entirely clear in his view of Microsoft's motives: "Microsoft came along and in an attempt to put us out of business, gave away the browser totally free, even for companies who wanted to use it for business. It definitely had an impact on us. As a consequence, we had to give away *our* browser."

For a company that in three years had browser revenues climb from zero to half a billion dollars, this is a serious adjustment. But in mid-1998, Clark was confident that Netscape had ridden out the blow: "We've done it now and we've made the transition just this quarter. This quarter (Q1/1998) we just finished is the first quarter where we've had *no* browser revenues."

In another historical irony, the nineties relationship between a nimble newcomer (Netscape) and a slower-moving, established company (Microsoft) mirrors the similar dynamic of the PC era in the early eighties. In Bob Metcalfe's opinion: "Netscape is the leader and Microsoft's playing the role of IBM, if I might go back to the mid '80s. So Microsoft is the big bumbling company who got taken by surprise with the Internet, and Netscape is the Microsoft. They switched roles. So Microsoft is now the dominant monopoly, which relies on, much too often I think, on its size rather than its excellence to succeed."

Whether the Microsoft browser is free or not, and whether Microsoft is attempting to create a browser monopoly to match its de facto operating system monopoly, goes to the very heart of competitive practices in American business; and therefore gets the attention of the U.S. government. According to both those directly involved (at Netscape, on the receiving end) and some outside observers, what Microsoft is doing is illegal. Microsoft, after belatedly rushing to the publicity barricades in mid-1998, has argued that it's just serving the customer by offering more, better, cheaper software.

Bill Gates suggests that the shared public-domain ancestry of Mosaic is an argument for distributing the browsers for free; and that Microsoft isn't competing for Netscape's market, because Microsoft had started work on its browser first. "Now Netscape is one of our competitors. It's been a great thing for customers, the pace at which all of these products have moved along."

Jim Clark of Netscape has the opposite view: "They're ruthless and vicious.... Ask anybody who's gone up against them directly. Of course, they weren't in our market when we started. So we were hardly going after a market that they were aware of, but they then realized that it could be a big market and it's their God-given right to own any big market in software."

Bob Metcalfe is a big believer in competition: "Giving it away is an anti-competitive technique. They're trying to kill Netscape by drying up its revenue sources. And it should be illegal. They should not be permitted to do that. If antitrust has any use, it's to go in now and say 'You spend millions and millions of dollars to develop the thing, and you give it away. Hmmm. Why are you doing that? Clearly you're doing that to damage Netscape. You're not allowed to do that.'"

On May 18, 1998, the Department of Justice filed an antitrust lawsuit against Microsoft alleging anti-competitive practices in the browser market. However the case is resolved—and however soon the case is resolved—it represents a watershed of the information age, perhaps a coming-of-age, in which the industry has become significant enough for the attorney-general, Janet Reno, to stand before a Washington press conference to announce: "The Justice Department has charged Microsoft with engaging in anti-competitive and exclusionary practices designed to maintain its monopoly in personal computer operating systems and attempting to extend that monopoly to Internet browser software."

In interviews conducted with Microsoft executives some six months before the Justice Department's case was filed, it was apparent that Microsoft was both sensitive and somewhat inconsistent on the question of whether their browser, Internet Explorer, is given away for free or is part of a more complex transaction. Bill Gates smiles when he says that Microsoft knows how to make money: "Now, in order to keep Windows very strong, we felt having a free browser that promoted our extensions, as well as providing all the power of all the other standards, that that was critical to our strategy. So the browser investment is totally paid for by the fact that it helps Windows—and Windows is a very good, quite profitable business."

Gates' longtime lieutenant, Steve Ballmer, was promoted by Gates in the summer of 1998 to become president and CEO of the company (to allow the chairman to spend more time on his first chosen focus, product development). He interprets the "free browser" somewhat differently: "Do we give away software? I don't think so. Nobody ever told us we were giving away the print manager, the thing that lets you configure printers in Windows. It's just a built-in piece of Windows. The browser, similarly, is really a built-in piece of Windows. Now, we sometimes update it when it's not time to update the rest of Windows. But you want our browser, you got to own Windows. So while the browser itself may be free, we're getting paid. It's a commercial proposition for us."

Microsoft's critics, and there are many, argue that Microsoft's reservoir of cash liquidity allows it to enter and dominate any market. Jim Clark is pragmatic, and has pushed Netscape to pursue markets outside Microsoft's orbit: "Well, let's face it. Any company in the software business, if Microsoft decides they want their market, you almost don't have a chance, because they do own the Windows business and the Windows business is 95 percent of the world, maybe 98 percent by now. It's very difficult to compete with a company like that, which is why as soon as we were directly in their crosshairs, we decided we had to start building other services. And we're being successful at that now."

John McAfee knows all too well, to his personal benefit, how free software and majority market share add up to an unassailable and highly profitable position: "When you're up against Bill Gates and his money, and he is following this strategy, the best bet is to get into another business. Just say, 'Okay, forget it. I'll do something else in life.' Because you cannot compete with that."

Marc Andreessen, with the brash confidence of a hugely successful twenty-six-year-old entrepreneur, enjoys denouncing Microsoft products, management strategies, and culture. It may not help Netscape win the so-called browser wars, but it helps rally the troops: "Microsoft has been a historically very isolated culture, with an environment of barely controlled anger and chaos and fear a big part of the set of management tools that they use. Netscape, being a creature of Silicon Valley, is—I think—much more open as an environment in which to work. For a lot of people, certainly more fun than working at Microsoft. Or at least that's what our ex-Microsoft employees tell us."

In previous antitrust dramas, matters have been resolved by the Department of Justice, the Federal Trade Commission, and the courts, but such cases—involving Standard Oil, IBM, Xerox, or AT&T—occurred before the accelerated era of the Web. This case may simply be resolved by the onrush of time, new products, better browsers, and newer ideas, which will make the issue obsolete before the relatively glacial pace of judicial intervention can make a mark. The Department of Justice does not operate in "dog years."

Chapter Sixteen
Really Good Vibes

IF A NONDESCRIPT HOUSE AT 3958 Sutherland Avenue, Palo Alto, is to gain the same recognition by the California Historical Commission as the birthplace of Hewlett-Packard, we may have to wait until the year 2045 to see the bronze plaque installed. Excite, the company that started out in the Sutherland Avenue garage, may gain lasting recognition from the historians in fifty years' time, or it may disappear as rapidly as it has grown in the first five years of its life. While Silicon Valley has become synonymous with the high speed of high technology development, the Web era has accelerated development cycles, market valuation, success, and failure; those involved have made the joke about measuring their lives in "dog years" into an instant cliché.

The acceleration of technological progress has also leveled the playing field between experience and youth, according to Rohit Khare. In 1997, no one had more than four years of Web experience. So in two years of working for the World Wide Web Consortium, at the age of twenty, Khare traveled around the world five times, was involved in half a dozen technical initiatives, ran over a hundred standards organization meetings and public events: "This is completely without comment. This is not out of the ordinary. That's just the pace of events, you expect to get two hundred e-mails a day. You expect to not be able to survive more than forty-eight hours out of e-mail connectivity."

The World Wide Web is not the first electronic-technological-media phenomenon of the 1990s to be touted as a revolution. Pen computing nosedived and interactive television failed to materialize as predicted. But the Web upheaval does appear to be real. It is a major twenty-first-century business zone in prospect and a revolution in the communications world—with effects potentially as profound as those of the telephone or television, and with some prospect of swallowing both of those "old media" along the way. Its success may be attributable to the very fact that it does not deliver one new "killer app," but rather provides a new, generally more convenient way to do a vast variety of transactions—informational, commercial and social. As Jim Clark of Silicon Graphics and Netscape concluded, " You got to be able to make money with 50 million people using your product." The World Wide Web is consequently fueling a frenzy of venture-capital speculation for the next Netscape.

Statistics and projections from industry groups, the U.S. Department of Commerce, and others demonstrate the growth is real. There are "early adopters," not least from the industry itself, who indeed use the Web for a growing number of their daily transactions: buying groceries, making travel reservations, reviewing their bank balance, filing their taxes, and buying and selling stocks. In 1997, the value of travel bookings via the Web was $827 million, according to the Travel Industry Association of America. The association predicts in five years it will multiply tenfold, to $9 billion a year. So far, all such predictions have massively underestimated the rate of growth. And there are dozens— or perhaps hundreds—of markets beginning to open up to Web transactions. And there are huge, unwired, or barely wired markets around the world where the growth has not even begun.

As the industry has grown, and the pace of development has grown with it, modest investments of a few hundred thousand dollars no longer make sense. If a venture firm has fifty, sixty, or a hundred million to invest each year (and venture firms have been able to raise tens of millions with a single phone call in the mid-nineties) it makes no sense to commit such small sums. The trend has been towards minimum investments of several million dollars: a sum that requires a high level of confidence in the entrepreneurs who get it.

Don Valentine has been investing in Silicon Valley for close to thirty years, and now bemoans the excess of money chasing a paucity of high-quality ventures. It used to be different: "There were very few available dollars to invest and we all used to collaborate to finance one company at a time, which is all we could ever muster enough energy for in a business. Now there are many venture capitalists—too many—and there's a great deal of money—far too much—and we now have no ability to collaborate. We are, unfortunately, preordained to compete. As a result, we end up with companies that are totally superfluous to the process of Darwinian selection. Business is accelerated and is very brutal, eliminating and weeding out companies that just have no real purpose in life."

By the mid-nineties, natural selection had caused the trend of new ventures to become heavily Web-centric. Rarely now do start-ups bring new ideas for hard-drives, or pen computing: now almost every application and device is Internet-driven.

At Draper Fisher Jurvetson, a Redwood City venture-capital firm, the steady stream of would-be entrepreneurs into the conference room has a mesmerizing quality. It takes a lot of work, planning, and credibility to get this far. Never mind that the first group into the room on June 18, 1997, Digital Post Office ("we are the outsource messaging service for the Internet"), had their last meeting with the VCs in the men's room, leaving the one woman member of the team, by definition, outside. Today their job is to convince the three politely skeptical investors (wearing ties) to part with a few million to endorse their vision of a new technology, a new service, or a new market. You can cut the anxiety with a knife. But there's no way around it. The money lies on the far side of this hurdle of coherence, technical skill, and self-abasement. It's a very polite form of torture.

"How big is the market? How are you going to make money? How long were you at Apple? Who's going to be the CEO? I still don't see how you are going to make money?" The questions are relentless, firm, and focused. The venture-capital community accepts the odds of failure in the companies they back. Two or three out of ten just fail; four or five out of ten do moderately well, and perhaps repay the investors over two to four years. But one out of ten has to hit the jackpot, returning to the investors ten, twenty, or fifty times their investment.

What about your background? You weren't in the bathroom there. What was your master's degree in?
Artificial intelligence.
Uh-huh...

Do you think you're going to lose out to the free e-mail?

I don't think anybody in their right mind's going to trust their business mail to a consumer mail service.

Our product addresses those needs that are highlighted in yellow. So we think we have analytic support to our position that there is a big opportunity in interactive broadcasting.

I'm very concerned unless you guys are going to pay yourselves, you know, $500 a year, it's hard for me to see this thing become a cash flow positive for four or five years.

This is the Silicon Valley mating dance, and entrepreneurs have to be ready to do it dozens of times. Each needs the other, yet it is the VCs who decide whether or not to mate. They call this dance "the pitch," and it can be the difference between total obscurity and a billion-dollar IPO. Some entrepreneurs do this dance a hundred times and never raise anything. Despite cautionary tales and horror stories that could outdo both Grimm and Aesop, this is a scene that is played out thousands of times a year in front of venture capitalists. It's horribly repetitive for the VCs: nine out of ten pitches fail.

No sooner do the pitches end than the brutal dissection begins—of the team's qualifications, of the product idea, and of the financial projections:

I think they have a good technologist and they have a good marketing director and they don't have a CEO. I think they need a CEO. But the one thing I was thinking is could we take this and change it and make it into a business? Because the technology's interesting. Could we mold it a little?

I think they're selling their product wrong.

They've got their pyramid flipped.

This is the kind of thing, I think, that we could potentially seed. And if we got a CEO and we remanipulated the business model...

It's hard to get a name. You got to go out and get it registered. And get the .com and all.

Seemed like a soft-market, laid back, "We're here to have fun together" kind of experience. Maybe there's a business that will come out of it and we'll acquire it early in life and we'll just get rich that way.

For the venture capitalists, it's mainly about the return. For the entrepreneurs, it's mainly about the vision. Both groups testify to the fact that the entrepreneurs driven by visions of wealth do not generally get funded; nor do they generally get rich. Start-up exponents willing to subject themselves to the mating dance have to be nerveless—or perhaps more useful—innocent and naive. The start-up venture in Palo Alto, California, called Architext, provides a perfect example—indeed, a fairy-tale case history—of people who didn't know enough to know that what they were attempting was practically impossible, that the odds were massively stacked against them, and that they had almost none of the experience or credentials to succeed. Ignorance is bliss.

Architext was a classic Silicon Valley garage start-up. In 1994, in a rented bungalow on Sutherland Avenue in Palo Alto, six recent Stanford graduates (five in computer science, one in political science) decided to start a company. The political scientist, Joe Kraus, was "CEO." It must have seemed like a game at the time: "We were just six guys who wanted to do something big. We got together in Redwood City at Rosita's Burritos. It was, 'We don't know what we want to do but we know we want to start a company and it's got to be big.

We're going to do something great, right?' And we had a theme in the early days that we were unencumbered by reality. We didn't know what reality meant. We didn't know we couldn't win. We didn't know we could fail."

In 1993, the Internet was the big new thing, and college students, especially at Stanford, knew all about its virtues, its scale, and its potential. But the browser was barely a factor yet, so the World Wide Web was yet to be fully exploited. Stanford, as we have seen, is a place where the tradition of taking intellectual capital out into the real world and starting businesses is positively fostered. The founders of Architext embarked on creating a product designed for the newly emerging market space of the Internet.

Just as libraries need catalogs, the Internet needs devices for users to find what they are looking for among the gigabytes and terabytes of information stored in all the servers and databases that the Net makes accessible. The search engine, invented to simplify and organize the Internet, is the solution and an immensely valuable new business opportunity. A user enters certain key words to tell the search engine what he or she is looking for, and the search engine combs all the available catalogs and indexes to match the key words with material from all the databases. The founders of Architext decided to enter the search-and-retrieval business, with a couple of value-added features: enabling a search with *or without* the keywords that most search engines require; and an automatic document-summary program. They called this notion Intelligent Concept Extraction, and patented it.

In April 1994, the six gathered in the Sutherland Avenue garage to review progress so far. The furniture was dingy, the computers competed for space with a washer, dryer, and baskets of unwashed laundry. The diet was reheated spaghetti eaten straight from the Tupperware, and bags of Halloween candy, supplemented by snacks of uncoooked rice from a fifty-pound bag. They bought one bag a month, for $12. They had spent less than $2000 of the $15,000 of funds they had scraped together from their parents or saved from day jobs.

The "company" was led technologically by Graham Spencer, a skinny blond kid with a passing resemblance to Bill Gates. Describing his social profile as "punk," Graham Spencer spent the time he wasn't writing code pondering the most effective way to dye his hair blue. But all six spent a great deal of time writing code: Spencer was lead designer, "fleshing out the high-level structure," assigning tasks, and defining the "interdependency between the components."

The "CEO" was twenty-two-year-old Joe Kraus, the political scientist with a steamrolling quantity of self-confidence, allied to a natural, winning charm. From the front, Joe appeared to have a short, businesslike haircut with the clean-cut looks which made him the natural pitch man for the project—"Phone Boy" as the less-presentable members of the team called him. From the back, Joe's concession to hip was visible: A long, thin, elegant braid of hair grew from the back of his neck; low down, where it could be tucked invisibly inside a dress shirt collar for business meetings.

The pitch was this: "Architext Software is a company that's dedicated to bringing information management to a new level, by making information retrieval very simple. We use a natural language interface (plain English) instead of arcane commands, and Intelligent Concept Extraction so that if you search for 'racket', you don't miss references to 'tennis.'"

Architext would also include features like automatic summarization of articles, research background tools, and automatic hypertexting tools. The staff planned to meet the urgent information needs of litigation-support departments, political campaigns, and public relations agencies. They hoped to get paid by selling licenses to large corporations that needed to execute rapid and extensive document searches and to navigate through ever-growing quantities of information held in internal or external databases. The search engine would exist as a piece of software, though distributed McAfee-style rather than packaged in shrink wrap.

The rest of the team—Ben Lutch, Martin Reinfried, Mark Van Haren, and Ryan McIntyre—looked like what they were: twenty-something hackers with shoulder-length hair, who were more articulate in code than in English, happy to live in grunge as long as the project seemed cool. What seemed cool in 1994 also had to be commercial. Most of the six founders had previously collaborated in a jazz-funk band named Where's Julio, and even recorded a CD, which sounds rather as if the same track was recorded twelve times. Music was not going to make their fortune.

Joe Kraus worked the phone, knowing from the grapevine that what the start-up needed was venture capital. What he did not know, and only learned by painful experience, was that they *first* needed a business plan. Meanwhile, the rest of the Architext team plowed on with writing the code that would get their start-up into the search-engine business, to take advantage of the global database environment as it grew daily. As Joe Kraus said in April 1994, "The problem with a start-up is that we have to think of so many things. It's hard to look beyond two or three months and 'We need a demo, and we need it now.' The rule is, if you're not sleeping, you're in here, working."

In the early days of a start-up, even small luxuries can seem like major milestones, as Kraus remembered: "My parents taking me to Office Max. How grateful I was that they spent $96 on this piece of carpet that we could put down on the ground. That was like a huge step."

In the spring of 1994, they were satisfied that they had created a core technology that worked, and felt that what was needed was a demo to prove it. They had recently heard of a competitor, an East-coast company with big military contracts. But after a momentary depression, Ryan McIntyre reported, "It's a little bit scary, but we're hoping we'll surpass them with what we have to offer." Mark Van Haren felt "We believed in ourselves enough."

And Joe Kraus announced "Commando Week," in which all six founders would work flat out—without underwear—until the demo was done. There was just one hitch, which revealed itself when venture capitalist (and Sun Microsystems founder) Vinod Khosla stopped in to visit the Architext team: "Fifteen minutes into my first meeting with them I said, 'Can you prove your technology really works?' And they said, 'I don't have a disk drive big enough.' I said, 'Call my secretary. Tell her to get you a $5 or $10 thousand disk drive and then let's meet next week.' They didn't have enough disk storage space to prove that their search engine could scale through a large enough index or document set."

Khosla's spur-of-the-moment decision to invest modestly (at first) in Architext paid off. It enabled them to prove that their technology did work; and began a rapid change in their fortunes. But why did he do so? "What made me spend $5 or $10 thousand in fifteen minutes on really two guys—Joe Kraus and Graham Spencer—who I was meeting for the first time, who had never had a job, never had any success, had completely crazy notions of what applications they wanted to pursue? There was something about them that said to me, they're good entrepreneurs. They were good listeners. They were good debaters. They were thoughtful about my comments. They didn't give in to everything I said. They didn't disagree with everything I said. And I really liked the vibrations, the vibes. There were really good vibes."

John Doerr, Vinod Khosla's partner at Kleiner, Perkins, saw that Excite had four of the five factors he regards as necessary for success: "They had terrific technology, a terrific team to start with; they had a large, rapidly growing market they wanted to address; and they had an incredible sense of urgency about them. The only one that was missing was a really complete and experienced management team." That was the one John Doerr knows how to provide.

In December 1994 the company secured $300,000 in venture-capital funding from Kleiner, Perkins that would enable them to grow. (Later, they would get several million more.) By 1995, Architext Software had moved into 5,000 square feet of real office space, on Garcia Avenue in Palo Alto, and had started hiring more people to develop their product. This company was firmly in the Silicon Valley tradition, little different from pioneers like Apple Computer or even Microsoft—a bunch of nerds who shared a dream. They transported the garage culture to the offices largely intact: hundred-hour work weeks, sleeping on couches or the floor instead of beds, guitars strewn about, and food remnants in unwashed Tupperware accumulating by the day. Mark Van Haren used a watch-cap for sleeping during the daylight hours when others were working; Joe Kraus tried to look alert at breakfast meetings when he had gone to sleep at 4 A.M.; Graham Spencer kept on hacking the code.

Their original prototype, which provided document search and summary services for law firms and businesses, was working well by 1995. Graham Spencer was able to demonstrate the technology by searching the Internet for "Hamlet," and making it much shorter than Shakespeare's version. The fifteen-line summary of the play captured at least some of the essential dramatic themes:

A mote it is to trouble the minds' eye. (Act I, Scene i)

It beckons you to go away with it,
As if it some impartment did desire
To you alone.
Look, with what courteous action
It waves you to a more removéd ground:
But do not go with it. (Act I, Scene iv)

I doubt it is no other but the main;
His father's death, and our o' erhasty marriage. (Act II, Scene ii)

Man delights not me: no, nor woman neither,
though by your smiling you seem to say so. (Act II,
Scene ii)

Alas, there was no sign of the most renowned soliloquy in the English language because, as Graham Spencer pointed out, "the software automatically ignores little words like 'to,' 'be,' 'or,' and 'not.'"

By the summer of 1995, the hype (and some measure of underlying reality) about the business opportunities thrown up by the Web created a storm of venture funding of start-ups, both promising and doomed. The El Dorado of Silicon Valley—Sandhill Road in Palo Alto—was inundated with, in the skeptical language of the time, "Internet toasters." Not least of the forces that fueled the rush to invest in Web ventures, good and bad, was the fact that Netscape's initial public offering had broken all records for the instant wealth of those who secured stock.

With the input of funding from venture capitalists, the founders found themselves owning a (nominal) $30 million worth of a company. At the same time, they began to have less control over their destiny, with the usual pressures that venture capitalists exerted: to allow professional management to run and build the company, while also to remain flexible enough to adapt to the rapidly changing Internet environment. In October 1995, halfway between Netscape's IPO and Microsoft's "Internet Day" realignment, Architext changed its name to Excite, Incorporated. Their products were also known as Excite, and could be found at http://www.excite.com.

Their search engine was a fine tool; but it was not a big enough deal to build a major investment triumph for the venture capitalists, who were starting to call the shots. So the founders interviewed candidates to find the person who would become their own boss. The choice they made was significant: they hired not a technology industry specialist, but a media man—former television producer and magazine publisher George Bell: "It's a very odd situation when you're interviewing with a twenty-three-year-old guy [then-CEO Joe Kraus], and trying to puff your chest out about all the things you've accomplished and all you've done. Here's a twenty-three-year-old guy who's well on

his way to being a multiple millionaire, and who's got a very
good view of business already at the age of twenty-three. And he
was not alone among the other founders. They also were very sophisticated in other ways."

George Bell started work at Excite in January 1996, at the same
time as the company moved again, this time to half of a building,
a 19,000-square-foot space in Mountain View. At the time of their
IPO, in April 1996, the company had grown to have sixty-five employees, and was valued at over $200 million. To mark the occa-
sion, Joe Kraus allowed cofounder Ben Lutch to cut off his hip
Indian braid.

As George Bell describes it, Excite had to make a major strategic shift in defining their business activity, all the while racing
forward: "We can make more money and grow a better identity
by establishing a brand around navigation, which was more
than search on the Internet: helping people find things, and
connect people with content, and people with one another on
the Internet."

They also had to decide whether this was a subscription-
sustained service (no) or an advertising-dependent medium (yes).
As the proliferation of Web-browsers made the Internet look increasingly like an informational TV screen, companies like Excite
began to look more like TV or cable channels every day, and that
transformation affected the revenues and economics of their business, as well as the user interface. Excite itself did some limited
TV advertising, mainly in the high-tech Bay Area market, with
Jimi Hendrix's "Are You Experienced?" as the sound track. One
of the Excite products was code-named "Purple Haze." Joe Kraus
describes the evolving business of Excite thus: "Basically, we call
ourselves Publishing on Steroids. Devoid of print, paper, or ink,
we do what a publisher does, or a cable provider does. We aggre-
gate consumers around our programming and then we sell that
demographic back to advertisers."

The growth of Excite has been remarkable, though not unique,
in its speed and scale. In the frenzied hyperactivity of Web ventures, it is difficult to determine whether Excite's success is real
or lasting. There is growth, there is volatile but generally upward
movement in the stock price; and their site has become the
second-most visited media channel on the Web. Their senior

competitor, Yahoo!, is another company that emerged from the Stanford University nursery.

By 1997, Excite had changed its business model from software creation to "internet media programming"; changed its revenue stream from user fees to advertising; and changed the character of the company from six grungy burrito-eating kids to a 200-plus staff, with a grown-up media CEO and a NASDAQ listing. At the time of writing, the six founders are worth about half a billion dollars, and the company three times that amount. Yet they are generally working in their first real job, other than selling lemonade and vacation lawn-mowing. As George Bell pointed out, adult supervision was essential: "You have to remember that for all six of the founders of Excite, this is still their first job. There's no reason to expect that people in a first job of any kind would be comfortable or qualified or succeed at managing growth where we've added perhaps close to two hundred jobs in the last fourteen months. This rate of growth is strong and extraordinary even for the Valley."

Despite new-found riches, the twenty-four-year-old founders had not, a year after the initial public offering of Excite stock, found very original ways to spend their money. Joe Kraus bought a StarTac phone, a digital camera, and a car. Not a particularly os-tentatious car, but a stylish black BMW M3. The license plate says "Excite." Mark Van Haren bought a $2,000 carbon fiber rac-ing bike, and took the plunge to buy a house—"A huge step: that's very grown-up."

Graham Spencer, still debating the blue-hair problem, set out to buy a car, but was confronted with an ethical dilemma: "I had a hard time making the decision. I wasn't going for a luxury-mobile, a Porsche or anything like that. But I wanted a pretty nice car and I wanted lots of gadgets. I like gadgets in my cars. But the problem was I'm also a vegetarian so I didn't want leather seats in my car. What I discovered was that there are almost no car manufacturers who put all the gadgets in a version of their car without leather seats. So you can either have leather seats and gadgets, or no leather seats and no gadgets. So it was a big dilemma for me to try and pick the right vehicle that had the fea-tures I wanted and the seats that I wanted."

In March 1997, the company underwent its latest transforma-tion along the road to corporate adulthood. Another move, this time into their own 80,000-square-foot building in Redwood City. Acquisition of two competitors—Magellan and WebCrawler—and deals with America Online, Netscape and Intuit Software were driving growth and physical consolidation of the company into one space.

Graham Spencer packed his own boxes, because the (paper) multimillionaire felt "way too guilty about having someone pack my office for me." The building had been renovated to their own specifications—and therefore included a large circular slide from the second floor, enough open space to play touch football indoors, a conference room (known as "The Garage") with its own up-and-over garage door, and enough free drinks to float the Titanic. Life has changed in material ways and remains the same in others. This is the nineties, so staff members drink more health juices than carbonated sodas; mountain bikes have displaced guitars, though some offices have both; Joe Kraus' stock in Excite is worth $100 million, but he still reenacts the "Death of Spock" scene from *Star Trek*—"Tell my wife...I love her"—behind the plate-glass walls of the Excite server room.

Joe Kraus calls the new building "our final resting place" but it's quite possible that Excite will move again, or build yet bigger premises, or fall back from their current position, or be acquired and swallowed by a larger company: Rumors abound of such prospects. Graham Spencer was bemused by the onward rush of events as they moved from their last location to the new headquarters: "I wouldn't even have guessed that we would have moved into the Garcia office that we were at, the 2,000-square-foot office with the little dingy cubes. That was a step up for us. Then to move in here and then to move into our very own building is just, you know, a surprise."

Excite is the visible proof of the Internet's accelerating progress from backwater to global media space and market. The company's growth mirrors the expansion of the wired world. Two statistics show the growth, and the space for growth: in the four years of Excite's life, the number of Americans using the Internet has risen from five million to 62 million, and shows no sign of leveling off. In 1996, Web-based media advertising in the United States was less than $200 million, while all media advertising amounted to well over $2 billion.

The acceleration of the Web phenomenon was fueled by money, technology, and the growing critical mass of major industry players—not least, Microsoft—who began to take the Internet seriously. While many of the technological breakthroughs came—and perhaps had to come—from tiny, passionate start-up exponents "unencumbered by reality," another major technological breakthrough came from a large and successful company that had first nailed its networking colors to the mast back in 1982: Sun Microsystems. Its slogan was "The network is the computer," and by 1995 the network had become global. Like anyone else, in all previous generations of networking efforts, Sun could recognize the technical difficulties inherent in a global computer network made up of multiple different systems.

The Internet grew in a haphazard way, and as Tim Berners-Lee found in writing the World Wide Web software, the computers that comprised the Net had different operating systems and hardware configurations, and used many different programming languages. The Web made it possible for them to inter-communicate, but what was needed next was a tool to make it easy. Like everything else on the Internet, it had a strange name—Java.

Bill Joy was the Berkeley programming wizard who became the fourth cofounder of Sun, though only employee #6. Sun's success (and networking technology) allows him to live where he pleases (Aspen, Colorado) and still work for Sun on new technological directions. Joy encouraged and supervised the project that became Java. Like many technological advances, Java began its evolution with a different intention—as a chip language to control hand-held devices, intelligent agents, and set-top cable boxes. But it became a computer language for the Internet era. Its appeal is twofold: first, it is a language that developers apparently find easier to use than previous languages; second and more importantly, it can be used to write programs for any platform, any chip, any application. Just what the multi-platform, multi-chip, multi-application Internet and Web needed.

Eric Schmidt watched Java develop at Sun: "Everyone knows that if you go to the computer store you have to buy software that runs on Windows, or a different piece of software that runs on the Mac. With Java, you could take a single program and it will run on both, and it will run on both well. That opportunity was created because of the Internet, because the Internet is a mixed network and it doesn't make sense to have twenty versions of your software on a single server. So the promise of the Internet coincided just at the right time with the great inventions by people like James Gosling."

James Gosling is the primary name attached to the invention of Java, though he is not its sole creator. The team was to include Patrick McNaughten, Mike Sheridan, Ed Frank, and Arthur Van Hoff, among a dozen members. No one would dispute that James Gosling is a nerd, who admits that he spends his time, and enjoys, "Sitting down at a keyboard and typing stuff. I get my kicks out of doing engineering." His first networking experiences were at Carnegie Mellon University (CMU) in Pittsburgh, in the early days of the ARPAnet. CMU was home to IMP #13.

According to Sun CEO Scott McNealy, the story began in 1991, when James Gosling arrived in his office, unhappy: "One of the most brilliant programmers on the planet—Bill Joy calls him the greatest programmer in the world—came to my office one day because I'd heard he was upset. I said 'What's the matter? Why aren't you happy?'"

Gosling was tired of trying to write software to fit the "legacy environment" of older languages and operating systems already in place. He told McNealy it was "like trying to fly by flapping your wings. I want to go out and create a new environment."

In one of the more renowned cases of a Silicon Valley blank check, McNealy told him to get started: "I don't care what you want to do. Wherever you want to do it, whenever, however long, with whoever, for as much money, I'll set you up in a room. I'll give you all the raw meat and Jolt Cola and potato chips you want, anything you need, for as long as you want. Just go do something great. He said, 'Really?' I said, 'Yeah. Get out of here.'"

As Gosling remembers, what they were attempting, or where they were headed, was far from obvious to the boss: "Certainly early on I don't think Scott had a good idea of what it was about or what it was for. It was sort of this group of rabble-rousers off in the corner doing something really odd that he didn't know how it related to their main business. And the truth is that in the early times, it didn't relate to the main business."

The boss wholly concurs: "It was like Groundhog Day. They'd

come out every now and then, they'd look around, and I'd look and see what they have. And I'd go, 'I don't get it.' And they go, 'Okay.' And so they'd go back in."

The Java project was planned to network devices together—this was Sun's core business—but the work began before it was at all clear that the Internet was the place where networking would be happening. Kim Polese was in charge of marketing Java for Sun, before leaving to set up Marimba: "It was conceived way back in the 1990-91 time frame by a few engineers at Sun Microsystems who wanted to create a better world in terms of software delivery, software deployment. They were frustrated with all these huge operating systems and all these incompatibilities and multiple-window systems and bloated code, and they were envisioning a world in which there would be something much better."

The Java team began as "The Green Team." The idea was that all the consumer electronics in the home—from VCRs and cell phones to PDAs and desktop computers—should inter-communicate. They all have microprocessors, which are small computers, inside. So the Green Team tried to build a prototype hand-held remote control to network these devices together. As James Gosling admits, it did not work very well. And fortunately Sun was not demanding that the project produce a marketable product: "It made absolutely no sense as a product. This was a remote control that, if you tried to manufacture them, would be $10 or $15 thousand each."

Somewhat like the unmarketable Alto computer from Xerox PARC, the prototype was an exercise in developing technology, and learning. James Gosling is a believer in building, rather than writing papers: "That's really what drove the Green Project, was to actually build something and try to understand where the issues really were because, as in many things, the devil is in the details. And unless you actually build something, it's just science fiction."

Next the remote control became a kind of sophisticated cable TV tuner. But that ran into all kinds of industry standards and market problems. The common theme was that there was a net-work involved, and Java, as Kim Polese describes it, was a lan-guage for efficient inter-networking: "There would be a ubiquitous network that connected everybody; and there would be small, very lightweight programs that would zip around the network and land on all sorts of different devices. It wouldn't matter what operating system those devices were running, or what chip set was in them. Everything would just work magically."

It is difficult to describe a computer language. James Gosling tries to describe Java thus: "Java's a building material. It's like concrete. It's something that you can use to build software out of. There's a bunch of different things that appeal to different people in different situations. I think the one that has gotten the most airtime is this thing about being 'write once, run anywhere' or being architecture neutral, where you can sort of write a program once and it will actually run on different machines and it can rove across the network."

The Green Project was planning for a technological world in which consumers were plugged into some kind of ubiquitous network of devices. Kim Polese, Sun's product manager for Java, says that "what they didn't realize at the time was, it was going to be the Internet."

Gosling and company recognized, and to a significant degree overcame, the perennial problem of networking: "One of the big issues when you're building a network of machines, you have a terrific problem when the different machines are of different types—and you want to be able to write programs that work everywhere. Java makes that work pretty well."

In 1994, with Web browsers beginning to get a lot of attention, Sun's John Gage and James Gosling demonstrated Java's capabilities to a technical conference in Monterey, California. At that time, Web pages mostly looked like pages of paper—static and print-filled. Gosling clicked his mouse on a molecular diagram on Sun's Web site, and woke the audience up to Java's potential: "I clicked on something and dragged it, and the molecule rotated. The whole audience just went 'Oh!' It changed people's view of what the universe was built out of. They had this view of the universe being just paper and pictures, and static. All of a sudden it was, these things can actually be alive. You can actually interact with them. That one demo, just being able to just get something to move and to interact with it, that snapped people's heads very quickly. It was the ten-second, emotionally grabbing explanation of why this was interesting."

Bill Joy, the godfather of the Green Project, concluded in 1995 that Sun had achieved something significant: "We've been trying to write a great language for a long time and I think we finally did. It wasn't planned, grew out of an attempt to do something else, but it feels great, the level of excitement is enormous, I can't return all the phone calls. It's got that feel of success, when people start calling you up and say, 'I don't know what it is but I gotta have it,' that's when you know you've got a real success on your hands."

Java has the authentically hip flavor of Silicon Valley, but its name came about almost by accident. The Green Project's language was first called Oak, because one day James Gosling was staring out of his window at an oak tree. But the lawyers rejected Oak as a trademark name. Gosling says: "We actually got to the point where the number-one thing blocking the release of a system was having a name."

Kim Polese called in a naming consultant, and after a marathon brainstorming session, Gosling reports, a list of about a dozen names was created: "We sent the dozen names off to the lawyers and said, 'Start from the top. We'll take the first name that passes the trademark search.' And Java was number four or five on the list."

Microsoft did not entirely welcome Java. The Washington company saw the arrival of Java as a threat to its own dominance in the operating system market, especially as the Web era has created a goldrush of new applications to be written. Microsoft's dominance of the PC operating system is a pattern the company loves. It has similar designs on the Web browser marker, as we have seen; and for Java to take over the web application writing market with the speed it has, provided something of a new challenge to Microsoft. Technically, Java is something more than a language to create instructions for computers. It also contains something known mysteriously as "the Java virtual machine," which its advocates regard as a helpful feature, and Microsoft regards as a Trojan horse into the operating systems and applications business.

Steve Ballmer, Microsoft's new CEO and president, differs from his fellow Detroit native Scott McNealy over many things, but especially Java:

> Java's two things in one. Java, as a programming language
> for tools, is a semi-big to big deal. There are things pro-

grammers like about it that they didn't like about some of these other languages. That's kind of arcane technical stuff, but some guys like Java. The second part of this thing, this operating system thing, that's like this funny layer that slows Windows down. And that's really the part McNealy likes best. He would say it's a breakthrough. I would say it's sort of a return to the dark ages of operating systems when they had no capabilities and they ran terribly slowly. That's what I would say. I think you would get different views on the level of breakthrough-ness of that piece of Java.

Bob Metcalfe sees Java as part of the continuing trend, always present in networking evolution, away from proprietary systems, into open systems: "The whole Java event is about sapping the energy out of the Windows juggernaut and moving the momentum for software development off the Windows platform onto the Java platform; off the proprietary Microsoft OS platform onto the open Internet platform."

By 1997, there was no denying the enthusiasm with which Java had been taken up in the development community. Even Microsoft had licensed Java. It was quite a payoff for a project designed to keep a talented programmer happy, and a project no one really understood. As John Doerr claimed in the fall of 1997: "It's taken the world by storm. It's very clearly now going to be in some 300 million computers just two years from now (2000). I think there's two hundred books on the market right now on Java. Four million programmers programming in it. And it's only seven hundred days old, so, that's phenomenal."

James Gosling is no longer unhappy with legacy environments. He now has the self-imposed problem of trying to restrain the hype for his own creation: "Marketing people and business people [are] going out and standing on platforms and saying completely outrageous things that have no relationship to the truth, and I end up having to put a dose of reality into some of these things."

On balance, James Gosling prefers the recognition for his work: "I've done many things that have gotten very popular but amongst a very sort of nerdy community. The kind of stuff I do is stuff that I have no idea how to explain it to my mom. So it tends to stay in a fairly closed community. And to have something that has touched people's everyday lives ... surprised me."

The creators of new technologies like Java work very long hours, away from the sunlight, eating poorly and drinking too much cola and coffee. Milestones and opportunities to let off steam are important, and perhaps explain Sun's April Fool's traditions, and Excite's newer practice of riding bicycles *inside* the office building. Throughout their long grind of eighteen-, or twenty-, or twenty-four-hour workdays, the Excite founders had always promised themselves a celebratory trip to Hawaii. But the moment never seemed to come. The first demo was completed, the Beta version ... even the IPO, which made them rich enough to *buy* a small Hawaiian island at least. As Joe Kraus recalls: "We had all said at some point, the six founders were all going to take a trip to Hawaii. And it always was, when we accomplish the next thing. And when we accomplish the next thing we'll do it. So when we get our funding we'll do it. We got the funding. We didn't do it. We get our strategic round of financing we'll do it. And we didn't do that. When we get this deal we'll do it. And we didn't do it."

But finally, in the spring of 1997, they did do it. From irritation at themselves for delaying, and because they always end up doing what they set out to do, they had their Hawaiian vacation. They sailed, surfed, and encountered the local marine life; Graham Spencer even kissed a dolphin. Excite's Silicon Valley saga may seem like a fairy tale, but it didn't turn into a princess.

Just after returning from Hawaii, the six founders gathered in The Garage—not on Sutherland Avenue, but the conference room in their new building—to reflect on the changes in their lives as entrepreneurs. One change was that they rarely found themselves all in one room at work any longer. Among a staff of 200, each was involved in different aspects of the technology, business, and content development. Graham Spencer said that "Three years ago, none of us would have ever imagined that we would actually be able to have a building like this, have all these employees.

Ryan McIntyre took pride in their collective creation: "Just looking around me and saying, 'Wow. We have all these fantastically dynamic people that we're working with and this company exists here because of us, because of something that we started.' That's insanely gratifying."

Joe Kraus recalled the strategic advantages of ignorance and naiveté: "When we were six guys in the garage, we were able to successfully compete against companies of much larger size because we had no baggage, meaning all the things that could be construed negatively—like no money, no customers—also had a positive aspect to it. When you have a lot of customers, that means you're serving their needs; it's harder to focus on sort of future opportunities."

Recently Kleiner, Perkins had sent some young, would-be entrepreneurs to consult the sage veteran, twenty-six-year-old Graham Spencer, who found the experience somewhat surreal: "So I was telling these guys the stories but at the same time I was listening to myself talk about this and thinking, 'Wow, are we really successful at this point? Have we really gotten that big so that now I'm telling small start-up companies how to do the same thing?' It was a very strange experience."

Joe Kraus believes that The Garage, both physical and metaphorical, is a useful reality-check for the company: "Remembering back to the garage helps keep you paranoid because you realize how quickly things can go from a garage to something like this. I think we all feel extremely proud and happy of what's been accomplished. But I think it reminds you that just as easily as you can make it here, you can make it back to the garage."

When Architext Software first developed its Intelligent Concept Extraction to search for documents, it used Mosaic and traveled on the Web, around the Internet, to find them. But today the Architext search engine is just one tool in use on a Web media channel named Excite. The company has succeeded by being flexible, not focused, as Graham Spencer admits: "We certainly had no clue that millions of people would be using the Web as a consumer experience on a day-to-day basis three years from back then. But I think that we did see there was text online. There was going to be more of it, and digital text was an interesting problem to look at."

People who work at Excite compare it to being inside a washing-machine on the spin cycle. There is both a need for flexibility, and an absence of models in this field. George Bell comments: "There's the absence of historic data. No one's ever done this before." The media phenomenon of the Internet is not being evolved by the creation of infrastructure, like previous media revolutions. It is being built almost entirely on existing infrastructure, and its virtual components are the product of intelligence, imagination, and stamina.

Bell came from the old media to the new, and has enjoyed his education: "I'm amazed what you can achieve if you take two hundred people, give every one of them ownership by way of stock in a company, tell them to use their wits and their intelligence and experience and cobble together a strategy, and tell them that going fast is a requirement of the business. You give me two hundred people like that, under any circumstances, I'll take that team any day of the week over the big media company teams that I've worked on before."

This is the Silicon Valley fairy tale. There are thousands more little gangs of dreamers eating burritos, working all night, and seeking venture capital, to make their fortunes in the wired world. Vinod Khosla sees his investment as a success, to say the least: "Six burrito-eating Stanford students turned into a couple-hundred-million-dollar enterprise two years later, that truly is reaching millions and millions of people—that probably has the media reach of *The New York Times*. Two years later! Pretty amazing phenomenon."

Chapter Seventeen
All Geeked Up

THE WEB LIFESTYLE IS BOTH AN INDUSTRY cliché and a growing so-cial phenomenon. In the high-tech industry, anyone working in product development has had to adapt to ever-more-rapid cycles of idea/prototype/release because the world is moving so rapidly. Since the advent of the World Wide Web—borrowing from Sad-dam Hussein's rhetorical repertory, Bob Metcalfe calls it "the mother of all applications"—the demanding schedules of high tech have become ever more rapid.

James Bidzos observes: "We saw the arrival of Internet time, which some people equate with dog years. It's seven times faster. But in Internet time there are no secrets. There is no time for delay. There are plenty of competitors who are going to eat you alive. Basically, what you need to do is get from the beginning to the end of a process, a mission, a sales effort, a product develop-ment cycle, you need to not take a breath, and start over and do it again as soon as you get done with one. And you need to jug-gle three or four of these all the time. That's how you compete and survive if you're in the software business on the Internet."

Christine Comaford is a self-described nerd; veteran of multi-ple consulting, software, and Web ventures; and now a venture capitalist with Artemis Ventures. To the cofounder of a Web-based grocery coupon venture, Planet U, Web-time is a powerful influence: "I'm physically thirty-five and my last year was a full Net year, which is about seven regular years. It's about a dog year, right? So that means that, thirty-five plus seven, so I'm virtually forty-two. So basically since I feel forty-two since I live so hard, I may as well have my mid-life crisis and get it all over with. Buy a motorcycle, right? Date a young guy...."

For users of the Internet and Web, the multiplication of infor-mational and commercial Web sites has put every conceivable type of information within the reach of a keyboard and modem.

In three years, from 1995, the number of commercial sites increased by a factor of thirty. Steve Ballmer, now president and CEO of Microsoft, is an exponent and devotee of the Web lifestyle: "I went on a camping trip two weeks ago with my family. How did I find the campground? They had a homepage! I got up there and it showed the nice little bunnies and the cabins and the tent sites. Boom! I reserved right there on the spot. Let's go camping!"

The cheerleaders of this new revolution are staking their companies on the notion all of us will follow their lead. Even Bill Gates has committed both himself and his company to the notion:

> You're living a Web lifestyle when you just take it for granted that any purchase you make, any new thing you'd want to plan, like a trip, you turn to the Web as part of that process. People today live a phone lifestyle and a car lifestyle. And they almost laugh when you say that to them, because it's just so taken for granted. Today not many people live a Web lifestyle. Their doctor doesn't let them set up appointments that way. Their accountant doesn't put the information up that way. The IRS doesn't make it that easy. But we're starting to see it happen. I've been bold enough to say that the next decade, the majority of Americans will be living the Web lifestyle. It'll just be there. They'll be getting lots of e-mail from their friends and relatives, for their business activities. Everyone you do business with, you'll expect one of the ways to interact with them will be over the Web.

Steve Ballmer argues that the Internet is profoundly changing the computer and high-technology market, for both the industry itself and its customers. He believes that home computer sales are stronger in the United States than in other parts of the world because Internet access is better and cheaper. For the computer industry itself, the Internet is the biggest new influence: "I can interact directly with my customers. I can hear their voice. I can provide them service. I can sell them something. I can take a transaction. It's a huge change. I can go to a Web site in Tel Aviv, Beijing, Paris, London, at no additional cost and just learn, check things out. It opens up phenomenal new opportunities."

Scott McNealy of Sun Microsystems sees the opportunities as mostly lying ahead—and being much assisted by the advent of his company's Java language: "The Internet boom hasn't even started. People are all geeked up about it but we're just beginning; I think we're in the Roaring Twenties. We're in the very early days. People are now just moving to the Web technologies all of a sudden, with Java browsers. People are going to start spending more time getting out on the network and using network-based applications, communicating out over the network, getting access to data out over the network."

In May each year, the Sloan School of Management at MIT has a contest for the best new business plan. Just like Stanford, MIT positively encourages students and alumni to develop intellectual property into business ventures, with faculty staff, entrepreneurs, and venture capitalists as advisers and team members. Each team must have at least one current MIT or Sloan student. The first prize in the MIT $50K Entrepreneurship Competition is a modest $20,000 of seed money. Along with the money, the faculty and alumni provide a quantity of invaluable advice and coaching to help shape, focus, and plan these ventures. The recognition of winning the contest can also be a helpful public relations platform on which to launch a start-up.

Bob Metcalfe is a longtime supporter of the competition, and an alumnus of the Sloan School. Each year, he hosts a party to launch the contest at his Boston townhouse, and another on the eve of the competition finals. He shares with the contestants his own insights into entrepreneurship: "Focus—but not too much." Everyone at these events is pumped-up with enthusiasm for the entrepreneurial life, from idea to seed money to mezzanine funding to IPO and exit strategy. By the mid-1990s, the majority of contestants, and winners, were devoting their attention to Internet and Web-related ventures above all.

A case in point is the 1991 winner, Stylus Innovations. The prize then was only $10,000, but in the seven years since their victory, its founders Michael Cassidy, John Barrus, and Krisztina Holly shifted the company focus to a new computer telephony software product, "Visual Voice," and sold the company to Artisoft for almost $13 million. In 1997, the contestants ranged from Imagen, an image-based retrieval application, to "The Perfect Underwear Company"—a non-Internet group devoted to getting more women into the right-size brassiere. Imagen won, with their content-based, automated image search technology for the Internet; in plain language, give their search engine a picture of a sheep, and (like a sheepdog) it will round up all the pictures of sheep—and sheep-like images— it can find on the World Wide Web. They would find a lot of them on Metcalfe's own Kelmscott Farm Web site.

The $50K Competition is no mere exercise. The winners of the 1996 contest, Pasha Roberts and Firdaus Bhathena, set up their company, Webline, and found a backer to develop the interactive Web site business service they invented. Victory in the $50K got them a hearing at every venture capital firm on the East Coast, but also an inevitable slew of negative responses—"months of rejection." Finally, they secured seed funding not from a venture-capital firm, but from a so-called angel—a wealthy individual. Angels traditionally are willing to risk money earlier in the development of a company than venture capitalists, in exchange for significant ownership stakes.

The Webline concept is one that could not have occurred before the browser, or Internet commerce. The idea is that as a customer visits a Web site to buy, for example, a car, a hotlink button allows her to summon the assistance of an online salesperson, and the two then talk, either by telephone or by Internet-tradition "chat" typing, with the screens of both participants linked and interactive. "Okay, let me show you the interior colors available," —and they're on the screen.

As the MIT $50K alumni literature states, "Webline is the leading developer of 'teleweb' solutions...to seamlessly integrate telephone and Web-based communication within their sales, service, and support organizations."

Their first steps were inevitably hesitant. As his partner Firdaus Bhathena says, "Pasha had a crude prototype and some idea of where we wanted to go, and no proven track record."

Angel funding enabled Webline's founders to attract a CEO with experience and proven success, whose last start-up had grown to a $400 million company. Bhathena and Roberts developed two options for how to advance the company: the "Bootstrap" and the "Wild Man." The former involved going slowly, but maintaining more ownership and spending less money; the latter, selling more equity for the funding that would allow rapid development of the product. Thanks to the pace of Web technology, they had no option but to take the Wild Man route.

It could be said that Pasha Roberts has the Web in his blood. His father is Larry Roberts, author of the original ARPAnet Request for Quotations, director of the Information Processing Techniques Office, and one of the chief architects of the interconnected world. Pasha Roberts likes to tell the story of how his twentysomething contemporaries at MIT would one-up each other about when they first started using the Internet: "It is weird. I remember visiting my dad in the Pentagon and walking through those big halls. He taught me how to program and how to build electronic stuff. I think then they were talking about what it would be like to build a galactic network and that was part of the vision. Any time we get into discussions about who was in the Internet first, I always win. I always say I was on in 1969. So that effectively wins. I was seven."

In the Pentagon in 1969, teleweb customer support was not foreseen. The accessibility of the Web, and the commercialization of the Internet, have created a vast array of information sources, content-providers, customer services, products, entertainment, and exploitation. The Internet itself is a medium too large to have a single killer application. But the number of connected computers and competing applications is growing at a breakneck pace. In the ten years from July 1988 to January 1998, the number of hosts connected to the Internet grew from 33 thousand to almost 30 million: a near thousandfold increase. In 1995, a year after the Web took hold, there were just 27 thousand commercial Web sites, and by 1998, three-quarters of a million—thirty times as many.

The potential neural overload of all the digitized content and services available to Web users has itself been made the subject of several books, and there are numerous magazines that do nothing more than describe and critique the best, worst, and weirdest of Web sites. Online services like America Online package and select materials, but also provide access to the unlimited Internet domains. Search services like Excite and Yahoo! select Web sites to save users the trouble of doing so for themselves. "Portals" to the Internet—a new designation—describes the commercial requirement, in an advertising-driven market, to capture viewers for the Web equivalent of channels or networks. As a result, the vast quantity of material is a matter of daily and hourly change, and this medium—the Gutenberg 1.0 technology—is not the place to attempt either a comprehensive or a current survey. But a few examples will provide some indication of the trends that either the nature of the technology or the culture of the new medium are bringing to the Internet.

Mail order has become e-mail order. Larry Ellison, founder and chairman of Oracle, likes to quote old-media shopping channel mogul, Barry Diller: "His comment was absolutely wonderful. He said that in terms of infrastructure costs, 'Buying underwear in your underwear is hard to beat.' If you buy the same underwear, you know exactly what the product is. You don't have to look at it. You buy Munsingwear 34's or whatever—kangaroo pouch—twelve pair. Please mail it to my house."

The commercial exploitation of the Web allows for virtual shopping on the grand scale. Amazon.com, the Internet bookstore, is generally regarded as the leading exponent of Web commerce, despite the fact that by 1998, after three years of trading, the company had yet to make a profit. But the venture funding Amazon received was intended to build market share and a marketing presence, with the benefits to be reaped later. The company went public in 1997, according to founder Jeff Bezos, for the same reason—to raise the money that would build the business to make money later: "The number-one reason for us to go public was so that Amazon.com could work on two things. Number one, further marketing its services and building its brand name is very, very important. Number two, increasing the level of services that we provide."

Amazon.com is a true garage start-up in Seattle, the brainchild of an ex-Wall Street wunderkind named Jeff Bezos. At Princeton he had taken astrophysics courses with his double major of electrical engineering and computer science, and noticed how the physicist part of the academic-scientific community used the Internet extensively. On Wall Street, where he worked for Bankers Trust Company, his peer group used e-mail; and in 1994, Bezos discovered the Mosaic Web browser and saw the astounding growth rate it was driving in World Wide Web usage.

"In the spring of 1994, I came across the statistic that Web usage was growing at 2300 percent a year, and, outside of a Petri dish, I hadn't seen anything grow that fast. So I decided I would try to find a business plan that made sense in the context of that growth. I made a list of twenty different products that you might be able to sell online, and force-ranked them according to several different criteria and picked books as the first best product, primarily because there are so many books."

Amazon is based on a simple, strategic idea. There are more different units in the category "books" (about three million) than there are in any other category. The next most numerous is CDs and music cassettes, of which there are about 300,000. The Internet is the ideal medium to gather, store, and present information about a very large number of items. The more choice one offers the customer, the more likely a sale: "There's no way to have a 2.5-million-title physical bookstore. The largest physical bookstores in the world only have about 175,000 titles. And there's no way to have a print catalog. If you were to print the Amazon.com catalog it'd be the size of more than forty New York City phone books."

This was Jeff Bezos' notion. When he went looking for venture capital, there was a tussle over who would fund him, between Hummer Winblad Venture Partners, and Kleiner, Perkins, Caufield, Byers. Ann Winblad recalls how Bezos pitched Amazon: "He said, 'I know nothing about the book industry. Nothing. I want to tell you that up front. But let me just tell you this: I know that I can get the books here and I can get them to the customers and forget about bricks and mortar. All I need to do is build an Internet site. My margins will be higher. I will change the economics of the book industry as a whole. My economies of scale will be so much more efficient that I can even withstand price wars.'"

Ann Winblad regards Amazon's performance as having delivered on those objectives, and says "the book industry is like a deer in the headlights." However, she has been a spectator, not a participant in this venture. The funding fight was won, perhaps predictably, by John Doerr of Kleiner, Perkins. Doerr today sits happily on Amazon's board, having put the necessary management team into place: "We had a superb CEO and founder, and a chief technical officer. But there was no VP of engineering, no VP-

CIO, no VP of business relations, no VP of finance, no VP of sales, no VP of marketing. Once we invested, we worked together with Jeff. We helped him recruit a really outstanding team of maybe ten vice presidents."

Amazon's big, noisy warehouse is located close by one of the biggest book wholesalers in the country. The relatively few desks are old doors on trestle legs. Jeff Bezos hired a staff of Generation-X bibliophiles, who give every appearance that body-piercing and tattoos are compulsory at Amazon. The books trundle out of the loading bays into U.S. Mail trucks, boosting the revenues of that delivery system. In less than three years since starting up in 1995, Amazon's valuation had risen to more than $1 billion. Jeff Bezos was vindicated in his decision to ignore the bricks and mortar: "If you look at revenue generated per operating employee, we generate something like $300,000 a year. Physical bookstores generate something like $95,000 per year per operating employee."

Amazon's prospects have driven up the stock price, to dizzying levels in mid-1998. As a result, and in a bid to dominate Web retailing in general rather than Web bookselling in particular, Amazon embarked on a round of acquisitions, mostly paid for with Amazon's golden stock. It is said that Jeff Bezos, having made a splash on the Web with books, has started working down his original list of twenty products, scaring many of his current and potential competitors in the world of electronic commerce.

The other key insight in Amazon's success is one that the history of networking has demonstrated repeatedly, and that Metcalfe's Law formalized: that the network becomes more and more useful as more and more people are connected. Amazon would not have worked before PCs were connected, for example. As Jeff Bezos points out, the key is not the technology: "The basic technology is fairly simple. The problem was the ubiquity of that technology. Because of that growth rate, this looked like the first time ever that the basic technology needed to do electronic commerce in an acceptable way would be ubiquitous. It turns out that the ubiquity of the Internet is more important than the technology of the Internet."

Although most people pay a subscription to get their Internet access from an Internet service provider, or ISP, the Web sites

they visit are not funded by the ISPs. Many Web sites, especially
those providing corporate information to clients and customers,
are sustained at the expense of the company as a marketing and
publicity service. Similarly, personal Web sites with family news
and photographs, can be organized and created very inexpen-
sively by individuals. But once Internet commerce began, three
other funding mechanisms took over: subscription services, pay-
per-view, and advertising. It took no time at all for the advertising industry to notice the growing numbers of eyes staring at Web
sites, and for Web site operators to start selling screen space to
the advertisers to catch the eyes in question. In 1999, online advertising revenue will exceed $1 billion, and the figure has been
doubling each year.

The Motley Fool is an example of a Web site that combines the
irreverent energy of the new medium with the advertising-
revenue model of the old. The Fool fosters an unconventional,
grassroots information exchange about investment and personal
finance. It was established by two brothers, Tom and David Gardner, whose expertise in the field was entirely free of Wall Street
experience or relevant educational qualifications. Dave Gardner
explains: "Advertising is the most frequent form of money-
making for us. And we have enough people coming to our various online sites that advertisers are interested. So that's been
[since 1995] the majority of our revenue. But then merchandise
as well. We have books. We have primers. E-mail services. We do
free massages as well."

Their own investment history consisted of managing their own
modest portfolios thanks to twenty-first-birthday gifts from their
parents. With that, and their English literature degrees, they have
built one of the most popular sites on the Internet by poking fun
at Wall Street conventions, and stating the obvious about the nature of investments, trading, and finance. The key idea is that
Wall Street depends on keeping the customer ignorant; so the
Fool Web site brings huge numbers of people together to share
their experiences and wisdom.

Tom Gardner sees the huge reach of the Internet as a financial
negotiating tool for Motley Fool's community of participants:
"Let's say we put 100,000 people together in a block that are
going to buy insurance or they're going to buy mutual funds. If

we can package them together, have everyone work together, we're going to be able to cut prices significantly."

Six hundred thousand households a week participate in this free exchange of information and opinion, though none of the advice is necessarily good advice. Hence the name, as Tom Gardner explains: "We pulled the Motley Fool from Shakespeare's *As You Like It*. In the Elizabethan court, the fool was the only guy who would go out there and tell people the truth, make some jokes, that was generally lovable and didn't get his head cut off for telling the king what was really happening out there in the court. So what we're doing with Wall Street is we're reminding people of how everyone's paid. We saw an industry that was getting really fat without a lot of light being shed on what they were doing. So we came and we said, 'We'll be fools.' It's a perfect disclaimer. If something goes wrong, well, we're fools. Unfortunately, you relied on the advice of fools."

As Howard Rheingold argues, this expansion of access is remarkable: "It's vitally important because it's a many-to-many medium. Every desktop, every computer that's connected to the Internet, even whether it's through an ordinary telephone line and a modem, is potentially a printing press and a broadcasting station and a place of assembly."

The Internet is no longer just an information medium; it is also a visual medium. As with every other new means of presenting pictures since still photography began, the item driving early adoption was none other than sex. So-called adult chat rooms were an influence on the spread of the Internet before the Web made pictures available, and an early trend once the Web made the Internet graphical was "adult content." No particular blame should be attached to the Internet for this: stills, motion pictures, and videos all went through the same growing pains in their time.

In October 1996, at a conference in London's Café Royal on the Internet and telephony, one lonely American raised his hand in response to the question "Who is making a profit on the Internet?" The burly gentleman in question was Dan Guess, CEO of Virtual Dreams, a Web-based peepshow: "I opened up my laptop; I dialed Virtual Dreams in southern California; and we had a beautiful model half way around the world waving to the audience, saying hello from Los Angeles. I said 'This is exactly how we're making money on the Net.' You could have heard a pin drop in the room. People were somewhat shocked."

As Dan Guess claims, warfare and sex are the twin forces that drive technology: "Sex sells. There is a market for it and it's true capitalism. If there's a market for it, it will be filled. It's legal and there's nothing wrong with it. In the beginning of this industry, people are willing to pay for adult content. The home video cassette industry was a prime example. Initially people were spending several thousand dollars back in the 1970s for machines to go home and basically watch adult content. Now, eventually that exploded into a whole big industry."

The Virtual Dreams Web site is just one example of the pay-per-view or subscription Web sites offering XXX photographs, live action, and chat. Here, the models disrobe in front of cameras they control with a keyboard and mouse, while also responding to the live instructions of customers online. The keyboard planted in the cheesy pseudo-boudoir of each model adds a surreal note; as do the technical challenges of the job, described by "Kat": "You want to have your nails manicured, and nails do slip a lot on the keyboard. But as long as you just write simple things like, 'Hi, how are you, babe?' You can just put 'R U.' You don't have to put the whole word down. And most of the time you're saying, 'Oh, yeah, baby....'"

After five years of the World Wide Web era, the Internet economy is still in the formative stages, and predicting which successes will last, and which will fade, is impossible. Certainly some current successes will fall by the wayside, and new unforeseen competitors will rise like meteors. Larry Tesler has observed every generation of networking from close quarters: "This is still a very early period in the development of the Internet. It reminds me of the late 1970s in personal computing, when we had companies that were on the front pages of the trade magazines that you never even hear of anymore. They're mostly gone."

Dan Guess is looking forward to an improvement in Internet technology that will allow a new venture to flourish: but one at the opposite end of the taste spectrum. Full video interactivity will facilitate his "Virtual Santa": "You can have your children dial up and can call the North Pole, and Santa can be sitting there. You might have an arrangement with a department store where there's a preset spending limit. The child talks to Santa using his computer and she tells Santa what she wants for Christmas. Santa's already got the preset spending limit and, next day, out comes the gift directly from Santa for the child."

Dan Guess' biggest problem at Virtual Dreams is not a lack of attractive models willing to remove their clothes, but a shortage of qualified technicians to program and maintain the software and hardware for the business. This is a familiar complaint across the entire high-technology industry. The success of Silicon Valley industries (both in the Valley and elsewhere) has resulted in a desperate shortage of qualified, skilled, English-speaking software engineers available to American companies. This has resulted in a number of intriguing consequences.

The first result can be seen in the growing popularity of cricket in Northern California. There are clubs in San Jose, Santa Clara, Sunnyvale, Berkeley, Davis, East Bay, Marin, and elsewhere that wander from field to field. The great majority of players are from India (and neighboring countries), drawn to Silicon Valley by the incomparable job opportunities for English-speaking, highly-educated computer scientists and engineers. In India, English is the language of higher education, and industry has for decades required technological training for tens of thousands of Indian graduates.

Throughout the 1980s and 1990s, Indian computer-science graduates have been finding jobs in Silicon Valley, either by migrating as individuals (though this is subject to Federal restrictions) or by being provided as temporary labor by Indian companies. The latter process is known in India as "body-shopping." So in the eighties and early nineties, programmers from India would arrive in Silicon Valley, where they introduced to suburban soccer and baseball fields the unaccustomed sights and sounds of cricket. As an Indian-born venture capitalist, Boston-based Sundar Subramanian explains: "India is the second-largest country in number of engineers, after the United States, in the whole world, so I think that is a factor. The second thing is it's an English-based system. It's a lot easier for people to come from India and integrate and do business in the United States. So I think given the education system and the large number of engineers, it's been a natural fit in the U.S."

The second consequence is that in the 1990s, venture capitalists have begun to look elsewhere than Silicon Valley to set up new ventures. Sundar Subramanian prefers to locate new ventures in Los Angeles. The talent pool in the Valley is now so competitive that almost any good programmer can change jobs and increase his or her salary with a single phone call. If a new venture with good programmers begins to look like anything other than a massive success, the staff quickly drop out and look for the next big opportunity. Almost all start-ups offer stock options, so there is little disadvantage to switching from a failure to a new potential success. Because of the talent shortage, there's also very little disapproval of people moving rapidly from job to job. It is the business culture of the Valley.

These circumstances have begun to change with the growing ubiquity of Internet access. Increasingly, as the growing number of American telecommuters testifies, it may not matter very much where you live or work. On a grander global scale, this permits American companies to sub-contract development work from companies elsewhere, or to set up subsidiaries in locations where there is still a pool of available and qualified staff. One of the places most often mentioned in this regard is Bangalore, in the Indian province of Karnataka. Oracle is one of the American companies that has followed this route, as Larry Ellison explains: "The original interest in Bangalore came about because it was pretty inexpensive, compared with Chicago or New York or San Francisco, to do software development in Bangalore. We have the remarkable situation that I work in an industry where there's zero unemployment. You can't get skilled labor at any price. There is no labor available. So we're scouring the world market to get programmers."

Bangalore is known as "The Garden City" and claims to be the fastest-growing city in all of Asia. It is elevated, cool, and green. The city is the traditional home of the Indian aerospace and defense industry, and of the venerable Indian Institute of Science. The city produces thousands of English-speaking engineering graduates each year: the saying in Bangalore is that "every second person writes code." Inevitably, it is known as the Silicon Valley of India. Although the cost of business here is lower—between 50 and 70 percent lower—than in the United States, there are other advantages Ellison identifies: "I thought it would cost us a tiny fraction of what we paid programmers here in the United States. As it turns out, it was more than half. The quality of the people is astonishing. The loyalty of the people and the work ethic, the quality of their English, everything just blew us away. We just have a fabulous experience in Bangalore and we're expanding our operations there very, very rapidly."

Today, many American companies besides Oracle are commissioning software development and product support from workers who operate twelve time zones from California's Silicon Valley. Novell is constructing a new headquarters building in Bangalore. Oracle has a major division there. In 1998, Microsoft announced a $60 million commitment over three years to develop the market in India, setting up a South Asian headquarters in the same building where Compaq, Sun Microsystems and Apple are located. Many more American companies contract work from Indian-based software shops there.

V. Chandrasekranan, the president of Wipro Systems in Bangalore, employs no less than 2000 Indian programmers to work for General Electric, Allied Signals, Sequent, Xerox, Putnam Investor Services, Tandem, Cisco, Stratacom, and others.

Sundar Sankaran is a typical young programmer in Bangalore who rides to work at Sonata Software on a motor scooter. It is the favored means of transportation in Bangalore, and the streets are choked with hundreds of thousands of scooters at rush hour, their riders honking aimlessly at the congestion. These streets present an odd mixture of images. At every corner there are banners offering training in C++, Oracle databases, workstation sales and service; while in the open market, cripples beg, holy cattle wander at will, and the knife-sharpener pedals his whetstone furiously. Bangalore seems to thrive on its contradictions. Sundar has benefited from the Indian education system's attention to technology, studying computer science since the equivalent of eighth grade, though today it starts in third grade. He got a bachelor's degree in computer science, and then continued with postgraduate training.

Sundar's boss at Sonata Software is Managing Director Srikan Reddy. In this company, like so many in Bangalore, the distance and time difference between India and the West Coast of the

United States is a boon in the Internet era: "You're working when your customer is sleeping. To that extent if he gives you a problem during his working hours, you'll solve it and send it back to him by the time he starts working. So I mean, it's a great advantage, especially if you're doing things offshore."

Vikram Shah, the head of Novell's Indian subsidiary, uses the Internet and Novell's own Internet software to achieve the same around-the-clock work cycle: "Novell Directory Services provides us a worldwide view of the Novell network. By sitting in here, I can look at servers all over the world and I can log into the servers. I can do the work here, upload the work that is done in India onto the servers in the U.S., download in the morning when we come in the work which is done there."

The Internet has in effect perfected the twenty-four-hour workday: "We get a call in the evening through e-mail saying there's a problem. Next day morning when people come to work the problem is solved. The customer gets surprised, saying 'I just told you at 5 o'clock in the evening, how come in the morning you guys solved it?' The problem is solved in the other part of the world by really using this twenty-four-hour development cycle."

It's not only cricket that the British Empire gave India. As the inscription on Bangalore's Vidhana Soudha (the State Legislature building) asserts, "Government Work Is God's Work." The Empire made English the language of government and of higher education. Which gives Indian engineers another great advantage, because English is clearly the language of the Internet. In India, the average person in school learns at least three languages: English, Hindi, and their local dialect. It's not unusual to know five or six languages. Even on the cricket fields of Silicon Valley, Indian players speak different regional languages; so on the cricket field they communicate in English, overcoming the incompatibility problem that has always held networking back.

An indirect result of the Internet's growth has been to open up the global market for engineering talent. While labor is in short supply in Californian and Massachusetts, there are qualified pools of labor in India, Israel, and Russia. As Larry Ellison says, "There's tremendous talent and tremendous competition for the talent. You have to follow the talent wherever they are in the world."

The computer, software, and Internet industry is indeed "all geeked up," and high technology has become not only what the industry produces, but also the medium in which it communicates. Throughout the industry, one learns of consulting work being conducted entirely by e-mail, or job interviews conducted online. The Web lifestyle is advancing rapidly; but perhaps no one has quite as much wild enthusiasm for it as Microsoft's Steve Ballmer: "I use the Internet to lead what we like to call around here, a Web lifestyle. I want to find out something nowadays, the first thing I do is turn to the Internet."

No one outdoes Steve Ballmer in his devotion to the Detroit Pistons. He uses the Internet to sweep up every scrap of information he can locate about the team. But above all, for him as for most users, the closest thing to a killer app in the nineties is the same killer app of networking in the seventies: "E-mail, baby! That's number one. I probably get a hundred pieces of e-mail a day but at least thirty of them nowadays come from outside. 'Hey, bud, I haven't seen you since you and I were in school together in fifth grade in Belgium!'"

The Internet is a global community; but who would have guessed that Steve Ballmer went to elementary school in Belgium?

Conclusion
Not A Fad

T HERE IS, OF COURSE, NO CONCLUSION to this story. This is only the beginning. The Internet is by now as diverse as the entire media industry, or the entire publishing industry, or the entire aggregation of people's whims and passions. The resources required to establish a Web site and begin communicating with like-minded people, or aggregating those people towards a common financial or cultural interest, are practically zero. The growth in the Internet is more rapid than the growth in any medium in history. Yet the iceberg of the Internet is still mostly below the water. It has many facets, but in these concluding pages we will address just four: commerce, community, the personal, and the political.

Commerce

As the number of people using the Internet increases, the opportunities to make money from providing them with services increases too. This is the marketplace of the third millennium: the prize for which all the hardware, software, and service providers of the Internet industry are competing, and a prime piece of what venture capitalists call "market real estate."

Ann Winblad, of Hummer Winblad Venture Partners, defines it thus: "We are market real estate investors. The opportunity has to be enormous. Because guess what? It always gets smaller. If you don't start with the state of Texas, you know, it may whittle down to the size of Nebraska. So if you start with Rhode Island, you're going to end up with Martha's Vineyard."

Community

The Internet has created virtual communities. For the first time since the population dispersal of the industrial revolution, there's a means for communicating with everyone in one's chosen community. The family or group may be geographically scattered, but they can remain virtually connected. Bulletin board systems allowed individuals to use a phone line and modem to connect to other people with similar interests. The WELL's founder, Stewart Brand, sees the wired world of the Internet as a marriage of 1960s ideology and the most modern technology: "The *Whole Earth Catalog* of the 1990s *is* the World Wide Web."

Larry Tesler, former Xerox PARC researcher and chief scientist at Apple Computer: "When we were human beings in small tribes hunting and gathering, everybody you had to deal with was somebody you saw every day. We're a species that's based on communication with our entire tribe. As the population grew and people had to split up into smaller tribes and separate, they got to the point where they would never see each other for their whole lives. The Internet is the first technology that lets us have many-to-many communication with anybody on the planet. In a sense, it's brought us back to something we lost thousands of years ago. So one reason I think the Internet's taken off so fast is that we always needed it. And we finally have it."

The service that The Motley Fool or thousands of other Web sites provide is a megaphone for conversations that otherwise might take place among only handfuls of people, over coffee or at the water-cooler. As Steve Jobs points out, the Web makes small businesses look the same as big businesses: nobody's Web site makes the computer monitor any larger. So in areas of personal importance, like investments, people are being exposed to bad, unaccountable advice as well as good. In medicine, Web sites offering or advocating extreme medical quackery pop up no more or less easily than those of regulated, professional bodies like the National Institutes of Health or the American Cancer Society. The torrent of information has no quality control; yet there are wonderful stories that emerge from the flood.

The Personal

Vint Cerf's wife, Sigrid, lost almost all her hearing after contracting spinal meningitis at the age of three. For fifty years she wore an amplification device. On the Internet, the couple researched cochlear implants, an experimental electronic inner ear, and she located people who had the implants, and by e-mail contacted a specialist at Johns Hopkins University. After some tests, in the spring of 1996, Sigrid Cerf had the implant. Some weeks later, she went back to the hospital, where they activated the inner ear implant. After they tinkered for twenty minutes she could hear. As Vint Cerf emotionally explains: "She makes a phone call. And she and I talk to each other on the phone for the first time in thirty-one years. She and I had this chance to talk. It wasn't a very profound conversation."

Vint and Sigrid Cerf had a good experience with the information resources on the Internet, though it was not the Internet that cured her deafness. The information is unregulated and uncensored, and its providers are largely unaccountable. It is a many-to-many dialogue that some people regard as the Achilles heel of the Internet; while others see it as the jewel in the crown. There are thousands of Web sites and usergroups that provide information and support to fellow sufferers from illness, fellow seekers after particular truths. On the Net, freedom of information is truly free.

The Political

Bob Kahn, who with Vint Cerf is as responsible as anyone for the global interactivity of networks, sees a struggle between political freedom and technological competitiveness: "Information is really power in many ways. Could a totalitarian regime even maintain control effectively if all the citizens had access to this? The reality was that when enough of the free world was able to adopt it, it made it even more difficult for the countries that were trying to resist it to continue to do it because they would only fall further behind in the space of possibilities."

Some argue that the early Internet, the offspring of the ARPAnet, perfectly fulfilled its original post-Sputnik role as an anti-Communist tool, by helping to bring down the Iron Curtain in the late 1980s.

Howard Rheingold, an early advocate of the virtual community, observes:

> The way the Internet has changed the means of distribution of information has really had profound political effects that haven't hit the history books yet. In 1989, Tienanmen Square, we watched television, we watched the networks. But I also watched UseNet. There were thousands of eye-

witness accounts that came out of China. Once they came out of China and hit one node of the Internet, they were everywhere else. The opposition to the counter-revolution in Moscow, when they had the battle at the White House there, used the Internet to organize. More recently in Serbia, when radio station B92, the opposition radio station, was shut down, it was up on the Internet within hours. It used to be possible for entire populations that occupied entire continents to be sealed off from the world. Word didn't get in, word didn't get out. That day is gone forever.

Before and since those events, people have been talking about an Information Revolution to match the Industrial Revolution. In this brief history of the Internet, we have perhaps seen that it is real.

In Conclusion

Bob Metcalfe is first among equals as a witness to the history of the future: "You've heard about the information age? It's here. It's the Internet. It's the Web. It's happening right in front of us. It's a privilege to be here watching it happen because I've been worrying about it for decades. It's happening right now."

Doug Engelbart, pioneer and visionary, has the limited satisfaction of seeing now, after almost fifty years in the field, how right he was: "It's frustrating to have it all go so slowly, and having such a hard time getting a story across. For several decades you could say, well, maybe my story is not right. There are lots of guys out there waving and pointing, the world can't listen to everybody. But now it's getting a little more frustrating when I realize I must have been more right than one could expect."

For the lay user of the Web, such as the author of this book, or to the new or uninitiated user, there is a paradox: while the riches and diversity of the information and media resources available on the Net are overwhelming, it doesn't work well *enough*. Most modems are too slow, most computers don't have the memory to allow pages to be rendered quickly, and the Web is hard to access away from home or workplace. Most people who are "wired" are also trying desperately to become "wireless," and one clear trend that will emerge in the next three to five years will be the advances in what some are calling "nomadic computing"—the successor to "distributed computing." Len Kleinrock, still pioneering after thirty years on the cutting edge of networking, calls his new company Nomadix, and he proposes to address the needs and obstacles of the technological nomads.

The networking of our computers with that generic entity "the Internet" has made possible something that was science fiction barely a generation ago: the universal gathering-together of any and all information, accessible to any and all users. There are dangers, of course, and abuses that may be more or less trivial; but the real and potential benefits are immense, and this brief history may only represent the beginnings of a cultural phenomenon that will justify the hype of comparisons to the printing press or broadcasting.

For all the fun that one can (and does) have at the expense of the geeky entrepreneurs who have created this enormous new medium and industry, it is worth noting that they have created immense numbers of new, relatively well-paying jobs; that the Internet is largely free of political, racial, and gender boundaries; and that it is beyond the control of any political movement, nation-state, organized labor or religious movement. It is, in its flawed and diverse fashion, a ubiquitous expression of human imagination, ambition, and individuality.

When I first began paying attention to this technological/media phenomenon in 1993, all the talk was about convergence—of computers, cable, and the Internet. With the advent of digital television, in 1998, that convergence is coming a step closer. But lacking a crystal ball, we remain unable to predict the next steps. If they were easier to predict, we would already be reporting them as history. It is clear that the two primary applications of the Net in 1999—one dating from its origins, the other from its recent liberation—are communication and commerce. Metcalfe's Law will continue to operate, ensuring that the more family members, colleagues, and friends go online, the more one will choose to communicate with them by e-mail rather than, or as well as, the old-technology methods. And the ease with which one can now buy almost anything online—be it Amazon's books sold at discounts to the customer, or the disposal of surplus industrial inventory in India—means that electronic commerce is sure to grow.

At the very least, the Internet's commercial future is the first truly global, truly unlimited market, potentially making NAFTA and the European Community modest by comparison. John Doerr, investor par excellence, revels in the size of this unprecedented business opportunity: "It's at least three times bigger than the PC was and the PC was the largest single legal creation of wealth we've ever seen on the planet. In year three of the Web, by my calculation, the new Web companies are worth more than $40 billion. That's four times what the PC companies were worth at this point in the decade of the PC. Some of it's undervalued. Some of it's overvalued. That's how markets are. But this is not a hula hoop. It's not a fad."

Cast of Characters
(those in italics, not interviewed)

Norm Abramson, University of Hawaii professor, developer of Alohanet, founder of Aloha Networks

Sam Albert, lifelong IBM salesman, Internet consultant

Paul Allen, cofounder of Microsoft and many other high-technology ventures, chairman of the Paul Allen Group

Marc Andreessen, coinventor of the University of Illinois Mosaic Web browser, cofounder of Netscape

Bill Atkinson, Apple Computer—Lisa and Macintosh design team member

Steve Ballmer, Harvard friend of Bill Gates, as of 1998 president and CEO of Microsoft

Paul Baran, _RAND Corporation researcher, cofounder Aloha Networks_

Andy Bechtolsheim, cofounder Sun Microsystems, founder of Granite Systems (later acquired by Cisco Systems)

George Bell, former magazine publisher hired as CEO of Excite in January 1996

Tim Berners-Lee, information technologist at CERN (the European particle physics laboratory), inventor of the World Wide Web

Jeff Bezos, founder of Amazon.com, the online bookstore; former Wall Street trader

Firdaus Bhathena, cofounder of Webline (winner of the 1996 MIT $50K competition)

Jim Bidzos, CEO of RSA Data Security, director on numerous Internet company boards, immensely successful Internet investor

David Boggs, _Xerox PARC Researcher, coinventor of Ethernet, Digital Equipment Corporation Systems Research Center researcher_

Congressman Frederick C. Boucher, _of Virginia's "Fightin' Ninth"_

District, introducer of legislation that allowed commercial traffic on the Internet

Len Bosack, cofounder of Cisco Systems, founder of XKL Technologies, formerly director of Stanford's computer science department

David Bradford, General Counsel of Novell Inc.

Stewart Brand, media entrepreneur, author, founder of *The Whole Earth Catalog* and the Whole Earth 'Lectronic Link (WELL)

Dan Bricklin, founder of Software Arts, coinventor of VisiCalc, founder of Trellix Corporation

David Bunnell, technical writer at MITS; founder-publisher of *PC Magazine, PCWorld* and *MacWorld*

Rod Canion, cofounder of Compaq, former Texas Instruments executive

Steve Case, founder and chairman of America Online (previously Quantum Computer Services)

Vint Cerf, coinventor of the TCP/IP Internet protocol; cofounder in 1986 of the Corporation for National Research Initiatives; senior vice president of Internet Architecture and Engineering, MCI Communications Corporation; president of the Internet Society, 1992–95; winner of the U.S. National Medal of Technology award in December 1997; former UCLA graduate student present at the creation of ARPAnet

V. Chandrasekranan, president of Wipro Systems, Bangalore, India

"Kat" Charrette, interactive adult Web site model, Virtual Dreams

Jim Clark, founder of Silicon Graphics, cofounder of Netscape Communications, former Stanford professor

Bernie Cosell, member of the BB&N ARPAnet team, master debugger

Steve Crocker, initiator of ARPAnet and Internet "Requests for Comments"

Will Crowther, programmer, member of the BB&N ARPAnet team

Eddie Currie, childhood friend of Ed Roberts, MITS staffer

John Doerr, venture capitalist; principal at Kleiner, Perkins, Caufield & Byers

Willie Donahoo, Novell executive from 1990 to 1998

Larry Ellison, cofounder and Chairman of Oracle

Doug Engelbart, inventor of the computer mouse, manager of ARPAnet Network Information Center at Stanford Research Institute, director of the Bootstrap Institute

Chris Espinosa, Apple Computer staffer from the age of fourteen

Fawn Fitter, freelance writer and cohost with Mary Elizabeth Williams of Byline, the WELL's conference for freelance nonfiction writers [www.well.com/conf/byline/index.html]

Bob Frankston, cofounder of Software Arts, and coinventor of Visi-Calc

Gordon French, *founder of the Homebrew Computer Club*

David Gans, musician, Grateful Dead art expert, radio deejay at KPFA Berkeley

David Gardner, cofounder of The Motley Fool financial advice Web site

Tom Gardner, cofounder of The Motley Fool financial advice Web site

Harry Garland, member of Homebrew Computer Club, cofounder of Cromemco

Bill Gates, cofounder and chairman of Microsoft

Chuck Geschke, *Xerox PARC researcher, cofounder of Adobe Systems*

Rob Glaser, Microsoft Network software executive, founder of Progressive Networks

Adele Goldberg, Xerox PARC researcher, founder of PARC Place Systems

Marv Goldschmitt, proprietor of Massachusetts computer store who sold the first copies of VisiCalc

Ralph Gorin, Manager of LOTSS (Low Overhead Time Sharing System) at Stanford University, XKL Technologies staffer

James Gosling, principal architect of Java, the Sun Microsystems cross-platform enhanced computer language

Andy Grove, cofounder of Intel in 1968, president from 1979, CEO from 1987 to 1997, *Time*'s 1997 Man of the Year

Dan Guess, CEO of Virtual Dreams, a Web-based "adult" interactive peepshow

Frank Heart, manager of the Bolt Beranek & Newman (BBN) team which invented and built the ARPAnet

Charlie Herzfeld, second director of ARPA, who authorized Bob Taylor to attempt the experimental ARPAnet

Rita Hurault, cohost of "Women on the WELL" conference, known as "WoW"

Steve Jobs, cofounder of Apple Computer and NeXT Computer, acting CEO of Apple in 1998

Bill Joy, cofounder of Sun Microsystems, Sun's chief technical philosopher

Robert Kahn, coinventor of the TCP/IP Internet protocol, cofounder and president of the Corporation for National Research Initiatives, winner of the U.S. National Medal of Technology award in December 1997

Rohit Khare, World Wide Web Consortium executive (1995–97), host of FORK (Friends Of Rohit Khare) Web site, Ph.D. student at UC Irvine developing new Web protocols and studying the process of Internet standardization

Vinod Khosla, cofounder Sun Microsystems; venture capitalist at Kleiner, Perkins, Caufield & Byers

Len Kleinrock, professor of computer science at UCLA, former director of the ARPAnet Network Measurement Center, Chairman and founder of Nomadix Inc.

Joe Kraus, cofounder and first CEO of Architext, senior vice president of Excite

Butler Lampson, Berkeley Computer Corporation staffer, Xerox PARC researcher, DEC Systems Research Center researcher

Sandy Lerner, cofounder Cisco Systems, founder of Urban Decay cosmetics, former director of computer facilities for Stanford Graduate School of Business

J.C.R. Licklider, first director of ARPA's Information Processing Techniques Office (1962–65)

Bill Lowe, head of the IBM Research Laboratory in Boca Raton, Florida, where the IBM PC was developed

Ben Lutch, cofounder of Architext; technical lead for software operations, Excite

Drew Major, SuperSet computer consultant for Novell Data Systems in 1981, chief scientist and vice president for Advanced Development at Novell Inc.

Mike Markkula, *former Intel executive, cofounder and first president of Apple Computer*

John McAfee, founder of McAfee Associates and Tribal Voice (PowWow)

Peter McColough, *Xerox Corporation president (from 1966) and CEO (1968–1981)*

Ryan McIntyre, cofounder of Architext; Tools Tsar, Excite

Scott McNealy, cofounder and CEO of Sun Microsystems

Roger Melen, member of Homebrew Computer Club, owner of Altair #002, cofounder of Cromemco

Bob Metcalfe, Xerox PARC researcher, coinventor of Ethernet, founder of 3Com, *InfoWorld* columnist

Gordon Moore, cofounder of Intel, author of "Moore's Law"

Ted Nelson, computer visionary, author of *Computer Lib/Dream Machines*, inventor of Xanadu

Ray Noorda, venture capitalist and company doctor, owner of a majority interest in Novell Data Systems in 1983; relaunched Novell and was its president, CEO, and chairman (1983–1994), chairman of the Canopy Group

Scott Oki, Microsoft senior vice president for Sales, Marketing and Services (1982–1992)

Severo Ornstein, software engineer, member of the BB&N ARPAnet team, researcher at Xerox PARC

Kim Polese, product manager for Java at Sun Microsystems, cofounder of Marimba

Jonathan Postel, *editor of ARPAnet and Internet "Requests for Comments"*

Srikan Reddy, managing director of Sonata Software (Bangalore, India)

Martin Reinfried, cofounder of Architext; technical lead in international engineering, Excite

Howard Rheingold, *Whole Earth Catalog* staff writer, author of "Tools for Thought," "Virtual Communities," etc.

Glen Ricart, Novell executive, former University of Maryland network technologies professor, coarchitect of SURANET

Ed Roberts, founder of MITS; inventor of the first personal computer, the Altair 8800

Larry Roberts, director of ARPA's Information Processing Techniques Office from 1969 to 1973; CEO of Telenet, the first packet-switching utility; founder and president of Packetcom

Pasha Roberts, cofounder of Webline (winner of the 1996 MIT $50K competition), son of Larry Roberts

Arthur Rock, venture capitalist; original investor in Intel, Apple Computer, etc.

Jack Sams, IBM PC executive

Sundar Sankaran, programmer with Sonata Software (Bangalore, India)

Eric Schmidt, chief technology officer Sun Microsystems (1983–97), chairman and CEO of Novell from 1997; former Xerox PARC Computer Science Laboratory researcher

Rich Seidner, veteran IBM programmer

Vikram Shah, managing director of Novell India

Jon Shirley, Microsoft president and chief operating officer (1983–89), former Tandy executive

Charles Simonyi, Xerox PARC researcher, inventor of Wordstar, first head of Microsoft applications group (1981), chief architect at Microsoft (1998)

Brian Sparks, president of Caldera, formerly head of advanced development team at Novell Inc.

Sparky Sparks, IBM PC sales executive

Graham Spencer, cofounder of Architext; chief technology officer of Excite

Sundar Subramanian, venture capitalist at Cambridge Technology Partners

***Ivan Sutherland,** second director of ARPA's Information Processing Techniques Office (1965–66), inventor of Sketchpad, University of Utah professor*

Bob Taylor, director of ARPA's Information Processing Techniques Office (1965–69), founder and associate manager of Xerox PARC

Computer Science Laboratory (1970–77), manager of Xerox PARC CSL (1977–83), and founder and manager of Digital Equipment Corporation's Systems Research Center (1983–96)

Larry Tesler, Xerox PARC researcher, chief scientist at Apple Computer (1980–97)

Chuck Thacker, *Berkeley Computer Corporation staffer, Xerox PARC researcher, DEC Systems Research Center researcher*

Ray Tomlinson, BB&N engineer who was first to send e-mail on the ARPAnet and invented the use of the @ sign in e-mail

Don Valentine, venture capitalist at Sequoia Capital; investor in Apple, 3Com, Cisco Systems, and dozens of other companies

Mark Van Haren, cofounder of Architext; technical lead at Spider Group, Excite

Dave Walden, software engineer, member of the BB&N ARPAnet team

John Warnock, Xerox PARC researcher, cofounder of Adobe Systems

Jim Warren, founder-editor of "Dr. Dobbs' Journal," founder-organizer of the West Coast Computer Faire

Ann Winblad, former software entrepreneur, venture capitalist, principal of Hummer Winblad Venture Partners

Irving Wladawsky-Berger, IBM Internet strategy chief

Steve Wozniak, cofounder of Apple Computer

Timeline

THIS TIMELINE IS DERIVED in part from a number of versions available on the Net, of which the most detailed is *Hobbes' Internet Timeline v2.5*, by Robert H'obbes' Zakon, "Internet evangelist." It is based primarily on material and events covered in this book. This timeline too will be posted, on the Nerds 2.0.1 Web site <http://www.pbs.org/nerds201>, together with other material from and relating to this book and the television series it accompanies.

August 23, 1937	Bill Hewlett & David Packard, first official business meeting.
1938	Hewlett & Packard's garage start-up. Designated a California Historic Landmark, "the birthplace of Silicon Valley" in 1989.
1945	First electronic digital computer created by Army-funded University of Pennsylvania team: ENIAC, Electronic Numerical Integrator and Calculator.
1951	Remington Rand combined with ENIAC inventors to create UNIVAC.
1951	Stanford Research Park, established on university land.
October 4, 1957	*Sputnik I* launched; Eisenhower Science Advisory Committee meeting follows.
1958	Eisenhower requests funds from Congress to set up ARPA. Approved as a line item in Air Force appropriations bill. ARPA established.
Late summer 1958	NASA appropriations approved. Space & missile programs transferred from ARPA to NASA. ARPA budget left at $150 million.
1960–1961	Ted Nelson proposes "Xanadu." First Paper on packet-switching theory by Len Kleinrock,

"Information Flow in Large Communications Nets," published by *RLE Quarterly Progress Report.*

1962   Paul Baran, RAND Corporation study, "On Distributed Communication Networks," or packet-switching networks.

August 1962   First paper on Internet Concept by J.C.R. Licklider & Welden Clark, "On-line Man Computer Communication."

1963   J.C.R. Licklider memo addresses "Members of the Intergalactic Computer Network."

1964   NASA (Bob Taylor) funds Doug Engelbart's "Augmentation Lab."

                Communication Nets, a book by Len Kleinrock, provides the network design and queuing theory necessary to build packet networks. This work was a major factor in designing the communications network for the ARPANET.

March 1964   First paper on secure packetized voice communications by Paul Baran "On Distributed Communications Networks," *IEEE Transactions on Systems.* It is from this paper that the false rumor was started that the Internet was created by the military to withstand nuclear war.

1965   "Moore's Law" first postulated by Gordon Moore; Donald Davies, National Physical Laboratory, UK packetizing data for store-and-forward communications.

February 1965   First network experiment: Ivan Sutherland, director of IPTO at ARPA, gives contract to Larry Roberts at MIT Lincoln Laboratory.

October 1965   First network experiments: Lincoln Lab's TX-2 tied to SDC's Q32. This experiment was the first time two computers talked to each other and the first time packets were used to communicate between computers.

1966   Bob Taylor wonders why his three computers should not be connected.

October 1966	First paper on network experiments, Larry Roberts & Thomas Marill, "Toward a Cooperative Network of Time-Shared Computers," Fall AFIPS Conference.
December 1966	ARPA Communications Program begins. Larry Roberts becomes ARPA chief scientist and begins the design of the ARPAnet. The ARPAnet program as proposed to Congress by Roberts was to explore computer resource sharing and packet-switched communications.
April 1967	ARPAnet Design Session held by Roberts at ARPA/IPTO Principal Investigator meeting in Ann Arbor, Michigan. It was at this meeting that Wes Clark suggested the use of minicomputers for network packet switches (IMPs) instead of using the mainframe computers themselves for switching.
October 1967	Original ARPAnet design paper, Lawrence Roberts, "Multiple Computer Networks and Intercomputer Communication," ACM Conference, Gatlinburg, Tennessee.
	First use of the word "packet," by Donald Davies, Roger Scantlebury et al, in their paper "A Digital Communications Network for Computers...," presented at ACM Gatlinburg. Donald Davies could not convince the British to fund a wide area network experiment.
1968	Doug Engelbart's "mother of all demos": the mouse, windows, videoconferencing.
	Robert Noyce and Gordon Moore quit Fairchild Semiconductor to found Intel Corporation. Intel's first chips store 256 bits.
August 1968	Request for Quotations released for ARPAnet by Larry Roberts, ARPA. The RFQ mandated the main packet-switching design elements for the ARPAnet.
September 1968	ARPAnet RFP responses received. Evaluation was by Roberts, ARPA staff, and a group of ARPA contractors.

December 1968	ARPAnet contract awarded to Bolt, Beranek & Newman (BBN) in Cambridge, Massachusetts. Frank Heart's group at BBN began to build the ARPAnet Interface Message Processors (IMPs). The BBN group proposed to use Honeywell 516 minicomputers for the IMPs. The team included Bob Kahn, Severo Ornstein, Dave Walden, and others.
	Senator Edward Kennedy's office sent a message of congratulation to BB&N re: "Interfaith" Message Processor.
1969	Department of Justice filed anti-monopoly suit against IBM.
April 1969	Host to IMP Specification #1822 released, written by Bob Kahn at BBN. The spec detailed the interface between ARPAnet host computers and the IMPs. The IMPs needed to be connected to each computer with this unique hardware interface. It needed to be designed and built for each different computer attached.
April 1969	Request for Comments (RFC) #1, "Host Software" released, written by Steve Crocker, covering host-to-host protocol, the first output of the Network Working Group (NWG).
September 1, 1969	First node of ARPAnet installed at UCLA Network Measurement Center, where Len Kleinrock's group connected the IMP to their Sigma 7 computer.
October 1, 1969	Second node of ARPAnet installed at Stanford Research Institute where Doug Engelbart's group connected it to their SDS 940 computer. The first ARPAnet messages passed that day: "LOG-IN . . . Crash!"
September 1969	Bob Taylor leaves ARPA for the University of Utah and Larry Roberts becomes fourth director of IPTO.
November 1, 1969	Third node of the ARPAnet installed at University of California, Santa Barbara, connecting to their IBM 360/75.

December 1, 1969	Fourth node of the ARPAnet installed at the University of Utah, connecting to their DEC PDP-10.
March 1970	ARPAnet first spans the U.S., connecting BBN (node #5) into the Net.
June 1970	Xerox PARC opened; Bob Taylor is founder and associate manager of the Computer Science Laboratory.
July 1970	First packet radio network, Alohanet operational at University of Hawaii under Norm Abramson using the Aloha concept of random packet retransmission.
1971	15 nodes on the ARPAnet: UCLA, SRI, UCSB, U of U, BBN, MIT, Rand Corporation, Systems Development Corporation, Harvard, Lincoln Lab, Stanford University, U of Illinois (Champaign-Urbana), Case Western Reserve, Carnegie Mellon, and NASA/Ames.
September 1971	First terminal interface processor (TIP) in ARPAnet permitting terminals to directly dial into the network, greatly increasing the network growth.
1972	Federal Trade Commission accused Xerox of illegally monopolizing the plain paper copier market.
March 1972	First basic e-mail programs, SNDMSG and READMAIL, written by Ray Tomlinson at BBN.
July 1972	First e-mail management program, RD, written by Larry Roberts at ARPA to list incoming messages and support forwarding, filing, and responding to them.
July 1972	File Transfer Protocol (FTP) specification (RFC 354) released by Jon Postel, the editor of the Request for Comments, and Abhay Bhushan, the chairman of the Network Working Group.
October 1972	First ARPAnet public demonstration at ICCC in Washington organized by Robert Kahn of BBN. Kahn was then hired by Roberts into ARPA. 29 nodes on the ARPAnet at the time.

1973	Both Bob Metcalfe and Larry Tesler, among others, join Xerox PARC; the first Alto built by Lampson, Thacker, etc. at Xerox PARC.
	First international connections to the ARPAnet: University College of London (England) and Royal Radar Establishment (Norway).
May 1973	First Ethernet operation at Xerox PARC designed by Robert Metcalfe. He had expanded the Alohanet packet radio concepts and applied them to cable technology.
May 22, 1973	Bob Metcalfe coins term "Ethernet" in Xerox PARC memo.
October 1973	Larry Roberts leaves ARPA, joining Telenet, the first packet-switching carrier, as CEO. Licklider returns to ARPA as Director of IPTO. Telenet proved that packet switching was far more economic than the telephone network for data.
1974	Intel launches the 8080 microprocessor.
May 1974	First internetworking protocol, TCP outlined in a paper by Robert Kahn and Vincent Cerf, "A Protocol for Packet Network Interconnection." Kahn and Cerf had started design in 1973.
June 1974	62 hosts on ARPAnet.
January 1975	*Popular Electronics* magazine featured what it announced as the world's first personal computer—the Altair 8800; Bill Gates and Paul Allen partner to write Basic for the Altair.
July 1975	ARPAnet management transferred to DCA, the Defense Communications Agency; Microsoft founded in Albuquerque, New Mexico.
1976	Atlantic Packet Satellite Network SatNet created; Apple Computer founded by Steve Jobs and Steve Wozniak; Queen Elizabeth II sends out e-mail
July 1976	Vint Cerf joins ARPA as program manager of the packet radio and packet satellite network.

March 1977	111 hosts on ARPAnet.
1978	The First West Coast Computer Faire, promoted by Jim Warren, took place in San Francisco's Civic Auditorium. Apple II launched—the first retail, mass-market personal computer.
March 1978	TCP protocol split into TCP and IP.
June 1979	Bob Metcalfe and others found 3Com—Computer Communication Compatibility.
October 1979	VisiCalc spreadsheet software goes on sale, designed for the Apple II.
December 1979	Steve Jobs visits Xerox PARC to see a demonstration of the Alto.
1980	Tim Berners-Lee writes a program called "Enquire Within"—the predecessor of his World Wide Web.
July 1980	NSF organizes CSNET, increasing it to 70 sites by June 1983 and integrating most computer-science sites by 1986.
1981	CSNET (Computer Science NETwork) built by collaboration of computer scientists at University of Delaware, Purdue University, University of Wisconsin, RAND Corporation, and BBN through seed money granted by NSF to provide networking services (especially e-mail) to university scientists with no access to ARPAnet.
January 1981	Microsoft has 40 employees.
August 1981	IBM announces the IBM Personal Computer; Microsoft creates the DOS operating system for the PC and its clones.
September 1981	213 nodes on ARPAnet.
January 1982	Sun Microsystems founded by Vinod Khosla, Scott McNealy, Andy Bechtolsheim, and Bill Joy; 3Com starts selling Etherlink connectors for IBM PCs.
Summer 1982	Novell Data Systems sells its furniture to meet payroll; John Warnock and Chuck

	Geschke (Xerox PARC computer-science researchers) quit to start up Adobe Systems; Sun I, the Sun Microsystems workstation, launched.
December 1982	Drew Major and SuperSet colleagues decide to network the IBM PC.
1983	ARPAnet and Defense Data Networks begin to use TCP/IP protocol: thus the Internet is born. Ray Noorda acquires control of Novell Data Systems and relaunches the company as Novell Inc.
	Bob Taylor leaves Xerox PARC to found and manage Digital Equipment Corporation's Systems Research Center.
	DCA splits MILNET from ARPAnet, leaving 68 nodes on ARPAnet and 45 on MILNET, the military network; NSFNet first established. Cisco Systems founded (incorporated in 1984); Quantum's Q-Link online service offered to Atari and Commodore computer users.
	Internet Activities Board (IAB) established.
June 1983	Novell's "Netware" first demonstrated in Houston, Texas.
September 1983	562 nodes on ARPAnet.
1983	Desktop workstations come into being, many with the Berkeley UNIX operating system, which includes IP networking software.
November 1983	Domain Name System (DNS) designed by Jon Postel, Paul Mockapetris, and Craig Partridge to support the e-mail addressing format, creating .edu, .gov, .com, .mil, .org, .net, & .int.
January 1984	Apple Macintosh launched; IBM and Microsoft jointly developing OS/2 for the next generation of IBM PCs.
1984	1,000 hosts on the Internet; Whole Earth's 'Lectronic Link (WELL) established.
October 1984	1,024 nodes on ARPAnet/Internet.

1985	NSF organizes NSFNET backbone to connect five supercomputing centers and interconnect all other Internet sites; Quantum launches bulletin board subscription service with graphical user interface (GUI).
March 15, 1985	Symbolic.com is assigned to become the first registered domain.
1986	5000 hosts on the ARPAnet/Internet.
1987	10,000 hosts on the Internet; first Cisco router shipped; Micorosoft and 3Com join forces to compete with Novell; 25 million PCs sold in the U.S.—one per six households.
December 1987	Sequoia Capital invests $2 million, in exchange for one-third of Cisco Systems.
1988	NSFNET backbone upgraded to T1 (1.544mbps).
1989	100,000 hosts on the Internet; Microsoft and Novell discuss merger/acquisition (and do so again in 1991–92); McAfee Associates founded; gives away anti-virus software to build market share; Quantum becomes America Online.
February 4, 1990	Cisco Systems goes public; at the IPO the company is valued at $288 million.
1990	ARPAnet is finally "deinstalled"after 20 years; Tim Berners-Lee creates the World Wide Web at CERN in Switzerland.
August 28, 1990	Sandy Lerner is fired from Cisco Systems (and Len Bosack resigns shortly thereafter).
1990	Bob Metcalfe retires from 3Com.
1991	U.S. High Performance Computing Act (sponsored by Senator Al Gore) establishes the National Research and Education Network (NREN); James Gosling embarks on "The Green Project," which would become Java; venture capitalists Technology Associates and Summit exchange $10 million for 50 percent of McAfee Associates; each gains a 2000 per-

	cent return; CERN publishes the code for the World Wide Web on the Internet.
June 9, 1992	Congressman Rick Boucher's amendment to the National Science Foundation Act of 1950 allows commerce to flourish on the Net (signed into law by President Bush on November 23, 1992); 1,000,000 hosts on the Internet.
1992	Sandy Lerner acquires Chawton Manor as headquarters for the Center for the Study of Early English Women's Writing.
1993	Mosaic browser developed by Marc Andreessen and others at University of Illinois, Champaign-Urbana (UICU). The Web grows by 341,000 percent in a year. Both the White House and the United Nations go online.
February 1994	Jim Clark and Marc Andreessen meet.
1994	Architext Software founded by Joe Kraus, Graham Spencer, et al, at Rosita's Burritos, Redwood City, California.
April 1994	Netscape Communications founded; Apple Computer launches e-world online service (decommissioned 1997); Jeff Bezos writes the business plan for Amazon.com, online bookstore; Java's first public demonstration in Monterey, California.
December 1994	Architext Software secures $300,000 in venture-capital funding from Kleiner, Perkins; Microsoft licenses technology from Spyglass to develop a Web browser for Windows 95.
January 1995	Microsoft invests $16.4 million in UUNet Technologies, an Internet service provider, to carry the traffic for Microsoft Network, to be included in Windows 95.
May 11, 1995	Bill Gates writes his watershed memo, "The Coming Internet Tidal Wave."
1995	NSFNET reverts back to a research network.

	Main US backbone traffic now routed through interconnected network service providers.
August 9, 1995	Netscape's IPO. Shares priced at $28 open at $70.
August 24, 1995	Microsoft's Windows 95 is launched.
October 1995	Architext changes its name to Excite.
December 7, 1995	Microsoft's "Internet Strategy Day" held on Pearl Harbor Day.
April 1996	Excite's IPO values the company in excess of $200 million.
May 1996	Pasha Roberts and Firdaus Bhathena win MIT's $50K Contest and establish their company, Webline.
1996	Bob Taylor retires from Digital Equipment Corporation.
March 1997	Excite moves into its own 80,000-square-foot building in Redwood City, California.
1998	Cisco Systems market valuation exceeds $60 billion.
May 17, 1998	United States Department of Justice and twenty states file suit against Microsoft for anti-competitive practices in the Internet-browser market.
September 1, 1998	The Starr Report published on the Internet; traffic jams ensue.

Glossary

Bandwidth: the capacity or scope available to process and transmit digital signals. The analogy of thin or fat pipes best conveys the variety of bandwidth in the digital world.

Bitmapping: a technique for relating on-screen images to memory. Each bit of memory is a binary switch; and each picture element (a single dot on the screen) corresponds to a single bit. By mapping the memory bits on screen, an image is created out of thousands of dots, whether it is text or graphical material.

Browser: a piece of software which navigates the Web, retrieves information, and presents a graphical image of the material on the user's screen.

Bulletin board: a digitized version of the cork-faced bulletin board on an office or dorm room wall, computers dedicated to providing information, news, gossip, and a forum for exchanging messages among a virtual community.

Circuit switching: the method whereby a telephone call can be made, with a wire circuit linking one user to another; whether one talks or not, the circuit remains switched through, until one party hangs up.

Data sharing: an original goal of computer networking, and of the ARPAnet, whereby individuals at different locations could access and share the data of others at other locations, and vice versa. Not, as it turned out, very much used.

Domain name: an address which enables a Net user to locate a server connected to the Internet. They end with .edu or .com, etc.

DOS: Disk Operating System, the operating system created by Microsoft for the IBM Personal Computer, which drives about 90 percent of the PCs in the world.

E-mail: electronic mail. Invented at Bolt, Beranek & Newman within weeks of the ARPAnet network creaking to life in 1969.

Ethernet: a technology invented by Bob Metcalfe and David Boggs at Xerox PARC, which used Alohanet and ARPAnet technology to create local networks of personal computers.

Graphical User Interface (GUI): the visual, icon-driven look of the Apple Macintosh and Windows that superseded the text-based, un-intuitive format of DOS. User-friendliness personified.

Hardware: the physical plant of computers, consisting of metal, plastic, silicon, and bulk.

Homepage: the entrance to a Web site, as a grand house has a fine hallway which leads to other, more intimate rooms. A homepage might have the address *homepage.com*, while more detailed categories of information will be at *homepage.com/detail*.

Hypertext: the "discovery" of Ted Nelson, originator of Xanadu, which allows links to be created between one word or passage of text and another, across the huge space of the Internet.

Killer application (app): the single, often limited, purpose for which a lot of people will buy a new technology.

Load sharing: another original goal of computer networking, and of the ARPAnet, whereby one user with an overloaded computer could use a distant computer to process his/her work. Not much used, after all.

Local Area Network (LAN): a group of computers in a single room, building or local area, connected together to share files, exchange mail, and allow collaborative work.

Mainframe: the big, high-powered computers, typically manufactured by IBM, which predated minicomputers and microcomputers (later renamed personal computers). This was the "big iron" of "Big Blue," so expensive that ARPA invented networking to reduce the costs of buying so many of them.

Message switching: a technology which was a hypothetical alternative to packet switching. It improves the utilization of expensive phone lines by saving material to be sent, dialing up the connection, delivering the information quickly, and hanging up.

Modem: modulator/demodulator. Because a computer is digital, and works with distinct electrical signals representing 1 and 0, but a phone line is analog, carrying a large range of signal variations, the modem is needed to convert from binary to analog at the input end, and from analog to binary at the output end of the line.

Metcalfe's Law: Where N is the number of nodes, the power of the network is N squared. If you double the number of nodes, you quadruple the overall value of the network. The network gets more valuable to each user as every other new user joins. The same is true of most networks: for example, the telephone network or the network of Federal Express locations.

Moore's Law: As generally reported, it states that the complexity of integrated circuits (microprocessors) doubles every year, and the price is halved every year. Gordon Moore is too modest to admit that he predicted exactly this, but if he had, he would have been largely right, consistently for thirty years.

Net/Internet: interchangeable terms for the entire global network of computers. Every computer with a modem connected to it is part of it.

Network operating system: the software which enables a network of computers to behave like a network, allowing file exchange, mail programs, etc.

Networking: communicating through computers instead of telephones or the mail.

Node: a location on a network. The ARPAnet's first nodes were UCLA, Stanford, UC Santa Barbara, and the University of Utah.

Packet switching: the most efficient way (so far) to send data, by breaking a block of information into smaller pieces called packets, and each packet makes its way through the network, to be put back together at the destination.

Protocol: the rules of diplomacy among computers and related machines. Protocols define how networks organize communication among their own nodes, or between networks.

Router: a descendant of the IMP, which directs traffic between networks, and made Cisco Systems into a near $100 billion company.

Search engine: Just as libraries need catalogs, the Internet needs search engines. A user enters certain key words to tell the search engine what he or she is looking for, and the search engine combs all the available catalogs and indexes to match the key words with material from all the databases.

Software: the instructions that tell computer hardware what to do, applications and programs consisting entirely of zeroes and ones, with no physical substance. A business worth scores of billions of dollars.

Web site: a virtual location, accessed by a string of letters and dots, which appears on a user's screen with the color and vitality of an interactive, constantly-evolving front page.

Whole Earth 'Lectronic Link (WELL): the virtual community which sprang from the Whole Earth community in Sausalito, California, to embrace technology and exploit it as a form of free expression, private conversation, and social activism.

Windows: generically, the organization of a computer screen display which allows multiple, overlapping documents or other files to appear on screen at the same time and to be moved around. In proprietary terms, it is the brand name of Microsoft's version of this user interface, though Macintosh did it first.

Workstation: the hybrid computer, bigger than a PC, smaller than a minicomputer, which exists only within a network. Sun Microsystems developed the workstation and coined its best slogan "The Network Is The Computer."

World Wide Web: the software Tim Berners-Lee invented to "translate" material from any computer, from any format, into a common language of words, images and addresses.

Acronyms

ACM: Association for Computing Machinery

AOL: America Online

ARC: Augmentation Research Center (of the ARPAnet)

ARPA: Advanced Research Projects Agency

BBN: Bolt, Beranek & Newman

BBS: bulletin board system

CD-ROM: compact disk-read-only memory

CERN: the European Center for Particle Research (Conseil Européen pour la Recherche Nucléaire)

CMC: Corporate Management Committee (IBM)

CMU: Carnegie Mellon University

CP/M: Control Program/Monitor

CPU: central processing unit

CSMA/CD: Carrier Sense Multiple Access with Collision Detection

DARPA: briefly, the name given to ARPA, for Defense Advanced Research Projects Agency

DEW: Defense Early Warning

DoD: Department of Defense

EARS: Ethernet-Alto-RCG-SLOT

ENIAC: Electronic Numerical Integrator and Calculator

FTP: File Transfer Protocol

GUI: graphical user interface

HTML: HyperText markup language

HTTP: HyperText transfer protocol

ICBM: Intercontinental Ballistic Missile

ICCC: International Conference on Computer Communications

IEEE: Institute of Electrical and Electronics Engineers

IIT: Indian Institute of Technology

IIS: Indian Institute of Science

IMP: Interface Message Processor

IPTO: Information Processing Techniques Office (a division of ARPA)

ISP: Internet service provider

LAN: Local Area Network

LOTSS: Low Overhead Time Sharing System

MAD: mutual assured destruction

mbps: megabits per second

MIT: Massachusetts Institute of Technology

MITS: Micro Instrumentation Telemetry Systems

MS-DOS: Microsoft Disk Operating System

MSN: Microsoft Network

NACA: National Advisory Committee on Aeronautics

NASA: National Aeronautics & Space Administration

NCSA: National Center for Supercomputing Applications

NIC: Network Information Center (of the ARPAnet)

NLS: oNLine System

NMC: Network Measurement Center (of the ARPAnet)

NPL: National Physical Laboratory

NSF: National Science Foundation

NSFNet: National Science Foundation Network

OS/2: Operating System 2 (for the IBM PC)

OTL: Office of Technology Licensing (Stanford)

PC: personal computer

PC-DOS: Personal Computer Disk Operating System (by Microsoft, for IBM)

PDA: Personal Digital Assistant

PI: Principal Investigator

POLOS: PARC on-Line Office System

RFC: Request for Comment

RFP: Request for Proposals

RFQ: Request for Quotations

SAGE: SemiAutomatic Ground Environment

SDC: System Development Corporation

SDS: Scientific Data Systems

SLAC: Stanford Linear Accelerator Center

SLOT: scanned laser output terminal

SNA: Systems Network Architecture

SRI: Stanford Research Institute

TCP/IP: transmission control protocol/Internet protocol

TIP: terminal interface processor

UNIX: the minicomputer operating system developed at Bell Labs and Berkeley

URL: Universal Resource Locator

USCISI: University of Southern California Information Sciences Institute

VC: venture capitalist

W3C: World Wide Web Consortium

WAN: Wide Area Network

WELL: Whole Earth 'Lectronic Link

WOW: Women on the WELL

Photo Credits

Index

About the Author

STEPHEN SEGALLER is a writer and television producer whose work has been published and broadcast all over the world. He produced both *Triumph of the Nerds* and *Nerds 2.0.1*, among many productions for PBS, the BBC, and Channel 4. He is the author of *Invisible Armies*, a study of terrorism and (with Merrill Berger) *The Wisdom of the Dream*, on the work of C.G. Jung. He lives in Massachusetts.